Dorset

Mark Glaister
Pete Oxley

A rock climbing guidebook to Portland, Lulworth, Swanage and Anstey's Cove in Devon

Text and topos by Mark Glaister and Pete Oxley
  with additional work by Ben Stokes
Computer artwork, design, layout and editing
  by Alan James, Chris Craggs and Mark Glaister
All uncredited crag photos by Mark Glaister
Action photos as credited
Original ROCKFAX design Mick Ryan and Alan James
Printed by Clearpoint Colourprint, Nottingham
Distributed by Cordee (www.cordee.co.uk)

All maps by ROCKFAX
Some maps are based on original source maps kindly
supplied by Collins Maps (www.collins.co.uk)

Published by ROCKFAX Ltd. July 2005
© ROCKFAX Ltd. 2005, 2004, 2000, 1994

ISBN 1 873341 90 3

www.rockfax.com

This page: Gavin Symonds on *Forensic Scene* (7a+)
Coastguard South, Portland - *page 118*. Photo: Mark Glaister
Cover: Danie Rushmer on *England's Dreaming* (7a+)
Blacknor North, Portland - *page 57*. Photo: Mike Robertson

GUIDEBOOK FOOTNOTE

CONTENTS

INTRODUCTION

The rock climbing scene on the cliffs of Portland, Lulworth and Swanage has evolved from a neglected backwater, into one of the most important areas in Britain. Dorset's attractions include a superb mix of both sport climbing and traditionally protected routes across the grade spectrum. This has drawn increasingly large numbers of visitors from all over the UK, and even from abroad, to sample what the area has to offer. It is a sign of the times that most of the visitors are interested in the superb selection of well-bolted sport routes that now exist here; there are 1225 sport climbs described in this book, the result of just over fifteen years of intense activity. In contrast to Portland, which caters almost exclusively for sport climbers, the extensive sea-cliffs at Swanage have long been a major destination for traditional climbing. This remains the case although the 'big' routes in this area are now interspersed with some

Dancing Ledge - *page 218*. Photo: Mark Glaister

extremely popular sport climbing arenas. High summer also sees the emergence of Deep Water Soloists - the warm-water-lovers - who are devoted to a branch of climbing that has been honed to a high level of refinement in Dorset and successfully exported worldwide. Bouldering has also taken hold like elsewhere in the country.

The amount of climbing available, coupled with a relatively mild climate has resulted in the establishment of an exceptional year-round climbing destination and, although approaching maturity, development continues. In the short time since the last Dorset Rockfax was published in 2000, developments have included events such as the South's first 8c and Portland's first confirmed 8b. Those who have not climbed in the area for a while will notice improved parking, well established paths beneath most of the cliffs and most importantly the way that much of the once dusty rock has cleaned up.

Once the haunt of locals only, the pull of the massive number of routes, the striking coastal scenery and amiable weather, mean that the area provides a reliable choice for weekend or longer trips throughout the year, without the need to cross The Channel. Visits to the area during high summer have the added attraction of beautiful beaches, gorgeous villages, ancient landscapes and countless numbers of pubs and cream-tea shops.

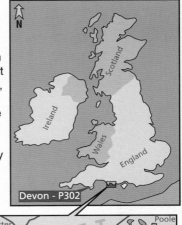

Devon - P302

Lulworth - P174

Swanage - P190

Portland - P38

Lee Proctor on the exposed final wall of *Buoys will be Buoys* (6b+) on Battleship Back Cliff on Portland - *page 83*. The tall walls and buttresses of Blacknor Central and South are visible in the distance. Photo: Mark Glaister

THE BOOK

It has only been five years since the last Rockfax guidebook to Dorset but things have moved on significantly during this time. There have been plenty of new routes added, lots of rebolting done, new boulder problems, new deep water solos and generally the area has matured into one of the major destinations on the UK climbing scene. More significantly for Rockfax, the way we present the information has changed with the full colour photo-topo format established in the Peak Gritstone guides, now becoming the accepted standard for most guidebooks. This has meant that we have had to get a full set of new crag shots in order to create the photo-topos. A combination of good planning and good fortune meant that most of these photos were taken from local climber Neal Heanes' boat during a few days of perfect weather. We hope you will agree that the end results are stunning and show the cliffs at their very best, hopefully inspiring you to visit all the far flung corners of Dorset climbing.

In a slight change from the last addition, we have added the small set of mainly-sport routes in Anstey's Cove and Torbryan Quarry in Devon. Although not geographically very close, the climbing is of interest to those who frequent Portland and both venues did appear in the original Dorset Rockfax of 1994.

PREVIOUS GUIDES

Dorset (2nd Edition - *right*) by Pete Oxley *(ROCKFAX - 2000)*
Into the Blue by Jonathan Cook, Mike Robertson, Steve Taylor and Damian Cook *(Climbers' Club deep water soloing guide - 1996)*
Swanage and Portland by Nigel Coe *(Climbers' Club - 1995)*
South Devon and Dartmoor by Nick White *(Cordee -1995)*
Dorset by Pete Oxley *(ROCKFAX - 1994)*
Swanage by Gordon Jenkin *(Climbers' Club - 1986)*
Dorset by R.J. Crewe *(Climbers' Club - 1977)*
Dorset Climbs by R.C.White *(Climbers' Club - 1969)*
Limestone Climbs on the Dorset Coast by B.Annette *(Climbers' Club - 1961)*

DORSET
by Pete Oxley

WEB SITE - www.rockfax.com

The Rockfax web site is a mine of useful information about climbing all over Europe. It contains the Rockfax Route Database (see below) plus many MiniGuides and updates both complementing the printed books produced by Rockfax and also covering new areas. These downloadable guides are stored in PDF documents - a universal format which can be viewed and printed out on all modern computers using the free application Adobe Acrobat Reader. For some MiniGuides there is a small charge to download but many are free. As things develop on the Dorset crags we will be producing updates and possibly extra MiniGuides covering any extensive new areas, so keep checking the web site.

ROCKFAX ROUTE DATABASE - This database contains a listing of every route in this book, and most other Rockfax books as well. The Dorset section has been there for nearly four years and has had a huge number of comments and votes on the routes. All this information has been vital in putting together this book, in getting the grades and stars right and keeping a check on developments. Thanks to all those who contributed.

The current version of the database has been updated to reflect the routes as described in this edition of the book so you can start using it again to keep everyone informed about any changes or your own opinions on grades, stars and the routes in general.

Don't forget that you can also use the database to construct a personal and printable tick list of routes by using the advanced search function to select a location, grade band and star range of routes and return a list with tick boxes, and page references in this guide.

Ken Palmer deep water soloing *Blue Planet* (7b+) at Long Quarry Point, Devon - *page 313.* Photo: Mark Glaister

GEAR and SAFETY

SPORT CLIMBING

For the sport routes a single rope of 60m is advised since there are several areas on the east and west coast of Portland with routes close to 30m in length. It is possible to climb on many other areas with a shorter rope but please take special care and, no matter what length of rope you have, ALWAYS tie a knot in the end and stand close to the face when lowering off.

A rack of 12 or 14 quickdraws is enough for any route on Portland and Anstey's Cove, however some lines at Swanage require more. Some of the sport routes at Swanage need the odd wire or two - this is clearly marked in the route descriptions. Certain sport routes require an abseil approach or are tidal as at White Hole, Coastguard South and Long Quarry Point - again this is clearly indicated with the route descriptions.

TRAD CLIMBING

Double 50m ropes are required for virtually all the traditional climbs in this guidebook. In addition, a 50m abseil rope is essential for many of the crags at Swanage. Often these abseils are free-hanging so make sure a thick rope is used. Take a good selection of extra slings for belays and to avoid rope drag over the ever-present overhangs at Swanage. For the big traditional routes take two sets of wires and some micro-nuts, plus a good selection of cams and some larger nuts (see photo). Include enough gear to belay yourself securely at the base of the cliffs (in case of a freak large wave).

THE ROPED CLIMBING SAFETY CHECKLIST

1) Helmets are very strongly recommended, especially at Swanage because of the looseness of the rock.

2) In summer many of the crags can be unbelievably hot so take lots of water, shades and a hat, and slap on the sun screen.

3) Take great care near to the cliff tops, especially in the wet when the grass and mud can be leathally slippery, or after long dry spells when the dry grass is frictionless!

4) On sport routes, take great care when lowering off routes and always have a knot tied in the end of the rope.

5) For crags requiring an abseil approach, do not assume that it is possible to abseil in on ropes to be used for climbing since frequently the abseil rope forms an integral part of the cliff-top belay.

6) In most areas prussik loops are essential since there is not always an easy escape route.

7) Take great care with loose material on the cliff edge when abseiling and topping out.

8) Remember when abseiling not to let the rope get caught in the sea around boulders and if it does, take great care when trying to free it.

9) When moving along the crag base above deep water, carry the rack and rope in a manner whereby they can be easily and quickly jettisoned. If you are in the water with them on you will sink VERY quickly!

Emma Medara soloing *Ixtlan* (E2 5b) at Cave Hole on the East Coast of Portland - *page 136*. Photo: Mark Glaister

DEEP WATER SOLOING

Little gear is need for the actual climbing apart from a good supply of spare boots and chalk bags in case of a wetting. For some of the routes it is necessary for an abseil to be made to reach sea level for which you will need a harness and a friction device (these should be left on the ab rope when you set off on your solo so that you aren't weighed down in the water).

THE DEEP WATER SOLOING SAFETY CHECKLIST

1) Always check tides before starting. Remember a neap high tide may not actually be that high. Check which routes need high spring tides carefully.
2) Never go deep water soloing on your own in case you get into difficulties in the water.
3) Always check below you before starting sections of routes to look out for ledges or exposed reefs and boulders. Just because a route has been soloed it doesn't mean that there is always deep water beneath every section it.
4) Check for exits from the water should you need them.
5) Keep an eye out for weather changes, a sudden change in wind speed or direction can quickly create rough and dangerous conditions.
6) In spring and early summer the water is very cold and it will suck the life out of you in no time at all. Make provision for getting dry and warm quickly if necessary.

BOULDERING

For the bouldering on Portland a padded mat is recommended to soften some of the high landings. A spotter or three is also a good idea.

TIDES

There is not a great tidal range in the area. The highest spring tides (new and full moon) have about 2 to 2.5m range whilst neap tides (1/2 moons) only vary between 1 and 1.5m. Portland has a double tide which isn't really obvious to the eye but has the effect of prolonging the time the water level is high or low. Overall the changes in water level are slow when compared to Cornwall, Devon and South Wales. The tides advance by about 45 minutes a day and there are two highs a day some 12-13 hours apart. The flood tide flows to the east and the ebb to the west which are most apparent in the huge tidal race off of Portland Bill.

At Swanage a knowledge of tides is essential for most of the cliffs although only a few areas are actually cut off by high water. For virtually all areas it is worth keeping well away when the sea is moderately rough or worse.

On Portland a knowledge of the tides is not essential unless visiting the cliffs on the east coast or Coastguard South. The Portland deep water solos need the highest tides possible so look for spring tides of around 2m or higher.

Tide tables can be bought in newsagents, Post Offices, or from the visitor centre passed on the Weymouth causeway. There are different tables for Swanage and Portland. A rough guide to tides can also be got from the easytide website at **www.easytide.ukho.gov.uk** which could be very helpful when planning a visit. Because of the very strong tidal races at Portland and Swanage swimming is not advised. However Anstey's Cove in Devon has safe swimming from the beach.

BOLTING

The bolting system predominantly used at the sport crags covered by this book is the U-bolt staple. These are made from marine-grade stainless steel held in with a special epoxy glue. They provide inexpensive, corrosion-resistant protection with a lifetime in excess of 25 years. In the last 15 years they have spread from Britain's first stapled route - *Sugar Ray* at Dancing Ledge - to many parts of the country.

Here are some things to keep in mind when using these staples:
1) Use high strength karabiners with a breaking strain of 2300kg and above.
2) Carry a screwgate or sling to use on bolts which are close to edges or in uneven rock.
3) The staples can be lowered off directly or by abseil. When lowering always thread both belay staples. Make sure you secure the end of the rope before untying to thread the belay to maintain your lifeline in case of mishap.
4) Never top-rope off a single staple.
5) Always belay close to the rock face so that your belay rope goes straight through the first bolt. People who belay a long way from the face put heavy outward loading on the bottom bolt which has caused problems with some bolts in the area. It is also a dangerous practice since leaders are likely to go a lot further in the event of a fall.
6) If any bolts look suspect please make this known to other climbers by reporting it.

Nearly all of Portland, Devon and much of Swanage is now properly geared but there are places, such as Blackers Hole Quarry, that still need work. Additionally existing routes need occasional maintenance and re-gearing.

B The 'B' symbol denotes a sport route that has old or unsafe bolts and/or poor fixed gear. Do not climb these routes in their current state unless it is apparent that they have been re-bolted.

DORSET BOLT FUND

For more information about the funding of bolting in Dorset, check the Rockfax web site - **www.rockfax.com**

A Dorset fossil.
Photo: Mark Glaister

Learn to climb through your letterbox.

When a copy of our latest brochure drops through your letterbox, it's a great opportunity to improve your climbing. You'll find we run courses for every level of climber at a pace and a price that's sure to be comfortable.

What's more, we're convinced you won't find a better place to learn. Here at the National Mountain Centre, deep in the heart of Snowdonia, everything we provide is maintained at an incredibly high standard. A standard that has to be seen to be believed.

We run a year round programme of **PLAS Y BRENIN**

courses, holidays and expeditions designed to suit climbers of all ages and levels of experience.

You can choose from over 160 different options including Winter Climbing, Alpine Climbing, Big Wall climbing and Ski Mountaineering along with many courses designed purely to improve your technique and judgment. And for the aspiring instructors amongst you, we also run a complete range of national governing body training and assessment courses .

For a brochure call 01690 720214, e-mail info@pyb.co.uk or visit www.pyb.co.uk

Capel Curig Conwy LL24 0ET Tel: 01690 720214 Fax: 01690 720394 www.pyb.co.uk Email: info@pyb.co.uk

ACCESS

Many of the climbing areas covered in this book have sensitive access situations but thanks to the BMC and their local volunteers most are currently accessible to all climbers - any area where there are potential problems or actual bans are noted within the text. However, people should be aware of their responsibilities and be careful not to abuse the access granted. In general, simple reasonable behaviour like not dropping litter, respecting restrictions, not making excess noise and using the described approaches is all that is required to ensure continued untroubled access to the climbing areas.

One notable area with problems is the Lulworth area. This area is owned by the Weld Estate who have announced a total ban on climbing on their land. This is for reasons of conservation and public safety. The BMC is currently trying to negotiate an access agreement acceptable to both climbers and land owner. Until this is done climbing is not allowed in the Lulworth Area. There are also some specific restrictions at Winspit Quarry and some of the Devon crags which are covered in detail in their introductions.

BIRD NESTING RESTRICTIONS

 To help avoid disturbance to nesting birds seasonal climbing restrictions have been placed on certain sections of the Dorset Coast. The nature of these restrictions varies from Portland to Swanage but it is essential that climbers abide by the restrictions and also take note of any changes that may occur further to the information contained in this book. Note that the restrictions are not just no-climbing restrictions - please keep away from these areas altogether.

Photo: Mick Ryan

Portland - The restrictions on Portland are variable and reviewed each year and in general are only applied to the sections of cliff where the birds (often peregrines) have actually nested. The restrictions usually apply from the 1st February until the birds leave the nest (usually the end of July or August). The current practice is to mark the affected routes by fixing a sign (laminated sheet) on the bolts at the edges of the restricted area. Before climbing on any of the buttresses marked with the restriction symbol above, please check the current information, either from the ROCKFAX website **www.rockfax.com** or from the BMC website **www.thebmc.com**. There is also a permanent restriction on the far end of the Azymuth Area on Coastguard South.

Swanage - Unlike the Portland restrictions, the bird nesting areas for Swanage are more well established and seldom change much, however it is still worth checking the above web sites if you are unsure. The affected routes are clearly marked in the text and all the bans apply from 1st March to 31st July. The crags with restrictions for nesting birds are Hedbury Big Cove, Smokey Hole, Guillemot, some of Cormorant, some of Blacker's Hole and several sections of the Boulder Ruckle.

Devon - There are no bird restrictions on climbing at Anstey's Cove or Torbryan Quarry.

The spectacular Durdle Door - *page 181*. Photo: Mark Glaister

PARKING

Only use the described parking places which are clearly marked on all the approach maps. Please respect the local residents on Portland, especially in the Weston estate and in Southwell plus the road leading from there to Portland Bill. Note that some of the places previously used for parking are now officially restricted and parking tickets are regularly issued.

CAMPING

No wild camping is allowed anywhere on Portland, Swanage, Lulworth or Torquay. Use one of the many local camp sites. All accommodation suggestions are on page 24.

CLIFF PLANTS

Minimise damage to fragile flora by not gardening routes. Make sure you check local information before developing any new areas. It is almost certainly the case that undeveloped areas on Portland have been left for a reason. Don't abseil over cliff-tops on Portland since this is where much of the rare flora grows on the Isle. Only use the described abseil points on Swanage. Do not access the top of Torbryan Quarry at anytime.

SANCTUARY ZONES and MOD AREAS

Do not climb, or even enter, any of the sanctuary zones on Portland and Swanage. Don't climb on any of the MOD property near Lulworth.

GRADES

In this book sport routes are given sport grades, traditionally protected routes are given trad (or British) grades and boulder problems are given bouldering grades. Deep water solos may have a trad grade or a sport grade, depending on whether the route is a bolted route or not, but they will also have an S-grade. The complicated-looking grade table below attempts to compare the main grading systems so that some idea can be gained as to what standard of route you should choose depending on your ability on other types of routes.

SPORT GRADE

A sport grade is simply a measure of how hard it is going to be to get up a certain bit of rock. It does not attempt to tell you how difficult the hardest move is, or how scary the route is. The routes in this book are graded for their first try by the easiest method hence on-sights can seem harder if you miss the correct sequence.

TRAD GRADE

Trad climbing is where you place your own protection as you climb and there are usually no bolts to clip. The trad grading system is divided into two parts;

The adjectival grade (Diff, VDiff, Severe, Hard Severe (HS), Very Severe (VS), Hard Very Severe (HVS), E1,.... to E9). This gives an overall picture of the route including how well protected it is, how sustained and an indication of the level of difficulty of the whole route.

The technical grade (4a, 4b, 4c, 5a,..... to 7a). This refers to the difficulty of the hardest single move, or short section, on a route.

ROUTE GRADES

BRITISH TRAD GRADE (For well-protected routes)

Adjectival grades (with technical grades) shown as overlapping diamonds:
Mod (Moderate), Diff (Difficult), VDiff (Very Difficult), HVD (Hard Very Difficult), Sev (Severe), HS (Hard Severe) 4a, VS (Very Severe) 4c, HVS (Hard Very Severe) 4c/5b, E1 5a/5c, E2 5c/6a, E3 5c/6a, E4 6a/6b, E5 6a/6c, E6 6b/6c, E7 6c/7a, E8 6c/7a, E9 7a/7b, E10 7a/7b

Sport Grade	UIAA	USA
1	I	5.1
2	II	5.2
2+	III	5.3
	III+	5.4
3	IV	5.5
	IV+	5.6
3+	V-	
4	V	5.7
4+	V+	5.8
5	VI-	5.9
5+	VI	5.10a
6a	VI+	5.10b
6a+	VII-	5.10c
6b	VII	5.10d
6b+	VII+	5.11a
6c		5.11b
6c+	VIII-	5.11c
7a	VIII	5.11d
7a+	VIII+	5.12a
7b	IX-	5.12b
7b+		5.12c
7c	IX	5.12d
7c+	IX+	5.13a
8a	X-	5.13b
8a+		5.13c
8b	X	5.13d
8b+	X+	5.14a
8c	XI-	5.14b
8c+	XI	5.14c
9a		5.14d
9a+	XI+	5.15a

Bouldering Grade: VB, V0-, V0, V0+, V1, V2, V3, V4, V5, V6, V7, V8, V9, V10, V11, V12, V13, V14

UK Tech Grade: 4c or easier, 5a, 5b, 5c, 6a, 6b, 6c, 7a, 7b

Font Grade: 3, 3+, 4, 4+, 5, 5+, 6a, 6b, 6c, 6c+, 7a, 7a+, 7b, 7b+, 7c, 7c+, 8a, 8a+, 8b, 8b+

A WORD OF CAUTION ABOUT TRAD ROUTES AT SWANAGE

1) Remember that Swanage, and Boulder Ruckle in particular, is a big and serious cliff. Until you are familiar with the place, it is highly recommended that you drop your leading grade by at least 2 notches when attempting a route there.

2) Trad routes are a very different proposition from routes which have something solid and safe to clip every 1.5m. If you get into difficulty then you cannot always just lower-off and try the next route.

3) DON'T expect to instantly lead the same equivalent trad grade as your best sport grade effort on a bolted route, especially if that bolted route was at a climbing wall!

BOULDERING GRADE

The boulder problems described in this book are given a V-grade. This grade gives an overall level of difficulty of the problem in a similar way to a sport grade, however it has more sub-divisions as illustrated on the lower table opposite.

DEEP WATER SOLO GRADE

Routes that have been classed as deep water solos are indicated by the splash down icon (left) with the individual route descriptions. These routes can be trad routes or sport routes but some may also only ever been done as deep water solos. In addition to their normal sport or trad grade, they are also given an S-grade at the end of the route description which gives an indication of the seriousness of soloing the route **UNDER OPTIMUM CONDITIONS**. An S-grade is NOT a green light to go ahead at any time for a deep water solo, as many factors will alter the seriousness of a route such as the depth of water, height above water, rough seas, strong currents, people in the sea below, swimming ability and water temperature. The S-grade definitions are:

S0 - Can be undertaken at most tide states with normally plenty of water under all parts of the route. Low difficult sections and an easy exit from the water.

S1 - Needs careful consideration of tides to ensure sufficent water under route. Some climbing may not be above water. May have hard moves high up and/or some poor rock.

S2 - As for S1 but it may require high spring tides for sufficient water. Possible that water maybe too shallow for a safe entry. High hard sections. For the very experienced only.

S3 - Shallow water solos which are never really safe.

GRADE COLOUR CODES

All routes and boulder problems are all given a colour-coded dot corresponding to a grade band. The colour represents a level that a climber should be 'happy' at, hence sport routes tend to be technically harder than the equivalent coloured trad routes.

❶ - Up to Severe / Up to 4+ / VB to V0-
Mostly these should be good for beginners and those wanting an easy life.

❷ - HS to HVS / 5 to 6a+ / V0 to V1
General ticking routes for those with more experience.

❸ - E1 to E3 / 6b to 7a / V2 to V6
Routes for the experienced and keen climber.

❹ - E4, 7a+ or V7 and above
The really hard stuff!

ROCKFAX

Another publication for the Dorset Area from ROCKFAX

CUTTINGS BOULDERFIELD MiniGUIDE (2004)
'One Hundred Ways to Stand Up', Ben Stokes's indepth guide to the Cuttings Boulderfield which is selectively covered in the Cuttings chapter on page 168 - check **www.rockfax.com**

Other ROCKFAX print guidebooks

CLYWD LIMESTONE (2005)
Published in the late summer of 2005, this book covers all the fine limestone crags in the Eglwyseg Valley to the north of Llangollen in North Wales, plus many outlying areas.

COSTA BLANCA (2005)
One of the most popular areas for travelling climbers seeking winter sun on the east coast of Spain. Mainly sport climbing but also long mountain pitches and some trad climbing.
"It's magnificent; the sleekiest, slinkiest yet. And yet, unlike other recent publications, it is not just fit for the coffee table .. it has got everything; it's the holiday climber's complete bible."
- Carl Dawson, March 2005

NORTHERN LIMESTONE (2004)
The most comprehensive guide ever published to limestone in England covering every major limestone crag between Dove Dale in the south, and Chapel Head Scar in the north.
" In terms of quality, it is what you would expect, as good as it gets."
- Adrian Berry, Planetfear.com, June 2004

WESTERN GRIT (2003) - *Outdoor Writers' Guild Guidebook of the Year 2004*
The superb climbing on the Western Gritstone edges; from Staffordshire to Kinder, Bleaklow and the Chew Valley. Also covering sections of Lancashire and Cheshire sandstone.
" virtually flawless climbing guide - an admirable and practical book - extraordinary clarity"
- OWG Judges, November 2004

COSTA DAURADA (2002)
A brilliant winter sun destination near Barcelona in northern Spain. Single-pitch sport climbing on perfect limestone in a gorgeous landscape.
"It is the most comprehensive and up-to-date guide available for this area."
- John Adams, Climber, March 1999

PEAK GRITSTONE EAST (2001) - *Outdoor Writers' Guild Guidebook of the Year 2002*
The most popular UK guidebook ever covering the magnificent eastern gritstone edges of the Peak District from Wharncliffe to Cratcliffe including Stanage, Burbage, Millstone and Froggatt.
"..this book is as close to perfect a guidebook as we are likely to get."
- Ed Douglas, Climber, February 2002

We also have books to **Yorkshire Gritstone Bouldering (2000)** and **North Wales Limestone (1997)** in the UK. In the USA the current titles are **Islands In The Sky - Vegas Limestone (2001)**, **Rifle - Bite The Bullet (1997)** and the **Bishop Bouldering Survival Kit (1999)**.

In addition to this we have nearly 50 more PDF MiniGUIDES on **www.rockfax.com** covering areas from **Lofoten** in Norway to **Kalymnos** in Greece.

Route Symbols

 A good route

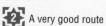 A very good route

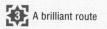 A brilliant route

 Technical climbing involving complex or trick moves

 Powerful moves requiring big arms

 Sustained climbing, either long and pumpy or with lots of hard moves

 Fingery climbing - sharp holds!

 A possible deep water solo - see page 10

 A route which requires some hand-placed gear or a full rack.

 Fluttery climbing with big fall potential

 A long reach is helpful/essential

Special Route Symbol

 B A route with old bolts. Do not climb unless you know that the bolts have been replaced.

Photo-topos

Approach or descent

Abseil descent point

Belay at the top

Lower-off

Mid-route belays

Easy scrambles

Alternatives for the same route

A

1   2   3

Crag Symbols

 Approach - Approach walk time and angle

 Sunshine - Approximate time when the sun is on the crag

 Approximate crag angle

 Access problems - climbing may be banned or restricted

 Bird restrictions - no climbing during the specified times

 Some multi-pitch routes

 A crag with dry climbing in the rain

 A sheltered/warm crag

 An abseil approach is needed

 A tidal buttress

Map (Inland)

Building

Fence

Track

A352   Main road

Path

Camping

Crags

Town/village

Wall

Lighthouse

P Main parking places

N

Grade Colour Codes

The colour-coded route numbers correspond to the following grade bands:

	Trad Routes	Sport Routes
1	Up to Severe	Up to 4+
2	HS to HVS	5 to 6a+
3	E1 to E3	6b to 7a
4	E4 and above	7a+ and above

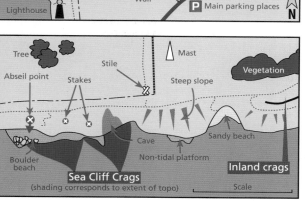

Tree

Stile

Mast

Abseil point

Stakes

Steep slope

Vegetation

Boulder beach

Cave

Non-tidal platform

Sandy beach

Sea Cliff Crags
(shading corresponds to extent of topo)

Inland crags

Scale

INTRODUCTION (Français)

Le domaine d'escalade du Dorset est probablement le plus important du sud de l'Angleterre. Les sites de Swanage et Portland possèdent des voies de styles très variés et partagent le doux climat permettant la pratique de l'escalade tout au long de l'année.

Depuis le début des années 90, Portland s'est dévelopé en site d'escalade sportive et comporte plus de 1000 voies équipées de qualité.

Swanage possède également un certain nombre de voies équipées mais est mieux connu pour ses 'trad routes' (voies traditionnelles) sans spits et nécessitant l'utilisation de coinceurs (nuts et friends). Ce guide couvre les meilleurs sites de 'Deep Water Solo', style de grimpe sans spits, coinceurs ou cordes, Il n'y a que vous, votre sac à magnésie et la mer au-dessous pour plonger en cas de chute. Lulworth Cove est un des meilleurs sites pour le 'Deep Water Solo' mais possede aussi d'excellente voies sportives. Le dernier chapitre traite de l'escalade sportive de haute difficulté dans le Devon. Ce guide contient toute l'information nécessaire pour accéder à tous les sites d'escalade, puis trouver et évaluer les voies. Chaque chapitre est richement illustrés de cartes, topos et symboles, donc si vous ne parlez pas bien anglais, vous ne devriez donc pas avoir de difficulté à vous orienter et à grimper confiant que vous êtes sur la bonne voie.

ÉQUIPMENT

Pour grimper à Portland, tout ce qu'il vous faut est une corde à simple (50 mètres sont suffisants pour la plupart des voies, mais 60 mètres sont préférables) ainsi que quelques dégaines. Pour les 'trad routes' de Swanage, apportez un jeu complet de coinceurs (voir matériel page 8) et vérifiez si une corde de rappel est nécessaire pour atteindre le pied des falaises (repérer les symboles de rappel). Pour le 'Deep Water Solo', vous n'avez besoin que de chaussons d'escalade et de sacs à magnésie de rechange et d'une serviette de plage.

SYMBOLES SPÉCIAUX

Il y a trois symboles de voies spéciaux a noter:

Ce symbole signifie que la voie est faisable en 'Deep Water Solo'. Cependant, soyez prudent et assurez-vous d'avoir lu toute l'information concernant la marée.

Ce symbole apparait sur certaines voies du secteur de grimpe sportive de Swanage. Il signifie qu'elles sont presque totalement equipées mais qu'il est préférable de prendre avec vous quelques coinceurs en cas où.

Ce dernier symbole est très important. Toute route avec ce symbole est sur le point de devenir un voie sportive entièrement équipée, mais lors de la réalisation du guide les spits existants sont vieux et non fiables. N'escaladez pas ces voies sauf si les spits ont l'air manifestement neufs.

COTATIONS

Les voies sportives reçoivent les notes sportives habituelles. Les voies nécessitant une quantité importante d'équipement sont classées selon le système britannique, lui-même divisé en 2 parties:

1) La note qualificative (Diff, ..., Very Severe (VS ou "très difficile"), ... E1, E2, ... jusqu'à E9). Ceci vous donnera une vue d'ensemble de la voie, y compris son niveau de protection, d'intensité, ainsi qu'une indication du niveau de difficulté de l'ensemble de la voie.

2) La note technique (4a, 4b, 4c, 5a, ... jusqu'à 7a). Ceci fait référence au niveau de difficulté du mouvement individuel ou de la portion la plus ardue de la voie.

INFORMATION SUPPLÉMENTAIRE

Pour plus d'informations sur l'escalade dans le Dorset voir le site Web ROCKFAX à **www.rockfax.com** Le site contient une banque de données complète des voies. Vous pouvez y vérifier les changements de cotations, les nouvelles voies et bien plus. Vous y trouverez aussi des mises à jour que vous pourrez télécharger.

ROCKFAX

Derrière ROCKFAX, il y a Alan James, Chris Craggs, Mark Glaister, et Mick Ryan. Cela fait 15 ans que nous publions des guides couvrant les lieux situés dans le monde entier. Toute information sur nos publications sont accessibles sur le site Web.

Symboles des voies

 Bonne voie

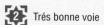 Trés bonne voie

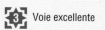 Voie excellente

 Escalade technique nécessitant des mouvements complexes et difficiles

Des bras solides pour des mouvements puissants

Grimpe intense, longue et très athlétique ou bien accumulant les mouvements difficiles

Grimpe sur le bout des doigts - la peau va chauffer

 'Deep water solo' (voir ci-contre)

 Coinceurs nécessaires (voir ci-contre)

Escalade Exposée avec un grand potentiel de chutes, mais, dans l'ensemble, pas trop de danger

 Les grands seront avantagés

Photo-topos

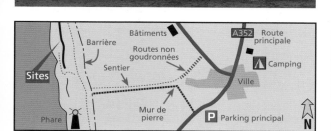

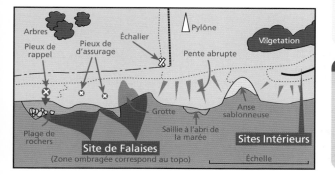

Symbole spécieux

 B Vieux spits non fiables lors de la réalisation du guide (voir ci-contre)

Symboles des parois

 Approche - Temps de marche d'approche, et angle.

 Soleil - Période approximative à laquelle la paroieest exposée au soleil

 Angle - Les angles de roche, de dalle à surplomb

 Restrictions - Escalade interdite pendant des périodes spécifiques

 Quelques voies de plusieurs longueurs

 Protége de la pluie

 Protégé du vent

 Approche en rappel nécessaire

 Atteint par la marée

Couleurs Différentes

Les numéros des voies en couleurs différentes correspondent aux bandes de cotations suivantes:

1 - Niveau 3+ ou au-dessous

2 - Niveau 4 à 5+

3 - Niveau 6a à 6c

4 - Niveau 6c+ et au-dessus

EINFÜHRUNG

Das Klettergebiet von Dorset ist wahrscheinlich das bedeutendste im Süden von England. Die Routen der beiden Hauptgebiete Swanage und Portland unterscheiden sich sehr stark im Stil der Kletterei. Beiden Gebieten gemeinsam ist ein warmes Klima, das sie zum nahen Ganzjahresziel für britische Kletterer macht. Seit den zeitigen 1990er Jahren hat sich Portland zu einem Sportklettergebiet entwickelt und verfügt gegenwärtig über mehr als 1000 voll abgesicherte Routen. Swanage bietet zwar ebenfalls einige eingerichtete Aufstiege, ist jedoch eher als traditionelles Gebiet bekannt, in dem der Kletterer seine Sicherungen selbst anbringt (Keile und Friends). Ebenfalls werden in diesem Buch die besten Gebiete für *deep water soloing* beschrieben, in denen man weder Bohrhaken, Keile noch Seile benötigt. Hier klettert man allein mit seinem Magnesiabeutel über dem Wasser, in das man sich im Falle eines Sturzes rettet. Lulworth Cove ist eines der besten Gebiete für *deep water soloing* und verfügt darüber hinaus über einige großartige und gut eingerichtete Routen. Das letzte Kapitel beschreibt die harten Sportkletterrouten in Devon.

Dieses Buch enthält sämtliche erforderliche Informationen, um in alle Klettergebiete zu gelangen und dort die Kletterein aufzufinden und einzuschätzen. Die Gebiete sind mittels Übersichtskarten, Topos und Symbolen umfassend illustriert. So wird es auch ohne Englischkenntnisse kein Problem sein, etwas zum Klettern auszuwählen und überzeugt zu sein, an der richtigen Route unterwegs zu sein.

AUSRÜSTUNG

Um auf Portland zu klettern, benötigt man ein langes Seil (50 Meter sind ausreichend für die meisten Routen, 60 Meter sind jedoch die bessere Wahl) sowie einige Expressschlingen. Für die *trad routes* in Swanage sind ein Satz Keile sowie Klemmgeräte (siehe Ausrüstung auf Seite 8) erforderlich. Man sollte außerdem darauf achten, ob ein zusätzliches Seil zum Abseilen benötigt wird, um an die Klippen zu gelangen (Abseilsymbol beachten). Für *deep water soloing* sind Ersatzschuhe, Magnesiabeutel und ein Handtuch ausreichend.

BESONDERE SYMBOLE

Drei Symbole sollten beachtet werden:

Dieses Symbol bedeutet: ein *deep water solo* ist möglich. Bitte die Sicherheitshinweise auf Seite 10 lesen und beachten (dieser Abschnitt enthält Informationen über die Gezeiten).

Dieses Symbol erscheint bei einigen Routen in Swanage und bedeutet, dass diese fast vollständig eingerichtet sind. Es empfiehlt sich jedoch, ein paar Keile zusätzlich dabeizuhaben.

Dieses letzte Symbol ist sehr wichtig. Routen mit diesem Symbol werden demnächst saniert. Zum Zeitpunkt der Drucklegung dieses Buchs waren einige oder alle Haken noch nicht erneuert und sind momentan alt und unsicher. Steige nicht in diese Routen ein, bis sie offensichtlich saniert worden sind.

SCHWIERIGKEITSBEWERTUNG

Die reinen Sportklettereien sind mit den üblichen (d.h. französischen) Bewertungen versehen. Routen, die man hauptsächlich selbst absichern muss, tragen die britische Bewertung, die wie folgt zu verstehen ist:

1) Eine adjektivische Bewertung wie "Diff" (schwierig), "Very Severe" (sehr ernst), [...], "E1, E2, ..., bis E9" (extreme Schwierigkeiten) stellt eine Gesamtbewertung der Schwierigkeiten bezüglich der Absicherung und der Länge der schwierigen Stellen der Route dar.

2) Die klettertechnische Bewertung 4a, 4b, 4c, 5a, ... bis 7a bezieht sich auf die Schwierigkeit des härtesten Einzelzuges (bzw. der härtesten Einzelstelle) der Tour.

ZUSÄTZLICHE INFORMATION

Weitere Informationen über Klettern in Dorset sind auf der Rockfax Webseite - **www.rockfax.com** - zu finden. Sie beinhaltet eine komplette Datenbank mit Bewertungsänderungen der Schwierigkeiten, neuen Routen und vieles mehr. Ebenso werden gelegentlich kostenfreie Updates im PDF-Format zum Herunterladen angeboten.

ROCKFAX

Rockfax sind Alan James, Chris Craggs, Mark Glaister und Mick Ryan. Wir veröffentlichen seit 15 Jahren Kletterführer von Gebieten in der ganzen Welt. Details zu all unseren Veröffentlichungen befinden sich auf unserer Web-Seite.

Symbole

 Lohnende Kletterei

 Sehr lohnende Kletterei

 Brilliante Kletterei

 Technisch anspruchsvolle Kletterei mit komplexen oder trickreichen Zügen

 Starke Oberarme für kraftvolle Züge erforderlich

 Durchgehend anstrengende Kletterei; entweder anhaltend schwer oder mit vielen harten Zügen

 Kleingriffige, rauhe Kletterei - nichts für zarte Hände

 Ein deep water solo (s. gegenüber)

 Kletterei, die Sicherung durch Klemmkeile u.ä. erfordert

 Heikle Kletterei mit hohem Sturzpotential

 Lange Arme sind hilfreich

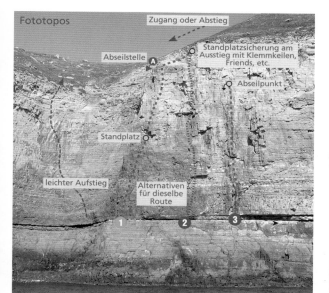

Fototopos

Zugang oder Abstieg

Abseilstelle

Standplatzsicherung am Ausstieg mit Klemmkeilen, Friends, etc.

Abseilpunkt

Standplatz

leichter Aufstieg

Alternativen für dieselbe Route

Besondere Routensymbole

 Route mit alten Bolts. Nicht in diese Route einsteigen, bis die Bohrhaken erneuert worden sind (siehe gegenüberliegende Seite)

Felssymbole

 Zugang - Zeit und Steilheit des Zugangsweges

 Sonnenschein - ungefähre Zeit, zu der der Felsen in der Sonne liegt

 Neigung - von geneigt bis überhängend

 Beschränkungen - Klettern ist zu manchen Zeiten verboten

 Vogelschutz - Klettern ist während der angegebenen Zeiträume verboten

 Einige Aufstiege mit mehreren Seillängen

 Trockener Fels bei Regen

 Windgeschützter bzw. warmer Felsen

 Zugang mittels Abseilen

 Vorsicht, Ebbe und Flut

Gebäude

Zaun

Schotterwege

Fußweg

A352 Hauptstraßen

Camping

Felsen

Stadt bzw. Dorf

Steinmauer

Leuchtturm

P Hauptparkplatz

N

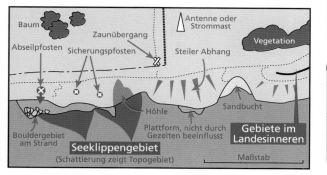

Baum

Zaunübergang

Antenne oder Strommast

Vegetation

Abseilpfosten Sicherungspfosten

Steiler Abhang

Höhle

Sandbucht

Plattform, nicht durch Gezeiten beeinflusst

Bouldergebiet am Strand

Seeklippengebiet
(Schattierung zeigt Topogebiet)

Gebiete im Landesinneren

Maßstab

Farbig markierte Routennummern

Die farbigen Routennummern entsprechen den folgenden Schwierigkeitsbereichen:

1 - Grad IV+ und darunter

2 - Grad V bis VI

3 - Grad VI+ bis VII+

4 - Grad VIII und darüber

INFORMATION

TOURIST INFORMATION OFFICES

For ideas on what to do on a rest day, accommodation advice, hiring a boat to look at some scary routes on Boulder Ruckle or if you are just interested in local history; take a look at one of the Tourist Information Offices listed below. These offices can provide much more useful and extensive information than it is possible to contain in these pages.

Tourist Information Weymouth - See map below. Tel: 01305 785747
Tourist Information Portland - Portland Bill Visitor Centre. Tel: 01305 861233
Tourist Information Purbeck - Town Hall, East Street, Wareham. Tel: 01929 552740
Tourist Information Swanage - Shore Road, Swanage. Tel: 01929 422885
Tourist Information Torquay - Harbourside, Torquay. Tel: 0906 6801268

PORTLAND ACCOMMODATION

No camping is allowed on Portland but there are a few sites close by. There are also several other caravan sites on the mainland.

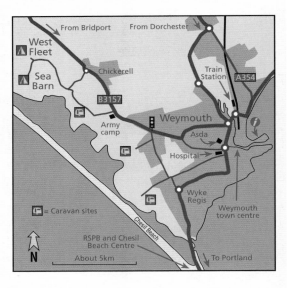

Sea Barn Farm Campsite - 🏕️🚿
Fleet, Weymouth. Tel: 01305 782218
Open - Mar. to Oct. - *advert opposite.*
Directions (see map) - Take the B3157 towards Bridport. After 3 miles turn left at a mini-roundabout on a bend towards Fleet. The camp site is 1 mile down here on the left.

West Fleet Holiday Farm - 🏕️🚿
Fleet, Weymouth. Tel: 01305 782218
Open - Mar. to Oct. - *advert opposite.*
Directions (see map) - Take the B3157 towards Bridport. After 3 miles turn left at a mini-roundabout on a bend towards Fleet. The camp site is 1 mile down here on the right.

Also worth considering are the following:
Dream Cottages - Tel: 01305 761347
Portland Holiday Cottages - Tel: 01305 861044
Cove Park Holiday Park - Tel: 01305 821286
Glen Caravan Holiday Park - Tel: 01305 823548

🏕️ - Tents
🚐 - Caravans for hire
🚿 - Showers
🚶 - Walk to pub

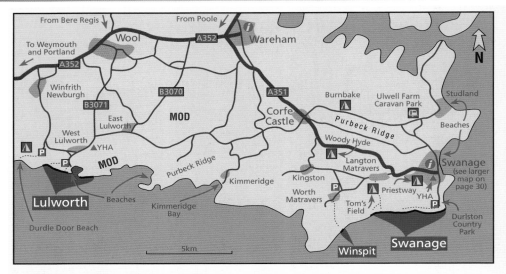

SWANAGE ACCOMMODATION

There are many camping and caravan sites in the area, several of the popular ones are listed below. Contact Swanage Tourist Information for more including non-camping options.

Tom's Field Campsite - 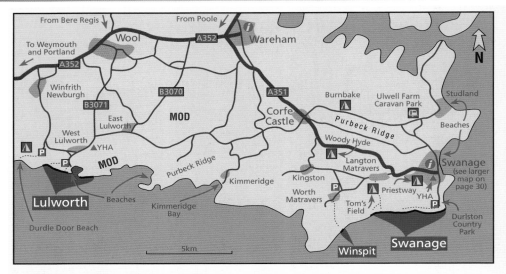 - *see advert opposite.*

Tom's Field Road, Langton Matravers, Swanage. Tel: 01929 427110. Open - Mar to Oct. Directions - Leave Swanage on B3067 (south of A351), for 2 miles to Langton Matravers. Tom's Field is on the left.

Priestway Holiday Park - 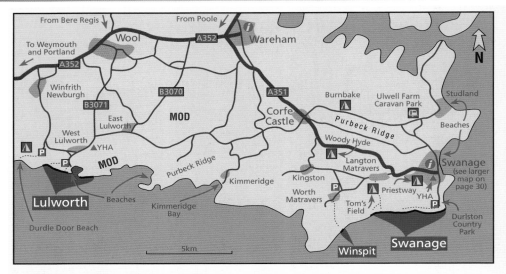 - www.shorefield.co.uk - *see advert opposite.*

Priests Way, Swanage. Tel: 01929 422747. Directions - Turn right on the approach to Swanage up the hill when you enter the edge of town. Drive through housing estate for 1km.

Burnbake Campsite -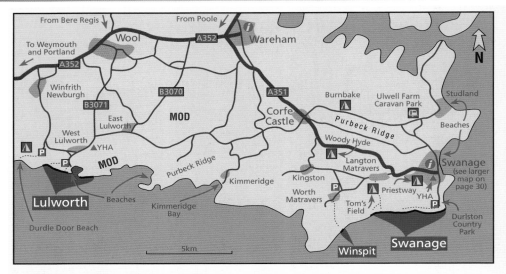

The Old Farmhouse, Rempstowe, Corfe Castle. Tel: 01929 480317. Open - Apr to Sept. Directions - Take B3351 from Corfe to Studland. Site is sign-posted down the 3rd turning on left.

Woody Hyde Farm Camping Park -

Corfe Castle, Wareham. Tel: 01929 480274. Open - Apr to Oct. Directions - Leave Corfe Castle towards Swanage. Campsite is 3/4 mile on the right.

Lulworth Area

Durdle Door Caravan Park -

West Lulworth. Tel: 01929 41200. Open - Apr to Oct.

	- Tents
	- Caravans for hire
	- Showers
	- Walk to pub

TORQUAY ACCOMMODATION

Torquay has many campsites, some of which don't allow all-male groups. One worth trying is **Widdicombe Farm** on the A380. (From Torquay, drive towards Newton Abbott). Another is **Landscove Campsite**, Staverton, near Totnes. (Turn left at first roundabout onto A380. The farm is on the right, 1 mile after the roundabout). A good alternative is to camp on the edge of Dartmoor at Holne Village which has a good pub near to the basic-but-pleasant site. The campsite also has a camping barn and is 30 minutes drive from the climbing.

PUBLIC TRANSPORT

South West Trains (SWT) run a fast service every hour from London Waterloo, via Wareham and Wool, to Weymouth. It may be possible to save one third on the fare with a *network card*. A cheap add-on ticket is also available from SWT stations which allows travel on Weymouth and Portland buses. (**www.swtrains.co.uk** **Tel -** 0845 6000 650).
Another rail service runs from Weymouth via Bath to Bristol. (**www.wessextrains.co.uk** **Tel -** 0845 6000 880).
More information is available from Traveline (**www.traveline.org.uk** **Tel -** 0870 608 2608) and from Dorset County Council (**www.dorsetcc.gov.uk/bustimes** **Tel -** 01305 225 165).

Portland Area

All the climbing on Portland is close to a regular bus service from Weymouth. The main service sets off from the riverside, just up and right from the railway station, or further along at the back of Debenhams department store. It runs at least every 15 minutes during the day time and will take you to Easton Square, for The Cuttings. It continues right at the Square and heads up, past the George Inn, to Weston Road. Get off at the third stop past the George Inn for the Blacknor Crags. It then loops round Southwell, closer to Battleship, Wallsend and the rest of the east coast cliffs. There is an evening service about every 20-30 minutes and the last bus is about 11pm. There is a different service which turns left, not right, at Easton Square, and passes closer to The Cuttings and the east coast cliffs.

Portland Bill Lighthouse. Photo: Mark Glaister

It also continues to Portland Bill on summer sundays during the day. Most services are currently operated by First Group (Services 1 and 1A). (**www.firstgroup.com/ukbus/south-west/dorset** **Tel -** 0870 608 2608).

Swanage Area

Swanage town is served by a bus service from Wareham Rail Station (north side) which runs hourly during the day and less frequently in the evening and on Sundays. It is a 1.5km walk from Swanage centre to Durlston Country Park for Subluminal, Boulder Ruckle and the other eastern crags. Usually each alternate bus serves Langton Matravers (Post Office) which is about 1.5 km from Dancing Ledge and the other western crags.
There is also a service from Swanage to Bournemouth via Branksome rail station. Be aware that this can be affected by delays on the Sandbank Ferry. Services are currently operated by Wilts and Dorset (services 142, 143, 144 and 150). (**www.wdbus.co.uk** **Tel -** 01202 673555).
There is a restricted bus service from Wool station to Lulworth Cove. Traveline (**www.traveline.org.uk** **Tel -** 0870 608 2608) or Dorset County Council (**www.dorsetcc.gov.uk/bustimes** **Tel -** 01305 225 165) are the best sources for information.

Torquay Area

Torquay is easily reached by rail from both London and the North. Bus services run from Newton Abbott to Ipplepen village that is within easy walking distance of Torbryan. Buses from Torquay or Newton Abbot Station to Babbacombe for Anstey's Cove run regularly.

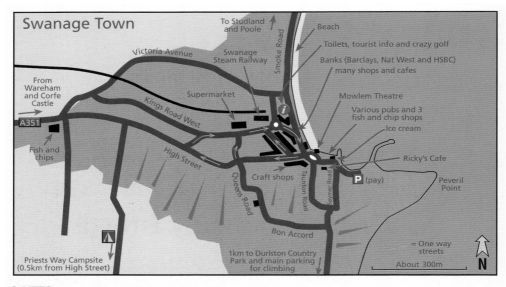

Swanage Town

To Studland and Poole

Beach

Toilets, tourist info and crazy golf

Victoria Avenue

Swanage Steam Railway

Smoke Road

Banks (Barclays, Nat West and HSBC) many shops and cafes

From Wareham and Corfe Castle

Kings Road West

Supermarket

Mowlem Theatre

Various pubs and 3 fish and chip shops

Ice cream

A351

Fish and chips

High Street

Craft shops

Queens Road

Taunton Road

Seymer Road

P (pay)

Ricky's Cafe

Peveril Point

Bon Accord

Priests Way Campsite (0.5km from High Street)

1km to Durlston Country Park and main parking for climbing

= One way streets

About 300m

N

CAFES

Portland Area

The Sugar Loaf in Easton gives good service and does a great fry-up.

The Blue Fish Cafe in Fortuneswell has good coffee.

The Church Ope Cafe is within 2 minutes walk of The Cuttings. Their tea cakes are huge and there is a beautiful flower garden to sit in.

The Tea Cosy in Fortuneswell is a pleasant place to start the day with a good full breakfast.

The Lobster Pot Cafe at Portland Bill is useful for the Coastguard and Cave Hole areas.

Lulworth Area

Lulworth has a very well situated cafe, right in the middle of the car park. There are some tea shops in Lulworth village just up the road from the Cove itself.

Swanage Area

Swanage town has lots of cafes with the best being *Ricky's*, *BeaveR* and *Hayman's*. Tea shops exist at the outlying venues of Langton Matravers and Worth Matravers.

Torquay Area

The best cafe is at Lymington Coach Station; a really good fry-up.

TAKE-AWAYS and RESTAURANTS

Portland Area

There are many fish and chips shops on the Isle. *Cafe India* in Fortuneswell is a good indian. *The Golden Island Chinese* in Easton is worth a look. There are three restaurants of note, *Giovanni's* (Italian) in Easton, *Vaughan's* in Weston and *The Blue Fish Cafe* also in Fortuneswell. *The Cove House Inn* also does good food.

Swanage Area

Head for Swanage town centre where you will find a good selection of take-aways and restaurants. If you are wanting to stop on the approach then try the Main Street in Wareham.

Torquay Area

Torquay is heaving with takeaways but the ones on the sea front are best avoided if you want a decent sized portion. There is a full selection (Indian, Chinese and pizza) next to each other on Market Street (off Union Street) in the town centre.

CLIMBING SHOPS

Portland

Ultimate Outdoor World, Southwell Business Park, Portland - *see advert on page 29*.
The Scuba Centre, Fortuneswell.

Dorchester

Great Western Camping, London Road, Dorchester - *see advert inside back cover*.

Exeter

Moorland Rambler, Fore Street, Exeter.

SHOPS

Portland Area

Weymouth is packed with every shop you could need. There is a large ASDA on the roundabout as you approach Portland. On Portland there are a few mini-markets. The largest is in the centre of Easton and there are another two on the main street in Weston. A Co-op is on the main street in Fortuneswell.

Swanage Area

There is a large Co-op supermarket in Swanage centre and also shops in Wareham on the drive to the crags.

Lulworth Area

In Lulworth there is one expensive local store - better to go to Wareham.

Torquay Area

There is a large Sainsbury's on the main approach road to Torquay and many other shops in the area.

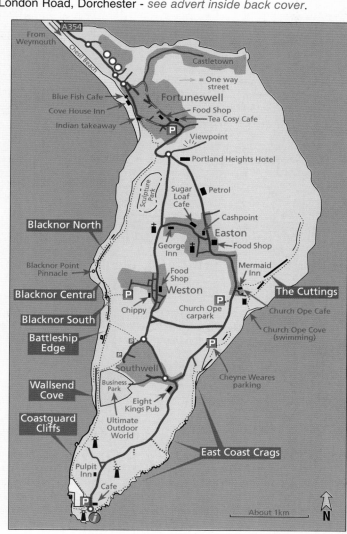

INFORMATION

GOOD PUB GUIDE

Portland Area
Portland has a pub on every corner, but many are 'locals only'. *The Cove House Inn* in Fortuneswell is a great place to sit outside as the sun sets over Chesil Beach. *The Mermaid* in Easton is also worth considering as is *The George. The Royal Breakwater Hotel* in Castletown has good food and serves until 10pm.

Lulworth Area
The Castle Inn is a nice pub with good food and a low slung roof.

Swanage Area
In Swanage town there is a whole cluster of pubs near the end of the pier. However the favourite haunt is situated directly above the cliffs - *The Durlston Castle Inn*. If you are climbing at Dancing Ledge or Winspit you can head straight for *The Square and Compass* at Worth Matravers which has a very 'olde world' atmosphere. *The Scott Arms* in Kingston (near Worth Matravers) is pleasant. Many of the pubs in Corfe Castle are excellent but possibly the best is *The Fox Inn*.

SQUARE & COMPASS

01929 439229

Worth Matravers

Real Ales • Ciders • Pasties Traditionally Relaxing Stunning Views over Winspit and Beyond

Worth Matravers, Swanage, Dorset

Torquay Area
The Cary Arms at the base of Babbacombe cliffs very close to Anstey's Cove is a great evening and lunch spot with a big beer garden and great food by the beach. *The Church House Inn* a stones throw from the top of Torbryan Quarry is a traditional thatched country pub with up market food and a peaceful beer garden.

CLIMBING WALLS

Q.E. Leisure Centre (The Edge) -
Blandford Road, Wimbourne, Dorset. Tel: 01202 888208. 8m high lead and top-rope wall plus bouldering room and a bar for après training. Best local wall to crags. Open weekday evenings and weekends all day.

Calshot Activities Centre -
Calshot Spit, Fawley, Southampton. Tel: 01703 892077. A large centre with a 20m leading wall. Open weekday evenings and weekend afternoons.

- Food
- Lead wall
- Bouldering

BEACHES
Along the coastline the variety of scenery is quite remarkable. Beautiful unspoilt sandy beaches occur at Studland, Sandbanks and Weymouth. There are also delightful stony coves at Lulworth, Worrbarrow Bay and Swanage Bay. The major venues have organised watersports such as water-skiing, parascending and windsurfing. Other areas which are popular for sunbathing and with families are Dancing Ledge Quarry and Church Ope Cove on Portland. Torquay has a lot of town beaches and coves but the beach beneath the climbing at Anstey's Cove is great for swimming.

ACKNOWLEDGMENTS

The crags of Devon and Dorset have been both home and away venues for all of my climbing life and have provided a few decades of fun that has been greatly enhanced by those who I have climbed with. My teenage days with Bruce Woodley, Brian Wilkinson, Mark Mallet and James Waddell were a mad mix of terror and pleasure never to be forgotten.

Many thanks to all who I have shared a rope with all along the coast, and to those who have helped with this guide and the development of climbing and climbs in the area, especially the following: all the Cooks, Mike Robertson, Barry Clarke, Steve Taylor, Mark Williams, Marty Hallett, Rich White, Rob Kennard, Dan Knight, Christine Forkin, Emma Medara, Gavin Symonds, Danie Rushmer, Dalvinder Sodhi, Ben Stokes, Nigel Tuckley, Bev Hull, Al Ashmore, Dave Pickford, Clare Dyson, Arran Deakin, Chris Gore, Rob Knight, Johnny Woods, Lee Proctor, Guy Blackwood, Steve Watt, Ken Palmer, Rob Sutton and Clarke Alston.

Damian Cook. Photo: Joff Cook

A huge amount of the information in this book has come from the Rockfax Route Database. I am very grateful to all those who contributed, keep the feedback coming in. Thanks to Nick Smith for his excellent technical work on the ROCKFAX web site.

The production of the guidebook is a long and complex process. Thanks to Alan James and Chris Craggs especially. Also, thanks to Carl Dawson for his proof reading, Mike Robertson for his excellent photography and also his proof checking. I am also grateful to Karsten Kurz and Arnaud Garçon for their help with the French and German translation pages. Others who I would like to thank are Dave Gregory, Colin Binks, Mick Ward, Jim Kimber, Roger Hill, all at Warners and Stuart Fletcher, Peter Garley and all at Clearpoint Colourprint.

A special thanks to Andy and Chegs for their great company and generosity and to Neal and Helen who have always been a great source of fun and brilliant company whether on the crag, at sea, or down the pub. A huge thanks to Pete Oxley for all his amazing routes and dedication and good luck in New Zealand. Finally my last thanks go to Rachel for yet again putting up with my travels and to promise that after we move to Devon my next guide won't be at the other end of the country (well not this country anyway)!

Mark Glaister, June 2005

For myself as one of the guidebook authors for the past three editions, it is also a pivotal moment for change as plans are in place to move to New Zealand at Christmas. The usual climbing crew of partners over the last 20 years must be thanked for a rucsac full of great memories. In very recent times special mention must be made of Andy Bell, Rob Kennard, Richard White and Dan Knight who have given great friendship both on the cliffs and off. Not forgetting of course a high five to my long-suffering partner Jan Rostron, here's to a beautiful new future Down Under.

Finally thanks must be made to all those who helped with donations to the bolt fund, and particularly Neal Heanes on Portland who has taken on

Brian Tilley. Photo: Pete Oxley

the bulk of recent work. Thanks also to Neal and Steve Taylor for the continued representations as BMC Reps to maintain good relations with landowners and management people alike. For sheer enthusiasm and regular production of interim guides published, Ben Stokes is also due a debt of gratitude for keeping a record of the ever-young Dorset scene.

DAMIAN COOK and BRIAN TILLEY

In particular I would like to dedicate this guide to the memory of both Brian Tilley and Damian Cook. It is with the greatest pride that I can say I climbed and developed these cliffs with both of them over the last twenty years. Both were warm and humble people, massively motivated and huge fun to be around. Their spirit lives on upon the cliffs of Swanage and Portland, spare a moment for reflection at their passing when you set foot on classics of theirs such as *Frazzled*, *Enchanted Path* and *Octopuss Weed*, man it hurts every time to think you are both gone.

So feel the weight of this guide there is no way anyone can say Dorset is ever a sleepy backwater. Enjoy the 1800+ climbs, act responsibly, and remember don't say the word rabbit on Portland.

Keep ya pipe lit, know what I mean pal to all the old skool, stay golden!

Pete Oxley, June 2005

ADVERTISER DIRECTORY

Rockfax is very grateful to the following companies who have supported this guidebook.

GEAR SHOPS

GREAT WESTERN CAMPING - Inside Back
28 High Street East, Dorchester.
Tel: 01305 266800
22 Catherine Street, Salisbury.
Tel: 01722 322100

ROCK ON - Page 199
Mile End Climbing Wall, London.
Tel: 0208 981 5066
Craggy Island, Guildford.
Tel: 01483 565635
www.rockonclimbing.co.uk

SNOW + ROCK - Opposite
Romford, Manchester, Sheffield, Birmingham,
Bristol, Portsmouth, Chertsey, Covent Garden,
Kensington, Holborn. Tel: 0845 100 1000
www.snowandrock.com

ULTIMATE OUTDOOR WORLD - Page 29
Southwell Business Park, Portland.
Tel: 01305 862228
www.ultimateworld.co.uk

COURSES and HOLIDAYS

ROCK & SUN - Page 25
Tel: 0871 871 6782
www.rockandsun.com

PLAS Y BRENIN - Page 13
Capel Curig, North Wales
Tel: 01690 720214
www.pyb.co.uk

CLIMBING WALLS

AWESOME WALLS - Page 33
St. Alban's Church, Athol Street, Liverpool.
Tel/Fax: 0151 298 2422
www.awesomewalls.co.uk

ENTRE-PRISE - Page 27
Entre-Prise (UK), Kelbrook.
Tel: 01282 444800 Fax: 01282 444801
www.ep-uk.com

THE LEEDS WALL - Page 25
100a Gelderd Road, Leeds.
Tel/Fax: 0113 234 1554
www.theleedswall.co.uk

ACCOMMODATION

PRIESTWAY HOLIDAY PARK - Page 27
Priestway, Swanage.
Tel: 01590 648331
www.shorefield.co.uk

TOM'S FIELD - Page 27
Langton Matravers, Swanage.
Tel: 01929 427110

WEYMOUTH CAMPSITES - Page 25
Sea Barn Campsite. Tel: 01305 782218
www.seabarnfarm.co.uk
West Fleet Holiday Farm. Tel: 01305 782218
www.westfleetholidays.co.uk
Bagwell Farm Touring Park. Tel: 01305 782575
www.bagwellfarm.co.uk

PUBS

SQUARE & COMPASS - Page 32
Worth Matravers, Swanage.
Tel: 01929 439229

MAGAZINES

CLIMBER - Page 2
Warners Group Publications. Tel: 01778 392004
www.climber.co.uk

OUTDOOR GEAR

BERGHAUS - Inside Front
Extreme Centre, Sunderland.
Tel: 0191 5165600 Fax: 0191 5165601
www.berghaus.com

BLACK DIAMOND - Outside Back
Tel: 0162 958 0484
www.blackdiamondequipment.com

Portland

Dave Pickford sampling the mighty *Beautiful South* (7c), at Wallsend. - *page 103*. Photo: Mark Glaister

PORTLAND

The Isle of Portland is a unique spot in Britain, jutting out into the English Channel with its only link to the mainland being via the narrow pebble strip of Chesil Beach. It is now part of the recently-designated Jurassic Coast World Heritage Coastline but for climbers the area's special environment and famous white stone are more well known as one of Britain's best sport climbing venues.

Circling the Isle's lofty fringes are around 6km of virtually unbroken limestone cliffs, a good proportion of which has been developed with hundreds of well-bolted sport routes throughout the grades. Early exploration did include some traditionally protected routes, however Portland's future always lay in sport climbing and the development has been dramatic in the last 20 years or so. More recently, deep water soloing has been added to the Isle's climbing heritage and not to be left out, the boulderers have also found some great little venues most of which are tucked away on the more-sheltered East Coast. As a venue for new routes, the Isle is finally reaching maturity; there are gaps left but most of these will be fillers in and of no great quality although this has been said before in previous guides and proved to be wrong on those occasions.

Portland itself is a place of rich history riddled with folklore about smugglers, quarrymen and shipwrecks. These legacies are now reflected in its unique population and oddly constructed terraces of stone cottages. Modern times have seen the closure of the local Naval base coincide with the development of a tourist industry based around diving and sailing and this is undoubtedly the direction that the future of the area lies. The landscape also provides an important habitat for a wide variety of plants and animals, some of which are nationally or even globally scarce. Because of this, the coastline is designated a Site of Special Scientific Interest (SSSI), is a European Special Area of Conservation (SAC) and also has its own dedicated warden. Often such designations bring with them problems for climbers but thankfully this area is not burdened by excessive access problems and there are only a few small issues to be aware of.

The climate on Portland is mild and there is the possibility for year-round outdoor climbing since there is limited seepage and lots of sunshine during the winter months. The east and west aspects mean that sun or shade can almost always be found and, unlike most sea cliffs, tides are not such a big issue here with only a few sections being affected.

The majority of the routes are well bolted with long life staples throughout so it is normally possible for climbers to push their grade to the limit without too much in the way of fear. Whether dedicated local, beginner, old hand, winter-sunseeker or holidaying family climber, Portland has something for all.

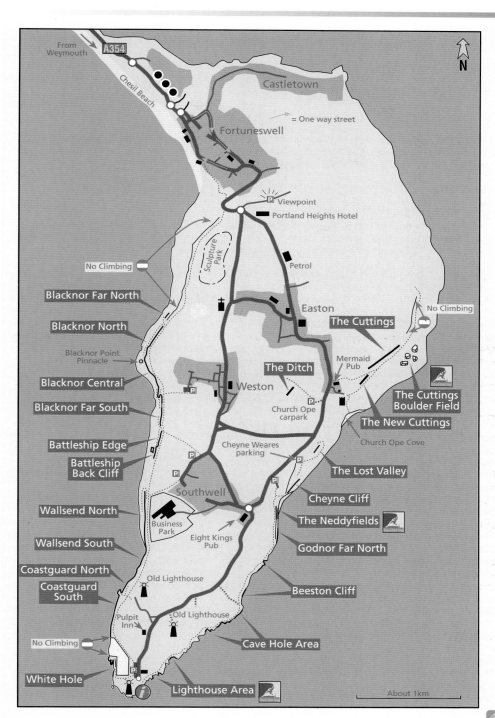

From Weymouth

A354

Chesil Beach

Castletown

Fortuneswell

= One way street

Viewpoint

Portland Heights Hotel

N

Sculpture Park

No Climbing

Petrol

Blacknor Far North

Easton

The Cuttings

No Climbing

Blacknor North

Mermaid Pub

Blacknor Point Pinnacle

The Ditch

The Cuttings Boulder Field

Blacknor Central

Weston

Blacknor Far South

Church Ope carpark

The New Cuttings

Church Ope Cove

Battleship Edge

Cheyne Weares parking

Battleship Back Cliff

The Lost Valley

Wallsend North

Southwell

Cheyne Cliff

The Neddyfields

Wallsend South

Business Park

Eight Kings Pub

Godnor Far North

Coastguard North

Coastguard South

Old Lighthouse

Beeston Cliff

Old Lighthouse

Pulpit Inn

No Climbing

Cave Hole Area

White Hole

Lighthouse Area

About 1km

PORTLAND *History*

Pre 1967 - Portland is ravaged by inland quarrying and the coastal crags were left to the peregrines and seagulls. A small band of locals establishes many of the easier routes at The Cuttings.

1967 - Mad Reverend Bob Shepton records first routes of real significance such as *Vesuvius*. Many loose cracks are ascended around the coast often involving horrendous top-outs. The first E1s and E2s are recorded by Shepton accompanied by Ian Kestin.

1972 - Murray Hodgson adds many routes to Blacknor South.

1977 to 1981 - Shepton's reign continues sometimes in the company of George Hounsome. This pair add several strenuous E2s. In 1980 Dave Jones hit E4 with *Kate* and Pat Littlejohn does likewise with *Bad Dream* at the Cuttings in 1981.

1983 - The first new route from a young Pete Oxley - *Two Fingers* at The Cuttings.

THE MINIMALIST DRILLED-PEG ERA
The clean white walls of Portland were first climbed using limited numbers of stainless steel drilled pegs, however most of the routes still required a very bold approach on mainly trad gear. Portland's early reputation was as a place to be wary of and nobody visited to repeat the routes.

1988 - Oxley puts up the first hard routes *Superfly Guy* (7a) and *Nothing but the Groove* (6c+) at Coastguard North, both with the odd drilled peg runner. *Colors*, the first E6 6b is found in Wallsend Cove. 7c arrives in the shape of *Keyboard Wall* at Battleship Edge which sees many new routes.

1989 - Martin Crocker opens up Blacknor Far South and Nigel Coe adds some easier lines. Oxley adds *Realm of Chaos* (7b+) and *Zum Zeaux* (7b+) to the Wallsend Area and the Coastguard crags are opened up. *Cocteau Phenomena* (7b) at Blacknor South by Oxley is the first pure sport climb on drilled pegs throughout. Late in year On The Edge mag profiled 'the new Pen Trwyn', as Portland was dubbed.

1990 - The Cuttings gets developed with some hard test-pieces from Oxley and Crocker. Battleship Back Cliff is opened up by Oxley with the likes of *Zinc Oxide Mountain* (7b+). Crocker puts up the second full sport route with *Wax Museum* (7b+).

1991 - Coastguard South receives attention from Oxley with some classics like *Quick as Rainbows* (7a+).

THE MODERN STAPLE BOLT ERA
Despite the wealth of new routes, Portland continued to be an unpopular backwater considered as having only bold, hard climbs on suspect rock. The decision was made by Oxley to fully bolt all his subsequent new routes. To do this required a cheap and long-lasting bolt system. Oxley introduced the first home made U-staples into Britain which were based on a system seen in Spain.
Retro-bolting - Many of today's classic clip-ups used to be gnarly trad routes. As the number of fully bolted new routes increased it seemed logical, albeit controversial, to start retro-bolting the older, neglected lines. Initially this was done on the routes which formerly required drilled pegs and has since spread to virtually all the lines. The general rule was to only retro-bolt with the first ascensionist's permission. Pete Oxley led the way with the retro-bolting over the next a few years, a huge task requiring massive financial investment on his part. Thanks are due to all who have contributed in any way.

1992 - Oxley opens up Blacknor North with popular classics such as *Reptile Smile* (6a+) and *England's Dreaming* (7a+). Word spreads and other locals join in such as the Cook brothers and Steve Taylor. 8a arrives in November with *Freaky Ralph*, by Oxley - after 5 days of effort.

1994 - Bay of Rainbows is opened up by Steve Taylor. Damian Cook lands his best route in the shape of *Hong Kong Phooey* (7c). Mike Robertson, with support from Oxley and Taylor, develops the atmospheric White Hole. Cheyne Cliff is opened by Oxley with classics such as *Road Rage* (7b+). Just before the 1994 ROCKFAX goes to press Oxley climbs *Vespasian* (8a+) the hardest route to date.

The East Coast of Portland offers a wide grade-span of quality sport routes and boulder problems that are nearly always in condition. Neal Heanes on *Consommé* (6a+) at The Cuttings - *page 165*. Photo: Mark Glaister

1995 - Neal and Helen Heanes become regular new routers at the Blacknor crags and eventually open Rockies Climbing Shack. Oxley turns his attention to the east coast with some super-steep routes in Cave Hole such as *King of the Swingers* (7c+) and visitor Grant Wright climbs *Resisting Mutiny* (7c+).

1996 - Londoner Nic Hellyer begins his campaign on the Blacknor crags. More hard routes in the 7c/8a range are added by Oxley. Sector Pom Pom is given the treatment by Oxley and Luc Percival with his superb *Big Blue* (7c+). *Illusions* (7c) at Cheyne Cliff gives Jon Cook his finest new climb to date.

1997 - Mike Vaicaitis (with members of the Basingstoke M.C.) put up some easier climbs at Godnor Far North. Heanes, Hellyer and Oxley all very active and Guy Dixon creates a classic with his *Detonator* (7c) at Cheyne and Chris Cubitt makes the first repeat of an 8a with *Breathing Method*.

1998 - Wallsend North has many easier lines added by Neal and Helen Heanes whilst Coastguard North and South are plundered of many last remaining hard classics by Oxley. Andy Long bags the best line left with his brilliant *Tennessee* (7c) at Coastguard South. James Dunlop, Jim Kimber and Oxley develop White Hole North. Dave Pickford, Long and Dixon are all active repeating Oxley's hard routes.

1999 - Gav Symonds helps clean up some projects with *Clockwork Orange* (7c) at Coastguard North. Neal Heanes gets *Wasted* (7b+) at Coastguard North and Oxley finally completes *Balance of Power* (8a) at White Hole. Pickford continues his repeat quest and late in the year a bouldering wave, centred on the New Cuttings, Sector Pom Pom and the Lost Valley, takes place with two V10s from Oxley and Kimber.

2000 - Dave Pickford repeats some hard test-pieces including *Magnetic Pull* (8a) and makes an impressive on-sight of *Zen Zero* (7c+) a feat equalled by Chris Cubitt. Then, without a rope, Pickford topped the DWS season with an ascent of *Nightmirth* (7c). Elsewhere the bouldering scene exploded, with Jim Kimber cleaning up old projects at The Neddyfields up to V9.

2001 - The arrival of the *Gary Gibson new route machine* sees a rapid cleaning up of outstanding lines down the West Coast, particularly at Coastguard South. The Cuttings Boulderfield is developed by Ben Stokes, Tim Crawshaw and friends with over 50 problems added up to V6. Martin Crocker returned with many serious shallow water solos at Beeston culminating with *Extreme Lives*, the Isle's first E7. Elsewhere Andy Long bagged a major classic prow aptly calling it *Beautiful South* (7c) at Wallsend.

2002 - The year of many Gibson ingenious routes as his new route tally grows, particularly at Wallsend North. Development continues at the Cuttings Boulderfield by Ben Stokes and friends.

2003 - A busy year with the prolific Gibson discovering many decent pitches and the odd classic such as *Olympus Mons* (7b) down in Wallsend. Nearby, Andy Long added the classic *Rush* (7b+) and Gavin Symonds completes the late Damian Cook's project naming it in his memory *To Hungary for Love* (8a) in Wallsend North. Other locals, Mick Ward and Neal Heanes, plug away with *Vin Chaud* and *Sang Chaud* standing out at 7a+. Heanes does a lot of retro-bolt work, especially at The Cuttings. Liam Halsey had a dream weekend bagging the second ascent of *Vespasian* (now 8b) where many had failed after repeating *Tuppence* in Devon the day before.

2004 - Yet more Gibson activity, especially at Battleship and Blacknor, with some surprisingly worthwhile finds. Mick Ward fills in a few other gaps and locals Steve Taylor and Mark Williams develop Beeston South. Strong John Gaskins brings the first V10 with a re-ascent of *Guy Fawlkes* after hold loss.

2005 - The popularity of Portland has not diminished with visitors and it is now firmly on the map as one of Britain's favourite sport climbing destinations. This confirms the vision Oxley had instigated back in the early 90s against stiff opposition. The latest Rockfax brings to light the full spectrum of Portland climbing adding DWS and the best bouldering all in full colour.

For the future who knows, surely there cannot be more new routes – can there?

Mark Glaister deep water soloing *Russian Roulette* (E4 6a) on the Ixtlan Area, Cave Hole on the East Coast - *page 136.* Photo: Mike Robertson

Since 2000 the routes in Dorset have been open for voting on stars and grades on the ROCKFAX web site and this graded list has been based on the many votes we have received. Some additional routes have been added to the list if the online database concensus wasn't sufficient. If you disagree with the list then please let us know by visiting the web site and placing your votes - www.rockfax.com. The routes are listed in descending grade order and with each route are three tick boxes. You can use these three tick boxes as you see fit but the intention is that box 1 is for clean ascents, box 2 for clean ascents but not first try, and box three is for all other styles!

1 2 3 8b
♦♦♦ ☐☐☐ Vespasian

1 2 3 8a
♦♦ ☐☐☐ Freaky Ralph
♦♦ ☐☐☐ The Breathing Method
♦♦ ☐☐☐ Fighting Torque

1 2 3 7c+
♦♦♦ ☐☐☐ Magnetic Pull
♦♦♦ ☐☐☐ Monoculture
♦♦ ☐☐☐ Bar Room Brawl
♦♦ ☐☐☐ The Big Blue
♦♦ ☐☐☐ Hurricane on a Millpond
♦♦ ☐☐☐ The Mind Terrorist

1 2 3 7c
♦♦♦ ☐☐☐ Beautiful South
♦♦ ☐☐☐ Screaming Skulls
♦♦ ☐☐☐ Shining Heart
♦♦ ☐☐☐ The Font of Knowledge
♦♦♦ ☐☐☐ Illusions
♦♦♦ ☐☐☐ Keyboard Wall
♦♦ ☐☐☐ Hall of Mirrors
♦♦ ☐☐☐ Crucifix Kiss
♦♦♦ ☐☐☐ Tennessee
♦♦ ☐☐☐ Hong Kong Phooey

1 2 3 7b+
♦♦ ☐☐☐ Running It In
♦♦♦ ☐☐☐ The Racing Line
♦♦ ☐☐☐ Subyouth
♦♦♦ ☐☐☐ Red Medicine
♦♦ ☐☐☐ Headwall Emptiness
♦♦♦ ☐☐☐ Wax Museum
♦♦ ☐☐☐ Info Freako
♦♦ ☐☐☐ Infernal Din
♦♦ ☐☐☐ Sign of the Vulcan

7b+ continued....
♦♦ ☐☐☐ Frenzied Detruncation
♦♦♦ ☐☐☐ Realm of Chaos
♦♦♦ ☐☐☐ Zinc Oxide Mountain
♦♦ ☐☐☐ Brooklyn Bimbo
♦♦♦ ☐☐☐ Road Rage
♦♦♦ ☐☐☐ Colors
♦♦ ☐☐☐ Coralized
♦♦ ☐☐☐ Cocteau Phenomena
♦♦ ☐☐☐ In on the Killtaker
♦♦ ☐☐☐ Mr. Natural

1 2 3 7b
♦♦♦ ☐☐☐ Want Out
♦ ☐☐☐ Corinthian Spirit
♦ ☐☐☐ Sparkling Bone Chamber
♦♦ ☐☐☐ Weakest to the Wall
♦ ☐☐☐ Rusty Chubblock Needs Oil ....
♦ ☐☐☐ Dumbfounded
♦♦ ☐☐☐ The Fun Factory
♦♦ ☐☐☐ Choco Loni
♦♦♦ ☐☐☐ Genuflection
♦♦♦ ☐☐☐ Twangy Pearl
♦♦ ☐☐☐ AeroForce
♦♦ ☐☐☐ Biscuits for Smut
♦♦♦ ☐☐☐ Halfway to Heaven
♦♦♦ ☐☐☐ Sweet Smell of Success
♦♦ ☐☐☐ Spare Rib
♦♦ ☐☐☐ Ryme Intrinseca
♦♦ ☐☐☐ Nihil
♦♦ ☐☐☐ Troll Team Special
♦ ☐☐☐ So Special
♦♦♦ ☐☐☐ Outside the Gate
♦♦ ☐☐☐ Stay Golden
♦♦ ☐☐☐ Olympus Mons
♦ ☐☐☐ Even Better than the Beatles

1 2 3 7a+
♦♦ ☐☐☐ Dreams Burn Down
♦♦♦ ☐☐☐ Dogtown Skate Team
♦♦ ☐☐☐ Psychic EMF
♦♦♦ ☐☐☐ Pump Hitler
♦♦ ☐☐☐ The Mouth Waters
♦♦ ☐☐☐ Humanoid
♦♦ ☐☐☐ The Bigger Piece
♦♦ ☐☐☐ Live By The Sword
♦♦ ☐☐☐ Cybernetic Orchard
♦♦ ☐☐☐ The Singing Bush
♦♦ ☐☐☐ Psychosomatic Addict
♦♦ ☐☐☐ Barbed Wire Kisses
♦♦ ☐☐☐ Forensic Scene
♦♦♦ ☐☐☐ Victims of Fashion
♦ ☐☐☐ Screw the Roses, Send me Thorns
♦♦♦ ☐☐☐ England's Dreaming
♦♦ ☐☐☐ Apple Turn Overload
♦♦ ☐☐☐ Bad Moon Rising
♦♦♦ ☐☐☐ Reverence

7a+ continued....
♦♦ ☐☐☐ Rocket from the Crypt
♦ ☐☐☐ Silage Clamp
♦♦ ☐☐☐ Great Barrier Reef
♦♦ ☐☐☐ Through the Barricades
♦♦♦ ☐☐☐ Quick as Rainbows
♦ ☐☐☐ Wurlitzer Jukebox
♦♦ ☐☐☐ Chaos UK

1 2 3 7a
♦♦ ☐☐☐ Haute Cuisine
♦ ☐☐☐ 1789
♦♦♦ ☐☐☐ Portland Heights
♦♦ ☐☐☐ The Holy Hand Grenade
♦♦ ☐☐☐ The Strobolising Scyphostoma
♦♦ ☐☐☐ Mechanoids
♦♦ ☐☐☐ Pining for Glossop
♦♦ ☐☐☐ Master of the Rolls
♦ ☐☐☐ Reve D'un Corbeau
♦♦♦ ☐☐☐ Vin Chaud
♦♦ ☐☐☐ Is Vic There?
♦♦ ☐☐☐ Modern Nightmare
♦ ☐☐☐ Tea Cakes Calling
♦♦ ☐☐☐ No me Comas el Coco
♦♦♦ ☐☐☐ Superfly Guy
♦ ☐☐☐ Loose Cannon
♦ ☐☐☐ Onto the Ice Flow
♦ ☐☐☐ Dirty Cow
♦ ☐☐☐ Kamikaze Moped
♦♦ ☐☐☐ Acid Jazz Disco
♦♦ ☐☐☐ Sacred Angel
♦♦ ☐☐☐ Jurassic Shift
♦♦ ☐☐☐ To Wish the Impossible
♦♦ ☐☐☐ Meltdown
♦♦♦ ☐☐☐ Forget Columbus
♦ ☐☐☐ Hot From the Forge
♦♦ ☐☐☐ Wolfgang Forever
♦♦♦ ☐☐☐ Medusa Falls
♦♦ ☐☐☐ Last Rose of Summer
♦ ☐☐☐ Bilboes
♦ ☐☐☐ Beer and Corruption

1 2 3 6c+
♦ ☐☐☐ Spontaneous Cattle Combustion
♦♦ ☐☐☐ The Oldest Profession
♦♦ ☐☐☐ Eight-Bar Blues
♦♦ ☐☐☐ Streaky
♦♦ ☐☐☐ Julie Ocean
♦ ☐☐☐ Cerebellum
♦♦ ☐☐☐ Isle of Slingers
♦ ☐☐☐ Come, Armageddon, Come
♦ ☐☐☐ Defcon One
♦♦♦ ☐☐☐ Nothing but the Groove
♦♦ ☐☐☐ El Poder De Un Coño
♦♦♦ ☐☐☐ Turned to Stone
♦ ☐☐☐ Serious Music
♦♦ ☐☐☐ Lost In Rock
♦♦ ☐☐☐ Scapa Flow
♦ ☐☐☐ Kill a Gent's Tart
♦♦ ☐☐☐ The Cutting Edge

Portland West | Portland East | Lulworth | Swanage | Devon | Blacknor N | Blacknor C | Blacknor S | Blacknor FS | Battleship M | Battleship B | Wallsend N | Wallsend S | Coastguard N | Coastguard S | White Hole

1 2 3 6c

- ◆ Evening Falls Direct
- ◆◆ Out of Reach, Out of Mind
- ◆◆ The Unworthy
- ◆◆◆ Flowers on the Razor Wire
- ◆◆ Where Silence Has Lease
- ◆◆ Downtown Julie Brown
- ◆ Pure Shores
- ◆ If You Should Go Skating
- ◆◆ Lefty Hoot 'n' Annie
- ◆◆ Always Have the Edge
- ◆◆ Bermuda Triangle
- ◆◆ Drowning on Dry Land
- ◆◆ Nothing is Cool
- ◆ Cliché Upon Cliché
- ◆◆ New Saladin
- ◆◆ Nobody's Hero
- ◆ Fantasy Island
- ◆◆ Protein Delta Strip
- ◆◆ Judge Jeffreys
- ◆◆ Blue Faced Booby
- ◆ Magical Mr. Mephistopheles
- ◆◆ No Man is an Island
- ◆ Blackthorn Winter
- ◆◆ Poop Scoop
- ◆◆ Wind in the Riggin'

1 2 3 6b+

- ◆◆◆ Burning Skies
- ◆◆◆ Buoys will be Buoys
- ◆◆ Enchanted Path
- ◆◆ Raise the Titanic
- ◆◆ Harpies and Quines
- ◆◆ Weird Shit, Keep Drilling
- ◆◆ Driven Like the Snow
- ◆ Bum Droplets
- ◆◆◆ The Jewel of the Isle
- ◆ The Sound of One Hold Snapping
- ◆ President Elect
- ◆◆ Reality Bites
- ◆◆ Bladerunner
- ◆ She's Going Down
- ◆◆ The Unknown Soldier
- ◆ Return to Roissy
- ◆◆◆ Walking the King
- ◆◆ Ausfahrt
- ◆ Seattle be the Day
- ◆◆ The Right Mix
- ◆ Peace in the Nineties
- ◆◆ The Empire State Arete
- ◆◆◆ Lord Stublock Deepvoid
- ◆ Hot Pants Explosion
- ◆ Losing My Sad Tomato
- ◆ Slumberland Direct
- ◆◆ Inch Perfect, Inchworm

1 2 3 6b

- ◆◆ No Place for Mambas
- ◆◆ Toe the Line
- ◆◆ Captain Lob Meets the Nipple Pincher
- ◆ Oblivion is Forever
- ◆ Retaining the Ashes
- ◆ One for the Gipper
- ◆◆ European Flavour
- ◆◆◆ The Watchman
- ◆ Cut Throat Jake
- ◆ Read the Small Print
- ◆ The Bournemouth Flyer
- ◆◆ Glamour Cat
- ◆ The Truth is Out There
- ◆ Crack My Bitch Up
- ◆◆ Kit Kat
- ◆ Wedding Daze
- ◆ Never Lose that Feeling
- ◆◆ Too Many Cooks Spoil the Broth
- ◆ Rag 'n' Bone Man
- ◆◆ Another Notch in the Gun
- ◆◆ Very Sleepy River
- ◆◆◆ Trad Free World
- ◆◆ Wonderlust
- ◆ Come In Alone, Go Out Alone

1 2 3 6a+

- ◆◆ Ocean Drive
- ◆◆ The Man Who Never Found Himself
- ◆◆ Lazy Days and Summer Haze
- ◆◆ Brief Encounter
- ◆ Lifeline
- ◆ Le Cranium Cassé
- ◆◆◆ Stalker's Zone
- ◆◆ Future Imperfect
- ◆◆◆ Reptile Smile
- ◆◆ New York Dolls
- ◆◆ Gaze of the Gorgon
- ◆◆ Punter's Way
- ◆◆ Consommé
- ◆ Evening Falls
- ◆◆◆ Pregnant Pause
- ◆◆ Young at Heart
- ◆◆ Talk

1 2 3 6a

- ◆ Screw You Hippy
- ◆ Fifteen Minutes to Fame
- ◆ Xavier Zoo
- ◆◆ Go With the Flow
- ◆ Grease Paint and Monkey Brains
- ◆ Margaret on the Guillotine
- ◆ Cosa Nostra

6a continued....

- ◆ Cake Walk
- ◆◆ Xavier's Wall
- ◆◆ Fear's Younger Brother
- ◆◆ Pinch an Inch
- ◆◆ Meg's Got Leukaemia
- ◆◆ Mother's Milk
- ◆◆ Coming of Age
- ◆◆ Never Drive a Car When You're Dead
- ◆ Captain Klutz and the Sailors of Fortune
- ◆◆ The Price of Silence
- ◆◆ The Lizard of Oz
- ◆◆ Underage
- ◆ Escape from the Dwaafee Room
- ◆ Indian Summer
- ◆◆ Shit Happens, Actually
- ◆◆ Monsoon Malabar

1 2 3 5+

- ◆ The Sod
- ◆ Chalkie and the Hex 5
- ◆ Little Chef

1 2 3 5

- ◆◆◆ Slings Shot
- ◆ Spare the Fern
- ◆ Diamond Geezer
- ◆ Jacob's Ladder
- ◆ It's My Life
- ◆ Ben
- ◆ Willem

1 2 3 4+

- ◆ The Bolt Factory
- ◆ The Great Hamburger Disaster
- ◆ Chips with Everything
- ◆ The Ramp
- ◆ Jasper
- ◆ This is This

1 2 3 4

- ◆ Three Fingers
- ◆◆ Six Good Biceps
- ◆ Vertical Thrill
- ◆ Opus
- ◆ Jam

1 2 3 3+

- ◆ Mystical Gill
- ◆◆ Tombstone

1 2 3 3

- ◆ Imperfect
- ◆ Suburban Dave
- ◆◆◆ Fallen Slab
- ◆◆◆ Fallen Slab Arete

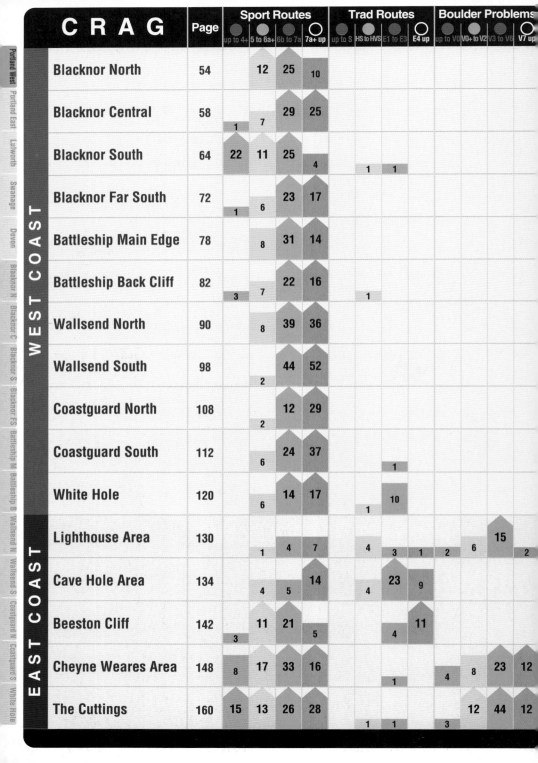

CRAG

Region	Crag	Page	Sport Routes				Trad Routes				Boulder Problems			
			up to 4+	5 to 6a+	6b to 7a	7a+ up	up to S	HS to HVS	E1 to E3	E4 up	up to V0	V0+ to V2	V3 to V6	V7 up
WEST COAST	Blacknor North	54		12	25	10								
	Blacknor Central	58	1	7	29	25								
	Blacknor South	64	22	11	25	4		1	1					
	Blacknor Far South	72	1	6	23	17								
	Battleship Main Edge	78		8	31	14								
	Battleship Back Cliff	82	3	7	22	16		1						
	Wallsend North	90		8	39	36								
	Wallsend South	98		2	44	52								
	Coastguard North	108		2	12	29								
	Coastguard South	112		6	24	37			1					
	White Hole	120		6	14	17	1		10					
EAST COAST	Lighthouse Area	130		1	4	7	4	3	1		2	6	15	2
	Cave Hole Area	134		4	5	14	4		23	9				
	Beeston Cliff	142	3	11	21	5			4	11				
	Cheyne Weares Area	148	8	17	33	16				1	4	8	23	12
	The Cuttings	160	15	13	26	28	1	1			3	12	44	12

Portland West · Portland East · Lulworth · Swanage · Devon · Blacknor N · Blacknor C · Blacknor S · Blacknor FS · Battleship M · Battleship B · Wallsend N · Wallsend S · Coastguard N · Coastguard S · White Hole

Approach walk	Sunshine or shade	Access	Sheltered	Tidal	Other	Best routes	Summary
15 min	Afternoon					Sport	One of the best and most popular areas with some spectacular flowstone formations. Long routes, a good grade spread and easy access make this a must-visit sector.
20 min	From mid morning					Sport	More good long routes and a great place for a bit of sun from late morning before it hits other sectors. Can be dusty at times although most routes are now cleaning up nicely.
12 min to 20 min	From mid morning					Sport	Large and varied area with the longest routes on Portland (a 60m rope is useful). There is also a good set of popular easier climbs including several well-devleoped slabby routes on the blocks down by the sea.
14 min	Afternoon					Sport	A superb set of mid-to-hard grade routes on fine rock. A great place for ticking technical 7s with short and intense crux sections. Easy and quick access.
10 min	Afternoon					Sport	A fine wall with excellent rock and many well-bolted routes. Another great quick-tick crag with easy access. Some routes are beginning to show over-use and it can be busy on bank holidays.
15 min	Afternoon					Sport	A great contrast to its neighbour with its long stamina climbs including one of the best training walls on the Isle. Also the Block Slab with its easier routes and shade in the summer.
10 min to 20 min	Afternoon					Sport	A series of fine walls perched above the slopes gradually trailing down to the boulder beach. Lots of routes to go at in the mid-to-hard grades and mostly they are now all well bolted.
40 min to 50 min	Afternoon	Birds		Tidal		Sport	The best of Wallsend cliffs including one of the finest walls on the Isle. Long and pumpy routes in the mid-to-high grades. A longish approach walk and slightly tidal access. **RESTRICTION** - A variable nesting restriction near the Colors Area.
8 min to 13 min	Afternoon					Sport	A fine compact wall above a non-tidal boulder beach with some very hard and technical walls. Quick and easy access. Not a hot day crag since many of the routes are very condition dependent.
12 min to 25 min	Afternoon			Tidal		Sport	The most atmospheric of the West Coast cliffs with many fine routes including a few in the easier grades. Easy access to the crag bases but becomes more tidal further along. Many of the harder routes are very condition dependent.
5 min	Afternoon			Tidal	Abseil in	DWS	Shorter routes and deep water solos on some pleasant bays near Portland Bill. Easy to reach but abseil approaches are needed for most routes. Very condition dependent but okay in most tides (not rough seas).
3 min to 5 min	Afternoon	Restrictions		Tidal		Bouldering	Several small bays with boulder problems and short boulder-style routes. Usually very quiet. Needs low tide. **ACCESS** - Keep away in Summer owing to a slight access dispute (the conditions are poor then anyway).
15 min to 20 min	Morning			Tidal		DWS	Atmospheric series of caves and passages. Several huge roof climbs plus some good solos. Awkward parking but usually very quiet. Needs low tides for the routes, high tide for the solos.
20 min	Morning			Tidal	Abseil in	Sport	Interesting bays and walls with some good shorter routes across the grade range including the easiest deep water solos around. There are also several very serious solos. Usually very quiet.
3 min to 10 min	Morning	Birds	Sheltered			Sport	Several small cliffs with great variety. The best has hard steep sport routes but there are three others with some great easy sport routes. Also home to some hard bouldering. **RESTRICTION** - Nesting Restriction on Cheyne Main Cliff.
5 min to 10 min	Morning		Sheltered			Sport	Compact rock and some fine technical climbs on one of Portland's most popular cliffs. Several easy sport routes and it is the best place for morning sun or shelter from the wind. Also includes an extensive boulder field.

BLACKNOR CRAGS

Laura Jones climbing *Last Rose of Summer* (7a) on Blacknor South - *page 63*. Photo: Mark Glaister

The first climbable sections of cliff that stretch virtually unbroken along the full length of the west coast of Portland are the Blacknor crags. These are also some of the most impressive and highly developed faces, with routes in all grades and, for the most part, on vertical or slabby rock. The style of climbing is typically fingery and technical, sometimes on flowstone, and at others on crimpy faces of fossil fragments. All of the routes are easily accessed along the cliff base paths and the area should be high on every visitor's hit list.

Blacknor North is justifiably one of the most popular areas on the Isle with fine lines in abundance that ascend some of the most amazing flowstone formations to be found anywhere in the UK. Blacknor Central has been the scene of a great deal of new routing and its popularity has been increased by the stabilisation and widening of the cliff base path beneath it making access to the central area easy from either end. Blacknor South has some brilliant wall pitches on delicate flowstone plus a number of particularly useful lower grade bolted routes. Below Blacknor South and Central are four popular slabby sea-level areas with a great set of easier climbs in a fabulous seashore location. The Far South area has received a complete overhaul and is now one of the best arenas for quality mid grade sport routes.

CONDITIONS

Blacknor Central, and some of Blacknor South, face south-west and are good late morning-sun venues. The other cliffs are all west facing and get plenty of afternoon sun with Blacknor North staying in the shade for the longest. There is little seepage apart from a few drainage streaks on the Niagara Wall section of the Go With The Flow Area, by *The Oldest Profession* on the Medusa Falls Area (also Blacknor South) and on the central section of Blacknor Far South - all are usually dry in the summer. The Blacknor cliffs are fairly exposed to the wind but can offer shelter if the wind is straight onto, or blowing over, the cliff line.

ACCESS

The main access problems here are to do with parking. Please follow the parking instructions described below, this will avoid the problems that have been created in the past by climbers parking randomly in the Weston estate. There are no longer any bird restrictions on the Blacknor Cliffs. The area to the north of Blacknor Far North is a sanctuary zone so please keep out. The local youths sometimes throw stones and other debris onto climbers below; the best advice is to take shelter. If you confront the youths on the crag top they usually run off.

APPROACH

All the Blacknor cliffs are approached from the designated Climber and Walker parking area at the far south west corner of the housing estate in Weston (see map opposite). Do not park anywhere else in the housing estate, especially not in Croft Road. If the car park is full then please park on the main street in Weston and walk through the estate to the car park. The main three approaches to the crags are described below. Individual area details are included with the route pages.

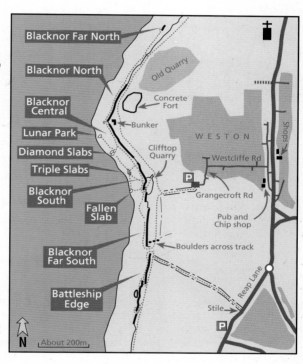

Blacknor North Approach - Walk towards the cliff-top path and turn right (looking out). Continue for about 500m, past an old bunker on the cliff edge and the walled concrete fort, before the path drops down slightly into a quarried area. Locate a small steep path at a break in the cliff line which doubles back leftwards (facing out) down the hill. This leads down to the first routes on the Drag Racing Area.

Blacknor Central and South, Quarry Approach - From the car park, walk to the cliff-top quarry just beyond the main cliff-top path. Scramble down into the quarry past a large block wall and then down a narrow gully at the far end of the quarry. This gully emerges below the Medusa Falls Area on Blacknor South. Blacknor Central is accessed by a small track that contours underneath the crags eventually joining up with the path beneath Blacknor North.

Blacknor Far South Approach - From the car park walk to the cliff-top path and turn left (looking out) along the cliff-top path. Continue for 400m to some blocks that lie across the path. Just beyond the blocks, descend steeply down a rough path and back right to below the crag.

Portland West | Portland East | Lulworth | Swanage | Devon | **Blacknor N** | Blacknor C | Blacknor S | Blacknor FS | Battleship M | Battleship B | Wallsend N | Wallsend S | Coastguard N | Coastguard S | White Hole

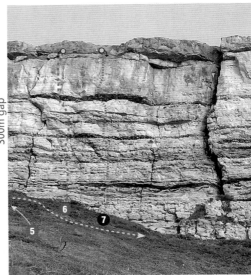

BLACKNOR FAR NORTH

This small, isolated sector is 300m north of the main area, on a leaning block, in front of the main line of cliffs. It is worth a visit if you want some peace and quiet. The best routes are all on solid rock, unlike the section of cliff behind which is anything but solid. No new routes here please.

APPROACH - From the cliff top continue walking along the coast path for 50m until opposite a quarry track branching inland to the right. Below here on the seaward side is the main descent to Blacknor North. Walk 40m further until just before the second quarry track on the right and a tiny track drops over the edge heading down to the fallen-away block.

🚫 The cliffs further north of this point are within a sanctuary zone so please keep away.

❶ Reinheitsgebot . . . . 🔲 **4**
11m. The line on the far left-hand side of the buttress. A poor route with a lot of loose rock, take care.
FA. Helen Heanes 7.5.95

❷ Another One for the Pot . . . 🔲 **6b**
12m. A pocketed sheet in the middle of the face. Reported to be a potential deathtrap.
FA. Neal Heanes 7.5.95

❸ Slim Fingers' Revenge 🔲 **7a**
12m. Super crux moves and the rock has cleaned up nicely. A pleasant pitch in a quiet setting. Finish with hands on top for the full tick.
FA. Neal Heanes 27.5.95

❹ Boiled Lobster . . . . 🔲 **6b**
12m. A worthy pitch if in the vicinity. The wall and groove on the right-hand end of the wall. Make sure you climb past the belay for the full tick.
FA. Neal Heanes 7.5.95

DRAG RACING AREA

❺ Absolute Beginners . . . . 🔲 **2**
6m. The first bolted line on the approach to Blacknor North. It follows the right arete of the gully with a square capstone wedged at the top. An exposed and bolted VDiff.
FA. Mick Ward 2002. Bolted later.

❻ Meltdown . . . . . 🔲 **7a**
16m. Good climbing with an ace bulge and upper crack. Don't walk by this one, it is well worth doing.
FA. Neal Heanes 2.7.95

❼ Quakin' in My Bones 🔲 **7a+**
16m. A good pitch often passed by. Worth a look with rock as good as anything else on Portland. The blind move to gain the rest below the bulge is a matter of luck not talent, and the upper groove is height dependant, however this does not detract from the quality of the climbing,
FA. Pete Oxley 4.10.92

There is a gap of 15m before the next routes.

❽ Death of Cool . . . . 🔲 **7a+**
22m. Surprisingly good climbing on some unpromising rock with an entertaining crux move. No lower-off.
FA. Pete Oxley 20.9.92

❾ Drag Racing Underground
. . . . 🔲 **6c+**
22m. A fine long route that passes a cave entrance at mid height. A tough finishing move and a holdless flowstone groove are the main (but not the only) problems to be encountered 'en-route'. A touch easier for the tall.
FA. Pete Oxley 28.4.93

DRAG RACING AREA

The first walls have some large blocky roofs and a number of excellent long routes on good rock. This area is often less busy than the sections further to the right.
APPROACH - The first two routes are encountered after about 150m, as you drop down the main approach path.

⑩ Seattle be the Day ... 6b+
21m. Some fine flowstone is the reward following on from a hard start.
FA. Pete Oxley 4.9.92

⑪ The Fabulous Bakery Boys
.... 6c
18m. A fine face of perfect flowstone. The crux is a bit bold.
FA. Paul Twomey 9.7.95

⑫ Captain Lob Meets the Nipple Pincher
.... 6b
18m. A pleasant open groove. Super technical and imaginative moves on the crux. High in the grade and a touch run-out.
FA. Neal Heanes 9.7.95 - The name tells of a gnarly first ascent for leader and belayer alike!

⑬ Grease Paint and Monkey Brains
.... 6a
18m. A long arete well endowed with some good jugs leads to a ledge with two technical options above. The best is to use the flake on the right.
FA. Neil Burton 14.10.96

⑭ Indian Summer. 6a
18m. A very nice climb. The long flake and groove with a crux juggy finish over a roof to a lower off 3m above.
FA. Helen Heanes 9.96

⑮ Blowing Chunks 6c
16m. A slabby wall, thin crack and roof, that involves some good climbing but is unfortunately a touch dusty. Reaching the crack is the crux.
FA. Neal Heanes 1997

⑯ Where's Blue Hippo 7a+
16m. The thin wall with an entertaining mid-height crux. The rock is a little on the crumbly side.
FA. Neal Heanes 15.8.96

⑰ Beer and Corruption .. 7a
17m. An excellent wall climb and a good route for those looking to break in to the 7th grade.
FA. Pete Oxley 20.9.92. So named because the second ascensionist promised a pint to Pete if he graded it 7a.

⑱ Henry Rollins for President ... 7a+
17m. Remember to break left early up the crack (crux).
FA. Pete Oxley 12.9.92

⑲ Wynona's Big Brown Beaver. ... 6c
20m. A poor route. Traverse left from second bolt on *Ximenesque.*
FA. Paul Twomey 19.7.95

⑳ Ximenesque. .... 6b+
20m. A very thuggy roof crack not too dissimilar to its namesake away to the east.
FA. Joff Cook 5.9.92

㉑ In Dust We Trust ..... 6c+
20m. Break right out of *Ximenesque* after its second bolt.
FA. Paul Twomey 3.8.95

WOLFGANG FOREVER AREA

A fine and popular area with two good sections of flowstone and some wacky conglomerate. It can be easily identified by the small stone shelter at its base

APPROACH - Continue along the cliff base from the approach.

❶ Ironhead . . . . . **7a+**
23m. A good but rather unbalanced line. The last few moves give the reach-dependent crux. Photogenic.
FA. Pete Oxley 4.9.92

❷ Meg's Got Leukaemia . **6a**
23m. Great jug hauling to a fingery finish, but what a terrible name (see below).
FA. Simon Vaughan 10.92. Named after a character in an Aussie soap.

❸ Cinema Paradiso **6a**
22m. Just right of *Meg's Got Leukaemia*. A highly enjoyable companion route although the start is a little dirty.
FA. Mick Ward 2002

❹ Captain Klutz and the Sailors of Fortune
. . . . **6a**
20m. Incredible conglomerate formation at the start gains more conventional rock and climbing on the upper wall. Take care at the start as the rock is not 100%.
FA. Steve Taylor 20.3.93

❺ Major Mushrooms and that Mentally Muffled Mentality **6c**
20m. The conglomerate wall right of *Captain Klutz* to a ledge. Tricky moves up a groove lead onto a wall via a slim overlap.
FA. Gary Gibson 9.5.2002

❻ Is Vic There? **7a**
21m. A super route that would rate 3 stars in many places. Much easier than it looks from below. Thin moves to the jug at the break and a brilliant move to get the stuck on block. Some great flowstone finishes this classy pitch.
FA. Steve Taylor 3.10.92

❼ Wolfgang Forever . **7a**
22m. A nicely sustained stamina route which is a memorial to Mr. Gullich. Spotting the good pocket on the crux is not easy if unchalked. Very good and very popular.
FA. Pete Oxley 4.10.92

❽ Apple Turn Overload **7a+**
22m. The lower wall has now cleaned up nicely which has increased the quality of the climb. The finish is as good as it has always been.
FA. Joff Cook 11.10.92

❾ Very Sleepy River **6b**
22m. Superb flowstone formations on the fingery and technical upper wall. A confident approach is needed on the lower crack which can be greasy.
FA. Damian Cook 12.9.92

❿ Edge Hog . . . . **7a+**
22m. A loose start and a contrived crux section have failed to promote this line to classic status!
FA. Steve Taylor 28.8.93

⓫ Toes Curl . . . . **6c+**
20m. Great technical face moves but the contrived start spoils the overall feel of the route. Don't touch the chimney, it is off limits.
FA. Will Jones 1996

⓬ Freaky Ralph . . **8a**
20m. A test-piece of the area with a long reach to a pocket at half-height being the crux. The reachy move can be climbed by a short person's sequence.
FA. Pete Oxley 3.10.92

REPTILE SMILE AREA

⓭ Aim High, Shoot Low . . . . **6a+**
21m. Not as dirty as it once was but is prone to dust being washed down from above. It is possible to add a tricky right-ward finish to the lower-off of *DJB* - 6c+
FA. Nic Hellyer 4.4.97

REPTILE SMILE AREA

The next bit of wall has the finest flowstone sheet on Portland and most of the routes here are classics of their grade.
APPROACH - This is the section just before the pinnacle.

⑭ Downtown Julie Brown
. . . . **6c**
22m. The first of the superb flowstone pitches on this section of crag. Excellent sustained and enjoyable face climbing. The flowstone can feel a little slick in warm weather.
FA. Pete Oxley 12.9.92

⑮ Reptile Smile . . . . **6a+**
22m. This classic route features an amazing set of flowstone 'organ pipes' and is probably the most popular route of its grade on the Isle. The first bolt is quite high up. *Photo page 49.*
FA. Pete Oxley 12.9.92

⑯ Talking Smack . . . . . . **5+**
22m. Useful if you have done the others. From the second bolt on *Reptile Smile* climb up and right to join *Slings Shot*.
FA. Will Jones 5.96

⑰ Slings Shot **5**
22m. A popular classic with great holds all the way and undeniably a classic grade 5.
FA. J.Tookey 1975. FFA. Nigel Coe 24.9.88. The line was bolted by Pete Oxley 11.5.94 and claimed as 'The Scales of Balance''.

⑱ Spanner Eyes **7b**
21m. Use the first bolt on *England's Dreaming* then climb through bulging flowstone on the left. A good addition.
FA. Will Jones 8.96

⑲ England's Dreaming . . . . **7a+**
21m. A stunning pitch on magnificent flowstone. The lower wall is fingery and the mid-section powerful although there is a sneaky sequence that utilises a hidden side-pull making the whole route a full grade easier. *Photo on cover.*
FA. Pete Oxley 4.9.92

⑳ Cake Walk **6a**
22m. The memorable bit of this line is the pumpy 3m flowstone phallus. The once loose lower section of the route has now cleaned up. Plenty of rests but a tricky finish.
FA. Steve Taylor 11.10.92

The route California Hot Licks used to follow the pillar but has suffered a rockfall in its upper section.

㉑ Doughnuts and Duvets . . . **6b**
21m. The technically awkward direct finish to *Apfel Strudel*.
FA. Steve Taylor 10.6.95.

㉒ Apfel Strudel . . . . **5+**
19m. A steady little face climb.
FA. A.Jende 13.3.93

㉓ Dwarf Lops . . . . **6b+**
14m. The slightly overhanging groove is loose and has been the undoing of many. Not recommended by anyone!
FA. Nic Hellyer 5.4.97

㉔ Suck, Don't Blow **6c**
21m. Has a frustrating move high up.
FA. Aiden Cook 31.10.92

㉕ Mother's Milk **6a**
21m. The closest you will get to a real crack in the area - white grit next to the sea! A top crack climb with bolts is both fun and pumpy. Watch out for the bolt hidden within the crack.
FA. Simon Cook 8.11.92

㉖ Do You Like Our Owls? . . . **6b**
21m. A weird conglomerate crack which is topped off with a committing roof finale. Not as cheesy as it used to be.
FA. Nic Hellyer 27.6.96

㉗ Hot From the Forge . . **7a**
20m. Sustained climbing on orange flutings. High in the grade.
FA. Pete Oxley 13.2.92

㉘ Onto the Ice Flow **7a**
20m. Good climbing with a hard but short lived crux section. Things are much easier above with the biggest jug in the world at the lower-off.
FA. Damian Cook 5.9.92

㉙ Imbolc . . . . **7b+**
21m. Badly bolted and therefore slightly run-out. Place a long quickdraw on the 4th bolt for a safer redpoint.
FA. Nick White 7.2.93

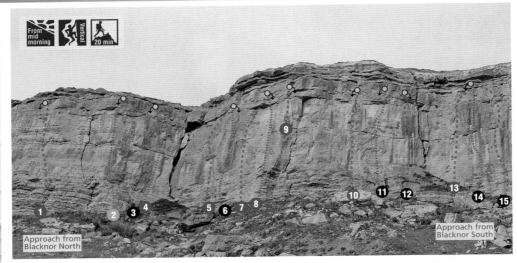

TWANGY PEARL AREA

This is a fine sector with some interesting flowstone which is especially useful as a morning crag on this side of the Isle. Sadly some of the routes have a tendency to be dusty.
APPROACH - This wall is just around the corner from Blacknor North. It can be approached from there or from the Blacknor South quarry approach since the cliff-base path is now very easy to navigate.

① Dudas sin nombres . . . 🔲🔲 ⬜ **6b+**
20m. A pleasant and worthwhile route that has now cleaned up. The start is a bit indifferent but the climbing then becomes an absorbing and technical challenge up the fossils to a hardish finish on the headwall.
FA. Nic Hellyer 20.3.99

② Shit Happens, Actually . . . 🔲 ⬜ **6a**
20m. A little gem that is low in the grade and has a cunning finish. The moves flow nicely and the rock is excellent.
Photo page 61.
FA. Mike Robertson 17.2.93

③ Unstuck On You (Flowstone Shuffle)
. . . . 🔲🔲 ⬜ **7b**
20m. A pumpy eliminate. Difficult to avoid *Shit Happens.*
FA. Joff Cook 1995. FFA. Pete Oxley 25.6.95 - This route caused much controversy when it was first climbed due to some glued-on holds being used! These are now long gone.

④ 21½ Weeks . . . . 🔲🔲 ⬜ **6b+**
19m. Fine climbing but it has become a bit unbalanced since losing a hold. The crux is now much harder than the rest.
FA. Mike Robertson 17.2.93

⑤ Hysterical Solitude . . . . . . 🔲 ⬜ **6c**
18m. Another good route that has cleaned up well, with some great moves.
FA. Mike Robertson 20.2.93

⑥ Crucifix Kiss . . . . . 🔲🔲🔲 ⬜ **7c**
17m. An excellent route featuring a powerful crux and an interesting groove to finish. The groove can be a bit dusty.
FA. Pete Oxley 6.3.93

⑦ Choc Speedway . . . . 🔲 ⬜ **6b+**
20m. A worthwhile route, now cleaned up.
FA. Gorden Jenkin, Francis Haydn 16.8.98

⑧ Nothing is Cool . . . . . 🔲🔲 ⬜ **6c**
19m. Virtually a slab climb although there is a roof at the top!
FA. Steve Taylor 6.3.93

⑨ Protein Delta Strip . . . 🔲🔲 ⬜ **6c**
19m. Great positions higher up with an exposed crux and a slightly committing section.
FA. Joff Cook 2.93

⑩ Kit Kat. . . . . 🔲🔲 ⬜ **6b**
22m. A super climb up a strong natural line. Some strange shaped holds aid progress on the powerful crux section.
FA. J.Walker 2.2.93

⑪ Whilst the Cat's Away. . . . 🔲 ⬜ **7a+**
22m. A good crux move but still a touch friable and a confusing line. Clip the bolt on the headwall then move left immediately.
FA. Neal Heanes 3.97

⑫ The Launch . . . . . 🔲🔲🔲 ⬜ **7b+**
19m. The loss of a good hold has not altered the overall grade. However the route is now high in the grade.
FA. James Dunlop 14.9.99

⑬ Fat Falling Pigs . . . . 🔲⬜ **6b**
14m. Weird tufa pipes and formations show the way. The
climbing is interesting but it can be a bit dirty at times.
FA. Gorden Jenkin 10.7.93

⑭ Twangy Pearl . . . . 🔲⬜ **7b**
16m. A well-travelled route now promoted to three stars by
popular demand. Superb flowstone climbing.
FA. Damian Cook 6.3.93

⑮ Boilermaker . . . . . 🔲⬜ **7c**
16m. Sustained climbing with a bouldery crux up a very blank
looking wall.
FA. Pete Oxley 14.2.93

⑯ Into the Sun . . . . 🔲⬜ **6c**
18m. A dusty slab which is unlikely to clean up but still has
some good climbing.
FA. Neal Heanes 24.3.96

⑰ Bring on the Night. 🔲⬜ **6c+**
21m. The middle of the blank wall has some nice climbing.
FA. Gorden Jenkin 22.6.97

⑱ Monsoon Malabar. . . . . . . 🔲⬜ **6a**
22m. A great outing with an easy start and an intricate finish up
the striking arete on the edge of this area. Move right around
the top roof. Atmospheric positions.
FA. Gorden Jenkin, Mike Robertson 22.6.97

PREGNANT PAUSE AREA

This wall has some scrappy routes on its left-hand side but is
dominated by the magnificent huge arete of *Pregnant Pause*.
APPROACH - This wall is now best approached via the good
cliff-base path from the Blacknor South quarry approach.
Take care when trying to gain the starts of routes 19 to 22.

⑲ Inbreeding . . . . 🔲⬜ **6b**
16m. The arete and slab to the right of the deep cleft has some
dubious holds and has, unfortunately, not cleaned up like many
of the routes on this wall have.
FA. Gorden Jenkin, Francis Haydn 16.8.98

⑳ We Are Not Men, We Are Roto Ⓑ⬜ **6c**
19m. A dusty pitch up the wall just right of a blunt arete. Old
bolts mark the line.
FA. Will Jones 6.94

㉑ The Stals on Me Pal . . . . . 🔲⬜ **7a**
20m. OK climbing on a weird conglomerate ramp of poor rock-
breaking right out of *We are Not Men We Are Roto*.
FA. Francis Haydn 16.8.98

㉒ Toothless Vampire . . . . 🔲Ⓑ⬜ **7b**
20m. A big flowstone pillar right of a large groove. Start by
scrambling up to a bolt below and left of the corner. It still has
some friable holds so don't pull too hard.
FA. Will Jones 7.6.94

㉓ Pregnant Pause . . . . . 🔲⬜ **6a+**
26m. The biggest arete on the island is a wonderful climb, that
is worth the long approach.
FA. J.Robertson, Mark Courtier 1993

Portland West | Portland East | Lulworth | Swanage | Devon | Blacknor N | **Blacknor C** | Blacknor S | Blacknor FS | Battleship M | Battleship B | Wallsend N | Wallsend S | Coastguard N | Coastguard S | White Hole

GO WITH THE FLOW AREA

This sector has some good flowstone and a number of very long routes that need a 60m rope. The right-hand side has a long dark streak which is often wet (hence the route *Niagara Wall*).
APPROACH - This sector can now be approached easily via the Blacknor South quarry and the solid path at the base of the cliff.

Pregnant Pause

Approach from Blacknor South

① **Valerian** . . . . 5+
26m. The line up the buttress right of *Pregnant Pause*. It has some superb flowstone on the upper wall.
FA. Mick Ward 2002

② **Natural Born Drillers** . . 6c
25m. A nice balancy flowstone face, but the lower section is awkward to cross. There used to be a knotted rope at the start but this has gone. It is best to get to the main section of the route via a top rope from *The Long Walk*.
FA. Pete Oxley 4.3.95

③ **The Long Walk** 6c
25m. A fantastic route; steep juggy tufas and more exposed than your average Portland 6c. It can be a touch dusty.
FA. Mike Robertson 8.12.95

④ **Mexican Stand-off** . . . . 7a+
25m. A quality route but it can be dusty. An easy start leads to interesting flowstone in the centre of the huge face.
FA. Pete Oxley 4.3.95

⑤ **One Fine Day** 6a+
25m. The right-hand side of the wall.
FA. Mick Ward 2002

⑥ **Skank Central** 6b+
25m. The right-hand arete, tackled via a thin crack. A bit 'cheesy' low down but better than it looks. The top crack and arete are exciting.
FA. Damian Cook 11.6.95. Includes bits of the trad route The Prow.

⑦ **Go With the Flow** 6a
22m. One of the best bits of flowstone on Portland. Scramble easily to a high ledge to start, but gear up first. Includes part of the old trad route *Last of the Summer Wine* (HVS 5a).
FA. Pete Oxley 6.5.95

⑧ **Ocean Rock** . . . . 6c+
22m. Right of *Go With the Flow*. Great flowstone.
FA. Mick Ward 2002

⑨ **Best Destiny** . . . . 4+
15m. The right-hand arete of the great flake. Generously bolted.
FA. Mick Ward 2002

⑩ **Aeroforce** 7b
26m. A tremendous find. Blast direct up the leaning rib on weird flowstone. Pumpy.
FA. Joff Cook 6.95

⑪ **Blame it on the Drain** . . 7a+
26m. A tricky number, breaking left out of *Niagara Wall*.
FA. Damian Cook 5.95

⑫ **Niagara Wall** 7a
26m. Climb from the right-hand side of the mid-height ledge past an amazing welded boulder.
FA. Mike Robertson 6.95

Approach from Blacknor South

Lana Lammiman reaching for the clip on *Shit Happens, Actually* (6a), perhaps not the world's most alluring route name but fine climbing nevertheless and one of a number of good mid-grade pitches on Blacknor Central - *page 58.* Photo: Mike Robertson

PORTLAND HEIGHTS AREA

A fine towering wall of mostly-excellent, if a little crisp rock, that provides a host of face climbing classics.

This area has now been completely developed to yield some excellent pocketed wall climbs and very long routes. It is one of the first and best west coast crags to receive the sun in the morning.

GEAR - The routes on this sector are very long. A 60m rope is essential if you are going to lower-off. Take great care and always tie a knot in the end of the rope when lowering.

APPROACH - Use the Blacknor South quarry approach and head right (looking out).

① **Gaze of the Gorgon . . .** 🗝️ 🪧 ☐ **6a+**
28m. A very long crack climb with spaced bolts.
FA. Tim Dunsby 3.10.92. Accidentally also claimed as as Vaziu by Damian Cook in 1995

② **Dizzy up the Girl . .** 🗝️ 🪧 ☐ **7a+**
28m. Break left out of *Gaze of the Gorgon*, on pockets, and fire up the groove on good clean rock.
FA. Gavin Symonds 8.2004

③ **Athenian Tactics . . . . .** 🗝️ ☐ **7b+**
28m. Start up the big crack, before heading direct up the wall at an obvious footledge over some flowstone bulges on undercuts and smears to a hard and reachy finish over the final bulge.
FA. Steve Golley 8.2004

④ **Corinthian Spirit . .** 🗝️ 🪧 ☐ **7b**
28m. Fine rock and a bouldery crux on a tightish line. Start as for *Cybernetic Orchard* before swinging left up a ramp at its fifth bolt.
FA. Pete Oxley 13.8.95

⑤ **Cybernetic Orchard . . .** 🗝️ 🪧 ☐ **7a+**
28m. A memorable pitch of escalating difficulty. Probably the best route of its grade on this sector. Good rock, interesting climbing and with great exposure.
FA. Pete Oxley 29.5.95

⑥ **Portland Heights. .** 🗝️ 🪧 ☐ **7a**
28m. An excellent and sustained climb up the centre of the large face. A tough mission that is found by many to be high in the grade.
FA. Pete Oxley 14.5.89

⑦ **Grand Larceny . . . .** 🗝️ 🪧 ☐ **7a+**
28m. The very steep prow right of *Portland Heights* on small pockets and edges to a slabby finish.
FA. Dave Pickford 9.99. Stolen from Nic Hellyer.

⑧ **Burning Skies. . . . . . .** 🗝️ 🪧 ☐ **6b+**
28m. First-class climbing featuring some great pocket pulling. Start up *Isle of Slingers* and break left. Originally it started up *Lord Stublock*.
FA. Pete Oxley 18.6.95

⑨ **Isle of Slingers. . . . . .** 🗝️ 🪧 ☐ **6c+**
28m. Good climbing with a technical head-wall.
FA. Nic Hellyer 18.4.99

⑩ **Lord Stublock Deepvoid Breaks the Chain of Causation . . .** 🗝️ 🪧 ☐ **6b+**
28m. A super pitch, sustained and a little draining. The finishing groove is particularly memorable.
FA. Pete Oxley 18.6.95

Portland West
Portland East
Lulworth
Swanage
Devon
Blacknor N
Blacknor C
Blacknor S
Blacknor FS
Battleship B
Wallsend N
Wallsend S
Coastguard N
Coastguard S
White Hole

Approach from
Blacknor South
quarry

⓫ Cocteau Phenomena
. . . . **7b+**
28m. A fine line direct up a dihedral wall. The lower-off is situated on the ledge above the route. Excellent.
FA. Pete Oxley 11.5.89

⓬ Ausfahrt . . . . **6b+**
28m. A much-travelled favourite which offers a long route with a couple of tricky sections.
FA. Mike Robertson 6.5.95

⓭ Screw the Roses, Send me the Thorns
. . . . **7a+**
28m. Some good, blind and fingery climbing.
FA. Nic Hellyer 1998

⓮ The Shells, The Shells . . . **7a**
28m. An eliminate up the narrow strip between two other routes. After a tricky start follow the wall then move leftwards onto the upper slabby face to a steeper finish.
FA. Gary Gibson 16.9.2004

⓯ Driven Like the Snow . . . **6b+**
28m. A Portland gem. Lots of great moves culminating in a tricky mantel to reach the belay.
FA. Pete Oxley 14.9.91

⓰ Return to Roissy . . . . . **6b+**
28m. A great line up the flake with a crux at the top where it is easier to clip the belay once the top is grabbed rather than struggling from below.
FA. Pete Oxley 13.8.95

⓱ Last Rose of Summer . . **7a**
28m. Another enormous pitch on a blank sheet of crimp-infested limstone. *Photo page 52.*
FA. Pete Oxley 21.8.88

⓲ Through the Barricades
. . . . **7a+**
27m. Fine climbing with the crux in the final groove giving a sustained section of thin climbing. Low in the grade. *Photo page 40.*
FA. Mike Robertson 19.4.98

⓳ Babelicious Redhead **6c**
26m. A friendly climb that is now stable and easier than when first climbed.
FA. Mike Robertson 1.12.95

⓴ Chasing the Sun . . . . **6c+**
24m. Pumpy climbing.
FA. Mick Ward 2002

㉑ The Angry Sea . . . . **6c+**
22m. Easy diagonal into *Chasing The Sun.*.
FA. Mick Ward 23.2.2003

Blacknor South quarry approach

Portland West · Portland East · Lulworth · Swanage · Devon · Blacknor N · Blacknor C · Blacknor S · Blacknor FS · Battleship M · Battleship B · Waitsend N · Waitsend S · Coastguard N · Coastguard S · White Hole

SACRED ANGEL AREA

A fine wall of good vertical rock suited to those with a technical bent and strong fingers. Some of the lines are useful for groups looking for easier grades.
APPROACH - Descend through the quarry and down the chimney to the right (looking in at the wall).

1 Dirty Cow. 7a
15m. A bit run-out, eyes on stalks stuff, especially at the top. Have fun, it is run-out but not really dangerous.
FA. Damian Cook 9.10.93

2 Spontaneous Cattle Combustion   6c+
15m. A pleasing wall pitch which is fairly reasonable at the grade if the correct sequence is unlocked.
FA. Pete Oxley 2.2.91

3 How Now Brown Cow 7a
15m. Straight up the wall to a fingery finale. Low in the grade.
FA. Gary Gibson 16.9.2004

4 Talk . . . .   6a+
15m. An enjoyable route with Interesting moves up the lay-back crack with the added extra of an exciting finish.
FA. Nic Hellyer 22.2.98. Includes some of a trad route called Reunion, E2.

5 Toe the Line. 6b
15m. Much easier than first appearances would suggest. Good, fun climbing which can be finished straight up or out right.
FA. Joff Cook 1.12.95

6 Sacred Angel 7a
15m. Another line that has now gained a reputation for quality.
FA. H.Venables 15.4.89. FFA. Steve Taylor 3.10.93

7 Pining for Glossop . . .   7a
15m. Similar to *Sacred Angel* but slightly better and tougher.
FA. H.Venables 8.7.89

8 I Love the Smell of Resin in the Morning
  6c
15m. The wall left of a big corner is a bit of an eliminate.
FA. Nic Hellyer 25.7.98

9 Draper's Henchmen . . .   7a+
12m. Step left to jugs at the bulge then back right immediately.
FA. Pete Oxley 19.8.95

10 Oblivion is Forever 6b
13m. The belay is a bit too low, so top-out first to get the tick. Only 6a if not climbed past the belay.
FA. Pete Oxley 8.8.88

The thin slanting crack is the trad route **Equinox, E3**.

11 Silent but Deadly . . . .   6c+
12m. A technical slab. Climb the top crux direct since it is probably only 6c if you escape to the left or right.
FA. Pete Oxley 19.8.95

12 Hot Pants Explosion . .   6b+
10m. The small bulge near the top gives the crux.
FA. Neal Heanes 25.7.92

13 Well Done Poppet. . . . .   4+
10m. The finish provides the crux.
FA. Jane Wylie 30.4.95

14 Do Ixtlan   5
10m. Once again, the finish is the crux but the run-out section in the middle gets the blood pumping.
FA. Damian Cook 30.4.95

15 Imperfect.   3
10m. Once the start is dispatched, cruise to the top. A good first lead. The route now has an extra bolt at the start.
FA. Joff Cook 30.4.95

16 Lifeline . . . .   6a+
11m. The photogenic right-hand side of the arete. 6a if you use the left-hand side of the arete at the top.
FA. D.Glover 25.7.96

17 It's My Life   5
10m. A good, well-trodden line, with interesting moves and a soft touch for the grade. A good warm-up.
FA. Jane Wylie 30.4.95

Steve Taylor tackling one of the best routes on Blacknor South, *To Wish the Impossible* (7a) on the Medusa Falls Area - *page 66*. Photo: Mark Glaister

Approach from Blacknor South quarry

MEDUSA FALLS AREA

A superb wall with stunning flowstone which has now been fully developed. This section of crag is one of the most popular 'mileage' walls on the west coast. It is also slightly less exposed to the weather than the other crags.

APPROACH - Walk through the Blacknor South quarry and descend the chimney. The Medusa Falls wall is above and left (facing out) from the base of the chimney.

❶ The Lizard of Oz . . . . 🔲🔲 6a
10m. Great fun. A popular introduction to the flowstone experience. The start is the crux but save something for the finale.
FA. Jan Rostron, Pete Oxley 24.8.95.

❷ Snakes Alive . . . . 🔲🔲 6a+
12m. Poorly bolted and not as good as *The Lizard of Oz*.
FA. Pete Oxley 16.4.94

❸ Medusa Falls . . . . 🔲🔲🔲 7a
15m. An incredible frozen sheet of flowstone pipes. The initial section is hard and slippery if taken direct.
FA. Crispin Waddy 8.8.87

❹ To Wish the Impossible 🔲🔲🔲 7a
20m. A superb pitch. Sustained and delicate climbing with a strenny finish. Some people enjoy this more than *Medusa Falls*. *Photo page 65.*
FA. Pete Oxley 18.4.94

❺ Psychosomatic Addict . 🔲🔲🔲 7a+
20m. Very similar to the last route, with escalating difficulties.
FA. Marty Hallett 16.5.98

❻ Crack My Bitch Up . . . . . . 🔲🔲 6b
22m. An easy corner leads to a hard, exposed finish.
FA. Marty Hallett 6.98

❼ Kamikaze Moped . 🔲🔲🔲🔲 7a
22m. A short-lived fingery section and a good finish.
FA. Pete Oxley 10.7.94

❽ The Oldest Profession
. . . . 🔲🔲🔲🔲 6c+
22m. Sometimes wet but it is worth waiting for.
FA. Pete Oxley 10.7.94

❾ Loose Cannon . . . . . 🔲🔲🔲 7a
22m. The black rib has some good moves.
FA. Mike Robertson 7.98

❿ Turned to Stone . . . . . 🔲🔲🔲 6c+
23m. Some thin pocket moves and a great finish. *Photo page 3.*
FA. Pete Oxley 22.4.89

⓫ Skids of Mark . . . . 🔲🔲🔲 7b
23m. The smooth wall has difficult moves over a bulge. Above it borrows holds off *Turned to Stone*. Finishing up *Turned to Stone* gives a worthwhile 7a+.
FA. Gary Gibson 24.8.2002

⑫ Bum Droplets . . . . 🔲 6b+
23m. An exciting route that looks like its name. The upper layback section takes a little working out.
FA. Martin Crocker 23.4.89

⑬ Cut Throat Jake . . . . . 🔲 6b
23m. Quality climbing with a pocketed lower wall.
FA. Helen Heanes 4.9.97

⑭ Cute Ass . . . . 🔲 7a
22m. A fingery headwall similar to the Battleship routes.
FA. Pete Oxley 10.7.94

⑮ No Ifs, No Butts . . . . . 🔲 6c
22m. The wall right of *Cute Ass* direct to a slim finishing groove and headwall.
FA. Gary Gibson, Hazel Gibson, Gordon Jenkin 15.9.2004

⑯ Seaman Stains . . . . . . 🔲 6c
22m. Similar to the others on this section of the crag.
FA. Neal Heanes 23.7.97

⑰ Master Bates . . . . 🔲 6b+
21m. A fine sustained groove leads to a swing left at the mid-height crux shelf. A couple of pokey clips provide interest.
FA. Helen Heanes 1.8.97

⑱ Captain Pugwash . . . . 🔲 6c+
21m. Varied with a balancy start leading to a wild finish through the roof on buckets. It is worth trying to add a bit to the finish by getting your hands on top first before grabbing the belay.
FA. Neal Heanes 29.7.97

⑲ Roger the Cabin Boy . . 🔲 6b+
21m. Similar climbing to *Captain Pugwash*. The flake on the crux is suspect so treat it with care. Low in the grade.
FA. Neil Burton 1.8.97

⑳ The Black Pig . . . . 🔲 7b
21m. The huge leaning arete at the end of the raised ledge is split by a rest ledge. Photogenic with fine moves high up.
FA. Neal Heanes 4.10.97

The next route is up a corner flake to the right. To reach the start, drop down from below the arete and follow a rough path around.

㉑ Still My Bleeding Heart . . . . . . 🔲 6a+
30m. The long corner flake is sometimes dirty.
FA. Nic Hellyer 26.1.97

Portland West
Portland East
Lulworth
Swanage
Devon
Blacknor N
Blacknor C
Blacknor S
Blacknor FS
Battleship M
Battleship B
Wallsend N
Wallsend S
Coastguard N
Coastguard S
White Hole

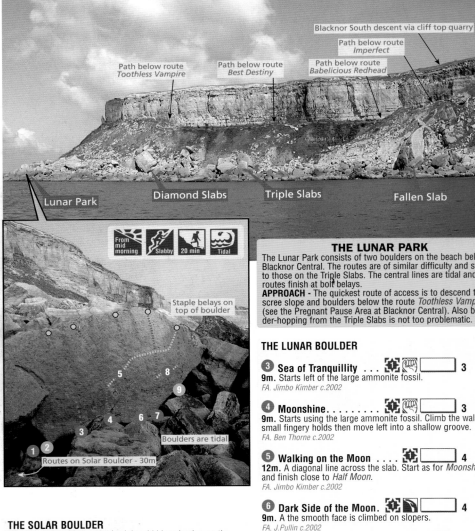

Blacknor South descent via cliff top quarry

Path below route *Imperfect*

Path below route *Toothless Vampire*

Path below route *Best Destiny*

Path below route *Babelicious Redhead*

Lunar Park

Diamond Slabs

Triple Slabs

Fallen Slab

From mid morning | Slabby | 20 min | Tidal

Staple belays on top of boulder

Boulders are tidal

Routes on Solar Boulder - 30m

THE LUNAR PARK

The Lunar Park consists of two boulders on the beach below Blacknor Central. The routes are of similar difficulty and style to those on the Triple Slabs. The central lines are tidal and all routes finish at bolt belays.

APPROACH - The quickest route of access is to descend the scree slope and boulders below the route *Toothless Vampire* (see the Pregnant Pause Area at Blacknor Central). Also boulder-hopping from the Triple Slabs is not too problematic.

THE LUNAR BOULDER

❸ Sea of Tranquillity . . . 🔷🐚 ☐ **3**
9m. Starts left of the large ammonite fossil.
FA. Jimbo Kimber c.2002

❹ Moonshine. . . . . 🔷🐚 ☐ **3**
9m. Starts using the large ammonite fossil. Climb the wall on small fingery holds then move left into a shallow groove.
FA. Ben Thorne c.2002

❺ Walking on the Moon . . . . 🔷 ☐ **4**
12m. A diagonal line across the slab. Start as for *Moonshine* and finish close to *Half Moon*.
FA. Jimbo Kimber c.2002

❻ Dark Side of the Moon. 🔷◣ ☐ **4**
9m. A the smooth face is climbed on slopers.
FA. J.Pullin c.2002

❼ Lunar Eclipse . . . . 🔷▮▮ ☐ **2**
9m. The massive pockets just right of the middle of the slab.
FA. Jimbo Kimber c.2002

❽ Half Moon . . . . ☐ **2+**
8m. A variation on *Lunar Eclipse*. Step right after 2m and foot traverse the lip until large holds are reached. Finish up a scoop.
FA. Jimbo Kimber c.2002

❾ Full Moon . . . . 🔷 ☐ **5+**
8m. A direct start to *Half Moon*.
FA. Jimbo Kimber c.2002

THE SOLAR BOULDER

The first two routes are set back in a hidden clearing on the steeper Sun Boulder which is about 30m north along the boulder beach from the Lunar Boulder.

❶ Solar Flare . . . . 🔷🔷📏 ☐ **3**
8m. Follow the line of large pockets.
FA. Jimbo Kimber c.2002

❷ Sun Spot . . . . 🔷🔷▨ ☐ **5**
8m. The tricky groove.
FA. J.Pullin c.2002

Danie Rushmer on the slabby block of the Triple Slabs. The route is *The Bolt Factory* (4+) - *page 71* - one of many pleasant low-grade bolted routes down on the jumble of boulders by the sea shore below Blacknor Central.
Photo: Mike Robertson

Portland West

Portland East

Lulworth

Swanage

Devon

Blacknor N

Blacknor C

Blacknor S

Blacknor FS

Battleship M

Battleship B

Wallsend N

Wallsend S

Coastguard N

Coastguard S

White Hole

DIAMOND SLABS AREA

Two clean and well-bolted slabs that are sure to become popular with those after some easier lines in a lovely setting.
TIDES - The lower slab is slightly tidal on the seaward face.
APPROACH - The quickest route of access is to descend the scree slope and boulders below the route *Toothless Vampire* (see the Pregnant Pause Area at Blacknor Central). Alternatively boulder-hopping from the Triple Slabs is not problematic.

1 Diamond Geezer . . . . 🔳 5
16m. The left-hand line of bolts up the attractive easy-angled face to a lower-off.
FA. Steve Taylor 22.2.05

2 Diamond Boulder . . . . 🔳 4
15m. The central line via the flake to a lower-off.
FA. Scott Titt 26.3.94

3 Diamond Edge . . . . 🔳 4
16m. Move out right and then back left to the lower-off.
FA. Steve Taylor 2005

4 Diamond Solitaire . . . . . . 🔳 3
10m. The left-hand line on the smaller Diamond Slab.
FA. Steve Taylor 1996

5 Portland Snowshine . . . . . 🔳 3+
10m. The right-hand line up the slab to a lower-off.
FA. Steve Taylor 27.2.05

TRIPLE SLABS AREA

6 My Little Buddha . . . . 🔳 2+
9m. The left-hand line is a very easy plod.
FA. K.Little 1995

7 Slabtastic . . . . 🔳 2+
10m. As the name suggests, it is just that.
FA. John Fletcher 1995

8 Suburban Dave . . . . . . 🔳 3
10m. Another fine outing at the grade.
FA. M.Bateman 1995

9 Mystical Gill . . . . 🔳 3+
11m. The right-hand of the bolted lines, on pockets and good friction.
FA. Pete Oxley 10.8.88 (solo)

TRIPLE SLABS AREA

The third of the sea-level sectors is located 100m north of the Fallen Slab area. It consists of three huge slabs running parallel to each other facing out to sea. The middle slab is the largest and forms a deep gully which keeps the routes out of sight until you are right on top of them.
TIDES - The main slabs are non-tidal but the seaward face is slightly tidal.
APPROACH - Cross beneath the Sacred Angel Area and locate a path beneath *Babelicious Redhead* which leads down to the slabs. Alternatively, boulder-hop along the beach from the Fallen Slab.

Change in viewing angle

Approach

10. **The Erogenous Stone** . 🔲🔲🔲 **VS 4b**
12m. The non-line 2m left of the crack right is the longest on the slab and has no protection.
FA. Nigel Coe 14.7.94

TRIPLE SLABS - THE SEAWARD FACE
The seaward boulder is reached by a scramble through a rock corridor and contains three more routes, not on the topo.

11. **Vertical Thrill** . . . . . . 🔲🔲 19.03.06 **4**
10m. The left-hand line direct up the seaward face.
FA. Nigel Coe 15.10.88

12. **The Bolt Factory** . . . . . 🔲🔲 19.03.06 **4+**
9m. The right-hand bolt line is just a touch tougher.
Photo page 69.
FA. Steve Taylor 26.8.93

13. **Last Suitcase Before the Holocaust**
. . . . 🔲🔲 **E1 5b**
10m. A deep water solo moving diagonally right from *The Bolt Factory* to finish midway along the sloping top of the face. (S1).
FA. Steve Taylor 28.8.93

FALLEN SLAB AREA
The Fallen Slab is located within the mass of huge boulders 'downstairs' from the main Blacknor South cliff, on the boulder beach. Since it was re-discovered and given a sport climbing overhaul, the area has become very popular.
TIDES - The slabs are slightly tidal on the seaward face.
APPROACH - The Fallen Slab, is reached by a steep track which leads straight down from below the route *Imperfect*. A gendarme marks the top of the buttress which forms a mammoth slab and starts at sea level.

14. **Six Good Biceps** . . . . 🔲 7/05 **4**
15m. A line of steep buckets. One pair of biceps should suffice.
FA. Joff Cook 28.5.95

15. **Losing My Sad Tomato**
. . . . 🔲🔲🔲 **6b+**
16m. Interesting and technical.
FA. Mike Robertson 27.5.95

16. **Le Cranium Cassé** . . . 🔲🔲 **6a+**
21m. The groove left of the arete is now adequately bolted but still has a sizeable fall potential.
FA. Damian Cook 27.5.95

17. **Fallen Slab Arete** . . . . 🔲🔲 7/05 **3**
25m. The huge ship's keel is exhilarating and photogenic. Stay as close to the arete as possible for maximum exposure.

18. **Fallen Slab** . . . . 🔲🔲 **3**
22m. The centre of the slab is a lovely outing. A classic in a beautiful location.

FEAR'S YOUNGER BROTHER AREA

A great crag packed with varied flowstone and pocketed walls, giving some very technical and often sustained routes.

APPROACH - From the car park walk to the cliff-top path and turn left (looking out). Continue for 400m to some blocks that lie across the path then descend steeply down a rough path and back right to below the crag. Alternatively it is possible to walk around from below Blacknor South.

❶ Where's My Washboard . . . 🔲 6b
14m. An overhanging groove with a tricky roof move.
FA. Neal Heanes 4.98. Originally graded 5+!

❷ Castle Anthrax . . . . 🔲 7a
15m. A left-hand variation to *An Arse..* over the final roof.
FA. Gavin Symonds, Ben Stokes 5.98

❸ An Arse With a View . . 🔲 7a
15m. A flaky technical groove to the smooth roof on its right.
FA. Neal Heanes 4.98

❹ The Singing Bush. . . . . 🔲 7a+
16m. One of the best on this section of wall. A pumpy and technical route following a faint rib.
FA. Joff Cook 2.6.96

❺ Bushwhacked . . . . 🔲 7a+
17m. Tasty-tufa-technicality on the black wave.
FA. Damian Cook 1.6.95

❻ Chaos UK . . . . 🔲 7a+
17m. A fine twisting groove packs in some good hard moves.
FA. Martin Crocker 19.5.89

❼ AKA UK OK . . . . 🔲 7b
17m. Climb the easy wall to the bulge. Good holds gain access to the upper wall which provides a fine fingery finale. It borrows holds off other routes.
FA. Gary Gibson 9.5.2003

❽ UK Subs . . . . . 🔲 7a+
17m. Pressing climbing up the blank wall.
FA. Pete Oxley 2.2.91

❾ The Unknown Soldier . 🔲 6b+
19m. Good climbing up flowstone above the mid-height break. Anyone going to own up to it? *Photo page 75.*
FA. The Phantom Bolter (still no claims 2005)

❿ Read the Small Print. . 🔲 6b
19m. The wall and fine upper groove.
FA. Steve Taylor 24.5.95

⓫ Fear's Younger Brother 🔲 6a
19m. A very popular line on some great rock. The crux takes a bit of working out but the rest is fine.
FA. Steve Taylor 2.2.91

⓬ Ocean Drive . . . . 🔲 6a+
19m. A superb sustained line with a stiff finish if taken direct.
FA. Helen Heanes 4.98

⓭ Kendo Nagasaki . . 🔲 7a+
20m. Challenging climbing with some blind moves at the bulge.
FA. Martin Crocker 7.5.89

⓮ Ryme Intrinseca . . 🔲 7b
20m. A direct and fingery test-piece. Keep right at the overlap.
FA. Martin Crocker 26.3.89

⓯ The Strobolising Scyphostoma
. . . . 🔲 7a
20m. Steep and varied climbing. A hard move to gain the roof is followed by a pleasant groove then a taxing finish. High in the grade.
FA. Martin Crocker 26.3.89

⓰ Kill a Gent's Tart. . . . . 🔲 6c+
20m. Take the easy flake to a hard pull to gain an unrestful groove. Swing right below the roof.
FA. Pete Oxley 12.6.94

⓱ Rag 'n' Bone Man. . . . 🔲 6b
20m. A very nice climb up the wall, scoop and roof.
FA. Pete Oxley 14.10.90

⓲ Steptoe and Son . . . . . 🔲 6c
20m. Pleasant climbing with an impressive finish. Climb the tricky initial wall to the roof. Take this head-on to finish.
FA. Gary Gibson, Phl Gibson, Hazel Gibson 7.5.2003

MECHANOIDS AREA

One of Portland's finest crags that has many superb routes across a wide spread of grades. This section of cliff is often in good condition and has a pleasant flat base.
APPROACH - As for Fears Younger Brother Area.

① Sparkling Bone Chamber ⬛⬛ ▢ **7b**
20m. Intense and blind climbing with a hard crux which is desperate to on-sight. The upper section is much easier.
FA. Martin Crocker 26.3.89

② Reality Bites . . . . ⬛⬛ ▢ **6b+**
20m. A stopper start needs some luck in finding the correct sequence. The remainder is delightful, assuming you find the good holds at the top.
FA. Janet Horrocks, George Ridge 6.4.98

③ Slumberland Direct . . . ⬛⬛ ▢ **6b+**
20m. A worthwhile line past a stuck-on ledge. Has a bit of a bogey move to enter the groove.
FA. Steve Taylor, Joff Cook, Damian Cook 10.6.95. Includes most of the trad route Slumberland (Nigel Coe 15.4.89).

④ Nobody's Hero . . . ⬛⬛⬛ ▢ **6c**
21m. A highly-rated outing up the juggy bulge and balancy upper section.
FA. Martin Crocker 19.5.89

⑤ Great Barrier Reef . . . . ⬛⬛ ▢ **7a+**
22m. Superb and intense moves, above the fossilized coral ledge, up a short groove.
FA. Martin Crocker 30.4.89

⑥ Crown of Thorns . . . . ⬛ ▢ **7a+**
21m. The thin blind seam high on the face.
FA. Pete Oxley 26.2.95

⑦ Wax on Wheels . . . ⬛⬛⬛ ▢ **7a+**
22m. Above the mid-height ledge, a big reach and high step gain the beautiful rising seam and flowstone finish. Up-graded due to the loss of a hold.
FA. Martin Crocker 7.5.89

⑧ Cerebellum . . . . ⬛ ▢ **6c+**
21m. A fine flowstone sheet with a couple of brain-like holds.
FA. Pete Oxley 26.2.95

⑨ Hollow Ground . . . ⬛⬛⬛ ▢ **6b+**
21m. The long-admired thin flake right of *Cerebellum*. The flake is very thin but has been tested by some heavy climbers.
FA. Ben Stokes 22.3.2002

⑩ So Special . . . . ⬛⬛ ▢ **7b**
20m. A testing route that is now climbed direct. Can be done by the short with a dyno.
FA. Martin Crocker 23.4.89

⑪ Mechanoids . . . . ⬛⬛ ▢ **7a**
20m. Another vertical challenge taking a 'gritstone-like' sequence up the ramp.
FA. Martin Crocker 23.4.89

⑫ Cliché Upon Cliché . . . ⬛⬛ ▢ **6c**
20m. A hard start and a hard finish. Move left to the lower-off.
FA. Martin Crocker 7.5.89

⑬ Senseless Thing . . ⬛⬛⬛ ▢ **7b**
20m. An reasonable pitch with a distinct crux.
FA. Martin Crocker 19.5.89

⑭ In on the Killtaker . ⬛⬛⬛ ▢ **7b+**
20m. A very good route taking in some unlikely climbing and with a sting in the tail.
FA. Pete Oxley 28.5.93

⑮ Think Black . . . . ⬛⬛ ▢ **7b**
20m. Follow the shallow black groove to a desperate finish. It can be covered in ivy.
FA. Pete Oxley 23.4.89

⑯ Paint a Black Picture ⬛⬛⬛ ▢ **7c**
20m. An almost impossible rock-over move (ok for shorties). It is often wet since it is on a drainage streak.
FA. Pete Oxley 28.5.93

⑰ Look on the Bright Side . . ⬛ ▢ **7a+**
20m. Start up *Paint a Black Picture* and break out right.
FA. Pete Oxley 1999

Mechanoids Area

Approach

MASTER OF THE ROLLS AREA

The tapering wall passed first on the approach has a number of popular routes at relatively friendly grades.
APPROACH - From the car park walk to the cliff-top path and turn left (looking out). Continue for 400m to some blocks that lie across the path then descend steeply down a rough path and back right to below the crag. Alternatively it is possible to walk around from below Blacknor South.

1 Carlos Fandango Belay 6b
18m. A technical wall leading to a balancy groove.
FA. Neal Heanes 3.2002

2 Paying It Forward 6a
19m. The technical wall and pleasant groove. There is a hollow block close to the top.
FA. Neal Heanes 3.2002

3 Escape from the Dwaafee Room 6a
19m. A popular piece of climbing.
FA. Ailsa Newcombe 8.4.99

4 Punter's Way . . . . 6a+
19m. A very nice line. Technical moves low down and delicate at the end.
FA. Steve Taylor 2.5.97

5 Blackthorn Winter. . . . 6c
20m. The loss of a crucial hold has pushed up the grade.
FA. Steve Taylor 28.5.96

6 Master of the Rolls . . . 7a
20m. A long, classy route with an exciting finish.
FA. Martin Crocker 23.4.89

The next line is a poor and escapable open project. It contains one very technical section.

7 The Loneliness of the Long Distance Driller 6b
18m. Now cleaned up to give another worthwhile grade 6. The top wall is superb.
FA. Nic Hellyer. 7.12.96

8 If You Should Go Skating . . 6c
15m. The butch overhang is followed by an easier layback.
FA. Nic Hellyer 19.10.96

9 Spare the Fern 5
15m. Follow the groove past a flowstone boss to the higher of two lower-offs. To the first lower-off is 4+.
FA. J. Leonard 30.7.96

10 Desireless 4
13m. Not one of the greatest on offer.
FA. Nigel Coe 13.5.89 - subsequently retro-bolted

There are two trad routes up the wall to the right. Further right again are two final bolt lines which are actually the first routes encountered on the usual approach to the crag.

11 Shoobedoobabadah 6c
10m. A short peapod groove.
FA. Steve Taylor 14.6.95

12 Blood and Chocolate 6c
8m. A thin and technical problem.
FA. Nigel Coe 27.3.89. Bolted and straightened by Neal Heanes

Gavin Symonds in the steep groove of *Unknown Soldier* (6b+) on Blacknor Far South - *page 72*. Photo: Mark Glaister

BATTLESHIP EDGE

The Battleship Edge area is the most popular on the whole Isle and is composed of four sections, the Main Cliff, the Middle Cliff, the Back Cliff and the Block, each with a very distinct character. The Main Edge itself is the most popular starting point for exploring the Isle's massive supply of well-bolted routes. It is an extremely friendly and inviting place with its gleaming white and grey-streaked faces and strong lines made up of the bounding corners and grooves. The crag base makes a pleasant place to sun-bathe, picnic or relax and it is possible to get a lot of mileage in here by nipping up and down the multitude of closely-spaced lines. If the crag is busy then it is worth looking at one of the other near-by venues such as the Back Cliff or nearby Blacknor Far South.

The Back Cliff offers some superb long pitches mixing fingery flint bands with well-positioned crux moves, often high on the wall. The left-hand side of the Battleship Back Cliff is a favoured place for those seeking out sustained pitches to pick up a bit of wall stamina. The right-hand side of the Back Cliff is shorter and has some easier lines and is one of the best sheltered areas on the west coast. Battleship Block has a number of nice, slabby pitches at friendly grades and on good rock.

CONDITIONS

The Main Edge and the Back Cliff face due west and get the afternoon sun. The Battleship Block receives only a sliver of sunshine at midday and gives some useful shade on summer afternoons. The rock dries very quickly and there is no real seepage. All the Battleship crags can be a bit more sheltered from the wind than the Blacknor crags because the cliff line is set back; however it can be a bit of a wind tunnel by the Back Cliff. Also note that the Battleship Block cuts the sun off the lower section of the Back Cliff in winter hence belaying may turn out to be a rather cold experience.

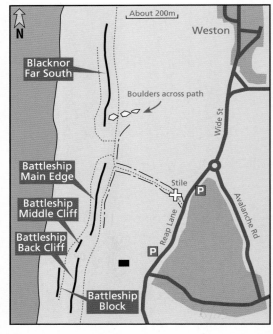

APPROACH

The Battleship cliffs are easy to reach from good parking spots on Reap Lane to the south of Weston. Drive through Weston to a small roundabout and turn right into Reap Lane and park on the roadside. **DO NOT PARK DIRECTLY OUTSIDE THE HOUSES AND DO NOT CHANGE CLOTHES IN FRONT OF THE HOUSES.** Walk carefully down a track with your eyes to the ground - it is a dog walkers' path! At the junction with the cliff-top path head slightly right, and then take one of two steep paths down the hillside. The cliffs are on left. It is also possible to approach from the Walkers and Climbers parking in the Weston Estate using the cliff-top path.

DRIVE A CAR AREA

The first section encountered on the approach has a tall central section tapering off to either side. The central routes are good and popular but the ones on either side tend to see less attention.
APPROACH - Follow the well-trodden path down and turn left just before the large grass mound below the crag.

❶ Another Trojan Horse . . . . ▮▮▭ **6b+**
12m. The left-most line up the wall past a reachy move to the break. The bulge above needs another long reach.
FA. Gary Gibson 14 9.2004

❷ The Black Pariah . ▮▮▮▭ **7a**
13m. The wall with a technical move to leave a ledge and fingery moves to reach easier ground slightly right.
FA. Gary Gibson 14.9.2004

❸ The Misanthrope . . ▮▮▮▭ **7b+**
14m. A ferociously hard pitch which needs a dry spell.
FA. Martin Crocker 1.4.89

❹ Silage Clamp . . . . ▮▮▭ **7a+**
15m. Two very technical moves into and out of the scoop.
FA. Martin Crocker 1.4.89

❺ Never Drive a Car When You're Dead
. . . . ▮▮▭ **6a**
17m. A delightful route, friendly, well-bolted and sustained but never desperate. Sheltered from the wind.
FA. Steve Taylor 17.4.93

❻ Wind in the Riggin'. . . ▮▮▭ **6c**
17m. A gnarly but rewarding pitch. There is at least one awkward clip high on the route.
FA. Martin Crocker 1.4.89

❼ Bawdy House . . . . ▮▮▭ **7a**
16m. A fierce start which is trickier for the short, this can be avoided by making a rightward detour. Another nasty clip.
FA. Martin Crocker 1.4.89

❽ The Ghost of Saturday Night
. . . . ▮▮▭6/05 **5+**
12m. The shallow groove has lost a block midway but this has not affected the grade.
FA. Steve Taylor 6.96

❾ Borstal Breakout. . . . . ▮▮▭ **6b**
10m. A square-cut groove at the top of the grass bank leads to a tricky finish.
FA. H.Venables 17.12.88

KEYBOARD WALL AREA

The central section of Battleship Edge is one of the most popular areas on Portland with a great supply of technical face and groove routes on excellent rock.
APPROACH - Follow the well-trodden path down and around the grassy mound to the base of the wall.

1 Citizen Dust 6c
10m. An entertaining eliminate with a short lived crux direct up parallel blind cracks.
FA. Nigel Coe 9.4.89.

2 Meet the Manatees . . . 6b+
12m. Follow a vague crackline up the wall, crossing an old trad route **Eyes in Your Navel Nigel**, which ran left to right.
FA. Gary Gibson, Phil Gibson, Hazel Gibson 7.5.2003

3 Bilboes 7a
13m. Good technical climbing although the sequence takes a bit of unlocking. Low in the grade.
FA. Martin Crocker 9.4.89

4 Keyboard Wall . 7c
15m. Tenuous moves on flowstone ripples.
FA. Pete Oxley 10.12.88

5 Choco Loni . . . 7b
16m. White hot fingery climbing on tiny holds. Steel fingers and good conditions are a must.
FA. Martin Crocker 9.4.89

6 Wurlitzer Jukebox . . . . 7a+
18m. Hard to start and a 'stopper' finish but a bit close to *Evening Falls* in the middle.
FA. Martin Crocker 9.4.89

7 Evening Falls . . . . 6a+
18m. The corner with a capping roof is deservedly popular.
FA. Pete Oxley 17.12.88

8 Evening Falls Direct 6c
20m. A good direct finish which includes the last move of *Wurlitzer* that seems easier with this approach.
FA. Nic Hellyer 1998

9 Victims of Fashion . . . . 7a+
18m. A superb stamina test up the blunt arete.
FA. Pete Oxley 10.5.89

10 Barbed Wire Kisses . . . 7a+
19m. A very hard technical crux move leads to a rest, followed by easier moves to finish.
FA. Pete Oxley 13.11.88

11 Monoculture . . 7c+
19m. A classic test-piece. Technical and extremely fingery with some blind moves over the bulge. Watch those tendons.
FA. Pete Oxley 12.88 FFA. 17.4.93

12 Reve D'un Corbeau . . . 7a
20m. The black streak. Difficult moves in the lower half and also a tricky clip. The upper section in the continuation groove, above a big rest, is also good.
FA. Pete Oxley 19.11.88

13 Lazy Days and Summer Haze
. . . . 6a+
18m. Varied climbing on a strong line, taking in the prominent layback and huge roof. *Photo page 77.*
FA. Pete Oxley 8.5.89

14 Norfolk Coast . . . . 7a+
18m. An eliminate up the steep slab just right of *Lazy Days*. Technical moves up the slab lead to a tricky finish.
FA. Gary Gibson 4.5.2003

15 Pinch an Inch 6a
18m. A nice warm-up with good holds arriving just when you need them. A reliable warm-up.
FA. Pete Oxley 21.8.88

16 Inch Perfect, Inchworm 6b+
18m. Technical moves in the middle and a bit polished.
FA. Crispin Waddy 8.8.87 and Pete Oxley 21.8.88

SERIOUS MUSIC AREA

More popular, high quality routes and a great place to get a lot of mileage in if the grade range is right for you.
APPROACH - Continue along the crag base path.

❶ Serious Music . . . . . .   6c+
18m. Stiff moves up and right gain the shallow arete. It can be started direct 1.5m to the right at **7a+**.
FA. Pete Oxley 19.11.88

❷ Margaret on the Guillotine .   6a
17m. Nice moves and pleasantly sustained. The first clip is a touch awkward.
FA. Pete Oxley 22.4.89

❸ Gratuitous Lies Here . .   6c+
17m. A very spicy finish on the headwall. Nasty.
FA. Martin Crocker 22.4.89

❹ Keel Haul 7b
17m. A disappointing eliminate.
FA. Damian Cook 16.2.93

❺ Out of Reach, Out of Mind
. . . .   6c
18m. The pocketed groove is enjoyable and has a technical start and a long reachy finish. A relic doorknob marks the line.
FA. Pete Oxley 13.11.88

❻ No me Comas el Coco .   7a
18m. Good sustained climbing with a pushy last move.
FA. Jon Biddle 7.2.93

❼ Come, Armageddon, Come
. . . .   6c+
18m. Layback the chunky pinch-grips, to a cool finish.
FA. Pete Oxley 22.4.89

❽ Defcon One . . . .   6c+
18m. A tricky groove at the bottom and a testing stretch for the break. Swing left on the flowstone to finish.
FA. Pete Oxley 17.7.90

❾ Blood Simple . . . .   6c+
17m. The scoop and slight groove to the right of *Defcon One* are gained via steep moves over the low bulge. Good rock.
FA. Gary Gibson 4.5.2003

❿ The Barton Fink 7b
17m. The wall just right of the wide black streak, with desperate moves at half-height. Easier for the tall.
FA. Gary Gibson 14.9.2004

⓫ Hipnition 7a
16m. A hard boulder problem start is worth perserving with to access the nice upper groove.
FA. Pete Oxley 22.4.89

HUMANOID AREA

⓬ Master of Ape Science
. . . .   7a+
16m. Has a bouldery start and is hard higher up as well.
FA. Martin Crocker 22.4.89

⓭ Dripping with Blood . .   6c+
17m. It's all over after the vicious start.
FA. Gorden Jenkin 5.8.89

⓮ Maud in Memoria .   6c+
12m. Once again, the hard climbing is short-lived.
FA. M.Ford 20.12.90

⓯ On the Wall . . . . . .   7a+
16m. The entertaining lichen-stained groove is often passed by.
FA. Pete Oxley 25.11.89

⓰ Trance Dance 7a
16m. A low crux past the pocket. Very bouldery.
FA. Pete Oxley 8.11.88

HUMANOID AREA

Lots of finger-strength testing vertical lines on some really good rock. Often empty when the lines to the left are crowded.
APPROACH - This is the far right-hand (looking in) end of Battleship Main Edge.

17 Judge Jeffreys . . . 6c
17m. Connecting the two flakes is a bit of a stopper move.
Photo page 87.
FA. Pete Oxley 19.11.88

18 Humanoid . . . . 7a+
17m. Fun and fingery from the word 'go', though a skin eater.
FA. Pete Oxley 19.11.88

19 One For The Gipper . . . 6b
17m. Don't miss the nice technical balancy moves on this line.
FA. Pete Oxley 19.11.88

20 President Elect . . . . . . 6b+
15m. A hard start to easier stuff above. High in the grade.
FA. Pete Oxley 19.11.88

21 Chappaquiddick 6b
10m. Hopefully the new grade will reduce the sandbag status.
FA. M.Ford 6.90

22 Coastguard Ron 7a
8m. A small route at the far right-hand end with a number of possible sequences.
FA. Mark Williams 26.4.98

BATTLESHIP MIDDLE CLIFF

23 Flickhead Goes Boing, Boing
. . . . 7a
14m. A nice bouldery crux with a blind reach.
FA. Steve Taylor 1996

24 Hats off to the Insane . . . . 6b+
14m. Probably the best route here with pleasant wall climbing.
FA. Steve Taylor 1996

25 Trashcan Man 6b
14m. Also a worthy pitch.
FA. Steve Taylor 1996

The next lines have a bolt belay on the raised ledge.

26 Setting the Date 6b
12m. An unusually wide groove.
FA. Steve Taylor 1996

27 Champagne Supernova 6a
12m. The narrow groove is short and awkward.
FA. Steve Taylor 1996

28 Andy Wallhole 6a
12m. Short and sweet, and also low in the grade.
FA. J.Waddington 1996

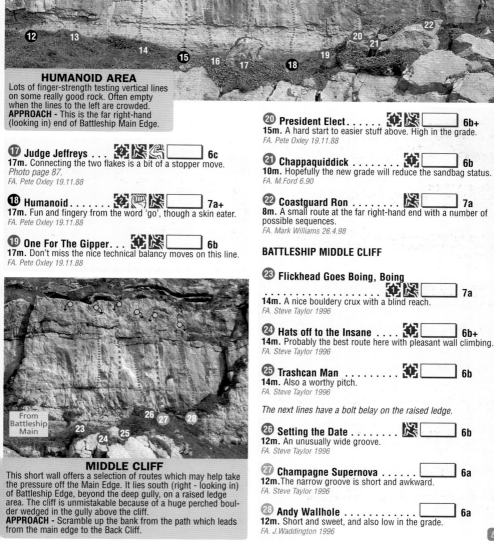

MIDDLE CLIFF

This short wall offers a selection of routes which may help take the pressure off the Main Edge. It lies south (right - looking in) of Battleship Edge, beyond the deep gully, on a raised ledge area. The cliff is unmistakable because of a huge perched boulder wedged in the gully above the cliff.
APPROACH - Scramble up the bank from the path which leads from the main edge to the Back Cliff.

BACK CLIFF - LEFT

This much-photographed wall features some brilliant long climbs crossing the flint knobs and breaks that cut across the wall. The climbing tends to be strength-sapping with technical moves on vertical rock which is more sustained than cruxy, although there are still some very hard moves! Many of the routes are more than 25m long so take great care when lowering off.

APPROACH - Follow the crag-base path below Battleship Main Cliff until it drops down towards the Back Cliff which towers above the Block Slab.

❶ Sex Cauldron. 7b
26m. Move left from the shared start and stretch away up the upper arete and wall on the left. Probably **7b+** if you can't do the reach.
FA. Joff Cook 2.5.98

❷ Even Better than the Beatles
. . . . 7b
26m. Good climbing in the high groove with a very blind crux. May feel harder until you spot the trick. Being tall also helps.
FA. Steve Taylor 19.4.97

❸ Arc of a Fridge . . . 7b
26m. A very technical crux. Watch your leg behind the rope on the crux.
FA. Pete Oxley 1.12.91. A very eventful first ascent involving a detachable fridge-sized block.

❹ Dreams Burn Down . . . 7a+
27m. A direct assault on the left side of the massive wall, finishing up the corner. An often overlooked pitch.
FA. Pete Oxley 27.1.91

❺ Nihil 7b
27m. Pocket-pulling up the exposed upper arete. Very photogenic and on some superb rock.
FA. Pete Oxley 16.4.93

❻ No Man is an Island . . 6c
27m. Tremendous climbing which finishes up the long thin flake. Some low down moves can prove tricky, above these it is just sustained pleasure.
FA. Pete Oxley 10.7.90

❼ Always Have the Edge 6c
26m. Another gem. Good climbing after a hard start. Clipping the second bolt is awkward but there are plenty of rests above. A deep pocket at the top often has a bird's nest.
FA. Pete Oxley 10.7.90

Colin Binks on *Buoys will be Buoys* (6b+) on Battleship Back Cliff - *below*. Photo: Chris Craggs

8 Pump Hitler . . . . . 7a+
26m. A Portland classic which has a complex crux section involving a slightly reachy clip.
FA. Pete Oxley 14.4.93

9 Buoys will be Buoys . . 6b+
27m. A sustained classic with a tricky section just above the mid-height crack. One of Dorset's best. *Photo above and page 5.*
FA. Pete Oxley 10.7.90

10 Jurassic Shift 7a
27m. An easy lower wall leads to a teasing shallow groove and a steep finish. One for the bridging technician.
FA. Pete Oxley 16.4.93

11 The Fun Factory 7b
26m. An almost 'Grit' like mid section. Excellent and varied groove climbing with the final reach sealing the grade.
FA. Pete Oxley 4.6.97

12 Info Freako . . . 7b+
27m. The searing crack in the headwall stops many. There are some very long moves especially at the top, the short may want to finish up the right arete on the final moves.
FA. Pete Oxley 18.7.90

13 Trance Mission 7c
30m. A hard hybrid which is high in the grade. Five crux moves and it includes the crux of *The Racing Line* and all the hard stuff on *Info Freako.*
FA. Pete Oxley 1.7.97

14 Rave Mission . . . . 7b+
30m. A counter-diagonal starting up *Info Freako*, reversing the traverse on *Trance Mission* and finishing up *Racing Line* giving another good stamina-based link-up.
FA. Jim Kimber 12.9.98

15 The Racing Line 7b+
27m. A superb direct version of *Trance Mission*, taking a central line that just touches *Zinc Oxide Mountain* at one point.
FA. Pete Oxley 4.6.97

16 Zinc Oxide Mountain 7b+
28m. A high class endurance test at the lower limit of the grade. The classic of the wall, taking on the white shield via some exquisite moves.
FA. Pete Oxley 25.7.90

17 Bending the Rules . . . . 7b+
30m. A massive traverse that forges a diagonal line starting up *Lost Army Expedition* (next page) and finishing up *Jurassic Shift.* Take a few long extenders. Hard for the grade.
FA. Pete Oxley 4.10.97

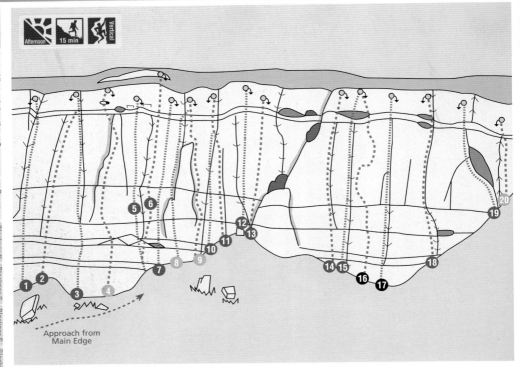

BACK CLIFF - RIGHT

Although shorter than the left side of the crag, this sector has a number of very worthwhile climbs and the friendlier grades tends to mean that it is more popular. The far right-hand end has a set of slightly steeper routes which have names that are almost longer then the routes themselves.
APPROACH - Approach as for the Main Edge and continue underneath it to the path for the Back Cliff which is opposite the Block Slab.

❶ Lost Army Expedition . 🔲🔲 🔲 **6c+**
18m. Tough in the top groove and a bit run-out as well.
FA. Brian Tilley 1992. Reclimbed after a rockfall by Steve Taylor 25.9.93

❷ Scapa Flow . . . . . 🔲🔲🔲 🔲 **6c+**
19m. A technical test-piece. Precarious groove climbing with nowhere near enough footholds for the right foot.
FA. Pete Oxley 6.90

❸ Raise the Titanic . . . . 🔲🔲 🔲 **6b+**
19m. The interesting groove is much easier than *Scapa Flow*, and almost as good.
FA. Steve Taylor 4.9.93

❹ The Price of Silence . . . . . 🔲🔲 14/8/05 **6a**
19m. A pleasing and very popular route. You need to search around a bit on the top section.
FA. M.Bateman 21.4.93

FIRST CLEAN 6A !

❺ Wave Dodging . . . . 🔲 🔲 **7a**
19m. This can be bold if climbed direct but it is only **6c+** if you slink off rightwards.
FA. Joff Cook 25.9.93

❻ Sink the Bismarck . . . . 🔲🔲 🔲 **6c**
21m. Quality climbing. It is possible to finish on the ledge of *Wave Dodging* but if you add the extra 5m it is probably worth **6c+**. Two old bolts.
FA. Pete Oxley 11.7.89

❼ Big Fish . . . . 🔲 🔲 **7a**
17m. A tight line featuring three hard sections but with good rests in between. Finish to the right of a blank section.
FA. Gary Gibson 14.9.2004

❽ Wiggi and Mopoke's Excellent New Hilti
. . . . 6/05 **5+**
19m. Unfortunately this line has suffered from a mud slide.
FA. Nic Hellyer 28.9.96

❾ A Dream of White Porsches 🔲 6/09 **5**
18m. A good easier route. The belay is tricky to clip for shorties.
FA. Pete Church 28.9.96

Change in viewing angle

Portland West | Portland East | Lulworth | Swanage | Devon | Blacknor N | Blacknor C | Blacknor S | Blacknor FS | Battleship M | Battleship B | Wallsend N | Wallsend S | Coastguard N | Coastguard S | White Hole

⑩ The Sound of One Hold Snapping . . . . . 6b+
16m. A nice route, similar to *Shed Head* but easier.
FA. Nic Hellyer 5.4.97

⑪ Electrically-Injected Shed Head
. . . . 6b+
16m. One of this wall's better routes, featuring some good pocket pulling.
FA. M.Ford 16.12.90

⑫ Splat the Cat . . . . 6c+
16m. Given 6b+ in previous guides but this was either wrong, or it has lost holds. Even at 6c+ it may be undergraded.
FA. Pete Oxley 16.12.90

⑬ Shallow End of the Gene Pool
. . . . 6b+
15m. An extended boulder problem.
FA. Nic Hellyer 30.11.97

⑭ Project 'A' 7a
17m. Greasy even on good days.
FA. Aiden Cook 25.6.95. Only his 3rd/4th route!

⑮ Searing Tunnel of Re-injury . . . 6b
17m. The groove is pleasant but a dusty break near the top spoils the experience as does an old lower-off. High in the grade.
FA. Pete Oxley 11.7.90

⑯ The Cones of Stress . . . . 7a+
20m. A poor eliminate to the old lower-off.
FA. Pete Oxley 16.1.94 Named after scaremongering by the anti-bolters.

⑰ Psychic EMF . . . . . 7a+
20m. The best route on this wall. The fine white dome is 'finger-wrenchingly good'.
FA. Pete Oxley 11.7.90

⑱ God Told Me to Skin You Alive
. . . . 6c+
17m. Good climbing on very pockety rock but a touch snappy and flaky.
FA. Pete Oxley 11.7.90

⑲ Roadkill on the Information Superhighway
. . . . 6b
10m. The left-leaning groove is awkward low down.
FA. Nic Hellyer 16.3.97

⑳ Error 404 . . . . 6a+
8m. Very short and awkward.
FA. Nic Hellyer 26.1.97

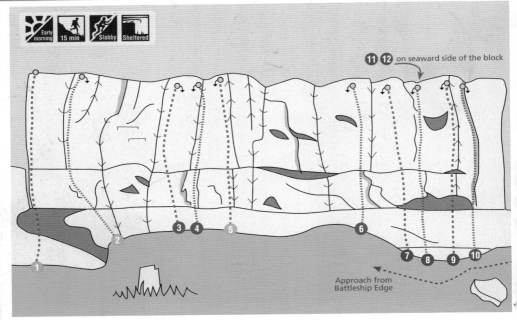

11 12 on seaward side of the block

Approach from
Battleship Edge

BLOCK SLAB

The short slabby side of the fallen block has some very popular routes which are useful for shade on summer afternoons.
APPROACH - Approach as for the main Battleship Edge but walk down the path towards the Back Cliff. The Block is obvious directly opposite Battlship Back Cliff.

1 U-143 . . . . **HVS 5a**
9m. The southern sharp arete of the block is started via the crack. This line will not be bolted.
FA. George Hounsome 1979

The rest of the routes are all resin-bolted with 2 bolt lower-offs. You can lower-off or sit on the top and belay in the sun.

2 Coming Unstuck . . **6a+**
10m. A testing series of moves defines this line that is short on length but high in difficulty.
FA. Steve Taylor 18.9.93

3 Braer Rabbit **6/05 4**
9m. A touch polished.
FA. Steve Taylor 18.9.93

4 This is This . . . . **09/05 4+**
9m. A very pleasant introduction to slab climbing.
FA. Pete Oxley 22.7.90

5 Wake Up, Time to Die . . . . **6a+**
9m. A bit short on bolts at the bottom. A large hex or nut may be needed by some to protect the easy bottom section.
FA. Pete Oxley 22.7.90

6 Like a Drowning Man . . 5 . **03/09 4 or 5**
9m. The grade depends on where you climb - left of the bolts is **5**, the layback seam is **4**.
FA. Pete Oxley 22.7.90

7 Hang Onto Your Ego . . **6b**
9m. The second bolt is a tricky clip for shorties.
FA. Steve Taylor 18.9.93

8 She's Going Down **6b+**
10m. A good test of off-vertical ability.
FA. Pete Oxley 22.7.90

9 Listing Badly . . . . **6c+**
10m. A wicked test of technique that has seen some tears over the years.
FA. Pete Oxley 22.7.90

10 I'm Doing it Anyway **6/05 4**
10m. This slick favorite requires good footwork and technique on the polished holds to guarantee a pleasant tick.
FA. Steve Taylor, Mark Williams 18.9.93

The next two routes lie on the seaward side of the block which is steep and loose in places.

11 Another Stone on the Pile of Choss **6c+**
10m. The steep undercut arete is a touch loose at the bottom but solid higher up.
FA. Jim Kimber 4.8.96

12 Welcome to the Gravity Program **6c**
10m. 5m further right.
FA. Nic Hellyer 28.9.97

There is a lone bolt further right again.

WALLSEND

The largest cliff on Portland is the huge arc of Wallsend Cove with its routes combining some superb climbing with bundles of atmosphere. The Cove is divided into two main areas that have close to two hundred routes on their various walls. Wallsend North's areas are all set back from the sea and vary between a short series of bays, around 15 to 20m high, to some larger sections toward the centre of the Cove. The spectacular Wallsend South areas are all at sea level and rise to a majestic thirty metres whilst exhibiting a geological gateaux of colourful strata. The climbs at Wallsend Cove span the grades well, providing many atmospheric climbs that cater for most teams visiting the area looking for a big cliff environment.

APPROACH

The Wallsend Cliffs have two main approaches, both of which can be quite hard going, especially the sections along the boulder beach; this is not somewhere to come with non-climbing friends.

Wallsend North Approach (all areas up to Laid Back Area) - Drive through Weston and at a roundabout turn right into Reap Lane (as for Battleship Edge) and park. From here, gain the cliff-top path via a path/track that heads towards the huge Southwell Business Park complex. Once at the cliff-top path turn, left (looking out) and walk on for 50m. Descend a path, which cuts back right, and at the end of this, head left underneath the So Hardcore Area, and then more sectors, before the path drops down to the boulder beach.

Coastguard Approach to Wallsend South (all areas from Bigger Piece south) - Drive to Portland Bill and park

in the pay car park. Walk back up the road past the Pulpit Inn and head out leftwards up the minor road towards the Coastwatch Lookout. Just before the Coastwatch Lookout, go down a grass slope to the cliff edge then descend a steep and precarious path onto a promontory to below Coastguard North. Walk north under this, past a gully, to reach Wallsend South. This approach is affected by high tide - see opposite.

CONDITIONS

All the Wallsend cliffs face west and catch the afternoon sun. The proximity of Wallsend South to the sea means that the holds can stay greasy until the sun burns them dry. This may take longer when it is humid. Wallsend North is set well back from the sea and is therefore less prone to dampness. There is little seepage but some black sections can remain wet for a time after rain due to the presence of a large grass slope on the top of the crag. The Downhill Spiral Area suffers badly from seepage but is usually dry by summer.

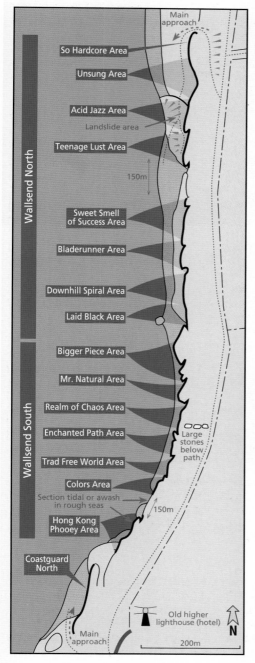

So Hardcore Area

Unsung Area

Acid Jazz Area

Landslide area

Teenage Lust Area

150m

Sweet Smell of Success Area

Bladerunner Area

Downhill Spiral Area

Laid Black Area

Bigger Piece Area

Mr. Natural Area

Realm of Chaos Area

Enchanted Path Area

Trad Free World Area

Colors Area

Section tidal or awash in rough seas

Hong Kong Phooey Area

Coastguard North

Wallsend North

Wallsend South

Main approach

Large stones below path

150m

Main approach

Old higher lighthouse (hotel)

200m

N

ACCESS

The only bird restriction currently on Wallsend affects the routes on the right-hand side of the Trad Free World Area and the Colors Area. No climbing from 1st March to 31st July. This restriction has been consistently applied in recent years. The situation can change though so check **www.rockfax. com** for up-to-date details.

TIDES

There are two tidal sections below Colors Area and Hong Kong Phooey Area. These cut off access for a short time at high tide and longer in rough seas.

SO HARDCORE AREA

Before the main quality cliffs start at Wallsend, there are a couple of isolated walls which are passed on the approach walk. These have a pair or routes each.

30m to left

❶ **Left Little Slapper** . 　　　　　 7b+
8m. Direct up the front face of the black streaked arete.
FA. Pete Oxley 28.4.96

❷ **Right Little Slapper** . . . 　　　　 7a+
8m. The right-hand variation.
FA. Pete Oxley 28.4.96

30m to the right is a short, clean wall.

❸ **They Walked In Line.** . . 　　　　 7b
8m. Directly up the wall. Lower-off the last bolt.
FA. Pete Oxley 5.7.92

❹ **So Hardcore** . . . . . 　　　　　 7c
8m. Utterly heinous and painful moves up the blank wall.
FA. Pete Oxley 11.5.89

Portland West | Portland East | Lulworth | Swanage | Devon | Blacknor N | Blacknor C | Blacknor S | Blacknor FS | Blacknor M | Battleship M | Battleship B | Wallsend N | Wallsend S | Coastguard N | Coastguard S | White Hole

So Hardcore - 50m

Acid Jazz Area

UNSUNG AREA

An often-deserted and friendly bay with some short and intense test-pieces on high quality rock. It is situated high above the sea and is reasonably sheltered and with a nice grassy belay area.
APPROACH - From the cliff-top path at the north (Reap Lane) end, drop down a path which cuts first back right and then left underneath So Hardcore to the Unsung Area.

❶ RP Screamers 7a
10m. At the start, clip the first bolt of *Alpenglow*. Also use the *Alpenglow* lower-off. This is now the best method of doing this line which was poorly bolted initially.
FA. Martin Crocker 6.5.89

❷ Alpenglow. . . . . 7a+
12m. The fading groove.
FA. Mick Ward 22.7.2003

❸ Topsy Turvy Land . . (7b)
14m. There are some amazing 'mono' holds on this route for which small fingers help. A crucial peg may be missing.
FA. Martin Crocker 6.5.89

❹ Weakest to the Wall . . . 7b
14m. A superb right-trending pocketed sheet is hard to flash.
FA. Pete Oxley 10.5.89

❺ Compromise . . . . 7b+
13m. The easiest way up the line of *Resisting Mutiny* is to the left of the bolts. A long reach is essential.
FA. Grant Wright. 12.95

❻ Resisting Mutiny 7c+
13m. Horrendous crimp-nasty sequence, directly above the shelf on *Right Mix*, staying exactly on the bolt line. An eliminate.
FA. Grant Wright 12.95

❼ The Right Mix . . . . . . 6b+
14m. Well worth seeking out for the interesting geology. There is also a direct start, up the wall right of the arete, at about **7a**. However the route could do with an extra first bolt for comfort.
FA. Martin Crocker 6.5.89

❽ Never Lose that Feeling 6b
13m. A technical delight with a 2nd move that will stump many.
FA. Pete Oxley 2.7.92

❾ Sing Something Simple . . . . . . 6c+
13m. The wall with a particularly hard move low down leaving a big ledge. Awkward to keep out of *Unsung*.
FA. Gary Gibson 20.5.2004

❿ Unsung 6b
11m. A short but action-packed line.
FA. Pete Oxley 18.8.92

⓫ Come In Alone, Go Out Alone
. . . . 6b
12m. A bouldery start followed by even more difficult climbing.
FA. Pete Oxley 6.5.89

⓬ No Soft Option 7b
11m. A very fierce crux, followed by an easier run-out section.
FA. Pete Oxley 10.5.89

⓭ Dial-a-Cliché . . . . 6c+
12m. This attractive shallow groove is a touch bold and has seen some nasty falls.
FA. Pete Oxley 6.5.89

⓮ Oscourt 6b
10m. The first ascent was virtually soloed. Weird stuff.
FA.. G.Jeffreys 13.7.90. The line was accidentally bolted and called 'The Web' as a new route (E.de Stefani 1994).

⓯ Can't Stop the Bosch . . . . . 6b+
8m. The short line on the right side of the bay.
FA. Joff Cook 8.5.94

⓰ Sgt. Ford's Roving Truncheon . . 7a
25m. A two pitch traverse starting up *Oscourt*, belaying above *The Right Mix*, and then continuing to the belay on *RP Screamers*. Bizarre.
FA. Joff Cook, Damian Cook 1994

ACID JAZZ AREA

A good open face which rather alarmingly is starting to gain height due to slippage of the earth and ledges below. However, this has recently stabilised but take care when negotiating your way along the base of the crag.

APPROACH - Continue carefully along the crag-base path from under the Unsung Area.

❶ Holding the Zero. . . . . [ ] **7a**
12m. Eases up after an interesting start.
FA. Mick Ward 2003

❷ Sniper in the Brain . . . . [ ] **7a**
13m. Move left from the second bolt of *Holding the Zero.*
FA. Mick Ward 2003

❸ Stay on Target . . . . [ ] **6c+**
13m. The old start is now awkward to get to. Start up *Holding the Zero* instead and move right.
FA. Joff Cook 28.4.94

❹ Dead Man's Click . . . . [ ] **7a**
14m. Move right from the first bolt on *Holding the Zero* to reach the wall on the far right.
FA. Mick Ward 2003

❺ Old Painless . . . . [ ] **7a+**
17m. The first route on the wall has some spaced bolts.
FA. Joff Cook 30.5.92. See the film 'Predator' to check the route name.

❻ Useless Generation [icons] [ ] **7b**
18m. Quality technical and fingery climbing.
FA. Pete Oxley 12.4.92

❼ My Love of this Land
. . . . [icons] [ ] **7b**
17m. This has lost a hold and become a bit harder. The third clip remains as gripping as ever.
FA. Pete Oxley 14.5.89

❽ Going Blank Again . . . . [icons] [ ] **7a+**
17m. There is only one hard move, but it's a tough one.
FA. Pete Oxley 12.4.92

❾ The Treacle Factory . . . . . [icons] [ ] **6a+**
19m. A much improved route.
FA. Aiden Cook 30.5.92

❿ Montreal Protocol . [icons] [ ] **7b**
19m. A direct start has been added to straighten the route out.
FA. Martin Crocker 20.5.89, Start - Pete Oxley 17.4.93

⓫ Cosa Nostra . . . . [icons] [ ] **6a**
20m. The corner line has a slightly dirty start but gives good climbing above; however it is often damp.
FA. E.deStefani 24.4.94

⓬ Acid Jazz Disco . . . . . [icons] [ ] **7a**
20m. A fine arete has a slightly broken start but improves dramatically higher up. The arete is climbed mainly on its right-hand side.
FA. Martin Crocker 20.5.89

⓭ Eight-Bar Blues . . [icons] [ ] **6c+**
19m. An excellent face of perfect blue rock that was somehow overlooked in earlier explorations. Easier for the short!
FA. Joff Cook 1995

TEENAGE LUST AREA

Some well-positioned routes above an elevated ledge although the approach scramble is a bit awkward.
APPROACH - From the Acid Jazz Area, the main path descends to the boulder beach. The Teenage Lust section is perched above a steep grass slope and a central knotted rope, leading to the base of *So Shoot Me,* is needed to access the thin ledge system from where most of the routes start. Once again, take care when using this approach.

❶ Precious to the Last
.... 7c
15m. Desperate 'grit-like' palming which needs good conditions for a successful ascent.
FA. Pete Oxley 11.5.90

❷ Ecstasy .... 7a+
15m. Trend right up the open scoop.
FA. Pete Oxley 27.3.90

❸ Live Now, Pay Later ... 7a+
15m. Directly up the sustained tilted wall
FA. Pete Oxley 5.7.92

❹ John Craven's Jumper Contest
.... 6c
16m. Fine laybacking up the groove. Good moves.
FA. Pete Oxley 7.6.92

❺ The Watchmaker's Hands
.... 7c
17m. Some very intense moves on small side-pulls.
FA. Pete Oxley 8.7.92

❻ Breakfast of Champions
.... 7b+
18m. Follow the right-hand line of bolts at the crux.
FA. Damian Cook 29.8.92

❼ Youth Body Expression Explosion
.... 7b
18m. A good route with a witheringly hard finish.
FA. Pete Oxley 15.8.92

❽ To Hungary For Love
.... 8a
18m. The blunt arete has some sustained moves on side-pulls and smears.
FA. Gavin Symonds 6.9.2003. A long-standing project which originally had been bolted by Damian Cook. Named in his memory.

❾ So Shoot Me .... 7a+
20m. Technical wall climbing with hard pocket moves.
FA. Joff Cook 8.5.94

❿ Lolita .... 7b+
26m. This big sweeping line up the ramp and flake breaks left from *Teenage Lust* at its 3rd bolt. Some find a stick clip necessary to extend the 3rd bolt.
FA. Pete Oxley 17.5.99

⓫ Teenage Lust.. 7b+
26m. It includes a killer move off 2 monos and is slightly bold low down with a tricky third clip (use a stick clip if unsure).
FA. Pete Oxley 12.4.92

SWEET SMELL OF SUCCESS AREA

A good area with a handful of very worthwhile pitches. The base of the crag is quite sheltered and stable. Some routes can be dusty.

APPROACH - Approach from the north end and scramble under the other sectors down to the boulder beach. The grass terrace below the wall is reached by a short scramble up the slope.

1 My Dog's Got Fleas 7b
20m. Excellent rock but old bolts.
FA. Martin Crocker 12.8.89

2 Poop Scoop 6c
20m. Climb a flake crack then move left onto the arete. The bolts are on a slightly different line which was added at a later date but is not really independent enough. It is around **6c+** if you stick religiously to the bolt line.
FA. Martin Crocker 12.8.89. Claimed as Yikes Shaggy by Gary Gibson in 2003.

3 Scoobydoobydoo . 6b
20m. The steep wall has a long move just before the roof finish.
FA. Gary Gibson 25.5.2003

4 Scooby Snacks 7a
20m. A striking arete. Climb the straightforward lower wall to a hand-ledge. Make a hard mantelshelf and further hard moves onto the arete proper. Fine open climbing leads to the top.
FA. Gary Gibson 25.5.2003

5 The Heanous Quest 6a
20m. Climb over the flake to a short groove. Follow this to a hand-rail which leads up right onto the headwall.
FA. Neal Heanes 5.6.2003

6 Hen's Tooth 7b
20m. Tackle the bulge to gain a scoop. Leaving this requires a long reach and the bulging rib on the right provides the finish.
FA. Gary Gibson 27.5.2003

The next line of bolts is a project.

7 So You Want to Be Happy . 7a+
20m. A bit soapy low down.
FA. Pete Oxley 17.7.90

8 Up on the Hill 7a
20m. Climb the wall and blunt rib then move onto the face above. Easier climbing remains. It has at least one airy clip!
FA. Gary Gibson 25.5.2003

9 Hallelujah 7a
20m. A good route which, despite being well-bolted, still feels bold. Approach it with your E5 head on.
FA. Pete Oxley 17.7.90

10 Old Speckled Hen . . . . 6c+
20m. A worthwhile pitch which is low in the grade. Climb the wall to gain a prominent flake hold. Reach the thin crack above and follow this to the slabby wall.
FA. Gary Gibson, Phil Gibson 2003

11 Stone Cold Sober . . . . . 7a+
20m. A good stamina climb squeezed in just left of *Stay Golden*, and sharing its start. Quite blind on the crux.
FA. Mike Robertson 18.8.98

12 Stay Golden 7b
20m. The first of three classics in this area features stylish climbing on great rock.
FA. Pete Oxley 17.7.90

13 Sweet Smell of Success
. . . . 7b
20m. A great route which overhangs gently all the way. One of the best lines on Portland.
FA. Pete Oxley 11.5.90

14 Frazzled 7b
20m. A stunning and difficult line up the faint streaked flake just right of the arete. Three cruxes and all are very different.
FA. Damian Cook 9.94

15 Streaky . . . . 6c+
20m. Not surprisingly this follows the streaky wall.
FA. Mike Robertson 5.8.94

16 Das Boot . . . . 6c+
20m. A good face climb. Follow the short steep wall to gain the blackened upper face. Intricate climbing up this leads to a bulge and a big jug above. The finish is harder than it looks.
FA. Gary Gibson, Hazel Gibson, Phil Gibson 27.5.2003

Portland West | Portland East | Lulworth | Swanage | Devon | Blacknor N | Blacknor C | Blacknor S | Blacknor FS | Battleship M | Battleship B | Wallsend N | Wallsend S | Coastguard N | Coastguard S | White Hole

BLADERUNNER AREA

This section was one of the last to be developed on Wallsend North and has suffered from mudslides in the past. This means that the routes can sometimes be a bit dirty but they are cleaning up with traffic. The climbing here tends to be good though, especially on the upper sections. Some of the starts are tough.

APPROACH - From the boulder beach, either walk along the grass bank from the Sweet Smell Area, or scramble up to the routes direct from the boulder beach.

❶ Falling with Style .... 6b+
20m. Break left at a low shelf to a tricky groove. It can sometimes be very dirty.
FA. Neal Heanes 16.8.98

❷ Screw You Hippy 6a
20m. The best of the slabs has good orange rock. High in the grade and the start can prove to be a bit of a 'stopper'.
FA. Neal Heanes 16.8.98

❸ Tanya's Sex Pot .... 6a+
19m. Very dirty at present.
FA. Neil Burton 16.8.98

❹ Gay Dog .... 6a+
20m. After a crunchy start, this one has some interesting groove climbing higher up.
FA. Neal Heanes 16.8.98

❺ Layback and Take It 6a
21m. A disappointing route up the flake. Still dirty.
FA. Neal Heanes 16.8.98

❻ Blackwind, Fire and Steel .... 6b+
20m. A tricky line up the centre of the big flake.
FA. Neil Burton 16.8.98

❼ Beefcake, Beefcake 6a
21m. An unusually long and thuggy flake climb.
FA. Neal Heanes 3.8.98

❽ Jungle Drums.... 6c+
22m. Some of the flakes ring hollow. A bold route.
FA. Joff Cook 29.8.92

❾ Aaron the Aardvark ...... 6b+
23m. Climb the centre of the face.
FA. Mike Robertson 6.5.95

❿ Bladerunner .... 6b+
24m. Break right out of *Aaron the Aardvark* to an arete-hugging finish. A good route.
FA. Mike Robertson 6.5.95

Portland West | Portland East | Lulworth | Swanage | Devon | Blacknor N | Blacknor C | Blacknor S | Blacknor FS | Battleship M | Battleship B | Wallsend N | Wallsend S | Coastguard N | Coastguard S | White Hole

Fixed rope

Approach

DOWNHILL SPIRAL AREA

The Downhill Spiral Area adjoins the last sector, immediately right of a huge chimney. The routes start from a raised grass bank beneath heavily stained black walls that are prone to seepage in the winter.

APPROACH - From the boulder beach, scramble up the bank to reach the grassy ledge below the face.

❶ Fatal Fibre . . . . 6c+
15m. Start from a bolt belay. The wall is followed with a hard move at the start to a lower-off on the right.
FA. Gary Gibson 4.5.2002

❷ Billy Bob's Way . . . . 6b+
15m. Start from the bolt belay of *Fatal Fibre*. Climb the prominent blackened-streak directly by pleasant sustained moves.
FA. Gary Gibson and Hazel Gibson 4.5.2002

❸ The Man Who Wasn't There 7b
16m. Climb steadily up the wall to reach the left-hand side of the arete. Continue up this until a swing up and right onto the face is possible. The rib has some hard moves on its upper section and is a little loose lower down.
FA. Gary Gibson 3.5.2002

❹ Hate Crime . . . . 7a+
17m. A fine, technical groove experience with one very hard move but it also has a few rests to compensate.
FA. Neal Heanes 9.5.98

❺ Lefty Hoot 'n' Annie . . 6c
19m. Good climbing up the yellow groove which requires some wide bridging moves before the nifty finish.
FA. Neal Heanes 2.5.98

❻ And the Boot Sails By 7a
19m. Sustained moves up the fine open face.
FA. Gary Gibson 30.3.2002

❼ Downhill Spiral
. . . . 7b+
20m. Run-out and pumpy.
FA. Pete Oxley 19.4.92

❽ Everything's Eventual . . . . 6c+
20m. A good pitch finishing up a shallow groove after a rather dusty start.
FA. Gary Gibson 1.4.2002

❾ By Mistake . . . . 7b+
20m. The thin left-hand finish to *More Than a Legend*.
FA. Andy Long 2005

❿ More Than a Legend . . 7b+
20m. A desperate technical sequence up the thin wall leading to a faint crack and more hard moves to the belay. Firable low down.
FA. Gary Gibson 1.4.2002

⓫ Under Crimson Skies . . 7a+
20m. Surprisingly sustained climbing up the right-hand side of the flowstone. A friable lower wall.
FA. Gary Gibson 1.4.2002

LAID BLACK AREA
This section of wall is the continuation rightwards from the Downhill Spiral Area and is just before the tall buttress of the Bigger Piece Sector.
APPROACH - Continue along the boulder beach below the streaks of the Downhill Spiral Area. Then scramble up the grassy slope to the base of the wall.

The next route starts about 8m right of Under Crimson Skies. which is the final offering on the Downhill Spiral Area.

❶ My Figure Head . . . . ▭ **6c**
20m. Climb dirty ground to a ledge. Gain the groove above with difficulty, then pull over the roof to the lower-off.
FA. Gary Gibson 11.5.2002

❷ The Shipping News . . . . . ▨ ▭ **7b**
20m. From the ledge of *My Figure Head*, step right and climb the technical wall past a deep break to the lower-off.
FA. Gary Gibson 11.5.2002

❸ Five Easy Pieces . . . . ▩ ▨ ▭ **6c+**
20m. A steep and intricate slab leads to an angled-ramp and steep, juggy headwall.
FA. Gary Gibson 3.6.2002

❹ Laid Black . . . . ▩ ▭ **6c+**
20m. Climb over cleaned ledges to below the black wall. Tricky moves through the bulge lead onto the wall. Climb this leftwards to the lower-off.
FA. Gary Gibson 11.5.2002

The last two routes are around 25m to the right.

❺ Wonderful . . . . ▩ ▭ **7a+**
18m. Climb a thin wall via a faint crack then move left to good holds at the top. Continue direct to a ledge and an awkward finish. Excellent rock.
FA. Gary Gibson 1.6.2002

❻ Wonder-Bra . . . . ▩ ▭ **6b**
18m. Trend right from the start of *Wonderful* and climb the scooped wall past a ledge to a steep finish.
FA. Gary Gibson 1.6.2002

en Stokes stretched out in glorious evening light on the superb *Vin Chaud* (7a)
n the Bigger Piece Area at Wallsend South - *page 98*. Photo: Neal Heanes

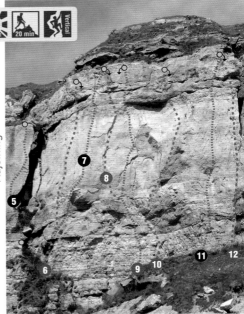

BIGGER PIECE AREA

A superb buttress of lovely rock providing some exhilarating climbs. Well worth the long walk-in. Routes from *The Bigger Piece* to *Mick Lovatt Stole My Trousers* are very long and require a 60m rope to lower-off.

APPROACH - This wall is about mid-way along the length of Wallsend hence it can be approached from either the north or the south (except at high tide). Either start from the boulder beach or scramble up the grass and vegetation to the right to reach the routes.

❶ The Bigger Piece . . . . . 🔲🔲 [____] **7a+**
30m. One of the longest lines on Portland up a huge pillar. The reach symbol is for clipping the bolts (tip - do Route 2 first and place the clips on your way down).
FA. Martin Crocker 13.8.89

❷ No Place for Mambas . . . . 🔲 [____] **6b**
30m. Quality face climbing on the headwall and generously bolted.
FA. Martin Crocker 2.5.92

❸ Opposites Attract . . . . 🔲🔲 [____] **6c**
30m. Good face climbing on quality rock high up.
FA. Martin Crocker 2.5.92

❹ Mick Lovatt Stole My Trousers 🔲 [____] **6b+**
30m. Follow the long layback crack at the top.
FA. Martin Crocker 2.5.92

The next routes are reached by scrambling up the steep bank (with knotted rope) to the belay bolts.

❺ Cool to be Uncool . 🔲🔲🔲 [____] **7b+**
15m. An unusual arete climb which feels bold. No lower-off.
FA. Martin Crocker 2.5.92

❻ Coconut Milk . . . . 🔲🔲 [____] **7a**
20m. A worthwhile route with good bolts now.
FA. Martin Crocker 16.7.89

❼ On a Desert Island Beach 🔲🔲 [____] **7a+**
21m. Great positions on a lovely curving arete.
FA. Martin Crocker 15.7.89

❽ Vin Chaud . . . . 🔲🔲 [____] **7a**
21m. A fine left-hand finish to *Accordians*.... up some flakes.
Photo page 97.
FA. Neal Heanes 16.6.2003

❾ Accordions Go Crazy . . 🔲🔲 [____] **6b+**
21m. Start to the left of the flake. Initially the rock is a bit crumbly but it improves dramatically above.
FA. Martin Crocker 15.7.89

❿ Basrah Blues Band . . . 🔲🔲 [____] **6c**
20m. Climb a flake to a ledge. Follow the groove above to a tricky bulge. The slab above leads to the lower-off.
FA. Neal Heanes 14.6.2003

⓫ Laughing Peter . . . . . . 🔲🔲 [____] **7a+**
20m. Very strenuous if you stay on the direct line.
FA. Martin Crocker 15.7.89

⓬ Sans Frontière . . . . . . 🔲🔲 [____] **6b+**
20m. A fine arete with a definite crux move.
FA. Helen Heanes 2003

Approach along boulder beach

MR. NATURAL AREA

This wall is also well-worth the effort of the long approach. The routes are all on good rock and have now received enough ascents for them to be clean.
APPROACH - The quickest approach is from the south along the boulder beach, unless the tide is high, in which case a longer approach will have to be made from the north.

❶ Parkhurst Dozen **6c**
18m. A good pitch up some layback flakes.
FA. Ben Stokes 8.2003

❷ Sang Chaud . . . . **7a+**
22m. Fine climbing up the wall and groove.
FA. Neal Heanes 8.2003

❸ Son of Mustang Ford **7a**
24m. Good flowstone near the top.
FA. Pete Oxley 26.4.92

❹ Mr Natural . . . . . . **7b+**
25m. A searing thin crack topped by a very hard move. Good, crimpy climbing.
FA. Pete Oxley 19.4.92

❺ Catatonic . . . . **6b+**
30m. An open face climb. Take care low down as the gear is a little spaced and the rock friable.
FA. Pete Oxley 19.4.92

❻ Moan, Moan, Moan . . . . . **7b+**
25m. A hideous mantelshelf over the roof spoils this route.
FA. Martin Crocker 20.4.92

❼ Injury Encyclopaedia . . **7b**
25m. A fine white wall.
FA. Martin Crocker 25.4.92

Portland West
Portland East
Lulworth
Swanage
Devon
Blacknor N
Blacknor C
Blacknor S
Blacknor FS
Battleship M
Battleship B
Wallsend N
Wallsend S
Coastguard N
Coastguard S
White Hole

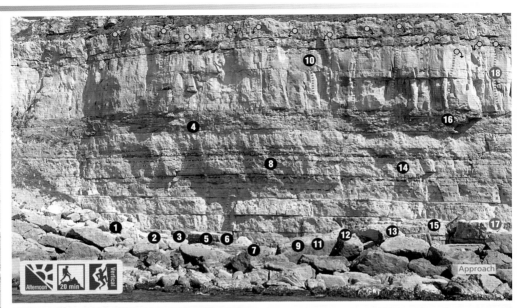

Afternoon | 20 min | Vertical

REALM OF CHAOS AREA

A big wall which should appeal to harder climbers. The pitches are long and sustained. Use 60m ropes.
APPROACH - The quickest approach is from the south along the boulder beach, unless the tide is high, in which case a long approach can be made from the northern end.

❶ Spinal Tap . . . **7b+**
27m. There is a safe but scary run-out at the top.
FA. Pete Oxley 26.4.92

❷ Million Watt Marshalls
. . . . **7b**
27m. Continually absorbing and very sustained.
FA. Pete Oxley 26.4.92

❸ Ariane V **7b**
28m. Direct and pumpy version of *Disintegration* with no real crux moves but plenty of hard moves. A very good route.
FA. Pete Oxley 9.5.96

❹ Disintegration . . . . **7b+**
28m. A drainage streak in winter and now virtually redundant.
FA. Pete Oxley 25.9.89

❺ Zum Zeaux . . . **7b+**
28m. A tremendous route with a burly start and a technical finish.
FA. Martin Crocker 16.7.89

❻ Magnetic Pull . . . . **7c+**
28m. An extremely demanding direct on *Zum Zeaux* with a power-packed first 10m. Save some energy for the last moves.
FA. Pete Oxley 14.9.96

❼ Realm of Chaos . . . . . . **7b+**
28m. A superb sustained route above a hard start.
FA. Pete Oxley 24.9.89

❽ Hombre Solaire . . . **7c**
28m. Another stamina monster. Start up *Realm of Chaos*, move out right at the 4th bolt for 4m, then climb straight up.
FA. Pete Oxley 6.6.96. The old direct start has been abandoned.

❾ Face the Truth . **7c**
28m. Amazingly steep initially, but it soon relents.
FA. Pete Oxley 1.9.89

❿ A Shadow on Mankind . **7b+**
28m. Slightly superseded by the next route.
FA. Pete Oxley 27.3.90

⓫ Saskatchewan Uranium Miner
. . . . **7c**
28m. A classic pump-out with a hard move low down and a demanding upper half.
FA. Martin Crocker 23.9.90

⓬ Troll Team Special **7b**
28m. A good pitch with a low crux and great climbing above.
FA. Pete Oxley 13.7.89

⓭ The Pickford Files . . . . **7b+**
27m. Start up *Breakbeat* then head left and up the headwall. Check with a local about the state of the rock on this pitch.
FA. Dave Pickford 9.99

⓮ Breakbeat . . . . **7b+**
27m. An unrelenting route with a fine upper groove.
FA. Martin Crocker 19.8.90

⓯ The Mask **7b**
27m. Nice and exposed pumpy climbing.
FA. Pete Oxley 30.4.90. Originally called The Mask of Self Hate.

⓰ Trent Reznor **7b**
20m. A wild version of *The Mask* with sensational exposure.
FA. Pete Oxley 14.10.95

Bevis
17 Bevis 6b
27m. The wall and soaring cracks give relatively easy access to some spectacular territory but it is a bit loose in the middle.
FA. Mick Ward 19.06 04

18 Moonfleet 6b
27m. Interesting, sustained climbing above the start of *Bevis*.
FA.Mick Ward 19.06 04

19 Gossip and Drool 7b
26m. Good rock throughout.
FA. Martin Crocker 13.8.89

20 Heat-stroke Groove . . . 6c+
26m. A fine white groove with a reachy finish.
FA. Pete Oxley 7.9.89

21 Summer Babe . . . . 7b+
26m. The right-hand rib has a slappy crux.
FA. Pete Oxley 21.5.92

ENCHANTED PATH AREA

22 Eternal Peace. 6c
28m. Climb the wall to a ledge and then head left and up the arete via some 'Grit-like' moves.
FA. Mick Ward 5.7.2003

23 Dark Play. 6b
28m. A direct on *Eternal Peace* from the midway ledge.
FA. Mick Ward 2004

24 The Bog Man . . . . 6b+
27m. The wall, overlap and flake-crack give good varied climbing. A long reach is useful at the top.
FA. Mick Ward 17.7.2003

25 Garstang . . . . 6c+
27m. The wall, groove and overlap. Good climbing with rests.
FA. Mick Ward 5.7.2003

ENCHANTED PATH AREA
A big wall with some essential ticks in the 6s. Use 60m ropes.
APPROACH - Approach from the southern end along the boulder beach, except at high tide.

26 Shibumi 7a
27m. Climb easy-angled rock to a good wall high up.
FA. Mick Ward 2004

27 Slave State . . . . . . 7b+
18m. Start by scrambling up to below the central gully. A bit run-out at present between bolts 2 and 3.
FA. Pete Oxley 2.5.92

28 Immaculata . . . . 6c+
27m. The wall and hanging groove.
FA. Mick Ward 30.3.2003

29 The Watchman 6b
28m. A great route for the grade. Start up the technical scoop just left of the corner.
FA. Pete Oxley 2.5.92 and 1.10.96 for the start.

30 Peace in the Nineties . 6b+
29m. Another hard start from the left with fine climbing above. The Direct Start is 6c and has a mean move on it.
FA. Pete Oxley 31.12.89 and 14.10.96 for the new start.

31 Enchanted Path . . . . 6b+
29m. A good route which has a big start over the initial roof but is much easier above this. Get a tall mate to place the first quickdraw.
FA. Brian Tilley 13.7.89. Brian's finest new route.

32 Best Fingers Forward . 6c
29m. Finger-jamming with bolts.
FA. Pete Oxley 11.7.89

33 Blue Faced Booby. 6c
29m. The upper arete is tackled 'au cheval' and is very exposed.
Photo page 105.
FA. Martin Crocker 13.8.89

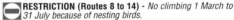

TRAD FREE WORLD AREA

This is one of the best areas on Portland, with long sustained pitches on good rock.
APPROACH - Approach from the southern end, along the boulder beach under Coastguard North.

❶ Tea Cakes Calling . 　　　　 7a
28m. The desperate start can be avoided by swinging in from *The Jewel of the Isle* - in this case it becomes a pleasant 6c.
FA. Pete Oxley 21.5.96

❷ The Jewel of the Isle . . 　　　　 6b+
28m. As good as the name suggests - superb and sustained.
FA. Pete Oxley 25.6.95

❸ Stalker's Zone . . . . . . 　　　　 6a+
28m. A very fine route for the grade. The first bolt is high.
FA. Pete Oxley 30.4.89

❹ Trad Free World . . . . . 　　　　 6b
28m. Immaculate rock throughout. Don't miss it!
FA. Pete Oxley 7.11.92

❺ Genuflection . . . . . 　　　　 7b
28m. A fingery crux but the difficulties are only short.
FA. Pete Oxley 11.5.96

❻ Reverence . . . . 　　　　 7a+
28m. The towering groove in the centre of the gold wall overhangs all the way. Harder if the groove is damp, aren't they all!
FA. Pete Oxley 5.7.89

❼ Outside the Gate . . 　　　　 7b
28m. A big pitch which gets harder all the way. Very sustained and varied.
FA. Pete Oxley 5.7.89

RESTRICTION (Routes 8 to 14) - *No climbing 1 March to 31 July because of nesting birds.*

❽ Halfway to Heaven . 　　　　 7b
28m. The central line is impressive and sustained.
FA. Pete Oxley 29.4.89

❾ Organic Snail Farming
. . . . 　　　　 7b
28m. Very hard for the grade.
FA. Martin Crocker 29.4.89

❿ Wave Graffiti . . . . . 　　　　 7b+
28m. A tough reach at the top. Strength-sapping.
FA. Pete Oxley 27.7.89

⓫ Hawaiian Pipeline . 　　　　 7b
28m. An attractive line which fires up the smart white groove after an easy start. It is slow to dry out.
FA. Pete Oxley 13.7.89

⓬ Running Down a Dream
. . . . 　　　　 7b
28m. The black-streaked groove gives good climbing, though it is a seepage line, which is often dirty.
FA. Pete Oxley 1.9.89

⓭ My Two Left Feet . . 　　　　 7c+
28m. A long and pumpy route with a withering finish.
FA. Pete Oxley 19.6.98 With two different shoes- check your sac!

⓮ Bob's Gold Run . . . . 　　　　 7a+
28m. A very blank-looking groove. Scramble up easy blocks in the gully to get to the start.
FA. Pete Oxley 1.9.89

Ledges awash at very high tide

Approach

COLORS AREA

A fine wall with some long climbs which are very condition-dependent. 60m ropes advised.

TIDES - The area below the face is covered by very high tides and also rough seas.

APPROACH - Approach from the southern end, along the boulder beach under Coastguard North.

RESTRICTION (except route 14) - *No climbing 1 March to 31 July because of nesting birds.*

① Fleshworld . . . . **7b+**
28m. The holds can be soapy at times but it's a cracking pitch.
FA. Pete Oxley 8.8.91

② Colors . . . . **7b+**
28m. An incredible line up the long crack in the headwall.
FA. Pete Oxley 8.11.88

③ Olympus Mons **7b**
28m. A fine route with a sting in the tail, that just merits the grade. Start up the wide crack right of *Colors*. There is a much easier variant just right of the bolts.
FA. Gary Gibson, Phil Gibson 2003

④ White Unconquerable . **6b+**
28m. A huge line up a towering flaky corner. Much better value on your arms than its Stanage counterpart. Can be soapy.
FA. Pete Oxley 1.10.95

⑤ Gedge . . . . **6b+**
28m. The wall just left of the central crack/chimney.
FA. Pete Oxley 8.8.91

⑥ Black'll do Nicely . . . . . **7a+**
28m. Good sustained climbing intially over bulges, then up the wall to a steeper finish. Close to *Gedge* on the crux.
FA. Gary Gibson 10.5.2003

⑦ The Empire State Arete **6b+**
28m. A huge adventure-style route up the right side of the towering arete. Often the location of a peregrine's nest.
FA. Pete Oxley 27.9.94

⑧ Dogtown Skate Team . . **7a+**
27m. The left-hand line is a brilliant route.
FA. Andy Long 15.9.2002

⑨ Rush . . . . **7b+**
26m. Start up *Beautiful South*. Move left to the flake crack.
FA. Andy Long 25.4.2002

⑩ Beautiful South . . . **7c**
26m. The impressive prow is gained from the right and gives a fine pitch. A long-standing project. *Photo page 38.*
FA. Andy Long 10.4.2002

⑪ Tarquill's Trollies **6c**
15m. The left-hand side of the wall only has one hard move.
FA. Mike Robertson 2.5.98

⑫ Flipper's Revenge . **7a+**
15m. A desperate cruxy route and even harder for the short.
FA. Gary Gibson 29.3.2002

⑬ Walking on Sunshine **7a**
15m. A brilliant climb up the isolated flowstone face 20m right of *Empire State Arete*. The first bolt may be missing
FA. Mike Robertson 5.8.94

The final pitch on this section is situated 30m to the right. There is a knotted rope in place to reach the start.

⑭ No Victory In Europe **6c**
17m. Has suffered from mud slides and can be dirty.
FA. Pete Oxley 7.5.95

Portland West
Portland East
Lulworth
Swanage
Devon
Blacknor N
Blacknor C
Blacknor S
Blacknor FS
Battleship M
Battleship B
Wallsend N
Wallsend S
Coastguard N
Coastguard S
White Hole

❶ Critical Mass 6b
25m. Pleasant climbing with a boldish finale.
FA. Gary Gibson, Hazel Gibson, Mick Ward 9.5.2003

❷ Rapid Response 7a
25m. A technical groove makes up the meat of this route.
FA. Gary Gibson, Mick Ward 9.5.2003

❸ Chert Noble. . . . . . 7a+
25m. The right-hand pillar is the best route of the three.
FA. Gary Gibson 10.5.2003

❹ Face in the Chert 6a
24m. A slight climb, maybe in need of another bolt. It follows
the flaky crack-line gained direct via a juggy wall and ledge.
FA. Gary Gibson, Phil Gibson 6.5.2003

❺ Glamour Cat. 6b
24m. A great face climb with lots of good climbing.
FA. Jan Rostron, Pete Oxley 25.7.96

❻ 1789 . . . . 7a
25m. Finish direct over the top roof. High in the grade.
FA. Pete Oxley 11.7.89

❼ The Bad Seeds . . . 7b
24m. An excellent wall and thin crack, beware the nest!
FA. Martin Crocker 23.9.90

❽ Magical Mr Mephistopheles
. . . . 6c
24m. Good climbing, heading for the open scoop right of *Bad
Seeds*. Swing left at the top to share a belay with *Bad Seeds*.
FA. Pete Oxley 1.11.94

❾ Clacichew 6b
25m. Traverse in carefully to the base. Follow the left-hand line
past the 'dripping collar' of flowstone. Slightly lichenous.
FA. Gary Gibson, Hazel Gibson 22.5.2004

❿ Calcite Compliment 6c
25m. The right-hand line with a testing central section.
FA. Gary Gibson, Hazel Gibson 22.5.2004

HONG KONG PHOOEY AREA
A fine set of stamina routes with a wide grade span.
TIDES - The area below the face is covered by very high tides
and rough seas.
APPROACH - Approach from the southern end, along the boul-
der beach under Coastguard North.

⓫ Jazz It Up . . . . 7a+
15m. Start at a bolt belay on a high ledge, accessed by a knotted rope. Worthwhile climbing with a very short hard section.
FA. Gary Gibson, Hazel Gibson 22.5.2004

⓬ Razzamatazz 7b
15m. A snazzy wall pitch from the same high ledge.
FA. Pete Oxley 6.11.94

⓭ The Great Pretender . . 6c+
23m. The blunt arete is sportingly bolted.
FA. Mike Robertson 5.8.94

⓮ Totally FOO to You 6c
21m. A prominent arete gained by tricky moves over an overlap
and leading to fine open climbing above.
FA. Gary Gibson 22.5.2004

⓯ Tunnel Vision . . . . 7b+
21m. A sister route to *Hong Kong Phooey* keeping close to the
bolt line. No escaping left at the top. Needs dry condtitions.
FA. Pete Oxley 2.4.99

⓰ Hong Kong Phooey. . . . 7c
20m. A sustained route which needs dry conditions and can be
terminally damp at other times. Plan an afternoon ascent.
FA. Damian Cook 20.3.94

⓱ Doolittle . . . . 6b+
18m. A great line.
FA. E.deStefan 2.2.94

⓲ Jane Says . . . . 6b+
17m. Climb the crack line which becomes increasingly steep as
height is gained.
FA. Joff Cook 1994

⓳ Relax . . . . 6b+
16m. Stay left of the bolts at the bottom for the best climbing.
FA. Nic Hellyer 10.99

Jane Weir enjoying *Blue Faced Booby* (6c), the Enchanted Path Area at Wallsend - *page 101*. Photo: Mike Robertson

COASTGUARD CLIFFS

Portland West
Portland East
Lulworth
Swanage
Devon
Blacknor N
Blacknor C
Blacknor S
Blacknor FS
Battleship M
Battleship B
Wallsend N
Wallsend S
Coastguard N
Coastguard S
White Hole

The Coastguard Cliffs are justifiably popular with their excellent set of routes in a remote and beautiful environment. Unlike much of the rest of the west coast of Portland, the Coastguard cliffs have a real sea-cliff feel about them, with all that this entails – tide-washed ledges and carefully planned approaches, slippery boulders and the constant noise of the sea very close by.

Coastguard North is best known for its collection of steep and powerful hard climbs, many in the high 7s and the area's hardest route - *Vespasian* at 8b.

Coastguard South offers more in the mid grades including the very popular Xavier's Wall area with a great set of mid-grade routes. The regular wave cleaning has left a huge crag of weathered rock; its major feature being the stunning sheet of organ pipe flowstone at the Quick as Rainbows Area.

APPROACH

Drive to the southern end of the island and park at the Bill car park (Pay and Display). Walk back up the road and, just after the Pulpit Inn, take a minor road on the left. As the road starts to level out, just before the Coastwatch Lookout, go left and down a grass slope to the cliff edge then drop down a steep and precarious path onto a prom-ontory. The path gains the boulder beach below the right-hand side of Coastguard North. To reach Coastguard South continue down to the boulder beach then double back left and scramble over a boulder jumble to a more level platform beyond.

ACCESS

There is a seasonal restriction because of nesting birds at the very far end of the Azymuth Area. Slightly further south is a sanctuary zone where there is a total ban on climbing.

Coastguard North — Old Lighthouse
Approach descent
Grip '89 Area
Coastwatch Base
Manhattan Skyline Area
Xavier's Wall Area
Private Road
Bad Moon Rising Area
From Southwell
Quick As Rainbows Area — Tidal trench
Azymuth Area
Pulpit Inn (no parking)
MOD
No climbing at anytime in this area
Pay and display
White Hole
Cafe
Lighthouse
Pulpit Rock
About 200m
Portland Bill
N

CONDITIONS

The cliffs receive sun in the afternoon from about 2pm onwards. Dampness can be a problem in the morning and on humid days, and the area is best visited in bright, fresh weather or late in the day. For the harder routes conditions, are crucial. There is seepage on the right-hand side of Coastguard North and on the black streaks right of Xavier's Wall.

TIDES

The first areas of Coastguard South are only affected for a very short time at high tide and the Grip '89 Area is clear from all but rough seas and very high spring tides. Beyond Xavier's Wall Area, the tide time window decreases and there is a low tidal trench before the Quick as Rainbows Area that allows access for 2 to 4 hours at low tide. The Azymuth Area is only really accessible for any significant time at low spring tide. Coastguard North is non-tidal.

Paul Twomey climbing *Wax Museum* (7b+) on Coastguard North - *page 108.* Photo: Mike Robertson

CHINA WHITE AREA
The first four routes are situated 30m north of the main crag and are well above the shore line atop a grass slope.

❶ El Poder De Un Coño. . 6c+
19m. The open groove just right of a huge prow has an airy climax. Needs good conditions.
FA. Mike Robertson 5.2.94

❷ 100% Colombian . . 7a+
19m. This lovely white wall has a stopper mid-height move and tricky finale.
FA. Pete Oxley 19.3.2000

❸ China White . . . . . 6c+
19m. An appealing thin seam up the white wall. A fine pitch that requires crisp conditions.
FA. Brian Tilley 11.7.89

❹ Pure Shores 6c
18m. A varied wall pitch that starts up the easy flake crack. Finish as for *China White*.
FA. Pete Oxley 1.5.2000

WAX MUSEUM AREA

❺ Meridian Line 7c
22m. Directly above the pillar, a blind crack leads to finger-burning mini-flakes which will completely drown your forearms in lactic acid, if they weren't already!
FA. Pete Oxley 3.10.98

❻ Ming the Merciless 7c+
22m. Very pumpy, with a desperate start that is best reached by nipping up the pillar to the left and stepping out right.
FA. Pete Oxley 7.11.98

❼ Headwall Emptiness. . . 7b+
22m. A classic in dry sunny conditions and worth waiting for, otherwise damp and best left well alone.
FA. Pete Oxley 12.7.92

❽ Glycerine . . . . 7c+
22m. A big stamina pitch with a complicated lower section and a hard finish. A stick-clip is useful to set the route up and no cheating with long slings on the belay! Good conditions needed.
FA. Pete Oxley 17.10.98

❾ Sand Castles . . . . 7a+
17m. A line of flakes left of *Wax Museum*. The gear is terminally old so avoid unless it has had new bolts added.
FA. Paul Twomey 9.7.95

❿ Wax Museum . . . . 7b+
18m. A magnificent route up the eye-catching sheet of orange flowstone. *Photo page 107.*
FA. Martin Crocker 1.4.90

⓫ Dr Phibes 7b
18m. More brilliant flowstone finger-flakes, after a slightly awkward start.
FA. Pete Oxley 28.4.93

⓬ Clockwork Orange 7c
22m. The power-packed blind crack leads to a blank headwall.
FA. Gavin Symonds 4.99

The next line of bolts is an old project.

⓭ The Nth Degree . . . 7c
22m. After the easy approach, blast up an overhanging scoop, past a big flake. Keep going, just right of the bolts, jumping to gain the break. Step back left to finish.
FA. Pete Oxley 4.6.98

⑭ Wasted . . . . 🖾🖾🖾 ☐ 7b+
22m. The open scoop leads into a left-trending undercut which can be very greasy.
FA. Neal Heanes 28.3.99

⑮ Last Orders . . . 🖾🖾🖾🖾 ☐ 7c
22m. A right-hand finish to *Wasted*. Move diagonally right on small holds then up to the finish of *Bar Room Brawl*.
FA. Pete Oxley 10.5.99

⑯ Bar Room Brawl 🖾🖾🖾🖾 ☐ 7c+
22m. An overhanging groove next to the huge black streak. So named after a couple of knee-bars on the route.
FA. Pete Oxley 23.4.95. Not the 8b that was predicted.

⑰ Vespasian . 🖾🖾🖾🖾🖾 ☐ 8b
22m. The hardest route on Portland which requires a BIG span for success. Repeated and upgraded.
FA. Pete Oxley 1.10.94. Dorset's first 8b was actually climbed in the mid 90s but was then only given 8a+.

⑱ Sale of the Century 🖾🖾🖾 ☐ 7b
22m. The central blind crack is very varied. Hold something in reserve for the last moves.
FA. Pete Oxley 8.9.96

⑲ Zero Tolerance . . . 🖾🖾🖾 ☐ 7b+
22m. A rightward line from the ledge on *Sale of the Century*, up an overhung ramp. Needs good conditions.
FA. Pete Oxley 23.9.98

WAX MUSEUM AREA
This clean and appealing wall is home to some great stamina test-pieces. One drawback is that most of the routes are very condition-dependent and need sunshine and no humidity. Plan a visit late in the day, or on fresh cool days, otherwise the damp and greasy conditions will be frustrating.
APPROACH - Approach from the southern end by dropping down the descent gully and then head right (looking out) along the boulder beach.

⑳ Mid-Strife Oasis . . . . . 🖾🖾 ☐ 7c
22m. Very hard climbing on its lower half.
FA. Pete Oxley 18.9.94

㉑ Eternal Spider . 🖾🖾🖾🖾 ☐ 7c+
22m. This route surges violently up the imposing white wall.
FA. Pete Oxley 18.4.93

The next line is an open project.

㉒ Happy to Go Blind . 🖾🖾🖾 ☐ 7b+
22m. A climb of two halves. Follow a tricky calcified-crack to a grass ledge, then contort up the innocent-looking blank groove.
FA. Pete Oxley 12.12.97

NOTHING BUT THE GROOVE AREA

A large sweeping grey-streaked wall with many excellent technical and sustained wall pitches. The area tends to be quite popular because it is the closest to the parking, but also because it has a good spread of quality routes across the grades.

APPROACH - From the lookout, drop carefully down the main approach path. This wall is the first encountered, above and to the right.

❶ Spare Rib . . . . 🔲🔲 **7b**
20m. Fine climbing, following a clean white tower of rock. Save your strength for the top.
FA. Mike Robertson 6.5.95

❷ Girl Power . . . . 🔲🔲 **7a+**
22m. A bouldery crux on compact rock, taking the right-hand side of the well-bolted arete.
FA. Pete Oxley 2.12.97

❸ Steve's Route . . . . 🔲🔲🔲 **7b**
22m. After an easy start, the central scoop gives an absorbing and intense chess game.
FA. Chris Cubitt 5.98 (but it was Steve Taylor's project).

❹ Retaining the Ashes . . . . . 🔲🔲 **6b**
22m. A varied and worthwhile line. Perhaps the route name is now more likely than it was back in 1993.
FA. Steve Taylor 7.3.93

❺ Into the Groove . . . . 🔲🔲 **6b+**
23m. A good link-up. Start up *Retaining the Ashes* then move right 'into the groove' past a single extra bolt.
FA. Pete Oxley 2000

❻ Nothing but the Groove 🔲🔲🔲 **6c+**
24m. A classic of the crag. The bouldery lower wall gains the stunning groove line.
FA. Pete Oxley 8.8.88. The first 'modern' route on Portland.

❼ Running It In . . 🔲🔲🔲🔲 **7b+**
23m. This blank-looking line has some fine fingery and intense sequences but the real difficulties are only short.
FA. Martin Crocker 10.6.90

❽ Superfly Guy . . . . 🔲🔲 **7a**
22m. A great pumper. Nicely sustained all the way, but a devil if not chalked.
FA. Pete Oxley 8.8.88

❾ Lost In Rock . . . . 🔲🔲 **6c+**
23m. Quality rock and good technical moves on this often over-looked climb. Climb the initial bulge to the right of the bolts.
FA. Pete Oxley 17.7.92

❿ The Man Who Never Found Himself
. . . . 🔲🔲 **6a+**
23m. The excellent central corner line is gained by a bouldery lower wall. Often wet after rain because of a drainage streak.
FA. Pete Oxley 15.8.88

⓫ Van People . . . . . 🔲🔲🔲 **7a**
22m. An enigmatic technical slab pitch that is a little run-out in places and has a hard finish.
FA. Brian Tilley 20.8.89

⓬ Dosvadanya . . . . . 🔲🔲🔲 **6c+**
35m. A rising diagonal traverse from *Fantasy Island* to the lower-off on *Retaining the Ashes*. A sling is needed to extend the 2nd bolt.
FA. Pete Oxley, Brian Tilley 27.11.99

⓭ Fantasy Island . . . . . . 🔲🔲 **6c**
22m. An unusually tough layback which is sometimes damp.
FA. Mark Higgs 28.5.93

Portland West · Portland East · Lulworth · Swanage · Devon · Blacknor N · Blacknor C · Blacknor S · Blacknor FS · Battleship M · Battleship B · Wallsend N · Wallsend S · Coastguard N · Coastguard S · White Hole

⑭ La Usurpadora . . . . 🎯🏃↗↗ ☐ 7c
20m. An artificial eliminate up the wall. For the full tick do not touch the flake of *Fantasy Island*.
FA. Pete Oxley 25.5.2000

⑮ Heartland . . . . . . 🎯🤚↗ ☐ 7c
19m. A good alternative start to *Shining Heart* from the first moves of *La Usurpadora*.
FA. Pete Oxley 17.5.2000

⑯ Shining Heart . . . . 🎯🤚↗ ☐ 7c
18m. Superb power climbing up the impressive rib.
FA. Pete Oxley 20.8.89

⑰ Frenzied Detruncation . 🎯↗ ☐ 7b+
18m. A great line with a thin bouldery start. Can be damp.
FA. Pete Oxley 27.7.89

⑱ Prison Sex . . . 🎯↗🤚🏃 ☐ 7c+
20m. Completely desperate from start to finish.
FA. Pete Oxley 28.5.93

⑲ Midnight Oil . . . . ☐ 7a
17m. A poor route with a run-out finish and often damp holds.
FA. Brian Tilley 5.69

⑳ Hang 'em High . . . 🎯🤚↗ ☐ 7b
15m. A smart test-piece which supersedes an older route called *Gunbarrel Highway* that gained the line by stepping out right from *Midnight Oil*.
FA. Pete Oxely 2000. FA. (Gunbarrel) Brian Tilley 5.89

㉑ Gun Runner . . . . ☐ 6a
10m. Often wet due to a drainage streak.
FA. Pete Oxley 19.3.2000

Portland West
Portland East
Lulworth
Swanage
Devon
Blacknor N
Blacknor C
Blacknor S
Blacknor FS
Battleship M
Battleship B
Wallsend N
Wallsend S
Coastguard N
Coastguard S
White Hole

Area of massive rockfall where *Grip '89* used to be

150m from the descent slope

GRIP '89 AREA

This excellent area is easy to reach and has some great rock. Sadly the central section fell down in the winter of 2000/01. It contained several great routes including *Grip '89*, the route this sector took its name from. Most of the other routes have now been re-geared.

TIDES - The wall is pretty much non-tidal, although it is best to keep away in rough seas.

APPROACH - Approach as for Coastguard North but turn left (facing out) at the bottom of the awkward descent path.

The first few routes lie 150m south of the approach slope, above a conglomerate-filled gully, behind a detached pillar. The most obvious feature is a weird suspended pillar of fused calcite and welded rubble on the left-hand side of the wall.

❶ Seat of Learning 🗝️📷🔦🏞️ [____] 7c
22m. Super technical and powerful climbing up a surprisingly difficult scoop on small layaways. Follow *Font of Knowledge* for the first 8m and stay just right of bolts 5 and 6.
FA. Pete Oxley 27.5.98

❷ The Font of Knowledge
. . . . 🗝️📷🔦 [____] 7c
22m. A big line direct up the impending face with some tough moves at the top.
FA. Pete Oxley 18.5.98

❸ Biscuits for Smut . . . . . 🗝️🔦 [____] 7b
22m. An attractive hanging groove which requires some thought and is difficult to flash.
FA. P Oxley 30.9.94

❹ Reactor Meltdown . 🗝️🏞️📷 [____] 7b
22m. Easier than it looks. Start up *Biscuits for Smut,* via its fused pillar of conglomerate, then move right to a hidden flake. Follow the arete above on its left-hand side in a great position. Technical and superb.
FA. Pete Oxley 27.5.98

The next section is where the bad rockfall was. The rock here has not yet stabilised sufficiently to offer any new routes.

❺ Guardian Angel . . . 🗝️🏞️🔦 [____] 7b+
27m. Superb face work with a complex blind crack in the headwall. Pass the third bolt directly for the **7b+** grade.
FA. Pete Oxley 2.5.98

❻ Brooklyn Bimbo . . . 🗝️🔦🏞️ [____] 7b+
27m. The lower half packs it in on amazing flowstone while the upper arete is exhilarating. It is slightly spoilt by a mid-height ledge and is much harder in greasy conditions.
Brooklyn Original, 7b+ - Starting up *Guardian Angel* and switch to *Brooklyn* is worthwhile still.
FA. (Original) Martin Crocker 29.6.91. Direct by Pete Oxley 12.5.98

MANHATTAN SKYLINE AREA

The continuation wall running right from the Grip '89 Area was initially ignored but has now had a number of worthwhile routes added.

TIDES - The base is covered at high tide. Keep away in rough seas.

APPROACH - Continue along the boulder beach and platform from the Grip '89 Area.

❶ From a Buick Eight. 🔲🔲🔲 ⬜ **7b**
25m. Immaculate rock and climbing, taking the undercut arete and then the right-hand side of the sharp upper arete.
FA. Gary Gibson 7.5.2002

❷ New York Dolls ...... 🔲🔲🔲 ⬜ **6a+**
25m. Exciting, clean and open climbing up the lovely grey groove which gets harder towards the top. High in the grade.
FA. Pete Oxley, C.Collins 9.5.98

❸ The Devil's Work .... 🔲 ⬜ **6b+**
25m. The recessed flake-line in the corner has now had a bit of traffic and is much cleaner than when it was first put up.
FA. Neil Burton 6.10.96

❹ Marshalling Amps ...... 🔲 ⬜ **7b**
23m. An impressive pitch up the finger-crack and wall. Split at half-height by a resting ledge but still high in the grade.
FA. Gary Gibson 15.9.2002

❺ Broadway .... 🔲🔲 ⬜ **E3 5c**
25m. The big crack gives an unpopular trad route. Three threads mark the line.
FA. Martin Crocker 10.11.91

❻ Manhattan Skyline ... 🔲Ⓑ ⬜ **6c**
25m. The fine undercut arete. Start up the wall and thin crack right of the arete then move onto the arete.
FA. Martin Crocker 10.11.91

❼ Skyscraper. .... 🔲🔲 ⬜ **7a**
25m. A sustained route breaking out right from *Manhattan Skyline* and following the crisp grey wall.
FA. Gary Gibson 28.8.2002

❽ H'electric Boogaloo .. 🔲🔲 ⬜ **6b**
24m. Start in a cave and climb out along the left wall. Pull around into a crack and follow this into a scoop. The groove above leads to the lower-off.
FA. Neal Heanes, Gavin Symonds 4.5.2000

❾ The Bronx .... 🔲 ⬜ **6c+**
26m. Climb up leftwards to a good ledge. The arete above gives the main interest of the route.
FA. Gary Gibson 7.5.2002

❿ American Beauty .... 🔲 ⬜ **6c**
25m. The big full-height arete is a fantastic line. Climb it mainly on its right-hand side. Great moves and still a touch friable.
FA. Gavin Symonds 7.5.2000

⓫ California Dreams ... 🔲🔲 ⬜ **6b+**
23m. Another full-height arete with a low and reachy crux.
FA. Alan Betts, Andy Long 25.5.2000

Tidal platform

XAVIER'S WALL AREA

A fine wall with a handful of the best easier routes on the Isle, plus a few steep lines through overhangs.
TIDES - The platform below is covered for a few hours at high tide which cuts off access to all the routes beyond this point.
APPROACH - Continue under the main Coastguard South cliffs along the wave-washed platform

❶ September Mourning . . 🔲🔲 [ ] **7b**
25m. A hard fingery start over the overlap leads to open climbing above, finishing up a thin crack in the head-wall.
FA. Gary Gibson 15.9.2002

❷ Wharfedale Boyz . . 🔲🔲🔲 [ ] **7c**
25m. The huge leaning wall and roof above the tidal shelf is very sustained and needs good conditions. Not possible at high tide.
FA. Pete Oxley 30.4.95

❸ Screaming Skulls. . . . . 🔲🔲 [ ] **7c**
25m. A long and sustained affair with a succession of bouldery moves between jugs in evermore spaced-out situations. Start up the rib just left of *Tennessee* and head for the steep hanging groove. Share the belay with *Wharfedale Boyz*.
FA. Pete Oxley 10.12.99

❹ Tennessee . . . . 🔲🔲 [ ] **7c**
25m. A brilliant route direct up the bulging face, starting from the tidal trench. It is an unrelenting arm-destroyer which is steeper than most hard routes on Portland. Low in the grade.
FA. Andy Long 7.98

❺ Darkest Before Dawn . . 🔲🔲 [ ] **7b**
24m. A desperate bouldery start stops most attempts. Above is an unusual long layback.
FA. Pete Oxley 23.5.97

❻ Actions Speak Louder 🔲🔲🔲 [ ] **7a+**
24m. Hard and fingery moves over the roof are followed by great climbing up the wall and rib. Three crucial pockets high up can be wet.
FA. Pete Oxley 21.9.94

❼ L'Odyssee Noire . . . . 🔲 [ ] **6c**
24m. Climb the technical wall left of *Xavier's Wall* to an overlap. Pull over and climb the shallow groove above to good holds. Move right to the lower-off.
FA. Gary Gibson, Jean Marc Anagnostidis 7.5.2002

❽ Xavier's Wall . . . . 🔲🔲 [ ] **6a**
24m. Superb climbing up a crack leading to a groove left of an arete. There is a tricky move near the top.
FA. Pete Oxley 21.9.94. Named after a young American boy whose father started ROCKFAX many years ago.

The next two routes share a lower-off which can cause problems when the wall is busy. Avoid top-roping them if possible.

❾ Coming of Age . . . . . . 🔲🔲 [ ] **6a**
24m. The black wall gives a good pitch with an awkward start.
FA. Jan Rostron, Pete Oxley, Mark Higgs (all led) 8.9.96

❿ Underage . . . . 🔲🔲 [ ] **6a**
24m. The direct line up the black wall has fine climbing throughout and a blind crux move.
FA. Jan Rostron 5.97

⓫ Xavier Zoo . . . . . . 🔲🔲🔲 [ ] **6a**
24m. A pleasant route taking a direct line up the wall to finish up a shallow groove. *Photo opposite.*
FA. Gary Gibson 8.5.2003

⓬ Young at Heart . . . . 🔲🔲 [ ] **6a+**
24m. The right-hand line wanders around a bit. This route has a prototype lower-off, called the Vulcan, which does not require untying, though the idea never really caught on.
FA. Pete Oxley 6.97

Gavin Symonds enjoying *Xavier Zoo* (6a), one of the superb mid-grade routes on the Xavier's Wall area of Coastguard South - *opposite*. Photo: Mark Glaister

BAD MOON RISING AREA

Lots of long, sustained wall climbs and some mean roofs are the main ingredients of this section of crag.

TIDES - The platform below is covered for a few hours at high tide which cuts off access to all the routes beyond this point.

APPROACH - Continue along the wave-washed platform.

❶ What Gives, My Son? . 🔲🅱🔲 **6b+**
23m. A disjointed crack-line.
FA. Pete Oxley 13.4.91

❷ Wavewatch . . . . 🔲🔲 **7b**
23m. Climb the straightforward wall to a final steepening. A hard sequence gains the lower-off.
FA. Gary Gibson 9.5.2002

❸ Full Fathom Five . . 🔲🔲🔲 **7b**
24m. A classic at the grade with a tough finish.
FA. Pete Oxley 13.4.91

❹ Bad Moon Rising . . . . 🔲🔲 **7a+**
25m. An impressive pitch up the blunt arete which gets harder as you get higher. Can be dusty and the first bolt is high.
FA. Pete Oxley 12.4.91

❺ A Ship Load of Moonies . . 🔲 **6c+**
24m. A fine pitch moving right from the start of *Bad Moon Rising* and finding a surprisingly easy way up this steep wall.
FA. Gary Gibson 15.9.2002

❻ Dead by Sunset . . . 🔲🔲🔲 **7b**
24m. Very sustained climbing which overhangs all the way. There is a difficult step left onto a shelf near the bottom.
FA. Pete Oxley 28.9.96

❼ Witchdoctor . . . . . 🔲🔲🔲 **7b**
24m. A route of two sections, pumpy low down and a technical headwall. At present it is a bold lead (**E6 6b**) since it needs two more bolts.
FA. Dave Pickford 3.5.98. His first bolted new route.

❽ Vampire Killers . . . . . . 🔲🔲 **7b**
23m. Another pumper with a delicate yet powerful scoop high up. Great climbing but it can be dirty.
FA. Pete Oxley 23.5.97

❾ The Lost Buoys 🔲🔲🔲🔲 **7c+**
24m. A 7a first half leads to desperate crimping up the leaning rib to reach an easier crack to finish. Needs cool conditions and sunshine. Easily spotted by the buoy on the belay.
FA. Pete Oxley 14.9.97

❿ No Survivors . . . . 🔲🔲 **7b+**
23m. Worthwhile climbing which is spoilt by a rest at half-height. Can get dusty at the top. Start above the huge steel plates from the hull of a shipwreck.
FA. Pete Oxley 15.9.96

⓫ A Meeting of Minds . . . 🔲🔲 **7a+**
23m. A massive roof test-piece at the bottom makes this one an unusual outing. A big half-height rest is the reward!
FA. Pete Oxley 15.9.96

⓬ Lip Service . . . . 🔲🔲 **7a**
25m. Great rock and a wild swing left on the lip of the roof provide the fun.
FA. Pete Oxley, Mark Higgs 15.9.96

⓭ Bermuda Triangle . . . . 🔲🔲 **6c**
24m. Start as for the last route but climb straight over the bulge and up the lovely grey slab.
FA. Pete Oxley, M.Higgs (both led) 8.9.96

⓮ A Bird in the Hand . . . . . . 🔲 **7a+**
24m. A crimpy lower wall leads to an easy upper slab. A bit unbalanced but great rock.
FA. Pete Oxley 14.9.96. Named after a dead bird found in a pocket.

⓯ Hasta La Vista . . . 🔲🔲🔲 **6b+**
25m. A fine start leads to a good finish but unfortunately it is spoilt by the big ledge in between. There is one awkward clip.
FA. Gary Gibson 4.5.2003

Portland West
Portland East
Lulworth
Swanage
Devon
Blacknor N
Blacknor C
Blacknor S
Blacknor FS
Battleship M
Battleship B
Wallsend N
Wallsend S
Coastguard N
Coastguard S
White Hole

Steep flowstone and sustained climbing are the main ingredients of the classic *Walking the King* (6b+) on the Quick as Rainbows Area at Coastguard South - *page 118*. Photo: GlaisterPhoto

Old pipe

Tidal trench access for only 2 to 4 hours at low tide

Platform covered at high tide

1 2 3 4 5 6 7 8 9 10 11 12 13 14 15 16

QUICK AS RAINBOWS AREA

A magnificent wall of immaculate flowstone. It sometimes suffers from seepage, can be dusty and has limited time access, but the routes are well worth the trouble.
APPROACH and TIDES - Continue under the main areas past the tidal trench which is uncovered for 2 to 4 hours at low tide. Wading in could gain you an extra hour. In calm seas it is possible to traverse the back wall to get in early, or out late but take great care!

❶ Small Talk Costs Walls ... 6c+
23m. The roof, juggy wall and flowstone tufa left of *Smashing Orange*. Start in a small alcove above the tidal trench. Best done at dead low tide otherwise the rope will get wet when pulled.
FA. Pete Oxley 27.5.98

❷ Smashing Orange.... 7a
23m. Classy crack climbing after a hard bulge above the trench.
FA. Pete Oxley 11.5.91

❸ Drive Blind .... 7a+
23m. A tough lower wall and a fine easier upper groove.
FA. Pete Oxley 11.5.91

❹ Forensic Scene ...... 7a+
24m. A fine flowstone arete. A useful rest before the top move is the well-deserved reward after the steep start. *Photo page 1.*
FA. Pete Oxley 14.5.95

❺ Quick as Rainbows.... 7a+
23m. A beautiful frozen wave of flowstone. Brilliant as long as the top is clean.
FA. Pete Oxley 17.7.91

❻ Red Medicine .... 7b+
24m. Sustained climbing on immaculate flowstone.
FA. Pete Oxley 14.5.95

❼ Aeon Flux 7b
24m. A hard lower half.
FA. Pete Oxley 17.7.91

❽ Under the Sky, Inside the Sea
. . . . 7a
25m. Unobvious moves on the sharp arete lead to a finishing corner. There is a new line finishing out right at around **7a+**.
FA. Pete Oxley 17.7.91. FA. (Right-hand finish) Andy Long 13.6.2005

❾ Forget Columbus 7a
25m. Magnificent tufa curtains and a huge flake.
FA. Pete Oxley 6.6.93

❿ Buried Violence...... 7b+
24m. Very hard moves on the lower wall lead to an amusing finish on organ pipes.
FA. Pete Oxley 2.11.93

⓫ Walking the King .... 6b+
25m. A classic pumpy wall of steep cracks and flowstone with the crux at the top. The best 6b+ on Portland. *Photo page 117.*
FA. Pete Oxley 20.4.93

⓬ An Ideal for Living . 7a+
24m. More quality rock. Pumpy and technical all the way.
FA. Pete Oxley 21.8.95

⓭ Time Bomb 7a
24m. The central line on the coral wall finishes up a slab.
FA. Pete Oxley 21.8.95

⓮ Winning at Rodeo. 7a
24m. An enticing line with an intriguing corner high up.
FA. Mark Higgs 21.8.95

⓯ Chevette de la Mer 6b
24m. More great rock in the groove.
FA. Andy Bell 9.5.98

⓰ Swimsuit Issue...... 6c+
24m. The arete is followed direct with some blind palming 'a cheval' to pass the mid-height bulge.
FA. Pete Oxley 9.5.98

COASTGUARD SOUTH *Azymuth Area*

Portland West | Portland East | Lulworth | Swanage | Devon | Blacknor N | Blacknor C | Blacknor S | Blacknor FS | Blacknor M | Battleship B | Battleship N | Wallsend N | Wallsend S | Coastguard N | Coastguard S | White Hole

AZYMUTH AREA

The final batch of routes on Coastguard South are on a superb steep buttress which ends at a sanctuary zone.
APPROACH and TIDES - Approach as for the Quick as Rainbows area and continue along the platform. This area is only accessible for 2 to 3 hours at low tide.

❶ Xistenz . . . . 7a+
24m. A worthwhile climb direct up the wall and arete.
FA. Gavin Symonds 2002

❷ Space Shanty 6b
24m. Fine and varied climbing tackling the shallow groove on the left of the buttress.
FA. Chris Parker, Pete Oxley 23.5.97

❸ Astra Blaze 6c
20m. A well-positioned climb direct up the arete.
FA. Pete Oxley 23.5.97

❹ Come In and Burn . 7b
24m. Pull away and roast up a stunning highway of increasing difficulties. Apply brakes at the belay.
FA. Pete Oxley 5.7.97

❺ Azymuth . . . . . 7a+
24m. A pumpy arete with a committing last move for added excitement.
FA. Pete Oxley 23.5.97

❻ L'Esprit du Vent . . . 7a+
24m. Entertaining climbing. It follows a big arching line up the side wall with a definite crux move.
FA. Pete Oxley 28.5.97

8m right again, past a shallow cave, is a pillar of excellent white rock above a flat platform.

⊖ RESTRICTION (Routes 7 and 8) - *No climbing 1 March to 31 July because of nesting birds.*

❼ Down to the Wire . . 7b+
24m. A fine pitch directly up the arete above an easy starting groove. There is a long reach from an undercut at mid height which is probably only 7b for the tall.
FA. Pete Oxley 12.2.2000. Completed the same day that the 2000 Rockfax guide was sent to the printers- it made it in!

❽ Dawn of a New Age
. . . . 7b+
24m. Starting 2m right of a flake line, hard, blind climbing on perfect rock takes the direct line up the front face of the white pillar. Very fingery and powerful on the crux.
FA. Pete Oxley 26.1.2000

⊖ RESTRICTION - *Directly below the large fence, where the boulders run out, is the beginning of a no-climbing sanctuary zone which continues for 300m to White Hole.*

There is a 30m gap from Dawn of a New Age to the sanctuary zone. Currently there is one project and there are likely to be more new additions soon.

WHITE HOLE

Memories Zawn | Faceache Area | Mirthmaid Zawn

White Hole is unique to the west coast of Portland being an area of well-defined and deeply-incised zawns. The walls of the zawns are relatively short compared to the neighbouring Coastguard Cliffs but have a set of good little routes with an atmosphere that is out of all proportion to their size. The rock is solid but also extremely rough and it can be a bit tough on the fingers. The best lines are in general committing routes and solos requiring blind approach abseils into the narrow zawns. Overall, White Hole is a small but worthwhile area with a lot of variety and a reasonable grade spread.

APPROACH

Drive to Portland Bill and park by the lighthouse (Pay and Display). From the lighthouse parking, walk west (right - looking out) next to a fence and above an old quarry, for 200m. Turn right at the cliff-top and follow the fence. The South Cliff is just below the top after 20m. Mirthmaid Zawn is the large square-cut prow further into the bay. It is reached by following the fence closely past a creek, before dropping down onto a large rock platform (see map on next page). To reach Memories Zawn and the Faceache Area, continue from the large rock platform by scrambling up to the top of the Mirthmaid promontory. Move along a narrow cliff-top ledge that runs right (looking out) around a square cut zawn to a narrow rift beneath the weird conglomerate rock bridge. More details are given with the route pages for the approaches from the cliff-top.

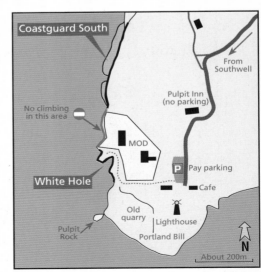

Coastguard South

From Southwell

Pulpit Inn (no parking)

No climbing in this area

MOD

White Hole

P Pay parking

Cafe

Old quarry

Pulpit Rock

Lighthouse

Portland Bill

N

About 200m

CONDITIONS

The routes can be damp so only visit in dry and sunny conditions. A calm sea is vital for abseiling into most of the lines. The routes are all non-tidal but high tide may be preferred for some of the deep-water solos. Take note that high waves and strong currents can be generated by the tidal race. Keep well away if the sea is even remotely rough.

The late Damian Cook on the first solo ascent of *Mirthmaid* (7a+) at White Hole - *page 124*. Photo: Joff Cook

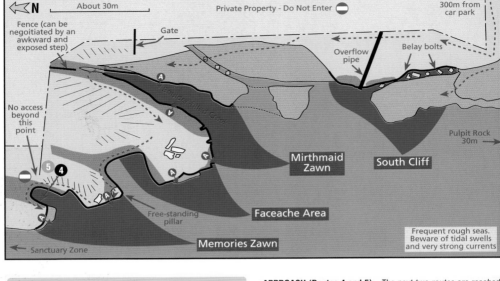

MEMORIES ZAWN AREA

The northern-most section of the *White Hole Area* is very atmospheric, consisting of a complex series of zawns and aretes rising from a cauldron of sea-washed boulders.
TIDES - All the routes are approached by abseil onto various ledges which are mostly non-tidal. Do not come here when the sea is rough and always bear in mind the abseil in will commit you so take prussiks down just in case.
APPROACH - Gain the lower ledges directly opposite Mirthmaid Wall. From the back of the zawn, scramble up to the ledges on the top of the Mirthmaid Wall. Walk above the Mirthmaid and Labyrinth Areas until you can step across Memories Zawn.
NOTE - The deep water solos here should only be attempted at high tide.

NO CLIMBING TO THE NORTH OF ROUTE 1 - This has been designated a bird sanctuary zone.

APPROACH (Routes 1 to 3) - *Move out to the end of the zawn and the large platform via a fixed line. Abseil from the fixed belay here to fixed belays on the ledge.*

❶ Second Attention . . . . ☐ 6c+
10m. A short groove above the big ledge in the seaward face.
FA. James Dunlop 7.8.98

❷ Crossing the Boundaries of Affection
. . . . ☐ 7a+
10m. This little gem weaves around the arete of the through zawn and is well worth the approach. **(S2)**
FA. James Dunlop 28.2.98

❸ Kinaesthesia . . . . ☐ 7a+
10m. The best route in the zawn. Swing right on a hand ledge and climb the blank wall above, requiring delicate footwork and powerful moves. Very atmospheric. *Photo page 127.*
FA. Jim Kimber 7.8.98

APPROACH (Routes 4 and 5) - *The next two routes are reached by abseil from the belay bolts at the start of the fixed line direct to a semi-hanging belay with a bolt.*

❹ Intricacies of Dreaming ☐ 7b
12m. A striking line blasting up the stunning crack-line in the centre of the wall. A hard start may foil many onsights.
FA. James Dunlop 24.8.98

❺ Memories . . . . ☐ 6a+
15m. An attractive diagonal crack in the left wall of the narrow section of the zawn. It is possible to bridge at times. A deep water solo at high tide only. **(S3)**
FA. Jim Kimber 28.2.98

APPROACH (Routes 6 to 10) - *The next routes start by abseiling from a single bolt to a small ledge and a semi-hanging belay below the left (looking out) arete of the zawn. There is a large perched boulder above the arete. The solos need high water.*

❻ Hung, Swung and Zawned Out
. . . . ☐ E2 5b
20m. An excellent introduction to deep water soloing. Move up left from the belay and follow a strenuous horizontal break leftwards, into the zawn, for 10m. Overcome a bulge then ascend the diagonal open groove. High tide only. **(S1)**
FSA. Pete Oxley 10.1.99

❼ Paraphilias . . . . . . ☐ E5 6a
14m. Start as for *Hung, Swung...*, then climb directly up to the arete. Follow this on its left-hand side. Tricky with a high crux. High tide only. **(S2)**
FSA. Chris Weedon 2.2.2000

❽ Aphasia. . . . . ☐ E3 5b
14m. From the ledge, solo leftwards and up to a ledge beneath a right-facing groove. Follow this to the top. A serious solo which should only be considered at high tide. **(S3)**
FSA. Chris Weedon 8.99

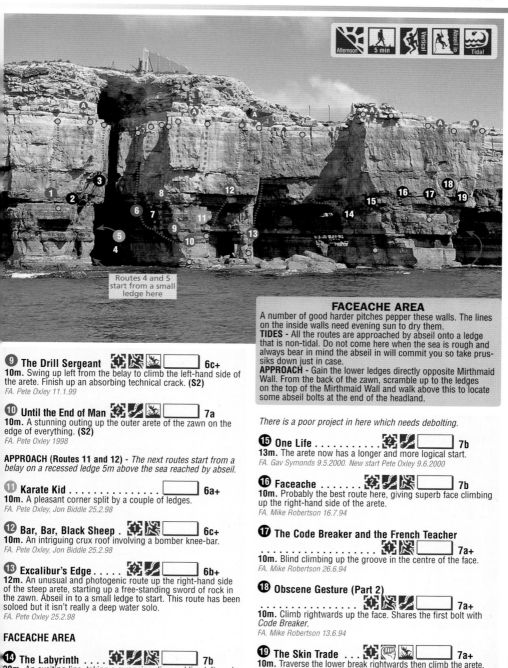

Routes 4 and 5 start from a small ledge here

FACEACHE AREA

A number of good harder pitches pepper these walls. The lines on the inside walls need evening sun to dry them.

TIDES - All the routes are approached by abseil onto a ledge that is non-tidal. Do not come here when the sea is rough and always bear in mind the abseil in will commit you so take prussiks down just in case.

APPROACH - Gain the lower ledges directly opposite Mirthmaid Wall. From the back of the zawn, scramble up to the ledges on the top of the Mirthmaid Wall and walk above this to locate some abseil bolts at the end of the headland.

⑨ The Drill Sergeant 6c+
10m. Swing up left from the belay to climb the left-hand side of the arete. Finish up an absorbing technical crack. **(S2)**
FA. Pete Oxley 11.1.99

⑩ Until the End of Man 7a
10m. A stunning outing up the outer arete of the zawn on the edge of everything. **(S2)**
FA. Pete Oxley 1998

APPROACH (Routes 11 and 12) - *The next routes start from a belay on a recessed ledge 5m above the sea reached by abseil.*

⑪ Karate Kid 6a+
10m. A pleasant corner split by a couple of ledges.
FA. Pete Oxley, Jon Biddle 25.2.98

⑫ Bar, Bar, Black Sheep 6c+
10m. An intriguing crux roof involving a bomber knee-bar.
FA. Pete Oxley, Jon Biddle 25.2.98

⑬ Excalibur's Edge 6b+
12m. An unusual and photogenic route up the right-hand side of the steep arete, starting up a free-standing sword of rock in the zawn. Abseil in to a small ledge to start. This route has been soloed but it isn't really a deep water solo.
FA. Pete Oxley 25.2.98

FACEACHE AREA

⑭ The Labyrinth 7b
20m. An exciting line, taking a sweeping diagonal line leftwards from the belay ledge on *One Life*. Swing left along a handrail to gain a hanging ledge above a roof. Move up and left to pass a bulge before finishing up a pocket laced slab. Fence belay.
FA. Pete Oxley 8.2000

There is a poor project in here which needs debolting.

⑮ One Life 7b
13m. The arete now has a longer and more logical start.
FA. Gav Symonds 9.5.2000. New start Pete Oxley 9.6.2000

⑯ Faceache 7b
10m. Probably the best route here, giving superb face climbing up the right-hand side of the arete.
FA. Mike Robertson 16.7.94

⑰ The Code Breaker and the French Teacher 7a+
10m. Blind climbing up the groove in the centre of the face.
FA. Mike Robertson 26.6.94

⑱ Obscene Gesture (Part 2) 7a+
10m. Climb rightwards up the face. Shares the first bolt with *Code Breaker*.
FA. Mike Robertson 13.6.94

⑲ The Skin Trade 7a+
10m. Traverse the lower break rightwards then climb the arete. Left of the bolts gives a less good **6c+**. DWS - high tide only. **(S2)**
FA. Mike Robertson 26.6.94. Steve Taylor soloed the easier version.

Portland West · Portland East · Lulworth · Swanage · Devon · Blacknor N · Blacknor C · Blacknor S · Blacknor FS · Blacknor M · Battleship B · Battleship M · Wallsend N · Wallsend S · Coastguard N · Coastguard S · White Hole

123

MIRTHMAID ZAWN AREA

The west wall of Mirthmaid Zawn gives some fine deep water solos above an undercut through cave. The eastern side of the Zawn is home to some lesser and easier routes.

TIDES - The various starting ledges are non-tidal although do not come here when the sea is rough and always bear in mind the abseil in will commit you to the chosen route so take prussiks down just in case. The deep water solos here should only be attempted at high tide.

APPROACH (Routes 1 to 10) - *Access the lower ledges opposite Mirthmaid Wall then from the back of the zawn, scramble up to the ledges on the top of the wall. Abseil in from here.*

The first 6 routes start from a ledge left of the through cave.

❶ Sad Young Biscuits . . . 🏔️ 🪴 [____] **7a+**
10m. Starting from a sentry box under the arete, climb up the right-hand side of the arete. **(S2)**
An alternative start can be made from the *Splendid Isolation* ledge at the same grade.
FA. Mike Robertson 13.6.94

❷ Dead in Europe 🏔️ 🏔️ 🪓 🪴 [____] **7a+**
12m. The blank wall leftwards from the belay. **(S2)**
FA. Mike Robertson 6.8.94.

❸ Splendid Isolation. 🏔️ 🪓 🪴 [____] **6c**
10m. Pull direct over the roof and then climb the crack to a hard finish. **(S2)**
FA. Steve Taylor 26.6.94.

❹ Just for a Day. . . . 🏔️ 🪓 🪴 [____] **E4 6a**
10m. The steep blunt rib. Start up *Splendid Isolation* and move right on the lip of the roof to gain the rib. **(S2)**
FSA. Pete Oxley 15.5.2000

❺ Mirthmaid. . . . . . . 🏔️ 🪴 🪴 [____] **7a+**
12m. Head rightwards over a roof and up an easier crack. **(S2)**
Photo page 121.
FA Damian Cook 6.94.

❻ Nightmirth 🏔️ 🪓 🪴 🪓 🪴 [____] **7c**
15m. A wild roof traverse extension to *Mirthmaid* out above the eerie zawn. **(S2)**
FA. Pete Oxley 7.4.96

The next three lines start from a small foot ledge in the middle of the east face to the right of Nightmirth.

❼ Sister of Night . . . . 🏔️ 🪴 🪴 [____] **E5 6b**
14m. Traverse left from the footledge for 8m until under the blank-looking banana-shaped groove. The groove requires a series of blind and bouldery moves. **(S3)**
FSA. Pete Oxley 24.6.2000

❽ Any Last Requests? . . 🪴 🪴 [____] **E4 5c**
12m. Traverse left from the footledge for 3m to reach the central groove. A hidden pocket near the top helps reduce the difficulties at the finish. **(S3)**
FSA. Pete Oxley 7.2000

❾ Spanish Air . . . . 🪴 [____] **E3 5b**
10m. Fairly straightforward climbing up the shallow groove directly above the footledge. Short but serious.
FSA. Pete Oxley 24.6.2000

❿ Tiny Smiles. . . . . 🏔️ 🪴 [____] **7a+**
10m. Start from ledges in the back left-hand corner of the zawn.
FA. Pete Oxley 24.6.2000

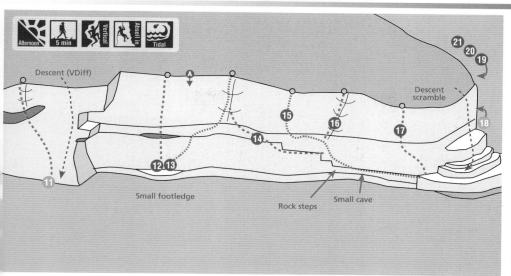

Descent (VDiff)

Descent scramble

Small footledge

Rock steps

Small cave

APPROACH (Routes 11 to 21) - *Gain the lower ledges directly opposite Mirthmaid Wall. The routes are located on the wall directly below reached by abseil or descent scramble (see topo).*

⑪ Totally Stoked . . . . **HVS 5a**
5m. Descend (VDiff) then swing out left and climb a short hanging groove.
FA. Pete Oxley 24.6.2000

⑫ Un-named **E3 5c**
5m. A direct line up the technical face above the ledge. **(S3)**
FSA. Chris Weedon 24.6.2000

⑬ Un-named **E2 5b**
5m. Move rightwards from the ledge to ascend a shallow groove. **(S2)**
FSA. Chris Weedon 15.6.2000

⑭ Get Some Air, Fatso! . . **E1 5b**
15m. A convenient traverse start to the previous route. **(S2)**
FSA. Ben Stokes, Mark Williams 17.8.2003

⑮ Un-named **E3 6a**
10m. Nice moves. Start up the wall then hang left along the lip for 4m, before making tough cranks to the top. **(S1)**
FSA. Pete Oxley 15.6.2000

⑯ Un-named **E3 5c**
10m. Start at the left side of small cave. Pull the roof using undercuts and then finish up the shallow groove just right. **(S1)**
FSA. Chris Weedon 15.6.2000

⑰ True to the Game **E3 6a**
5m. A smart little route. Pull the roof on its right-hand side. Move out left before making fingery moves up the wall above the roof apex. **(S1)**
FSA. Pete Oxley 15.6.2000

The next climb is more of a caving expedition, delving into the tiny zawn, right of True to the Game - Portland's answer to Preposterous Tales in Pembroke.

⑱ Dragon's Lair . . . . **VS 4a**
25m. Crawl into the dark sea-level chamber. Follow the water-worn tube for 20m until daylight can be seen above. Chimney out the blowhole. Low tide and calm sea essential.
FDescent! Pete Oxley 7.2000

The next cluster of three short lines are located just south of the main zawn above a deep Jacuzzi Pool. Do not fall off these routes.

⑲ Un-named **E2 5c**
5m. Traverse in as for *Dragon's Lair* and climb up the left side of the bay with tricky moves going for the top.
FSA. Chris Weedon 24.6.2000

⑳ Un-named **E2 5c**
5m. Traverse in as for *Dragon's Lair* and climb the central line up the steepening wall to a slight groove.
FSA. Chris Weedon 24.6.2000

㉑ Un-named **E2 5c**
5m. Traverse in from the right above the pool then take a line up the steep rib on the right side of the small bay.
FSA. Chris Weedon 24.6.2000

Portland West | Portland East | Lulworth | Swanage | Devon | Blacknor N | Blacknor C | Blacknor S | Blacknor FS | Battleship M | Battleship B | Wallsend N | Wallsend S | Coastguard N | Coastguard S | White Hole

SOUTH CLIFF

This is the short wall underneath the approach path starting from a ledge. Most of the routes don't have lower-offs but there are belays above including some staples.
TIDES - The ledge below the wall is non-tidal but keep away in rough seas.
APPROACH - Scramble down easy ledges on either side of the cliff. The first four routes need to be approached from the left-hand side (looking in) and start from a belay in the cave.

❶ Balance of Power. ⬛⬛⬛ [___] 8a
10m. The pillar above the cave offers a fine technical challenge.
FA. Pete Oxley 21.11.99

❷ The Pipers of Portland. ⬛⬛ [___] 6c
10m. Pull out of the cave and climb the groove to the left of the large pipe.
FA. Pete Oxley 16.9.94

❸ Funnel Web . . . . ⬛ [___] 6a+
10m. Shares the first two bolts with *End of Season Sale*, then climb the groove just right of the pipe.
FA. Pete Oxley 16.9.94

❹ End of Season Sale . . . . [___] 6b
10m. Traverse right from the cave into a hidden groove.
FA. Pete Oxley 16.9.94

The rest of the routes are approached by scrambling down the right-hand side (looking in) of the cliff.

❺ The Reign of Steel . . . . [___] 6b+
10m. Clip the first bolt on *Red Raw* then break left and climb a groove.
FA. Pete Oxley 16.9.94

❻ Red Raw . . . . ⬛ [___] 7a+
8m. Move leftwards to the blank rib.
FA. Pete Oxley 5.9.94

❼ Tickled Pink . . ⬛⬛⬛⬛ [___] 7c
8m. The short groove capped by a twin roof is desperate.
FA. Pete Oxley 5.9.94

❽ Wafer Thin . . . . [___] 6b
8m. From a higher ledge, climb a flake to a tricky finish.
FA. Pete Oxley 5.9.94

❾ Run, Rabbit, Run . . . . [___] 6b+
8m. Climb direct up the steep slab.
FA. Pete Oxley 5.9.94

❿ Staple Diet . . . . [___] 6b
8m. The blank slab is not as tricky as it looks.
FA. Steve Taylor 1.10.94

⓫ Painted Lady . . . . [___] 6a+
8m. Good climbing between jugs on the faint rib.
FA. Mick Ward 9.8.2003

⓬ The Feather . . . . [___] 6c
8m. Another thin slabby wall..
FA. Steve Taylor 1.10.94

⓭ The Cruel Sea . . . . [___] 6a
8m. The shallow corner is surprisingly awkward.
FA. Steve Taylor 1990s. Bolted and claimed by mistake by Mick Ward 2003.

⓮ Adonis Blue . . . . [___] 6b+
8m. The centre of the wall with a 'grit-like' crux.
FA. Mick Ward 15.8.2003

⓯ Chalk-hill Blue . . . . . . ⬛⬛ [___] 6a+
8m. Deceptively innocuous - make a long reach or improvise.
FA. Mick Ward 15.8.2003

Jimbo Kimber climbing, Dave Pickford belaying, on *Kinaesthesia* (7a+) above a turbulent sea at White Hole - *page 122.* Photo: James Dunlop

East Coast

Ken Palmer pulling the lip on the classic Portland deep water solo *Crab Party* (E4 6a) at Cave Hole on the East Coast - *page 137*. Photo: Mark Glaister

LIGHTHOUSE AREA

On the east coast of the southern tip of the Isle are four small areas nestling under the lighthouse. Barrel and Hidden Zawns are pleasant little bouldering areas above pebble and shingle beaches. They offer some intense and powerful problems on slopers and tiny crimps or pockets. The beach level can vary in height and the problems are at their best when the beach is low.

Sector Pom Pom offers a similar style of extended boulder problems and short power-packed routes situated in another delightful little bay with a frozen wave of grit-like stone pitted with infrequent pockets. Sadly neither place holds anything for beginners but both are great for a spot of sunbathing or a picnic and are only 200m from the car park.

ACCESS

There have been a few minor problems with an over-zealous local sheriff at Sector Pom Pom. The best advice is to adopt a voluntary ban from March 31st to October 1st when he is around and the conditions are too greasy anyway.

APPROACH

The various small bays are all best approached from the Portland Bill car park (Pay and Display).

Pulpit Rock
Park at the main Portland Bill car park. From the lighthouse, walk rightwards a little way (looking out to sea) until Pulpit Rock comes into view.

Barrel Zawn and Hidden Zawn
Park at the main Portland Bill car park, walk towards the headland and turn left just past the cafe. The zawns are to be found 100m left (looking out to sea) along the coast path, just before a large quarried rock platform.

Deep Zawn and Sector Pom Pom
Park and approach as for Barrel and Hidden Zawns. Deep Zawn is just beyond and directly below a cliff-top crane. Sector Pom Pom is 70m further along the coast path.

CONDITIONS

This is a good venue to get some early-season action on crisp winter mornings when the friction is good and Sector Pom Pom and Hidden Zawn offer great sun-traps with little seepage. Barrel Zawn faces east and

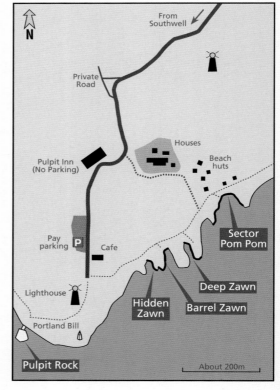

requires warmer conditions but remember to keep away in summer (see access above). Both Sector Pom Pom and Barrel Zawn require a very low tide.

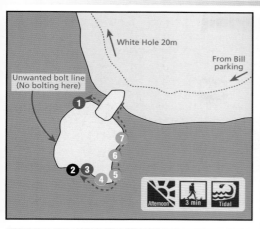

Scramble descent

PULPIT ROCK
The much-photographed Pulpit Rock now has several lines on it plus one illegal bolt route that is to be debolted.
TIDES - High tide is essential for both of the routes.
APPROACH - Park at the main Portland Bill car park. From the lighthouse, walk right a little way until Pulpit Rock comes into view. Bridge across the zawn underneath the fallen block and traverse steeply either left or right to the routes.
BEWARE OF STRONG CURRENTS THAT PASS PULPIT ROCK.

1 Tombstonin'.....   **E3 6a**
10m. A fine route which tackles the striking undercut arete right of the fallen block. A steep start leads around onto the sharp arete with difficulty. Ascend a thin crack on the left side with mounting technicalities to finish up a small groove in the capping bands. Good rock throughout. **(S1)**
FA. Pete Oxley 25.6.2000

2 End of the Land.......   **E4 5c**
10m. The south-west arete of Pulpit Rock forms a jutting prow. This climb is very serious as there is a rock shelf underneath the crux and it has a remote feel about it. Traverse around to a high ledge right of the arete then step left over the void and commit to a blind sequence up the arete that quickly eases towards the top. Good rock.
FA. Pete Oxley 25.6.2000

3 The Good of Sleep **E1 5a**
10m. Ascend a vague rib via flakes and nodules. Great rock. **(S1)**
FSA. Mick Ward 13.5.2004

4 Chymerie.............   **HVS 4c**
10m. Climb the shallow hanging groove just left of the southern arete. **(S1)**
FSA. Mick Ward 12.5.2004

5 Edge of Beyond .....   **HVS 5c**
10m. The faint grooveline just right of the southern arete. **(S1)**
FSA. Mick Ward 16.5.2004

6 Rapture of the Deep ..   **HVS 5b**
10m. The middle of the east face. Climb past an overlap, up a slab and into a short groove. A well-positioned crux. **(S1)**
FSA. Mick Ward 17.5.2004

7 Swirling Pool ....   **HVS 5a**
10m. The crack in the right-hand side of the east face.
FSA. Mick Ward 19.5.2004

HIDDEN ZAWN
This attractive little zawn has a small number of good but high-ball boulder problems. A mat is essential. The base of the cove is tidal but the wall gets lots of sun. The are many other problems on the surrounding low walls.
TIDES - Lowish tide is essential.
APPROACH - Park at the main Portland Bill car park. From the lighthouse, walk behind the cafe. The zawn is to be found 100m left (looking out) up the coast path just before a large quarried rock platform.

8 Problem 3 ....   **V4**
5m. A technical wall with a hard move high up. Move left of the small overlap.

9 Problem 4 ......   **V3**
5m. Climb past a small niche and then take a line just right of the small overlap.

10 Problem 5 ......   **V4**
5m. A tight line up the wall left of the thin face crack via a difficult rockover move. Start at a good hand ledge.

11 Problem 6 ......   **V3**
5m. The crack is awkward to start and may need a jump to gain the first break if the beach is low.

12 Problem 7 ....   **V1**
5m. The groove on the left side of the overhangs.

13 Problem 8 ......   **V1**
5m. A fine problem linking the start of the previous route with the finish of the next climb via a wild traverse.

14 Problem 9 ......   **V1**
5m. The height of the jump start is dependant on the beach level.

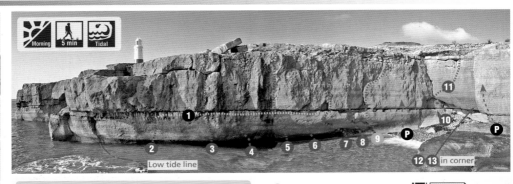

Low tide line

BARREL ZAWN

This is a neat clean-cut wave of rock in an isolated and rec-
cessed zawn. Good conditions and a bouldering mat are essential. Some problems are more like small routes.
TIDES - Only come here at low tides.
APPROACH - Park at the main Portland Bill car park. From
the lighthouse, walk behind the cafe. The zawn is 100m left
(looking out) up the coast path just before a large quarried
rock platform, and just after Hidden Zawn.

❶ Problem 1....... ▮▮▮ **V8**
10m. A pumpy and bold traverse. **(E4 6c)**

❷ Eranu............. ▮▮▮ **V6**
5m. A jump start to the hanging nose above. **(E3 6b)**

❸ Uvarvu.......... ▮▮▮▮ **V5**
5m. From a jump start, gain the hanging groove. **(E2 6b)**

❹ Problem 4 .... ▮▮ **V3**
5m. A long groove on finger flakes. **(HVS 6a)**

❺ Problem 5 .... ▮▮ **V4**
5m. The sustained groove.

❻ Problem 6 .... ▮ **V4**
4m. The seam and finger flake.

❼ Problem 7 .... ▮▮ **V6**
4m. Make a hard sitting-start on pockets then tackle the undercut groove.

❽ Problem 8 .... ▮ **V3**
4m. A sitting-start to the slab.

❾ Rampline................. **V0+**
4m. The left-to-right line.

❿ Corner Layback............. **V0**
4m. The flake-line.

⓫ Problem 11 .... **V3**
10m. From the flake, move right to gain the hanging corner.

⓬ Cornflake................ **V0-**
4m. The corner.

⓭ Problem 13 .... ▮ **V5**
44m. The centre of the bulging wall, gained from the corner.

DEEP ZAWN

⓮ White Pony.......... ▮▮ **V2**
4m. Step off the ledge and climb the crack. **(S0)**
FA. Pete Oxley 24.6.2000

DEEP ZAWN

The best swiming and diving spot on the east coast of Portland
is the narrow inlet under the red jib crane. These short walls,
that drop straight into the water, now have a few micro deep
water solos.
TIDES - Only come here at very high tide.
APPROACH - Park and approach as for Barrel and Hidden
Zawns. Deep Zawn is just beyond and directly below a cliff-top
crane. Sector Pom Pom is 70m further along the coast path.

Scramble descent

Descent by rusty chain

⑮ The World's Best Mono 🔲🔲 V5
9m. Worth doing for its cool crux! Step off the ledge at the end of the headland and traverse right under the large prow. Move 3m left along the break before tackling the blank bulging wall via a lone deep mono. **(S0)**
FA. Pete Oxley 24.6.2000

⑯ Sugar Daddy 🔲🔲🔲 V3
10m. Descend down the face by the rusty chain and traverse left around a prow via a vague foot break. At a slight layback climb the technical wall using pinches and layaways. **(S0)**
FA. Ben Stokes 25.6.2000

⑰ All Things Being Relative 🔲🔲 V1
8m. An easier version of *Sugar Daddy*. As for *Sugar Daddy* around the prow, then launch up the face on spaced holds. **(S0)**
FA. Matt Stammers 25.6.2000

⑱ The Red Crane Traverse 🔲🔲 5
12m. Start from the ledge at the bottom of the chain. Traverse right along the break, right around the headland to a ledge just above sea level. Many variations have been climbed on the wall above the traverse (4c to 6b). **(S0)**
FA. Ben Stokes, Matt Stammers 25.06.2000

SECTOR POM POM
The first two lines are situated in a walled corner, just past an undercut buttress, on the right (looking out) side of the bay.

⑲ El Scorchio . . . . 🔲🔲 6c
8m. Start just right of a big cave and climb the short bulging wall slightly leftwards. There are two ways of climbing the crux.
FA. Rob Godfray 23.1.2000

⑳ Maximum Grrr... 🔲🔲🔲 7b
8m. Make fierce moves up the blank wall, starting from a slot near the corner and finishing via a short layback.
FA. Pete Oxley 23.1.2000

㉑ L'Eau Profile . . . . 🔲🔲 7c
8m. Make contorted moves directly over the roof on the front of the undercut buttress.
FA. Pete Oxley 4.4.96

㉒ Private Dancer 6b
8m. The technical short groove on the right of the buttress. Top-out or lower-off last bolt.
FA. Pete Oxley 4.4.96

All the remaining climbs are situated on the wave of rock on the left side(looking out) of the bay.

㉓ Thirty Years Young . . . 🔲🔲 E3 6b
7m. A short solo up the right-hand side of the left-hand arete with a desperate start to gain the pocket and a committing move out right to gain a jutting ledge. Bring a bouldering mat.
FA. Pete Oxley 4.4.96

㉔ Burbage Belle . . . . 🔲🔲🔲 7c
7m. Pure bouldering. Jump to the break to start then tackle the Fontainebleau-like bulge.
FA. Pete Oxley 27.3.9

㉕ The Big Blue . . . . . 🔲🔲🔲 7c+
7m. A tremendous test-piece that blasts up the central hanging groove by some very hard moves. Probably 8a for the short. Jump to the break to start.
FA. Luc Percival 26.10.96

㉖ Ninth Wave . . . . 🔲🔲 7a+
7m. A very aesthetic problem taking the hanging crack right of the prow. Jump to the break to start. It has been soloed but it isn't a deep water solo.
FA. Luc Percival 6.95

㉗ Zimmerframe with Attitude . . . 🔲 7c
8m. A desperate V8 boulder problem start leads to the awkward corner. Used to be 6c but a rockfall altered the start,
FA. Luc Percival, Neal Heanes 6.95. Reclimbed by Andy Long 2004.

㉘ The O'lympets . . . . 🔲🔲 6c+
8m. A pleasant climb taking the vague crack in the side-wall after a hard start.
FA. Neal Heanes, Luc Percival 6.95

㉙ Honorary Froggatt . 🔲🔲🔲 7b+
8m. A hard bulging start then teeter up an 'Artless-style' ramp.
FA. Pete Oxley 19.3.96

㉚ Pocketful of Shells . . . . . . 🔲🔲 7b
8m. A strenuous start then technical stuff up the corner.
FA. Pete Oxley 19.3.96

㉛ The Waveband 🔲🔲🔲🔲 V9
14m. The best boulder traverse on the Isle. Start from a hand ledge below *Zimmerframe*... then traverse the break leftwards with hard moves out of *Ninth Wave* (spotters needed). A desperate finish where you eventually body-bridge onto the far ledge. Could be **V10+** if it were finished up *Thirty Years Young*.
FA. Pete Oxley 6.11.99

SECTOR POM POM
A pleasant bay with some short, hard routes that are very bouldery, including the fabulous traverse of *The Waveband*. Good conditions are needed.
TIDES - Only come here at very low tide.
APPROACH - Park and approach as for Barrel and Hidden Zawns. Sector Pom Pom is 70m further along the coast path from the crane of Deep Zawn.

CAVE HOLE

Cave Hole is a long low line of super-steep sea cliffs that are tucked away on the far end of the Isle. It is a fascinating area that is made up of a labyrinth of caves, ledges and tunnels that are worth exploring for their scenic value alone. For the climber however, the Cave Hole area dispels the myth that Portland is all about vertical walls full of crimpy holds. Many powerful routes cross the huge banded roofs whilst others take on the vertical ground in between and, although not much more than ten metres in height, the nature of the climbing packs in the moves. The area includes a couple of the biggest bolted roofs anywhere in the south-west. In addition to the bolted climbs, there are plenty of good deep water solos and this is a great spot to spend time in the summer although the tide window is limiting.

APPROACH

The series of sea caves and ledges that make up Cave Hole lies below fields on the east coast of the Isle 1km north-east of Portland Bill. The conspicuous jib cranes on the cliff-top of Cave Hole can be spotted from the road. Parking is not easy since it is illegal to park on the main road. There are spots in Southwell but care is needed not to block anyone in and be aware that parking tickets are regularly issued here. The best parking, albeit with a longer walk-in, is in the Portland Bill car park (Pay and Display - see page 130).

From Portland Bill Car Park - Gain the coast path on the east side of the Isle and continue for 300m beyond Sector Pom Pom to reach the jib cranes.

From Southwell - Reach the cliff-top by walking along the main road towards Portland Bill before taking the first quarry track on the left to the coast path. At the coast path, walk south (right, looking out) for 500m to reach the jib cranes which mark the top of the area.

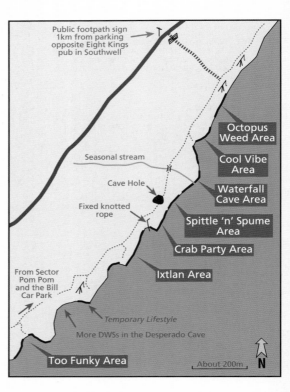

CONDITIONS

Morning sunshine is essential to dry the rock out and avoid the area completely on humid days. Seepage can be a problem on some sections, especially the Waterfall Cave for obvious reasons. The area is very tidal; mid-to-low tide will give enough time for the routes and high tide is essential for the solos. More details are given with the route descriptions.

TOO FUNKY BEACH AREA

This is a delightfully secluded little bay with one excellent sport route and some pleasant deep water solo traverses. It is situated some way to the south of Cave Hole.

TIDES - Routes *Up,Up and Away* and *Once Were Warriors* can be done at any tide. Routes *Too Funky For Me* and *Marine Boy Direct* need low tide. The solos need high tide.

APPROACH - Gain the coast path as for *Sector Pom Pom* and head up the east coast to the last group of three beach huts situated behind a rocky bay. Descend into the bay and the low cave is found on the left (facing out).

The first route described is on the right-hand (looking out) side of the bay.

❶ Memory Lane ▨▨ ☐ **E1 5b**
30m. A very amenable sideways expedition following any line you wish along the wall. Best done at high tide. At low tide the holds are more plentiful and the climbing easier (4c). **(S0)**
FSA. Mark Williams, Mike Robertson 6.8.94

❷ Up, Up and Away ▨ ☐ **E2 6b**
7m. A strenuous problem which is not a deep water solo and is too airy to be a boulder problem. Hand traverse the break leftwards then move up the arete on the edge of the cave. It can be started direct - easier.
FA. Pete Oxley 1995

❸ Once Were Warriors ▨▨▨ ☐ **7c**
13m. A memorable test of strength and ingenuity which takes the central 10m roof. Reverse for the gear.
FA. Pete Oxley 16.9.95

❹ Too Funky For Me . . . . ▨▨ ☐ **6b+**
8m. Only possible at low tide and in calm seas. Stake belay. It is **S3** with a high spring tide.
FA. Mike Robertson 6.8.94

❺ The Big Boss . . . . ▨▨ ☐ **E5 6b**
8m. A serious solo crossing the roof just right of *Too Funky*. No water to speak of! **(S3)**
FSA. Paul Savage 8.98

❻ Marine Boy . . . . ▨ ☐ **E2 5c**
8m. Swing right from the start of *Too Funky*. High tide only so to reach the start you have to traverse in from the beach. **(S1)**
FSA. Mike Robertson 10.6.95

❼ Marine Boy Direct . . . . ☐ **6c**
8m. Started direct at low tide only. This is the bolted method of climbing *Marine Boy*.
FA. Luc Percival 6.95

❽ Godzuki . . . . ▨ ☐ **E2 5c**
7m. The line of pockets left of the arete; a high tide solo only. **(S1)**
FSA. Damian.Cook 9.6.95

❾ Makin' Bacon . . . . ▨ ☐ **E1 5c**
7m. The short arete is also a high tide solo only. **(S1)**
FSA. Mike Robertson 5.8.95

❿ Penny Lane . . . . ▨▨ ☐ **E1 5b**
14m. Traverse the break from the beach to the quarry beyond *Makin' Bacon*. High tide only. **(S1)**
FSA. Mark Williams 6.8.94

The next section of cliff line, as far as the cliff-top jib cranes, is characterised by a bay of extremely overhung rock supported by some only marginally less-steep pillars and fringed by some particularly crumbly capping overhangs - the most impressive is the Desperado Cave. A good many of the spectacular lines here are very serious solos, although the line of **Desperado, E2 6a (S0)** *itself is more reasonable.*

At the northern end of the Desperado Bay is a lone route, Temporary Lifestyle.
APPROACH - *Drop down a fixed ladder directly beneath the southern-most jib crane.*

⓫ Temporary Lifestyle . . ▨▨ ☐ **HS 4b**
12m. A spanking little route that is easy to find and gives a very good introduction to the fine art of deep water soloing. Descend the fisherman's ladder to the ledge and then drop down the iron rungs to a point where a traverse left can be made to a groove. Climb this and then head merrily off leftwards under the capping overhangs, to a point where the top can be gained. **(S0)**
FSA. Mike Robertson 31.7.94

Portland West | Portland East | Lulworth | Swanage | Devon | Lighthouse Area | Cave Hole | Beeston Cliff | Cheyne Weares | The Cuttings

135

IXTLAN AREA

A good area of deep water solos on an atmospheric series of steep walls and buttresses. Only a small selection of the best routes on this section are included.

APPROACH - From the Portland Bill car park, gain the coast path and continue for 300m beyond Sector Pom Pom to reach the jib cranes. Descend leftwards (looking out) towards ledges below.

TIDES - All of the lines need very high water for solos.

Descend down ledges

Crab Party Area

Temporary Lifestyle

The Ixtlan Wall

---

❶ Babes and Bedsheets **E5 6a**
8m. A nasty bit of stuff not to be taken on lightly. Insecure with potential for a fatal fall.
FSA. Mike Robertson 6.8.94

❷ Foxy Chicks **E2 5c**
7m. A cracking but short-lived problem. From the ledge, reach the only crack you can find and yard up it. **(S0)**
FSA. Mike Robertson 6.8.94

❸ Reel 'Em In **E2 6a**
7m. Make a reach around the lip and campus or heel-hook away to the top. Not one for the weak. **(S0)**
FSA. Damian Cook 21.5.95

❹ Aquamarina . .   **E4 6b**
8m. A full-on bouldery wall climb with tiny crimps. Make sure the water underneath is adequate and pick your landing. **(S1)**
FSA. Steve Taylor 11.8.95

❺ The Little Hard   **E3 5c**
12m. Climb *The Big Easy* past its hard moves and then take a deep breath and fire up the weakness 2m left of the arete. High tide needed. **(S2)**
FSA. Mike Robertson 15.5.95

❻ The Big Easy **E1 5c**
21m. The approach traverse to the following routes is a great outing in its own right. The wall to the arete is the crux. Once the arete is rounded, steep juggy moves lead past ever-more impressive ground. Continue as far as you like and then retrace your steps back again, or swim. **(S0)**
FSA. Mike Robertson 6.8.94

❼ Ixtlan **E2 5b**
30m. Not too fluttery but it is worth checking out the final holds on the ledge before starting out. From the end of *The Big Easy*, move right to the steep corner with flowstone at its top, just beneath the capping roofs. Good holds make upward progress rapid. Once your chin is over the top the fun begins! **(S1)**
Photo page 10.
FSA. Damian Cook 23.4.95

❽ Karma **E3 5c**
33m. A more serious undertaking. From 3m right of the corner of *Ixtlan*, climb the wall to a flowstone crack in a roof. Move over the roof to a flake and finish via a hard rockover. **(S2)**
FSA. Mike Robertson 8.5.95

❾ Mad About You   **E3 6a**
36m. A fine but serious trip. Traverse about 7m beyond the corner of *Ixtlan* and climb the increasingly-difficult yellow and grey groove to a tough move and then a jug. Carry on up steep rock before a move left below the capping overhang allows access to the top. Take care there are large boulders below. **(S2)**
FSA. Mike Robertson 15.5.95

❿ Russian Roulette . .   **E4 6a**
40m. A wonderful climb with lots of brilliant moves in a great location. Crank it out along the base of the face beyond the corner of *Ixtlan* until all looks lost at an overhanging arete. The flowstone crack above is climbed with difficulty to more friendly ground. At the top of the wall move left and pull through the final overhangs on good holds. A great find. **(S1)** *Photo page 45.*
FSA. Mike Robertson 11.6.95

Descent Rope for Crab Party Area

Portland West
Portland East
Lulworth
Swanage
Devon
Lighthouse Area
Cave Hole
Beeston Cliff
Cheyne Weares
The Cuttings

CRAB PARTY AREA

A brilliant area of bicep-busting deep water solo pump-outs on excellent rock. Not for the faint hearted. The wall right of Crab Party offers a nice contrast with its technical and fingery climbing, also on excellent quality rock.

TIDES - All routes need a very high tide and calm seas.

APPROACH (Routes 1 to 6) - *Locate the chunky knotted down-climb rope roughly 60m north of the southern-most jib crane.*

❶ Captain Haddock **E2 5b**
9m. A good route for a first taster of this area. Climb across the rope and scuttle up the wall just right of the rope to a slightly crunchy finish. Needs a high tide. **(S1)**
FSA. Mike Robertson 19.5.95

❷ Flipper Force **E3 6a**
9m. Move up the arete and then pull around left onto the face. Follow this to the top. Needs a high tide. **(S0)**
FSA. Damian Cook 19.5.95

❸ Up the Grotto. **E5 6a**
9m. Traverse right from the rope to below a roof. Pull into the overhung niche and crank out the roof. Pull out right to finish on the right side of the arete. Not a deep water solo.
FSA. Mike Robertson 19.5.95

❹ Water Wings **E4 6b**
8m. A crowd pleaser up the arete with a very on/off move to finish. Needs a high tide. **(S1)**
FSA. Gavin Symonds 27.7.2001

❺ Ooh, Lovely! **E3 5c**
8m. Start right of the arete and climb leftwards through steep territory to the more reasonably angled upper face. A right-hand finish is also possible. Needs a high tide. **(S0)**
FSA. Mike Robertson 19.5.95

❻ Crab Party **E4 6a**
40m. A fantastic expedition which is one of the best deep water solos around. Check the water depth below the lip before you start out. Make a long traverse to below the roof rail. Climb up to and out along the rail to the lip. A contorted move gains the flat top. Requires a high tide. **(S2)** *Photo page 128.*
FSA. Mike Robertson 19.5.95

APPROACH (Routes 7 to 10) - *Abseil (staple at ground level) or down climb roughly 50m north of the chunky descent rope.*

❼ Intimate Dancing **E1 5a**
10m. Not a safe solo but good all the same. No gear.
FSA. Mike Robertson 13.6.93

❽ Robertson's Jam . . . . **HVS 5a**
7m. A good line up the vertical wall. Requires a high tide. **(S1)**
FSA. Steve Taylor 13.6.93

❾ Spittle 'n' Spume **E1 5c**
12m. Lots of fun is to be had on this super little rightward traverse on the lip of the roof. The wall looks totally blank but has some small positive holds. Requires a high tide. **(S0)**
FSA. Mike Robertson 13.6.93

❿ Bare Reputation **E4 6b**
20m. Extend the traverse of *Spittle 'n' Spume* via more brilliant and intense climbing. Requires a high tide. **(S0)**
FSA. Mike Robertson 15.5.95

WATERFALL CAVE AREA

This area has some of the best roof climbing on Portland, in an atmospheric cave, that belies its modest height. In winter a spectacular cascade pours over the lip, whilst in the summer it is a good swimming and jumping spot.

APPROACHES and TIDES - The Waterfall Cave is most easily reached by descending via the amphitheatre to the *Cool Vibe Area* and then making a short traverse around the promontory at low to mid tide and during calm sea conditions only. This gives access to the routes 9 and 11. Low tide is needed to cross the tidal trench below *King of the Swingers*. Beyond here there is a hidden through-cave which leads to the rest of the routes. Alternatively abseil directly into the left-hand side (looking in) at mid to low tide, from the bolt at the back of the ledge or from blocks.

❶ The Green Bearded Roof 🪨📶 ☐ **7a+**
11m. Start from a single bolt belay at the base. Belay at the back of the cliff-top ledge.
FA. Pete Oxley 6.6.96

❷ Supergeek . . . . . 🪨📶📶 ☐ **7b+**
11m. The best of the routes hereabouts. Start from a single bolt belay at the base. Belay at the back of the cliff-top ledge.
FA. Pete Oxley 28.7.96

❸ Pilot of the Future . . . . 📶📶 ☐ **7b**
11m. A very unlikely hanging roof on which shorties may need a bunk up to attain the first holds on the lip. Start from a single bolt belay at the base. Belay at the back of the cliff-top ledge.
FA. Pete Oxley 18.7.96

❹ Zen Zero . . . . 🪨📶📶 ☐ **7c+**
16m. A great route for roof thugs with 15m of escalating, bicep-death! It needs good dry conditions. Start from a single bolt belay and finish at a block belay. It used to be 8a but Mother Nature made the finish easier.
FA. Pete Oxley 28.8.96.

❺ Zombie Nation . . . . 🪨📶📶 ☐ **7c**
10m. Features an arm-stretching bouldery start. Block belay.
FA. Pete Oxley 12.8.2000

❻ Air Hoodlum . . . . . 🪨📶📶📶 ☐ **7b+**
10m. A dramatic grooved-arete which needs calm seas. Gets plenty of sun into late afternoon and early evening.
FA. Pete Oxley 7.5.95

❼ The Cult of John Craven 🪨📶 ☐ **7b**
10m. The fierce wall left of the escape route.
FA. Pete Oxley 24.1.2005. Pete's last new route in Portland? - Maybe!

❽ Escape Route . . . . ☐ **HVS 5a**
11m. If caught by tides, solo out up this.
FA. Pete Oxley 1995

❾ Osaki Dolphin . . . . 🪨📶📶 ☐ **7c**
11m. An 8m roof with wild moves. Needs dry conditions.
FA. Pete Oxley 7.8.95

Law of the Jungle and King of the Swingers start from a communal single bolt belay just inside the cave. The Swinging Nineties starts from a ledge just below the cliff-top.

❿ Law of the Jungle . 🪨📶📶 ☐ **7b+**
10m. Short and hard. Head right over the 3m roof to emerge on the promontory ledge. A good solo but only at high tide. **(S0)**
FA. Pete Oxley 6.5.95

⓫ The Swinging Nineties
. . . . 🪨📶📶 ☐ **7b**
10m. Good fun. Possible at any tide since it starts from the promontory ledge. Reverse down the last jugs of *Law of the Jungle* then swing along the 8m roof to emerge on the cliff-top. Reverse to get the gear if you used any. A deep water solo at high tides only. Block belay at the start and finish. **(S1)**
FA. Pete Oxley 29.5.95

⓬ King of the Swingers 🪨📶📶 ☐ **7c+**
20m. The biggest roof challenge on Portland. Start up *Law of the Jungle* then continue forever along the horizontal break to a no-hands knee-bar rest. Finish diagonally leftwards over the big roof. Reverse to retrieve the gear.
FA. Pete Oxley 27.8.95

COOL VIBE AREA

⓭ C.C. Backstabbers . . . 🪨📶 ☐ **E2 5c**
10m. A solo problem over the widest roof on the left.
FA. Pete Oxley 15.7.96

⓮ Different for Girls . . . . 🪨📶 ☐ **5**
10m. A neat little pitch on some excellent rock.
FA. Mike Robertson 10.6.95

⓯ Kisses and Lies . . . . . 🪨📶 ☐ **5+**
10m. More flowstone fun.
FA. Mike Robertson 10.6.95

⓰ High Klicks . . . . 🪨📶 ☐ **6a+**
10m. A fine little route on flowstone pockets. Quite beefy.
FA. Mike Robertson 10.6.95 .Named in memory of Paul Williams, High Klicks was the name of his photographic business.

⓱ 100 Reasons to be Cheerful 📶 ☐ **6c+**
9m. A powerful roof problem. Lower off from the wall well below the top or continue to belay on blocks.
FA. Mike Robertson 10.6.95

⓲ Bachelor Boy and the SR 500 📶 ☐ **5+**
9m. Steep climbing over the right-most roof.
FA. Mike Robertson 10.6.95

Mid-tide calm-sea approach to Waterfall Cave

⑲ One Cool Vibe ...... 🖼️🖼️ ⬜ **E2 5c**
12m. Direct up the arete, at very high spring tide only. **(S3)**
FSA. Pete Oxley 11.5.89

⑳ This is the Life ... 🖼️🖼️🖼️ ⬜ **E3 5c**
13m. Strenuously traverse in to gain the hanging groove. Very high spring tide only. **(S3)**
FSA. Pete Oxley 11.5.89

㉑ Fly the Friendly Skies 🖼️🖼️🖼️ ⬜ **7c**
14m. The biggest line here which tackles the 8m cave roof. Best to reverse for the gear. An abandoned and de-bolted project took a more direct line after the same start.
FA. Pete Oxley 13.5.95

㉒ Seeing is Believing 🖼️🖼️🖼️ ⬜ **7c**
11m. An impossible-looking double roof stack. Reverse for the gear.
FA. Pete Oxley 31.5.95

OCTOPUSS WEED AREA

㉓ Walking the Plank. 🖼️🖼️🖼️ ⬜ **E3 5c**
14m. An exciting solo traverse, from left to right, across the first big cave. Very high tide needed. **(S2)**
FSA. Pete Oxley 22.7.96

㉔ Staring at the Sea .... 🖼️🖼️ ⬜ **7a**
9m. A big roof challenge taking the left-hand line in the first cave below the jib crane. Low tide required.
FA. Pete Oxley 8.96

COOL VIBE AREA
This is the tiered overhang in the bay immediately south of the jib crane with an 'easy' vertical wall next to it.
TIDES - Calm seas and low-to-mid tide are needed.
APPROACH - Walk and then scramble down rock steps in the second amphitheatre to the right (looking out) to a wide belay ledge beneath the roofs.

㉕ Underwater Love .... 🖼️🖼️ ⬜ **7a**
9m. The right-hand roof line is the most aesthetic.
FA. Pete Oxley 8.96

㉖ Leave my Sole Alone . 🖼️🖼️ ⬜ **HVS 5a**
12m. Solo the pillar and overhung ledge right of the cave. **(S2)**
FSA. Pete Oxley 25.7.90

㉗ Octopuss Weed ..... 🖼️🖼️ ⬜ **E3 6a**
12m. A deep water solo in the right-hand cave. Starting on the left, crawl across the suspended ceiling. Halfway along, swing out across the roof above the water. Good clean fun. It is 3 stars or your money back. **(S0)**
FAS. Damian Cook and team 1.5.95

㉘ Tentacle Master 🖼️🖼️🖼️ ⬜ **E4 6b**
10m. A fierce early exit from the main section of *Octopus Weed* will take most a few attempts to crack the sequence. **(S0)**
FSA. Joff Cook 27.7.95

A number of other minor solos and boulder problems have been done in this cave.

OCTOPUSS WEED AREA
Another popular deep water solo spot.
TIDES - Calm seas and low tide are necessary for the lead routes. High tide is needed for the solos.
APPROACH - Go down rock steps in the first amphitheatre to the right (looking out) of the jib crane.

BEESTON CLIFF

Beeston Cliff is a fine series of interesting and secluded bays with some short, quality routes on excellent rock and some particularly good easier and mid-grade lines. With the exception of one wall, the climbs are bolted, with a number doubling up as decent deep water solos. This is a quiet area that is often overlooked and is consequently worth considering on busy Bank Holidays.

The Golden Pants Area and Limekiln Cave have some good technical sport routes although the latter area is quite tidal. The Bay of Rainbows is great for soloing or easy routes on fantastic flowstone. The exception to this friendly picture is The Great Escape Wall which is a totally different ball game, having one very atmospheric staple-bolted traverse as well as being home to some very serious shallow water solos.

APPROACH

The cliffs are situated on the east coast of the Isle just south of the village of Southwell. Parking places can be found in Southwell but be very careful not to block anyone in, and be aware that parking tickets are regularly issued here. The best parking is in Cheyne Weares car park - see page 146.

From the Cheyne Weares Car Park - Walk south (right looking out to sea) along the coast path for 15 minutes, past the Neddyfields and above Godnor, until a dome-shaped spoil heap is reached above a promontory.

From Southwell - Walk towards Portland Bill along the main road for 400m to a boulder-blocked quarry track on the left. Walk down the track for 300m to the coast path.

The Bay of Rainbows is situated on the promontory below and to the left (looking out) of the spoil heap. The amphitheatre which separates the Bay of Rainbows from the Great Escape Wall is to the right (looking out). The Limekiln is below the next promontory beyond this to the right (looking out). The Golden Pants wall is a further 200m south above a boulder beach.

TIDES

The Bay of Rainbows area is non-tidal owing to the raised belay ledge but high tide is needed if deep water soloing the routes. Limekiln Cave needs a very low tide to expose the boulder beach. The Great Escape Wall needs ultra-high spring tides to give any small degree of safety when deep water soloing. Do not visit this area if the seas are rough. The Golden Pants wall is non-tidal.

CONDITIONS

There is no seepage but avoid coming here on humid days. Bay of Rainbows faces north-east so it can be handy on very hot days; the other areas face east and go into the shade about mid morning. The bays provide a quiet sheltered environment.

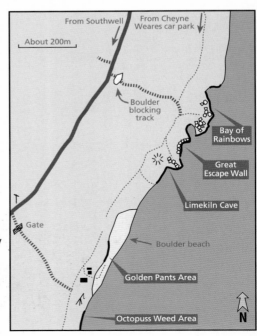

From Southwell
From Cheyne Weares car park
About 200m
Boulder blocking track
Bay of Rainbows
Great Escape Wall
Limekiln Cave
Gate
Boulder beach
Golden Pants Area
Octopuss Weed Area
N

Danie Rushmer enjoying one of the pleasant easier bolted routes at Beeston Cliff.
Etna (3) on the Bay of Rainbows Area - *page 145.* Photo: Mike Robertson

Approach via easy descent scramble

GOLDEN PANTS AREA

This outlying area is situated 200m south of the main cliffs, and a similar distance north of Cave Hole. It is a short, smooth, non-tidal, orange wall of good rock which faces south east.

APPROACH - The Golden Pants wall is 200m south along the coast path from the promontory by the spoil heap. It is situated above a boulder beach.

① Always a Little Further 　　　　6c+
8m. Interesting moves between prominent jugs.
FA. Mick Ward 20.6.2003

② Social Lepers . . . . . . 　　　　7a+
8m. Much harder for the short.
FA. Neal Heanes 1.97

③ Suits you Sir! . . . . 　　　　7a
8m. Tough stuff.
FA. Neal Heanes 5.96

④ Winterset . . . . 　　　　6c
8m. The prominent crack has a testing move.
FA. Mick Ward 26.2.2002

⑤ Skin Up . . . . 　　　　6a+
8m. A good one to get started on.
FA. Al 'Arthur' Ashmore 9.96

⑥ Sea Pink . . . . 　　　　7a
8m. The beautiful pink wall, with a brutal move. Lower-off shared with *Skin Up*.
FA. Mick Ward 26.2.2002

⑦ Eva Luna . . . . 　　　　7a+
8m. The faint weakness has some elegant moves.
FA. Mick Ward 12.3.2002

⑧ Fight the Good Fight . . . . . 　　　　7a+
7m. Another weakness featuring combative moves.
FA. Mick Ward 15.6.2003

⑨ Strategem . . . . 　　　　6b+
6m. Climb the wall.
FA. Mick Ward 15.6.2003

⑩ Burnt Sienna . . . . 　　　　6b
6m. The wall past an oblique move.
FA. Mick Ward 12.6.2003

Portland West | Portland East | Lulworth | Swanage | Devon | Lighthouse Area | Cave Hole | Beeston Cliff | Cheyne Weares | The Cuttings

Portland West
Portland East
Lulworth
Swanage
Devon
Lighthouse Area
Cave Hole
Beeston Cliff
Cheyne Weares
The Cuttings

LIMEKILN CAVE AREA

This is the series of low and tidal cliffs which run south from the *Great Escape Area*. Most of the routes are on good, compact, and well-bolted vertical rock although limited access to many of the routes (even at low tides) means that a visit must be well-timed.

APPROACH and TIDES - From the promontory above *Bay of Rainbows*, walk right (looking out) around the amphitheatre. By a block wall, head out to another promontory which overlooks the *Limekiln Cave*. Abseil from blocks to the boulder beach below which is only really advisable at low spring tides. For the right-hand routes (looking out), walk another 50m and locate a good ledge just beneath the cliff line which has a large rusty chain hanging from above it. It is best to abseil to the boulder beach from the staple in the back wall. A possible down climb from the right end of the ledge is not recommended as the final step down is on to a large rounded seaweed-covered boulder.

1 Flake Break . . . . 🔧🗲 ▭ **6c**
8m. Move up right through the roof, then break through the upper overhang to gain the ledge.
FA. Mark Williams 16.9.2004

2 Lardman . . . . 🗲🔧🗲 ▭ **6a+**
8m. Hard initial moves up the leaning arete are followed by much easier ground trending leftwards to the ledge.
FA. Mark Williams 11.9.2004

3 East Coast Epic . . . . . . 🔧🗲 ▭ **6b**
9m. Climb up the small corner just right of the arete to the tricky headwall.
FA. Steve Taylor 16.9.2004

4 Return to Form . . . . . . 🔧🛠 ▭ **6a**
9m. The flake crack just left of the large corner to a long move on the headwall.
FA. Steve Taylor 11.9.2004

5 Rusty Wall . . . . . . 🔧🗲🛠 ▭ **6b**
9m. The weakness just right of the arete is followed by some difficult moves on the headwall. A very intense pitch.
FA. Steve Taylor 16.9.2004

6 Dirty Dog . . . . . 🔧🗲🛠🗲 ▭ **6c**
9m. Climb the blank wall direct.
FA. Steve Taylor 16.9.2004

7 Pavane . . . . 🔧🛠 ▭ **6a**
9m. The corner and wall is best climbed direct. It is also possible to move in from the left when the tide is wrong.
FA. Mick Ward 16.9.2004

8 Aquaserene . . . . . 🔧🗲🗲 ▭ **7a**
9m. A smart test-piece with a blind crux.
FA. Pete Oxley 6.7.97

9 Te Taniwha . . . . 🔧🗲 ▭ **6b**
9m. Climb the blind crack and groove.
FA. James Dunlop 9.8.97

10 Silence of the Deep . . 🔧🗲 ▭ **6b**
9m. The calcite-encrusted face is nicely sustained.
FA. Pete Oxley 20.7.97

11 Lucky Day in Hell . . 🗲🗲🗲 ▭ **7b+**
9m. A very tough boulder problem which needs good conditions. Shares the final moves of *Silence of the Deep*.
FA. Pete Oxley 9.9.97

12 Heart Full of Nails . 🔧🗲🗲 ▭ **7a+**
9m. A miniature pump-route up a steep leaning face.
FA. Pete Oxley 20.9.97

13 Konked Out . . . . 🔧🛠 ▭ **7a**
9m. The bulging nose is very photogenic.
FA. Pete Oxley 9.9.97

14 Rags to Rags, Rust to Rust . . . ▭ **5**
9m. An amenable wall pitch past two old mystery pegs.
FA. Pete Oxley 9.9.97

15 The League of Gurus . . 🗲🛠 ▭ **7a**
9m. Avoid the tricky crux on the left for an overall grade of **6c**.
FA. Pete Oxley 27.9.97

16 Sea of Tears . . . . 🔧🗲 ▭ **6c**
10m. A photogenic arete with a blind crux. Only possible at dead-low spring tides.
FA. Pete Oxley 27.9.97

17 The Underhill Mob . . . . ▭ **6a+**
10m. A strenuous layback. Dead-low spring tides only.
FA. Pete Oxley 27.9.97

THE GREAT ESCAPE WALL

This snaking wall is partially tidal and has a number of unusual lines, some of which are serious undertakings. It also has some fully-bolted traverses in atmospheric positions.
TIDES - All routes can be done at any tide but high spring tides are needed for the solos though they still won't be safe!
APPROACH - The Great Escape Wall is to the left (looking out) of the spoil heap. All the routes require abseil approach from above as indicated on the diagram.

APPROACH (Routes 1 to 5) - *Abseil to a horizontal break just above high water.*

❶ Depth Gauge . . . . 🔲🔲🔲 **E4 6a**
13m. The flowstone face between two flake-grooves above shallow water. Step left to start then climb direct up the thin wall and over a bulge, using a layaway to go for the top.
FSA. Martin Crocker 3.10.99

❷ Esperanto . . . . 🔲🔲 **E1 6a**
13m. Step left and make a hard move to a jug in a groove. Follow the groove to the top, exiting rightwards.
FSA. Martin Crocker 3.10.99

❸ Bastinado . . . . 🔲🔲🔲 **E4 6a**
13m. Move right then rock up and climb the thin wall to a bulge (3 bolt belay to the right). Pull through and climb to the top.
FSA. Martin Crocker 3.10.99

❹ The Machine . . . . 🔲🔲🔲 **E5 6b**
13m. Probably the best of the new routes but with a crux at the top! Climb a scoop then move right between 2 bolts. Continue upwards past a bulge to a hard finish on the flowstone.
FSA. Martin Crocker 3.10.99

❺ Deep Water Drug Bust . 🔲🔲🔲 **E4 6a**
13m. Move up and right across the wall towards the arete. Use this to gain the crack above which leads to the top. A low crux.
FSA. Martin Crocker 3.10.99

APPROACH (Routes 6 to 9) - *Abseil from a thread in the stone wall to a small ledge just above high tide (but not high waves).*

❻ Nutters' Way . . . . 🔲🔲🔲 **E5 6b**
11m. A solo, effectively climbing the second pitch of *Esmeralda's Monkey* starting from the lower ledge. The hard bit is passing the second belay on *Esmeralda*. **(S1)**
FSA. Martin Crocker 3.10.99

❼ The 6.03 . . . . 🔲🔲🔲 **E3 6a**
9m. A solo start to the last section of *The Great Escape*.
FSA. Martin Crocker 3.10.99

❽ Scrubs . . . . 🔲🔲🔲 **E4 6a**
9m. A steep face with a low crux to gain a pocketed break.
FSA. Martin Crocker 3.10.99

❾ Borstal Brake-in . . 🔲🔲🔲🔲 **E3 6a**
9m. Good climbing above dodgy water. From the right-hand end of a narrow ledge, climb the wall above passing a bolt and small roof, to an easier flowstone finish. **(S2)**
FSA. Martin Crocker 3.10.99

APPROACH (Routes 10 to 12) - *Abseil from bolts on the blocks to the non-tidal beach below in the amphitheatre.*

❿ The Great Escape . 🔲🔲🔲🔲 **6c**
An atmospheric traverse. Take some wires to get to the first bolt. The beach has dropped and the start may be much harder.
1) 6c, 15m. Climb the pocketed wall above the roof, then traverse left along the lip to a hanging stance near the arete.
2) 6c, 15m. Continue traversing left around the arete, then trend upwards to a large square block.
FA. Mike Robertson 19.3.94

⓫ Beach Madness . . . . . 🔲🔲🔲 **6a**
15m. Follow the *Great Escape* to the 6th bolt, then climb direct through the roof to a belay on a block. Note that the crux is on *The Great Escape*.
FA. Mike Robertson 19.3.94

⓬ Esmeralda's Monkey . . 🔲🔲🔲 **7b**
50m. An extension to *The Great Escape*. From the belay at the end of pitch 1 of *The Great Escape*, drop down and follow the line around the headland through caves and bays. Eventually you emerge on a promontory overlooking Limekiln Cave. A great expedition for a competent party.
Pitch grades - 6c, 7b, 7b, 6a+.
FA. Mike Robertson 16.3.96

Belay bolts in blocks

Descent

Portland West
Portland East
Lulworth
Swanage
Devon
Lighthouse Area
Cave Hole
Beeston Cliff
Cheyne Weares
The Cuttings

BAY OF RAINBOWS AREA

A fine wall with some pleasant and relatively easy bolted routes, plus a few scary solos rising from a sea-filled cove below the gearing-up ledge.

APPROACH and TIDES - The Bay of Rainbows is situated on the promontory below and left (looking out) of the spoil heap. All routes start from non-tidal ledges. High tide is needed for the soloing.

APPROACH (Routes 1 to 4) - *Descend an easy flake to the small starting ledge.*

1 Extreme Lives . E7 6b
15m. Very serious climbing up the impressive undercut prow of the amphitheatre. Traverse left, as for *Staplebite,* then go 2m left of the arete itself. Power through the bulges above until moves rightward gain a finish up the arete.
FSA. Martin Crocker 17.10.2000

2 Staplebite E4 5c
12m. Traverse left to just short of the arete and climb to the top with difficulty. Watch out for hidden boulders in the water.
FSA. Martin Crocker 8.7.2000

3 The Portland Screw E1 5a
10m. The thin crack has a hard move to start.
FSA. Martin Crocker 8.7.2000

4 Ethical Vacuum E4 6a
9m. Step left from the descent and climb straight up the steep face to an easier finish. An eliminate.
FSA. Martin Crocker 8.7.2000

APPROACH (Routes 5 to 13) - *Abseil to a ledge with a bolt belay.*

5 Krakatoa 4
8m. Follow a diagonal line leftwards off the ledge. Watch out for the ledge if soloing. **(S2/3)**
FA. Steve Taylor 23.4.94

6 Etna 3
8m. Climb the flake above the ledge. Watch out for the ledge if soloing. **(S2/3)** *Photo page 141.*
FA. Steve Taylor 23.4.94

7 Popacatapetl 6a
8m. The wall and small roof. Watch out for the ledge if soloing. **(S2)**
FA. Steve Taylor 23.4.94

8 Fifteen Minutes to Fame 6a
9m. Start as for *Bay of Rainbows* but trend right. **(S1)**
FA. Steve Taylor 21.8.94

9 Bay of Rainbows . . 6c
12m. From the ledge head rightwards up the wall. **(S1)**
FA. Damian Cook 4.94.

10 Belly Button Traverse 6a+
11m. Traverse the low break to the far ledge and finish up *Bungle, Zippy and George,* or reverse the traverse. **(S0)**
FA. Mike Robertson 25.4.94.

11 Bay of Peegs . . 7a+
11m. Head along *The Belly Button Traverse* for two bolts and then surge straight up the technical face. **(S1)**
FSA. Joff Cook 08.2001

12 Cornflake Girl. . . . 6b+
9m. A tricky pitch. Start from near the end of *BBT.* **(S1)**
FA. Mike Robertson 25.4.94.

13 Bungle, Zippy and George 4+
9m. Start from the end of *BBT.* Mantel to finish. This is only really an easy way out since the approach is 6a+. **(S2)**
FA. Mark Williams 21.8.94

The next two routes are accessed by abseil.

14 Gyonyuru E4 5c
12m. The arete to a steep crack. Needs a very high tide. **(S3)**
FSA. Damian Cook 08.1995

15 Gyttja E5 6a
12m. The impressive arete right of *Gyonyuru.* Features a high crux and very shallow water. A solo really; do not fall. **(S3)**
FSA. Martin Crocker 8.7.2000

An isolated route is situated 40m north of the Bay of Rainbows. It is reached by abseiling from quarried blocks to a belay.

16 Portland Exclusion Zone 6c
13m. Climb the steep wall over a roof to a tricky finish.
FA. Steve Taylor 26.3.95

145

The section of coast near Southwell and the large Cheyne Weares car park, has a number of different cliffs which offer contrasting styles and grades of climbing. Godnor Far North has been developed into a low-to-mid-grade sport route playground and the Neddyfields Main Cliff offers routes in a similar vein. Both these cliffs were mainly developed by members of Basingstoke M.C. and they have become extremely popular although it should be noted that Neddyfields can be over-run by outdoor groups at times. The biggest crag in the area is Cheyne Cliff which looks scruffy from a distance but in fact harbours some fine flowstone faces and orange coral. The routes here are mostly for the fitter climber looking for ultimate stamina tests. The Lost Valley is a sheltered location in a deep inland ravine with an eerie quiet atmosphere. It also suffers from ivy growth from time to time but this is usually cleared away by the locals especially now that it is been developed as a good hard bouldering venue as well. There is more bouldering on the small vertical wall above the Neddyfields Main crag.

ACCESS

There is a variable climbing restriction on Cheyne Cliff because of a nesting peregrine although it has been consistently applied in recent years. The restriction is from 1 February to 30 September and goes from the route *Drowning on Dry Land* to *Pandemonium*. The Road Rage Wall is not restricted although it should only be approached by abseil from above during the restricted times. Please do not top out or abseil at Godnor Far North as cliff-top fauna will be disturbed.

CONDITIONS

All the areas face east and get the morning sun, which is great in winter, but can be hot on summer mornings. They offer some welcome shade in the afternoons. There is no seepage and all the cliffs dry quickly after showers. The Lost Valley is also particularly sheltered if it is windy but the other areas are not particularly exposed. The sea level crags can be greasy, especially Godnor Far North, so avoid these on humid summer days. Cheyne Cliff can become dusty in the summer. None of the areas are tidal.

APPROACH

The two main parking areas for these crags lie on the main road from Easton just to the north of Southwell. The first is the main Cheyne Weares car park which is clearly marked. The second limited spot (2-3 cars) is in a short track, on the seaward side of the road, 300m south of Cheyne Weares car park, and also 300m north from Southwell. This track is adjacent to the isolated Cheyne House opposite a quarry entrance. A good coast path track leads south down from here to the cliff-top. More details for the approaches to the individual crags are included with the sections.

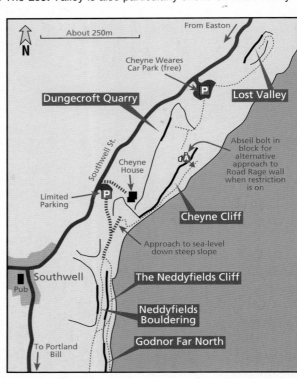

Jeremy Allen on *Jacob's Ladder* (5) on a busy morning at Godnor Far North - *page 151* - one of a number of good mid-grade pitches that get plenty of morning sun. Photo: Mark Glaister

NEDDYFIELDS BOULDERING WALL

This short accessible wall of superb rock receives morning sun and is very sheltered from westerly winds. All the lines are of a vertical nature and highly fingery and technical. The base of the wall is flat but a mat is recommended. All the problems end at a good horizontal break where it is best to hand traverse to a reasonable downclimb.

APPROACH - See Cheyne Weares Approach on page 146.

1 Foreboding V4
The right-hand side of the arete.

2 Hari-kiri V5
Up the bulge above the boulders. Dangerous.

3 Great Bear V3
Undercut, side-pull and up the arete.

4 Little Bear V1
The friable arete just right of the wide crack.

5 Solar Stone V7
Orange flowstone past an undercut.

6 Indian Summer V5
The fingery wall. Don't touch the tufa.

7 Totem Pole V0
The tufa is short-lived but very aesthetic.

8 Papoose V3
The arete and crack. Keep off the boulder.

9 Wampum V5
From the left or middle of the ledge - both are the same grade.

10 Vacillate V5
From the right-hand side of the ledge.

11 Jimbo's Wall V9
Direct to the boss without touching the ledge.

12 Jimbo's Right Hand V8
The wall between *Pock Mark* and *Jimbo's Wall*.

13 Pock Mark . . . . . . 🔲🔲🔲 [ ] **V8**
The slim groove and pock mark hole.

14 Colossus . . . . 🔲🔲 [ ] **V6**
Slap right off an undercut via a long move.

15 Stoic Existence . . . . . . 🔲🔲 [ ] **V5**
The grey arete rightwards.

16 Fontanel . . . . 🔲🔲🔲 [ ] **V7**
The slight groove right of the arete.

17 The Flake . . . . 🔲🔲 [ ] **V4**
From the flake below break and finish leftwards.

18 Pete's Groove . . . . . . 🔲🔲 [ ] **V6**
Climb the reachy groove from an undercut.

19 Taming the Flow . . . . . 🔲🔲 [ ] **V1**
The thin grey tufa.

20 Fountain of Youth . . . . 🔲🔲 [ ] **V0-**
The deep line of flowstone. Easy but great.

21 Stopcock . . . . 🔲 [ ] **V0**
Up through the small overhang.

22 Amoeba State . . . . . . 🔲🔲 [ ] **V1**
The scoop rightwards.

23 The Arete . . . . 🔲🔲🔲 [ ] **V6**
The blunt flowstone arete direct.

24 Ripples . . . . 🔲🔲 [ ] **V2**
The lovely flowstone ripples.

25 Razor . . . . 🔲🔲🔲 [ ] **V5**
The sharp pocket and thin crack.

26 Pete's Rib . . . . 🔲🔲 [ ] **V7**
The blank groove is superb.

27 Stairway Direct . . 🔲🔲🔲 [ ] **V3**
Use side-pulls to gain the hand ledge.

28 Stairway . . . . 🔲 [ ] **V0+**
Start from the low break and move up left to a flake.

29 Touched by God . . 🔲🔲🔲 [ ] **V7**
The blunt arete. Slappy and necky.

30 Quick Step . . . . 🔲🔲 [ ] **V0+**
Between the flake and crack.

31 The Mantel Piece . . . . 🔲 [ ] **V0-**
Past the flake.

32 Close Encounters . . . . . 🔲🔲 [ ] **V8**
The very shallow groove. No touching the flake on the left.

33 The Groove . . . . 🔲🔲 [ ] **V6**
Miss out the top incut for a V8 tick. Eliminate double dyno from low edges to high edges - V7.

34 Straight and Narrow 🔲🔲🔲 [ ] **V5**
A direct finish from the edge on *Diversion*.

35 Diversion . . . . 🔲🔲🔲 [ ] **V3**
Up to an edge then rightwards and up.

36 The Pod . . . . 🔲🔲🔲 [ ] **V0+**
Past a pod via a thin seam.

37 Disenchanted . . . . 🔲🔲 [ ] **V6**
A scary solo that needs spotters. Takes the surprising black roof that is passed on the way to the main bouldering wall.

38 Chocolate Orange . 🔲🔲🔲 [ ] **V9**
Traverse from *Touched by God* to *Ripples* and finish up it.

39 Savage Traverse . . . . 🔲🔲 [ ] **V8**
Traverse the low break from *The Arete* to *Stoic Existance* or to the ledge.

40 Janus . . . . 🔲🔲 [ ] **V6**
Traverse from *Quick Step* to *The Pod*.

GODNOR FAR NORTH

Godnor Far North has some useful quick-ticks that are very popular with those looking for easier lines.

APPROACH - Descend to the beach boulders as for the Neddyfields Main Cliff. Then head right (looking out) for 150m along the beach, past a large outfall pipe, to where the main crag starts. The boulders can be greasy and eventually they become tidal.

Do not abseil in or take short cuts due to rare fauna on the areas around the cliff.

Beyond here the boulder beach drops down round a corner to become very tidal. There are a number of short and easy trad routes here for the enthusiast (not described).

①　Gi' It Laldy . . . . 🔲🔲🔲 **6c**
13m. Make a hard start over the undercut roof. Steep, blind climbing and much harder than its neighbour.
FA. George Ridge 15.8.97

②　Harpies and Quines . . 🔲🔲🔲 **6b+**
14m. A good atmospheric little route which is worth seeking out. There is nothing hard but it is pumpy all the way.
FA. Janet Horrocks 22.8.97

③　Any Day Mike? . . . 🔲🔲🔲🔲 **7b+**
13m. Start as for *Harpies and Quines* and continue directly up the shallow rib.
FA. Jimbo Kimber 07.2000

④　One Day, James . . . . . 🔲🔲🔲 **6b+**
13m. A good route featuring a nice crack that has now cleaned up. Tricky for the grade.
FA. A.O'Boyle 21.9.97

⑤　Pathfinder . . . . 🔲🔲🔲 **6b**
13m. An excellent little pitch which is quite tricky at the top.
FA. Mike Vaicaitis 14.9.97

⑥　Sidewinder . . . . 🔲🔲🔲 **6a**
14m. A good subtle line that is unfortunately a little dusty.
FA. Mike Vaicaitis 20.9.97

⑦　Dreamscape . . . . . . 🔲🔲🔲 **6a**
13m. A popular route that can be made harder by climbing direct past the first bolt at **6b**.
FA. Mike Vaicaitis 20.9.97

The next five routes all have technically difficult moves at half-height. These moves tend to be much harder than anything else and have given the routes a reputation for being 'stoppers' at their grades.

⑧　Ben . . . . 🔲🔲🔲 **5**
12m. The central section of the route is the difficult bit.
FA. P.Cunningham 10.8.97

⑨　Willem . . . . 🔲🔲🔲🔲 **5**
12m. A tricky mid-height move again.
FA. P.Cunningham 10.8.97

⑩　Jasper . . . . 🔲🔲🔲🔲 **4+**
12m. A more sustained pitch that still has a tricky mid section. Perhaps the easiest line on this section of the crag.
FA. P.Cunningham 20.4.97

⑪　Jody Sunshine . . . . 🔲🔲🔲 **4+**
12m. Beware of the crux move (about half way) it is harder than you might expect although the top half is straightforward.
FA. P.Cunningham 20.9.97[1]

⑫　Wave Warrior . . . . 🔲🔲🔲 **4+**
20m. High in the grade but the top moves are not as bad as they appear from below.
FA. S.Robbins 20.9.97

⑬　Valerie's Patio . . . . . . 🔲🔲🔲 **3**
13m. The right-to-left rising diagonal line.
FA. P.Cunningham 25.8.97

Portland West | Portland East | Lulworth | Swanage | Devon | Lighthouse Area | Cave Hole | Beeston Cliff | Cheyne Weares | The Cuttings

Portland West · Portland East · Lulworth · Swanage · Devon · Lighthouse Area · Cave Hole · Beeston Cliff · Cheyne Weares · The Cuttings

⑭ Starbuck **6a**
12m. Very dusty at the moment but it may clean up with more traffic. A tricky move at mid-height, involving crimpy holds to the left, gains easier climbing above.
FA. Mike Vaicaitis 25.8.97

⑮ Last Human **6c**
12m. Thin wall climbing.
FA. Mike Vaicaitis 26.8.97

⑯ Tin Man . . . . **5+**
12m. Fingery and dusty around the bulge. Not a great route.
FA. Mike Vaicaitis 25.8.97

⑰ Tombstone . . . . **3+**
14m. A beauty for the grade which is a nice relaxing climb for a hot summer day. The start looks unlikely but persevere.
FA. S.Robbins 20.7.97

⑱ Where Silence Has Lease
. . . . **6c**
15m. The best pitch here up the blunt arete on its right-hand side. Tough at the top and requiring a long reach.
FA. Mike Vaicaitis 31.8.97

⑲ Wedding Daze **6b**
15m. Clean climbing throughout. One brief hard move at the top to a massive jug.
FA. J.Parsons 10.8.97

⑳ Future Imperfect . . . . . **6a+**
15m. A highly regarded route. Straightforward moves leading to a nice finishing crack.
FA. Mike Vaicaitis 10.8.97

㉑ Jacob's Ladder **5**
15m. This line has cleaned up well and gained a star.
Photo page 147.
FA. Mike Vaicaitis 3.5.97

㉒ The Truth is Out There . **6b**
15m. A good jug-haul to start with gains a delicate top section. The small crimpy bits at the top are the key to success.
Photo page 11.
FA. Mike Vaicaitis 20.4.97

㉓ Resistance is Futile **7a+**
13m. A desperate technical roof problem. By far the hardest move (or two) here.
FA. Mike Vaicaitis 20.7.97

㉔ Car Parts, Bottles and Cutlery
. . . . **6b+**
12m. Keep left near the top, out of the groove.
FA. Nic Hellyer 22.2.98

㉕ Factor 15 . . . . **6a+**
10m. A reasonable pitch which can be a bit dusty.
FA. Pete Church 8.2.98

Portland West
Portland East
Lulworth
Swanage
Devon
Lighthouse Area
Cave Hole
Beeston Cliff
Cheyne Weares
The Cuttings

Neddyfields Bouldering

1 2 3 4

Godnor Cliff 100m

NEDDYFIELDS MAIN CLIFF

The Neddyfields Main Cliff is a popular morning crag with plenty of friendly grades. It is quick to reach, has a pleasant outlook, is sheltered from strong westerly winds and offers shade on summer afternoons and evenings.

APPROACH - From the limited parking spot, walk 200m down the coast path to where the long Bouldering Wall appears on the right (2 mins from the road). The Main Cliff lies directly below the bouldering wall. Use a good steep track which cuts back left (looking out) along the cliff base, opposite the far end of the bouldering wall. Scramble down the gully and scree towards the boulder beach. For the first four routes cut back south (right looking out) down steep scree. The cliff base is in a hollow 10m above beach level, attained by a short scramble.

1 Lucy's off the Wall 8/05 5
8m. A stout route that requires a lot of effort between the mid-height breaks.
FA. P.Cunningham 13.8.97

2 Nothing's Shocking TR 6a+
10m. A fun climb. The last few moves often provide an 'anxious' moment.
FA. Steve Taylor 1995.

3 First Contact 6b
10m. A clean pitch tackling the front face of the buttress.
FA. Mike Vaicaitis. 13.8.97

4 Brace Yourself Sheila . 8/05 5
9m. The vague undercut arete. A lovely climb with a top section that may catch you out.
FA. P.Cunningham 13.8.97

Neddyfields Bouldering

Approach

Neddyfields Left 30m

5 6 7 8

9

Neddyfields Bouldering

Approach

Portland West

Portland East

Lulworth

Swanage

Devon

Lighthouse Area

Cave Hole

Beeston Cliff

Cheyne Weares

The Cuttings

5 The Accelerator .. 🔲🔲🔲 **7a**
7m. This micro-route starts halfway down the descent. Don't be deceived by its length; it packs a lot in. Low in the grade.
FA. Mike Vaicaitis 10.8.97

6 Nameless .... 🔲🔲 **6c**
7m. A very bouldery route with just the one hard move. It is easier to top out and walk around than lower off.
FA. Mike Vaicaitis 1997

7 Thick as Thieves. .... 🔲 **6c**
8m. Easy climbing to one 'nails' move.
FA. Guy Dixon 1995

8 Three in a Bed 8/05 **5**
8m. May be harder since the loss of a hold.
FA. Steve Taylor 1995

9 Wonderlust .... 🔲 **6b** ow!
16m. A fine addition which has become very popular. It is low in the grade but don't underestimate the finish.
FA. Pete Church 26.2002

10 Shit Route .... 🔲🔲 **7a**
17m. The route name says it all. A difficult bulge and finishing crack supply what little interest there is.
FA. Andy Long 07.2001

11 Julie Ocean ..... 🔲🔲🔲 **6c+**
17m. A well-positioned headwall. The lower moves are easy but the climbing builds up nicely to a first-class crux sequence.
FA. Mike Vaicaitis 28.3.97

12 Lugwiler's Dismal Itch. 🔲🔲 **6c**
15m. A worthwhile route with good moves all the way. The moves on the bubbly wall can sometimes be damp.
FA. Nic Hellyer 14.2.98

13 Ecosystem .... 🔲 **6b+**
15m. Quite a pleasant climb with some interesting moves over the roof on clean rock. Low in the grade.
FA. Mike Vaicaitis 26.7.96

14 Time of the Month 🔲🔲🔲 **6b**
15m. A lovely climb which has an intricate middle section. Much easier at the top.
FA. Nic Hellyer, Christine Forkin 18.4.99

15 Inception .... 🔲🔲 **5+**
15m. The mid-height bulge gives food for thought but keep something in reserve for the last move.
FA. B.Slattery 1996

16 Ocean Boulevard .... 🔲🔲 **4+**
15m. Start by a low overhang and an iron ring on the ground. There is a difficult opening move over the roof. The wall above is still tricky. It may be a poor relation to its Swanage namesake, but it is not a bad route at all.
FA. B.Slattery 20.7.96

CHEYNE WEARES AREA *Cheyne Cliff*

Portland West

Portland East

Lulworth

Swanage

Devon

Lighthouse Area

Cave Hole

Beeston Cliff

Cheyne Weares

The Cuttings

CHEYNE CLIFF
A superb wall covered in great flowstone. The harder routes have been used by locals for training purposes and many variations have been done.
APPROACH - The crag can be approached from either of the two parking spots. Head toward the Neddyfields Main Cliff but double back down a steep slope which leads to the crag base. All the sectors can be reached from here.
🚫 **RESTRICTION (all routes up to Pandemonium) -** No climbing 1 March to 30 September because of nesting birds. The Road Rage wall must only be approached by abseil from above during this period.

CORALIZED AREA

❶ Mirror of the Sea . 🔲🔲🔲 6c
20m. An awkward move on the lower wall is followed by easy but adventurous climbing above. Finish up the superbly-positioned seaward arete. Lower off in two stages via a double bolt belay on ledge at two-thirds height.
FA. Mick Ward 2003

❷ Silver-studded Blue. . . 🔲🔲 6b
20m. A pocketed coral wall followed by a pleasant groove.
FA. Mick Ward 2003

❸ Raptor . . . . 🔲🔲🔲 6c
20m. The coral wall and overhanging prow.
FA. Mick Ward 2003

❹ Drowning on Dry Land. 🔲🔲 6c
20m. A flowstone classic taking a long line up the calcite face and high groove.
FA. Mike Robertson 9.94

❺ Rocket from the Crypt. . 🔲🔲 7a+
20m. A big pitch that is worth seeking out as a first sample of the harder routes hereabouts. Start 6m right of the tunnel.
FA. Pete Oxley 22.7.94

❻ Coralized . . . . 🔲🔲🔲 7b+
20m. A good sustained climb with amazing coral on the lower wall and more good rock above.
FA. Pete Oxley 22.7.94

154

Adjoining

Fixed ropes

Approach from above
1 March to 30 September

PIGSKIN BUS AREA

7 **The Pigskin Bus Pulls Into Tuna Town**
. . . . 🔲🔲 **6a**
20m. A slightly dirty start is worth persevering with since the rest of the pitch gives good flowstone climbing.
FA. Pete Oxley 22.7.94

8 **Dutch Courage** . . . . 🔲🔲 **6c**
20m. Break out right from *Pigskin Bus* at the third bolt.
FA. Marty Hallett 13.1.98

PANDEMONIUM AREA

9 **Found Under Carnal Knowledge**
. . . . 🔲🔲 **7a**
20m. A friable start but better above. High in the grade.
FA. Mike Robertson 1995

10 **Fireblade** . . . . 🔲🔲🔲🔲🔲 **7b+**
20m. A good pitch which is very blind on the crux. High in the grade.
FA. Guy Dixon 17.9.95

11 **Dynomite** . . . . 🔲🔲🔲🔲 **7c+**
20m. An impressive line up the steep orange scoop, gained by swinging right from the 3rd bolt on *Fireblade*.
FA. Pete Oxley 24.4.99

12 **Pandemonium.** 🔲🔲🔲🔲🔲 **7c+**
20m. Sustained and reachy climbing with hard moves right at the top. Approach using the fixed rope.
FA. Pete Oxley 28.8.94

ROAD RAGE AREA
A great location for a clear winter's morning, or when a screaming westerly is blowing, or even on a hot summer afternoon.
APPROACH - *There is no restriction on this wall but please only approach these routes from above when the restriction is on the rest of the crag - 1 March to 30 September.*

13 **Road Rage** . . . . . . 🔲🔲🔲🔲 **7b+**
20m. A fine climb up the orange sheet of flowstone which is usually chalked up and in good condition.
FA. Pete Oxley 18.7.94

14 **Detonator** . . . . 🔲🔲🔲🔲 **7c**
20m. Hard and pumpy climbing up superb flowstone. High in the grade, and especially so for the short.
FA. Guy Dixon 1997

15 **Illusions** . . . . . 🔲🔲🔲🔲 **7c**
20m. Another fantastic stamina test with a debilitating reach near the top - shorties beware!
FA. Joff Cook 30.4.96

16 **Yesterday's Dreams**
. . . . 🔲🔲🔲🔲🔲 **7b+**
20m. The wall and V-groove on the far right-hand side of the face, starting as for *Illusions* then breaking right at its 2nd bolt. The original start collapsed but it is still a very good pitch.
FA. Mike Robertson 10.12.95. Reclimbed by Pete Oxley 18.11.96

Portland West
Portland East
Lulworth
Swanage
Devon
Lighthouse Area
Cave Hole
Beeston Cliff
Cheyne Weares
The Cuttings
Abseil in
Morning
10 min
Vertical
Sheltered

DUNGECROFT QUARRY

A very minor venue, short and with only three routes but worth a visit if you are into boulder-problem-style climbs. It is situated on the back wall of the quarry, which is effectively the land above Cheyne Cliff. The routes start in a narrow gully so be careful not to jump out if you fall off.

APPROACH - Park in Cheyne Wears Car Park and walk south towards Cheyne Cliff Main. The quarry is on your right.

1 Truly, Madly, Steeply . . . 🔲🔲 ☐ **7b**
7m. A neat tufa. Unusual climbing but with good moves.
FA. Mike Vaicaitis 1997

2 Lifesigns . . . . 🔲 ☐ **7a+**
7m. Very blind climbing.
FA. Mike Vaicaitis 1997

3 Sex, Lies and Videotape . . 🔲 ☐ **7a**
7m. The gritstone-like grey wall.
FA. Mike Vaicaitis 1997

LOST VALLEY

There are a number of problems up to about V5 on the excavated wall left of Quite Nice Actually.

4 Quite Nice Actually . . . . ☐ **6b+**
6m. The first line of bolts on the left.
FA. Neal Heanes 17.3.96

5 Little Pinky . . . . 🔲 ☐ **6b+**
6m. One hard move needing a mono-undercut.
FA. Mike Robertson 9.4.94

6 Clamped Aggression . . . . . 🔲 ☐ **6b+**
6m. The good little route. The sit down start is a **V5** problem.
FA. Mark Williams 9.4.94

HEAVEN WALL BOULDERING - *The next short problems are on the wall between Clamped Aggression and the big flake. They are complicated and well packed in.*

7 Back Door to Heaven . . . . ☐ **V4**
Start up *Clamped Aggression*. Traverse right from the high jug into the groove of *Heaven Sent*. Finish as for this.
FA. Ben Thorne 1999

8 Return to Sender . . . . ☐ **V5**
Do the sit-down-start to *Clamped Aggression*. Traverse low and to the right into the start of *Heaven Sent*.
FA. Jim Kimber 21.11.99

9 Heaven Sent . . . . 🔲 ☐ **V6**
Gain a groove via holds on the wall to the left. Continue to the breaks (or to the lower-off of *Clamped Aggression* for a full route tick - **E3 6b**).
FA. Jim Kimber 21.11.99

10 Straight to Heaven . . . . . . 🔲 ☐ **V7**
Climb the groove direct.
FA. Jim Kimber 21.11.99

11 Garden Force . . . . ☐ **V1**
The flake. This can be done as a route by continuing to the lower off of *Clamped Aggression* - **HVS 5c**. There is a direct variant to the left at **V4**.
FA. Ben Thorne 1999

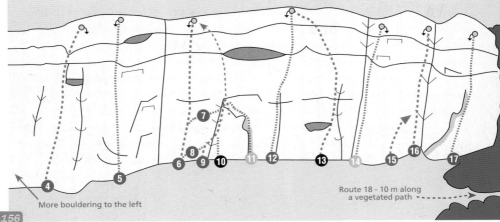

More bouldering to the left

Route 18 - 10 m along
a vegetated path

Portland West
Portland East
Lulworth
Swanage
Devon
Lighthouse Area
Cave Hole
Beeston Cliff
Cheyne Weares
The Cuttings

⑫ Bastard Crack . . . . [____] **7a**
6m. The name says it all.
FA. Steve Taylor 9.4.94

⑬ Plystalker . . . . 🖾 [____] **V7**
A hard boulder problem direct past the (missing) first bolt
(there is another bolt and a lower-off above). The route itself is
worth hard **7c** if it has a full set of bolts.
FA. Dave Henderson 2.97

⑭ No Chutney on His Ferret . . . . . [____] **5+**
6m. An awkward crack.
FA. Neal Heanes 17.3.96

⑮ LR Traverse . . . . [____] **V3**
The left-to-right traverse.
FA. Ben Thorne 1999

⑯ Chapter and Verse . . . . [____] **4**
6m. A very short groove.
FA. Helen Heanes 17.3.96

⑰ Oatsheaf, Chief . . . . [____] **4**
6m. A slight rib.
FA. Helen Heanes 17.3.96

LOST VALLEY
A hidden ravine with a good selection of sheltered sport routes.
The left-hand side of this wall has been developed as a
bouldering venue and some of the problems have been
included here.
APPROACH - From the main Cheyne Weares car park, walk
north (left - looking out) along a ridge for 250m, which gives a
view into a rocky ravine on the left engulfed in vegetation - this
is the Lost Valley. Drop down a steep chute at the far end to
gain the right-hand side of the cliff.

⑱ Training for Hubble . . . 🖾 🖾 [____] **6a+**
8m. A grand name but not quite as tricky.
FA. Pete Oxley 31.7.92

⑲ The Stoning of St.Stephen
. . . . 🖾 🖾 🖾 [____] **7b+**
8m. Buoux-like pocket pulling with a bouldery start (**V6**) which
can be extended by a sit-down start at **V7**.
FA. Pete Oxley 31.7.92

⑳ Mono y Mono . . . . 🖾 🖾 [____] **7a+**
8m. A bouldery route which keeps just right of *St.Stephen*.
FA. Jim Kimber 5.9.96.

㉑ Cadwallader . . . . 🖾 [____] **6b+**
6m. Bolted crack climbing!
FA. Steve Taylor 10.4.91

㉒ Redundancy Crack . . . . . . 🖾 [____] **E1 5b**
6m. The right-hand crack.
FA. J.Haine 7.90

㉓ The Martyr . . . . 🖾 🖾 [____] **7a+**
8m. A good test-piece.
FA. Steve Taylor 5.7.92

㉔ The Secret Garden . . . . . . 🖾 [____] **6b+**
8m. The steep wall to the break, then easier.
FA. Steve Taylor 6.11.93

㉕ The Beauty of Decay . . . . . 🖾 [____] **6b+**
8m. The last line on the cliff - before the ivy takes over.
FA. Mike Robertson 6.11.93

Portland West · Portland East · Lulworth · Swanage · Devon · Lighthouse Area · Cave Hole · Beeston Cliff · Cheyne Weares · The Cuttings

Portland West
Portland East
Lulworth
Swanage
Devon
Lighthouse Area
Cave Hole
Beeston Cliff
Cheyne Weares
The Cuttings

THE CUTTINGS

The Cuttings is an excellent and popular inland crag with a fine aspect looking out towards the Purbecks across Weymouth Bay. The crag is in fact an old railway cutting that has left several contrasting walls rising directly from a flat clear base. These offer climbing which is mostly of a sustained and technical nature on good clean vertical rock. The majority of the lines link up numerous features giving routes that need lots of finger strength and tenacity. The Cuttings is an excellent morning venue (often too hot in the summer) with routes to suit all grades of climber from 2 to 8a. There is also a beginner's wall set up for groups and individuals to cut their teeth on, which has an array of short bolted easy routes. Below the track that runs along the base of the Cuttings is a massive boulder field that has now been developed and provides lots of good problems which are also covered here.

CONDITIONS

The Cuttings provide an important colder weather venue for visitors to Portland. When the wind is blowing a strong westerly or north westerly (the prevailing wind directions) this crag is the place to be. The Cuttings catch the morning sun and are very quick drying with virtually no seepage. Additionally in very hot weather, when the west coast crags are red hot, the Cuttings are a haven of shade from mid-afternoon.

APPROACH

The Cuttings are 5 minutes from the road behind the terraced houses in Easton. Park considerately in the main street near the Mermaid Inn. Alternatively park down the road, around the bend from The Mermaid Inn, in Church Ope Car Park. (Car break-in potential here). By the Mermaid Inn, next to the bridge, a track leads east for 30m toward waste ground alongside houses. A small track ducks through some bushes to join up with a wide dirt track. Follow the wide dirt track up an

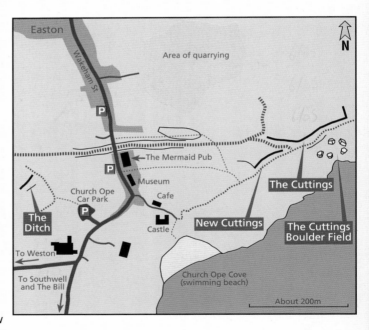

incline for 150m to just before it flattens out. A track on the right leads down rightwards to reach the Main Cuttings above a covered pipeline. The shorter New Cuttings is just to the right (looking out).

Another more direct approach is to follow a track heading directly east along the side of the Mermaid Inn which leads to the coast path running past the New Cuttings.

The boulder field is extensive but the developed section is just beyond the main cliff.

The superb upper groove of *New Saladin* (6c) at The Cuttings, Portland - *page 165*. Photo: GlaisterPhoto

Portland West
Portland East
Lulworth
Swanage
Devon
Lighthouse Area
Cave Hole
Beeston Cliff
Cheyne Weares
The Cuttings

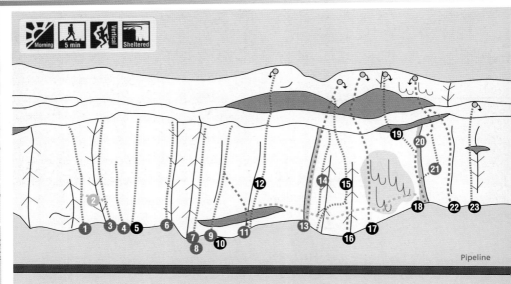

Pipeline

THE NEW CUTTINGS

A great little crag which is almost always in condition and has a good set of short and technical routes in the higher grades and some hard bouldering. It is very sheltered, away from the sea and gets sun from early in the day. The landings are good but bring a mat since some pf the problems are quite high. Descent for the boulder problems is usually by jumping off or traversing to something easier.
APPROACH - This wall is situated under the sloping track beneath the Sod Area of the main crag which is the section you encounter first when approaching The Cuttings.

❶ Phats and Bigs V5
6m. Climb direct up the blank face left of the crack of *The Fat Controller*. Don't touch the ledge on the left or the undercut on the right. It gets quite high.
FA. Jim Kimber 11.99

❷ The Phat Traverse V2
6m. A fine, fingery traverse from *The Fat Controller* to the ledge left of *Phats and Bigs*.
Weight Watchers, V7 - The low extension. The ledge above head height is not allowed.
FA. Jim Kimber 10.99

❸ The Fat Controller V3
6m. The technical blind crack.
FA. Tim Dunsby 13.5.89

❹ Phat Slapper V6
6m. A tight eliminate just left of *Pastoral*, not touching the crack. Very dynamic.
FA. Jim Kimber 26.10.99

❺ Pastoral V8
6m. A SDS can be added but there is no real increase in grade.
FA. Pete Oxley 11.5.91. Once the Isle's hardest problem.

❻ Descent Horizon V3
6m. The corner crack.
FA. Nigel Coe 5.3.89

❼ White Baron V5
6m. A low start. A **V6** variation breaks right at the sloper at head-height.
FA. Pete Oxley 5.11.90 and 11.99

❽ White Baron Left V5
6m. The left-hand side of the arete with a committing move near the top. There is also a harder low start at **V7**.
FA. Pete Oxley - early 90s

❾ Gunpowder Plot V5
6m. A very good problem.
FA. Pete Oxley 5.11.90

❿ Guy Fawkes V10
6m. The direct start to *Gunpowder Plot*, from a low jug, past two hideous crimps. Now harder since loss of holds.
FA. Jim Kimber 9.10.99. Reclimbed by John Gaskins.

⓫ Firestarter V6
6m. An extended boulder problem left from the pocket on *Subyouth*.
FA. Pete Oxley 11.4.96

The next few lines are fully-bolted routes although some new problems and projects have been added between them.

⓬ Subyouth . . . . 7b+
10m. The start is **V7** to a jug.
FA. Pete Oxley 7.11.90. Reclimbed in 1993 after losing a hold.

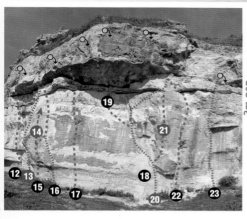

3m gap

⑬ Flowers on the Razor Wire
..... 🔲🔲🔲 ▢ **6c**
10m. Climb the corner with difficulty and then take the roof via a troublesome sequence.
FA. Pete Oxley 7.11.90

⑭ Nu Skool .... 🔲 ▢ **V6**
6m. An eliminate up the centre of the right wall starting from the pocket on *Stompin'* using the right arete and side-pulls on the left. Reverse down *Flowers on the Razor Wire*. A bit long for a boulder problem.
FA. Pete Oxley 7.11.99

⑮ Stompin' with Bez . 🔲🔲🔲 ▢ **7b+**
10m. Hideously hard as a route or a problem. The start is **V8**. It can be started direct by dynoing to the crimps and not swinging in from the pocket, at about **V9**.
FA. Pete Oxley 7.11.90. Direct start Jim Kimber 11.99

⑯ The Fibonacci Sequence
..... 🔲🔲🔲🔲 ▢ **V10**
6m. Climb direct up the arete right of *Stompin'* with a desperate move to gain the layback on *Stompin'*. Can be finished to the top at **7c+**.
FA. Jim Kimber 23.12.99. Reclimbed after hold loss by John Gaskins 2004

⑰ Lats, Babes and Bolts
..... 🔲🔲🔲🔲 ▢ **7b+**
20m. Do the (reachy) first 3m and you've ticked the **V8**.
FA. Pete Oxley 29.8.92

⑱ Razorface .... 🔲🔲🔲🔲 ▢ **V8**
6m. A fingery traverse from undercuts on *Unworthy* to the pocket on *Subyouth*. Use a high crimp on *Lats*, .. or go low (easier). The second half of the traverse from *Fibonacci* to *Subyouth* is a good V2.
FA. Pete Oxley 12.99

⑲ Bogus Roof .... 🔲🔲 ▢ **7b**
11m. Start up *The Unworthy* then fly leftwards over the roof.
FA. Pete Oxley 4.5.98

⑳ The Unworthy.... 🔲🔲🔲 ▢ **6c**
11m. A cracker. Short but steep, varied and surprisingly pumpy.
FA. Joff Cook 29.8.92

㉑ The Vulcanites ...... 🔲🔲 ▢ **7a**
11m. A good alternative first half to *The Unworthy* finish.
FA. Pete Oxley 29.6.96

㉒ Deadlosski Must Die 🔲🔲🔲 ▢ **7b**
11m. Unusual climbing up a layback pod. The start is **V3**.
FA. Pete Oxley 25.2.95

㉓ Leer of Beethoven .... 🔲🔲 ▢ **7b+**
8m. A very hard sequence from the mid-height undercut. There is a **7b** left-hand variation by-passing the crux via a groove. There is also a **7a+** variation on the right.
FA. Mike Robertson 7.5.94. Variations - Pete Oxley 29.6.96

㉔ Tipping the Scales 🔲🔲🔲 ▢ **7a**
7m. The short blank wall is a very tough little cookie.
FA. Steve Taylor 23.4.94

㉕ Nobody Runs for Free .... Ⓑ ▢ **6b**
10m. A flowstone ramp. The short arete to the left is **V4**.
FA. Pete Oxley 1997

㉖ The Running Man ...... 🔲 ▢ **6c**
10m. A link of the routes on either side joining *Bend Sinister* at its second crux.
FA. Mark Williams, Gavin Symonds 10.4.98

㉗ Bend Sinister ...... 🔲🔲 ▢ **7a+**
10m. A fine little route with a stout start and a tricky sequence to surmount the flowstone.
FA. Pete Oxley 7.11.90

㉘ Plyometrically Speaking
..... 🔲🔲🔲 ▢ **7b+**
10m. One for wood merchants. Good climbing.
FA. Pete Oxley 12.6.94

㉙ The Blandford Weasel ... 🔲 ▢ **7b**
6m. A miniature grit arete with wicked moves. Lower-off the third bolt.
FA. Pete Oxley 28.4.96

Portland West
Portland East
Lulworth
Swanage
Devon
Lighthouse Area
Cave Hole
Beeston Cliff
Cheyne Weares
The Cuttings

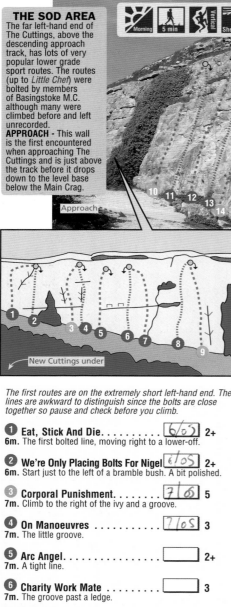

THE SOD AREA

The far left-hand end of The Cuttings, above the descending approach track, has lots of very popular lower grade sport routes. The routes (up to *Little Chef*) were bolted by members of Basingstoke M.C. although many were climbed before and left unrecorded.

APPROACH - This wall is the first encountered when approaching The Cuttings and is just above the track before it drops down to the level base below the Main Crag.

Approach

New Cuttings under

The first routes are on the extremely short left-hand end. The lines are awkward to distinguish since the bolts are close together so pause and check before you climb.

❶ Eat, Stick And Die. . . . . `6/o5` **2+**
6m. The first bolted line, moving right to a lower-off.

❷ We're Only Placing Bolts For Nigel `6/o5` **2+**
6m. Start just to the left of a bramble bush. A bit polished.

❸ Corporal Punishment. . . . . . . `7/o` **5**
7m. Climb to the right of the ivy and a groove.

❹ On Manoeuvres . . . . `7/o5` **3**
7m. The little groove.

❺ Arc Angel. . . . . **2+**
7m. A tight line.

❻ Charity Work Mate **3**
7m. The groove past a ledge.

❼ Magical Misty Tour . . . . **3+**
7m. Climb to the right of a grassy ledge.

❽ Bonsai. . . . . **3+**
8m. A short groove to a wall. Take care not to stray onto the finish of *Sting in the Tail*.

❾ Sting in the Tail . . . . **5+**
8m. The line just left of the ivy. Steady climbing turns difficult just before the finish.

❿ Juggernaut . . . . `6/o5` **5**
10m. The tricky wall past ledges and one hard move.

⓫ Rock Lobster . . . . `6/o5` **4+**
10m. The slim groove is not a very pleasant exercise.

⓬ Amazonia . . . . `1/o5` **4+**
10m. The groove and flake line give a fun route.

⓭ The Great Hamburger Disaster ⚡ `5/o5` **4+**
11m. A slim corner crack is the best of the three 4+ routes.

⓮ Definitely Maybe . . . . ⚡ **6a**
12m. The narrow wall is best taken to the right of the bolts.

⓯ Little Chef . . . . ⚡ `6/o5` **5+**
12m. The groove with an old peg is hard to enter.

⓰ The Sod . . . . ⚡ 🧗 `6/o5` **5+**
12m. The big corner at the base of the descent track has many long reaches. Although it has become polished, it is still about right at the grade.

⓱ Mindmeld . . . . . . ⚡🧗🪝 **7a+**
12m. Direct up the arete, keeping out of the corner all the way to the ledge. At the top, head left to join *The Sod*.
FA. Mike Vaicaitis 19.7.95

⓲ Sign of the Vulcan . ⚡🪢🪝 **7b+**
10m. A thin crux with a split pocket gives a terrific test-piece. However no-one can decide how hard it is. Some find it desperate and worthy of 7c, others find it a path and 'only 7b'. We have opted for the middle ground.
FA. Pete Oxley 4.9.94

⓳ Hillman The Hunter. . . . . . ⚡ **6b+**
13m. Pass the brickwall with one peculiar hard move. Watch your leg behind the rope.
FA. Steve Taylor 13.1.91

Change in viewing angle

Morning | 5 min | Vertical | Sheltered

THE CUTTING EDGE AREA

The main section of the crag has a few good routes, interspersed with some easier corners and patches of ivy. It is one of the few walls anywhere that has a grade range from 4 to 7c+ with all of them being reasonable routes.
APPROACH - The wall begins as the track below the crag levels out. The first feature is the prominent square-cut arete of the excellent *Cutting Edge*.

1 The Cutting Edge . . . . ☀️ 🧗 ⬜ **6c+**
12m. The striking arete is short but immaculate. Most finish on the left at the top of the arete but the right-hand side also goes, although it is a bit tougher.
FA. Pete Oxley 18.12.88

2 Dumbfounded . ☀️🧗✊🧗 ⬜ **7b**
12m. The blank-looking wall just to the right of *The Cutting Edge* is possibly 7b+ for shorties but only 7a+ for the tall.
FA. Martin Crocker 15.4.90

3 Chalkie and the Hex 5 . ☀️🧗 ⬜ **5+**
12m. A very appealing finger-crack.
FA. C.Ellison, H.Venables 1981. Bolted in 2002.

4 The Ramp . . . . ☀️ S/oS ⬜ **4+**
12m. The ramp right of *Chalkie*. Pass the roof and move back left to the lower-off.
FA. Unknown. Bolted in 2002.

5 Lusty Wedlock Needs Coil of Prevention
. . . . ✊🧗 ⬜ **7b+**
10m. A hard and fingery sequence well suited to the boulderer.
FA. Pete Oxley 27.10.94

6 Rusty Chubblock Needs Oil of Lubrication
. . . . ☀️🧗 ⬜ **7b**
10m. This route has stumped many over the years. The first bolt is shared with *Lusty Wedlock*.
FA. Martin Crocker 15.4.90

7 Evening Mistress . . . . ☀️✏️ ⬜ **6b**
12m. Climb the blank dihedral by some interesting bridging and layback moves.
FA. Pete Oxley 18.12.88

8 Amen Corner . . . . ☀️✏️🔧 ⬜ **VS 5a**
10m. The corner is well protected. At the top, move right to finish at the lower-off of *Mousefolk*.

9 Mousefolk . . . . ☀️🧗 ⬜ **6c**
10m. Delicate arete climbing. Keep out of the groove.
FA. Martin Crocker 15.4.90

10 Too Many Cooks Spoil the Broth
. . . . ☀️🧗✊ ⬜ **6b**
11m. A good little wall climb with a distinct crux. Keep away from the crack.
FA. Pete Oxley 5.11.90

11 Jam . . . . ☀️ S/oS ⬜ **4**
11m. Climb the jamming crack right of *Too Many Cooks...*
FA. Unknown. Bolted in 2002.

12 Chips with Everything . . . . ☀️ S/oS ⬜ **4+**
11m. The crack.
FA. Dave Jones, J.Kenton 21.6.81. Bolted in 2002.

13 The Mind Terrorist . ☀️🤸✏️ ⬜ **7c+**
10m. The flying arete is bouldery, powerful, hard and very good.
Photo page 47.
FA. Pete Oxley 13.1.91

14 Knockout Punch . . . ☀️🧗🧗 ⬜ **7b+**
10m. A short-lived but intense test-piece direct up the centre of the face.
FA. Pete Oxley 2.10.96

HALL OF MIRRORS AREA

This brilliant bit of crag has the best climbing on The Cuttings with some fine routes across the grades. The rock is clean and high quality and the sheltered location makes this a prime venue for hot afternoons or cold mornings for winter sun. With the harder routes, good conditions are usually crucial for a successful ascent, since the climbing is technical, requiring good finger friction.
APPROACH - Continue along the track past the Cutting Edge area to the tallest section of unbroken wall beyond.

❶ Blowing the Gimp . . . . 🔲🔲🔲 **7a+**
15m. A difficult-to-read crux requiring some blind moves.
FA. Pete Oxley 23.11.94

❷ The Sears Tower . . 🔲🔲🔲🔲 **7b+**
15m. Hard sustained crimping and smearing.
FA. Pete Oxley 4.11.90

❸ The Holy Hand Grenade
. . . . 🔲🔲🔲🔲 **7a**
15m. Fine sustained climbing up an open groove. Hard for its grade since a flake disappeared.
FA. Mike Robertson 26.11.95

❹ Brief Encounter. . . 🔲🔲🔲🔲 **6a+**
16m. A great piece of climbing. The wide groove, mainly on its right-hand side. The start is a boulder problem at about **V2**.
FA. Tim Dunsby 6.10.91

❺ Infernal Din . . . . . 🔲🔲🔲 **7b+**
17m. A hard direct start gives a better route than the old left-hand version. There is a slightly easier option on the lower crux to the right if needed - but that's cheating of course.
FA. Pete Oxley 2.10.96

❻ European Flavour . . . . 🔲🔲 **6b**
17m. A well-regarded route with a lot of varied climbing.
FA. Pete Oxley, Barry Clarke 2.10.96

❼ Europe Endless . . . . 🔲 **E2 5c**
17m. The corner is a seldom-climbed trad route. Don't top out, use the lower-off to the left.
FA. Pete Oxley 3.11.90

❽ The Breathing Method
. . . . 🔲🔲🔲 **8a**
18m. The second 8a put up on Portland is the hardest route at The Cuttings.
FA. Pete Oxley 24.4.94

❾ Hall of Mirrors. . . . 🔲🔲🔲 **7c**
18m. An impressive route that needs crisp conditions and features some unusual moves.
FA. Pete Oxley 3.11.90

❿ Want Out . . . . 🔲🔲🔲 **7b**
18m. An excellent stamina test with a few technical sequences thrown in for good measure. High in the grade.
FA. Martin Crocker 24.3.91

Portland West | Portland East | Lulworth | Swanage | Devon | Lighthouse Area | Cave Hole | Beeston Cliff | Cheyne Weares | The Cuttings

Portland West

Portland East

Lulworth

Swanage

Devon

Lighthouse Area

Cave Hole

Beeston Cliff

Cheyne Weares

The Cuttings

⑪ New Saladin ⬛⬛⬛ **6c**
18m. Wild moves up the crack and hanging corner above the start of *Want Out*. A fine pitch but avoid the prickly bush on the right. *Photo page 159.*
FA. Pete Oxley 13.1.91

⑫ Hurricane on a Millpond
........⬛⬛⬛⬛ **7c+**
16m. The most technical face moves in Dorset are best done on an ice cold day. Almost ungradable.
FA. Pete Oxley 21.11.96

⑬ Consommé ..... ⬛⬛⬛ **6a+**
17m. The long, thin layback flake is an outstanding line. The start is the hardest section. *Photo page 43.*
FA. Unknown. Unearthed and reclimbed by Jim Kimber 6.9.97

⑭ Haute Cuisine ...... ⬛⬛ **7a**
16m. Technical face moves based around the very thin crack after a hard start.
FA. Martin Crocker 16.4.90

⑮ The Mouth Waters . ⬛⬛⬛ **7a+**
16m. A pleasant crimpy face climb with some good rests.
FA. Martin Crocker 16.4.90

⑯ Two Fingers .... ⬛⬛⬛ **6a**
16m. Up and right of *The Mouth Waters* are three finger-shaped flakes above a wide ledge. Climb easily to the ledge then follow the groove behind to the lower-off.
FA. Pete Oxley, Tim Dunsby 16.10.83. Pete's first new route on Portland.

⑰ Three Fingers .... ⬛⬛ **4**
16m. From the ledge climb the right-hand side of the flakes.
FA. Unknown. Bolted in 2002.

⑱ Bob Hunkhouse ... ⬛⬛⬛ **V7**
45m. An excellent low-level boulder traverse. Stay low on crimps below the juggy break. Great stamina training.

⑲ Opus .... ⬛⬛ **4**
17m. The wide groove left of *Disobedience Contest*.
FA. Unknown. Bolted in 2002.

⑳ Rusty the Red Neck Takes
One for the Team .... ⬛ **6a+**
17m. Starts up *Opus* before moving right onto the wall and up the arete.
FA. Neal Heanes 2002

㉑ Disobedience Contest .... ⬛ **6b**
18m. One for the 'old school' who revel in jamming.
FA. Mike Robertson 17.11.95

Ivy is often stripped back

MODERN NIGHTMARE AREA

At the far end of The Cuttings is a large roof-capped corner flanked by some clean walls and aretes. Most of the routes here are in the higher grades and consequently the area is not often busy; however a few grade 6s to the left are worth a look.

APPROACH - Continue under the Main Crag to the far end where the long groove taken by *Modern Nightmare* is a prominent feature.

❶ Live By The Sword . . . . 🔲🔲 ☐ **7a+**
18m. Fine climbing on the headwall.
FA. Pete Oxley 5.2.94

❷ Another Notch in the Gun 🔲🔲 ☐ **6b**
18m. Good climbing all the way. The first bolt is right of the crack because of suspect rock.
FA. Pete Oxley 14.1.91

❸ Figgy Dropwise . . . . . 🔲🔲 ☐ **6c+**
18m. Technical moves but spoilt by the possibility of escape onto *Another Notch in the Gun* when the going gets tough. Try to keep right. Start from the high ledge.
FA. Mike Robertson 23.11.95

❹ Dusty Fred's Winter Collection
. . . . 🔲 ☐ **6c**
17m. A varied climb which has lost holds at the start and is still a bit loose.
FA. Joff Cook. 23.11.95

The next line is a mystery project.

❺ The Bournemouth Flyer 🔲🔲 ☐ **6b**
18m. Are you any good at bridging - if so this is the route for you? There is one desperate clip for shorties.
FA. Tim Dunsby 29.4.90

The first bolt on the next two routes is shared and is also a krab snapper - use a long sling.

❻ Nightmare Scenario 🔲🔲🔲 ☐ **7c**
18m. Very sustained and technical, especially on the crux.
FA. Pete Oxley 25.2.95

❼ Modern Nightmare . . . 🔲🔲 ☐ **7a**
19m. The big corner has a hard start and a superb pumpy finish. High in the grade. The ivy needs stripping back from time to time.
FA. Pete Oxley 29.4.94

❽ Fighting Torque 🔲🔲🔲🔲 ☐ **8a**
18m. A ferocious test-piece with unlikely moves.
FA. Pete Oxley 14.4.94

❾ Shiver Me Timbers 🔲🔲🔲 ☐ **7a**
17m. The finger crack. Loose at the bottom, painful at the top.
FA. Pete Oxley 7.12.85

❿ Weird Shit, Keep Drilling 🔲🔲 ☐ **6b+**
17m. Fine arete climbing which is well worth the wander around from the main section of the crag.
FA. Joff Cook 14.3.94

Descent from track

THE DITCH

This little crag is probably only worth considering if you have climbed everywhere else although some of the routes are pleasant enough. The wall can be dusty so bring a brush.
APPROACH - Park in Church Ope Car Park. Take a path out of the back which leads straight to the crag.

❶ Rock Logs . . . . ☐ **6b+**
10m. The tricky end slab.
FA. Joff Cook 1995

❷ Gold Dust . . . . ☐ **7b**
10m. A worthy test-piece. The finishing jug is above the belay.
FA. Joff Cook 1995

❸ Ditch the Bitch . . . . ☐ **7a**
10m. A good crux move.
FA. Damian Cook 14.4.95

❹ Pitch in the Ditch . . . . ☐ **6a+**
10m. A pleasant open groove
FA. Joff Cook 1995

❺ The Dump Pump . . . . ☐ **6a**
10m. Some interesting flowstone.
FA. Joff Cook 1995

❻ This Shit's Something . . . . ☐ **6c+**
10m. A tricky layback.
FA. Joff Cook 1995

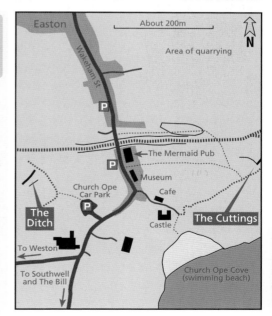

Side tabs: Portland West · Portland East · Lulworth · Swanage · Devon · Lighthouse Area · Cave Hole · Beeston Cliff · Cheyne Weares · The Cuttings

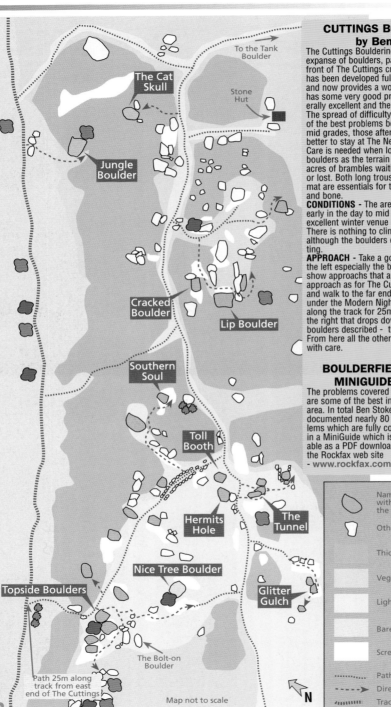

CUTTINGS BOULDERFIELD
by Ben Stokes

The Cuttings Bouldering lies amongst the huge expanse of boulders, paths and scrub located in front of The Cuttings crag itself. The bouldering has been developed fully over the last five years and now provides a worthwhile circuit which has some very good problems. The rock is generally excellent and the setting is very pleasant. The spread of difficulty is fairly wide with many of the best problems being in the easier and mid grades, those after harder action would do better to stay at The New Cuttings.

Care is needed when locating the individual boulders as the terrain is complex and has acres of brambles waiting to snare the careless or lost. Both long trousers and a bouldering mat are essentials for the preservation of skin and bone.

CONDITIONS - The area gets lots of sun from early in the day to mid afternoon and is an excellent winter venue in clear cold weather. There is nothing to climb here in the rain although the boulders dry quickly after a wetting.

APPROACH - Take a good look at the map to the left especially the blue dotted lines which show approaches that are not paths. Park and approach as for The Cuttings (see page 158) and walk to the far end of the main crag. From under the Modern Nightmare Area, continue along the track for 25m to a small path on the right that drops down to the first area of boulders described - the Top Side Boulder. From here all the other areas are accessible with care.

BOULDERFIELD MINIGUIDE

The problems covered here are some of the best in the area. In total Ben Stokes has documented nearly 80 problems which are fully covered in a MiniGuide which is available as a PDF download from the Rockfax web site - www.rockfax.com

Map labels

The Cat Skull
To the Tank Boulder
Stone Hut
Jungle Boulder
Cracked Boulder
Lip Boulder
Southern Soul
Toll Booth
Hermits Hole
The Tunnel
Nice Tree Boulder
Topside Boulders
Glitter Gulch
The Bolt-on Boulder
Path 25m along track from east end of The Cuttings

N

Map not to scale

Legend

Named boulders or boulders with lines only covered in the Rockfax Miniguide

Other Boulders

Thick vegetation

Vegetation

Light Vegetation

Bare ground

Scree, rubble

.... Path

- - - -> Direction (NO PATH)

⊔⊔⊔⊔⊔ Track (Below Cuttings)

Portland West
Portland East
Lulworth
Swanage
Devon
Lighthouse Area
Cave Hole
Beeston Cliff
Cheyne Weares
The Cuttings

TOP SIDE BOULDERS

① Blue Skies . . . . 🔲🔲🔲 V1
The scooped wall without the big pocket is a nice problem.
Start with both hands on the low sloping ramp.
FA. Ben Stokes 11.2001

② Jo's Arete . . . . 🔲🔲🔲 V0
The fine prominent arete above the smooth flat rock
FA. Jo Laver, Ben Stokes, P.Harris 11.2001

③ Nu Breed . . . . 🔲🔲🔲 V4
Make a powerful move to gain a wide pinch on the arete and a
good finger ledge at the same height. Further tricky moves via a
slopy ledge gain the finishing slab. The right side of the arete is
also worth doing from a standing start **(V1)**.
FA. Ben Stokes, Tim Crawshaw 7.2002

④ Global Underground 🔲🔲🔲 V4
Starting from a rough crozzle and a low pinch, slap up to a
good ledge, then a jug. Rock-over onto the slab with difficulty.
FA. Ben Stokes 11.2001

⑤ Made in the Shade . . . . . . 🔲🔲 V4
An eliminate breaking out of *Rocky and Diesel*.
FA. Ben Stokes 11.2001

⑥ Rocky and Diesel . 🔲🔲🔲 V2
The quality arete with mainly sloping holds. Start from a good
side-pull and a poor low pinch.
FA. Ben Stokes, Jo Laver, P.Harris 11.2001

THE TOLL BOOTH
*The main arete of the Toll Booth is a fine feature and is easily
identifiable from the main Cuttings track.*

⑦ Lonely Vidual . . . . 🔲🔲 V0
The juggy arete on its left side.
FA. Ben Stokes 19.6.2002

⑧ Tommy Cliffhanger . . . . . . 🔲🔲 V3
The left side of the face from a contorted sit-down start. At this
grade, the arete to the left is out-of-bounds.
FA. Ben Stokes 19.6.2002

⑨ Toll Booth Arete . . . 🔲🔲🔲🔲 V7
The dominating undercut arete from a sit-start with hands on
the lip of the roof.
FA. Tim Crawshaw 12.2000

⑩ The Dominator . . . . 🔲🔲 V3
The juggy line on slightly suspect rock to the right of the main
arete. Start on the lip of the roof under the line of jugs.
FA. Katie Dominey 12.2000

Portland West
Portland East
Lulworth
Swanage
Devon
Lighthouse Area
Cave Hole
Beeston Cliff
Cheyne Weares
The Cuttings

Portland West
Portland East
Lulworth
Swanage
Devon
Lighthouse Area
Cave Hole
Beeston Cliff
Cheyne Weares
The Cuttings

THE SOUTHERN SOUL BOULDER

❶ Southern Soul ... 🎫🔷💀 [____] **V4**
An excellent traverse leftwards along the lip of the steep side.
FA. Adam Slatter 12.3.03

HERMIT'S HOLE
A large boulder with a deep cave under its west face. All the problems on the boulder are worth attempting.

❷ Doogy Howser Gets Laid 🎫💀 [____] **V3**
A lay-down start with both hands on a good edge at the very bottom of prow. Move up the very edge of the prow before swinging onto the left face.
FA. Tim Crawshaw, Ben Stokes 19.6.2002

❸ Doogy Howser Gets VD 🎫💀 [____] **V5**
The right side of the prow. Move up and right with difficulty to good slopy sidepulls around a slight rib.
FA. Tim Crawshaw, Ben Stokes 26.6.2002

❹ Lightning Strike 🎫🔷💀 [____] **V7**
The fine undercut prow above the cave is the classic of the Boulderfield. Start with both hands on a good handrail at the back of the cave. Steep moves on weird jugs lead to a hard pull around the lip. Finish up the nose.
FA. Gavin Symonds 11/2002

❺ Relativity ..... 🎫🔷💀 [____] **V4**
Start as for *Lightning Strike*. Move out right along a jug rail to a hard move around the right lip of the roof.
FA. Matt Stammers, Gavin Symonds, Ben Stokes, Tim Crawshaw 11.2002

THE TUNNEL BOULDERS
On the opposite side of the valley path to The Toll Booth are The Tunnel Boulders.

❻ Streamline .... 🎫💀 [____] **V2**
The dominating arete on its right side is a fine problem.
FA. Tim Crawshaw 12.2000

❼ Bling, Bling .... 💀 [____] **V4**
The short arete at the entrance to the tunnel. Start at a 'Vulcan' pocket and a rough sloper on the left.

❽ In Ya Face .... 🔷💀 [____] **V4**
Takes the steep arete on the opposite side of the tunnel entrance. Rock-over onto the left face to gain the top.
FA. Tim Crawshaw, Ben Stokes 26.6.2002

❾ Pornographic Beats 🎫🔷💀 [____] **V4**
An excellent lip traverse through the tunnel and around the corner. Start up *Bling, Bling*. Only holds on the lip itself should be used at this grade (i.e. not the big pocket near the end).
FA. Ben Stokes 3.2002

GLITTER GULCH
A hidden valley with a handful of quality problems.

⑩ Neil Armstrong... 🎲🤚📷⬜ **V6**
Start at a positive jug. Swing left to an obvious edge and make hard moves up the blunt arete.
FA. Tim Crawshaw, Ben Stokes 13.3.2003

⑪ Lemon Jelly..... 🎲🤚📷⬜ **V3**
The central groove has a trick move. Start from the positive jug at the base of the groove. Use a hidden slot to pull over onto the slab.
FA. Ben Stokes, Tim Crawshaw 13.3.2003

⑫ The Death of Kings 🎲✂️📷⬜ **V6**
A right to left lip traverse starting from a good hold above the right arete. Follow the lip past *Lemon Jelly* and *Neil Armstrong* to jugs around the arete. Step off onto the pile of rocks.
FA. Ben Stokes 7.2.2004

THE NICE TREE BOULDER
This area has one of the best collection of hard problems in the Boulderfield. Beside a sizeable tree is a large boulder with a wide, leaning main face.

⑬ Pinky Power... 🎲🎯📷⬜ **V6**
A powerful sit-start on an obvious undercut and an edge leads to flakes and then a jug. A tricky mantel finish.
FA. Gavin Symonds, Tim Crawshaw, Ben Stokes 12.2001

⑭ Liquid Sunshine .. 🎲🎯📷⬜ **V7**
The obvious rising right to left lip traverse. Start on the nose of the prow on the right and strenuously traverse leftwards on slopers. Mantel the lip as for *Pinky Power*. **V8** if you start up the arete.
FA. Gavin Symonds 12/2001

⑮ The Prow...... 🎲🤚📷⬜ **V4**
The steep prow under the start of *Liquid Sunshine*. Start from a good side pull on the left side of the prow and a reasonable pinch low on the right side.
FA. Jimbo Kimber 1.2002

⑯ Rain Dodging .. 🎲🎯📷⬜ **V3**
Start just to the left of a rib using a high crimp. Move to a sloper just right of a wide pinch (see topo). Now reach/lunge to the top.
FA. Ben Stokes, Gavin Symonds, Tim Crawshaw 12.2001

⑰ A Bracing Dampness 🎲🎯📷⬜ **V4**
Gain the sloper, but this time grab the pinch itself with the left hand and reach right to a good side pull. Finish rightwards.
FA. Gavin Symonds, Ben Stokes, Tim Crawshaw 12/2001

THE CRACKED BOULDER
The Cracked Boulder faces away from the valley path and is a steep face split by a conspicuous crack line .

⑱ The Lip Traverse..... 🎲📷⬜ **V2**
Traverse the lip of the boulder without using the crack. At this grade make a standing start where the lip changes angle. A sit-start can be added at V4.
FA. Tim Crawshaw, Ben Stokes 12.2000

⑲ The Crack ...... 🎲🤚📷⬜ **V0**
The obvious thin crack to an easy mantel.
FA. Tim Crawshaw, Ben Stokes 12.2000

⑳ The Arete .... 🎲🎯📷⬜ **V3**
The right arete is fine and balancy. Mantel over the nose. At this grade the crack is out-of-bounds.
FA. Tim Crawshaw, Ben Stokes 12.2000

Portland West
Portland East
Lulworth
Swanage
Devon
Lighthouse Area
Cave Hole
Beeston Cliff
Cheyne Weares
The Cuttings

THE LIP BOULDER
The large pocketed roof was one of the first boulders to be developed and is one of the best venues in the Boulderfield.

❶ Trout Pout . . . . 🔲 **V3**
A left-hand start to *Petty Thief* from the lip.

❷ Petty Thief . . . . . . 🔲 **V6**
The centre of the roof. Start from a good undercut and a pocket-pinch. Reach for jugs on the lip. Turn the roof using good pockets and a flat jug high on the left. Starting at the lip is **V2**.
FA. Ben Stokes 2001

❸ Split Lip . . . . 🔲 **V7**
The centre of the roof. Start as for *Petty Thief*. Reach for jugs on the lip. Turn the roof by an ungainly move rightwards on small pockets and edges. Starting from the lip is **V4**.
FA. Ben Stokes 2001

❹ Lip Service . . . 🔲 **V7**
A left-to-right lip traverse starting up *Petty Thief* and finishing up *Cavity Search*. No supporting boulders. Strangely the arete feels easier with this approach.
FA. Ben Stokes 2001

❺ Cavity Search . . . . 🔲 **V7**
The right-hand side of the roof using a deep mono. Start at good undercuts with feet on a block in the back of the cave. Use the deep mono pocket to gain two finger pockets either side of the arete, just above the lip. Struggle up the arete. Starting at the lip is **V4**.
FA. Jimbo Kimber 2002

THE CAT SKULL
A face with some good, steep problems.

❻ Tour de Bloc . . . 🔲 **V4**
Start on the left arete as for *Eco Terrorists*. Traverse right, across *Cat Killer* to join the lip of the boulder at the far right-hand end. Finish up *Nine Lives Lost*.
FA. Jimbo Kimber 9.2002

❼ Eco Terrorists . . . . 🔲 **V3**
The left arete on its right-hand side. Watch your back.
FA. Ben Stokes, Jimbo Kimber 8.2002

❽ Cat Killer . . . . . 🔲 **V3**
In the centre of the steep face are two big slots. Use these to yard up the face. Gain the lip and mantel the top.
FA. Ben Stokes, Tim Crawshaw, Jimbo Kimber 8.2002

❾ Nine Lives Lost 🔲 **V3**
Start at a jug on a boulder to the right of the main face. Reach onto the lip and traverse leftwards along the lip. Turn the left arete to finish.
FA. Neal Heanes 31.1.2004

THE JUNGLE BOULDER
The Jungle Boulder gives a number of good quality problems.

❿ Hope Slide . . . . 🔲 **V5**
The left-hand side of the bulging face, starting from good side pulls. Use the sloping flowstone ledge to gain the top.
FA. Tim Crawshaw 2001

⓫ Cheese Grater . . . 🔲 **V6**
The right-hand side of the bulging face. From a sit start, use the pocket to reach a sloper and then the top.
FA. Jimbo Kimber 2001

⓬ Grate Escape . . . . 🔲 **V4**
Start just right of *Cheese Grater*. Use a kneebar to stretch right to a good pocket and finish straight up.
FA. Jimbo Kimber 2001

⓭ Napalm . . . . 🔲 **V1**
The juggy groove from a sit start off a big side-pull.
FA. Tim Crawshaw, Ben Stokes 2001

⓮ I'm a Swinger Baby, Yeah 🔲 **V2**
Start from the big low flake. Make a wild swing up and left to a distant jug.
FA. Tim Crawshaw, Ben Stokes 2001

15 Tripomatic Fairytales . 🔲🔳🔲 **V4**
Start with both hands on the big low flake. Slap your way straight up the rounded arete above you. A tricky mantel.
FA. Ben Stokes, Tim Crawshaw 2001

16 Downwards Spiral 🔲🔳🔲🔲 **V4**
Start with both hands on the big low flake. Move right to a wide slopy pinch and slap for the lip. Mantel with difficulty.
FA. Ben Stokes, Tim Crawshaw 2001

THE TANK
An isolated boulder that provides good steep problems on unusual rock. To reach The Tank take the path in the direction marked on the map on page 168 and, at the second of two stone huts, turn right along the coast for 25m to the boulder.

17 Pocket Traverse . . . . 🔳🔲 **V2**
Traverse of the left wall without using the lip of the boulder.
Finish up *Tufty*.
FA. Ben Stokes 2001

18 Tufty . . . . 🔲🔳🔳🔳 **V2**
A good little number. Climb the left arete on good holds.
FA. Tim Crawshaw, Jimbo Kimber 2001

19 Crouching Start, Hidden Agenda
. . . . 🔲🔳🔲 **V4**
The line up the middle of the boulder has a tricky start.
FA. Tim Crawshaw, Jimbo Kimber 2001

20 Hard Labour . . . . 🔲🔳🔲 **V1**
The line of jugs right of centre.
FA. Tim Crawshaw

21 Captain Cook . . . . 🔲🔳🔳🔳 **V2**
The right arete has a long reach.
FA. Tim Crawshaw 2001

22 The World's Best Mono II! 🔲🔳🔲 **V4**
Use the start of the previous problem to gain the obvious pockets on the west face.
FA. Ben Stokes 13.09.02

23 Christopher Columbus . 🔲🔳🔲 **V6**
The fine left-to-right traverse of the main face. Start up *Tufty* and follow the low lip with difficulty for the **V6**. Finish up *Captain Cook*.
FA. Jimbo Kimber 2001

THE COLLO BOULDER
If you have visited The Tank, instead of going straight back to the main Cuttings track, it is worth following the coast and searching out the Collo Boulder. There are only two established problems on it as yet, but both are excellent. To get to The Collo boulder continue along the coast path from The Tank and just before Church Ope Cove, The Collo Boulder is off to the left.

24 Ménage a Trois . . 🔲🔳🔳🔲 **V2**
The left arete of the landward face. Sit down on the quarried block to start. Keep to the right side of the arete for a more satisfying problem.
FA. Ben Stokes, Matt Stammers, James Wharton 28.2.04

25 Collo Della Terra . . 🔲🔳🔳🔲 **V7**
The right arete of the landward face is superb. Start 'au cheval' the arete. Move up to a small, high edge on the arete before swinging left onto the face.
FA. Ben Stokes 28.2.04

26 The Cutting Room . . . . 🔲🔳🔲 **V6**
The south side of the right arete starting as for *Collo Della Terra*
FA. Gavin Symonds 3.2004

Portland West
Portland East
Lulworth
Swanage
Devon
Lighthouse Area
Cave Hole
Beeston Cliff
Cheyne Weares
The Cuttings

Lulworth

Mike Robertson making the first ascent of *Window of Opportunity* (E5 6b) on Stair Hole at Lulworth - *page 186*. Photo: Joff Cook

LULWORTH AREA

Mark Williams trying to avoid the drink on *Hornier than Thou* (E6 6b) at Stair Hole - *page 186*. Photo: Joff Cook

The unique landscape of the Lulworth area lies at the heart of the 'Jurassic Coast' and is popular with many visitors attracted by the remarkable scenery, fine coastal walks and attractive beaches. This 'geological battlefield' is a fine example of marine erosion on rocks of very unequal resistance, which has left the spectacular formations such as Stair Hole and Durdle Door, where the result is some fantastic overhanging faces above through-caves. The position of the walls perched above the sea not only adds atmosphere to the bolted climbing, but also allows the area to be used as a great deep water soloing venue, for which the area has become world famous in recent years.

On the eastern side of Lulworth Cove itself is another roof playground known as the Amphitheatre Roofs. To the west lies a high ridge of steep pinnacles (Dungy Head) and a huge boulder on the sea shore known as Church Rock. These provide a complete contrast in style with generally easier pocketed wall climbs which may be an attractive option when the arms can no longer lock-off at Stair Hole or for those in search of lesser grades. The final area is Durdle Door with its famous arch which is home to several sustained pump-outs in a spectacular position.

ACCESS

The Lulworth area is owned by the Weld Estate who do not wish climbing to take place on their land. This is for reasons of conservation and public safety. Officially climbing is not allowed and the descriptions are only included here for reasons of completeness.

There is also a ban on climbing on the cliffs within the MOD range which starts to the right of the Amphitheatre Roofs.

Paul Twomey starting out on the popular pumpout *Animal Magnetism* (7a+) in the Stair Hole West Cave - *page 185*. Photo: Mike Robertson

CRAG	Page	Best routes	Sport Routes				Trad Routes				Boulder Problems			
			up to 4+	5 to 6a+	6b to 7a	7a+ up	up to S	HS to HVS	E1 to E3	E4 up	up to V0	V0+ to V2	V3 to V6	V7 up
Durdle Door	181	Sport			1	3								
Dungy Head	182	Sport		4	6	3						1		
Stair Hole	184	DWS		1	2	19		1	5	9				
Amphitheatre Roofs	188	Sport	1		2	12								

	Approach walk	Sunshine or shade	Access	Tidal	Abseil in	Summary
Durdle Door	10 min	Lots of sun	Restrictions			A spectacular rock formation forming an arch out into the sea. Just a few excellent hard routes. **Restrictions** - The Lulworth Estate have requested that no climbing take place on their land.
Dungy Head	10 min	Lots of sun	Restrictions			Some well-positioned pinnacles with a good set of mid-grade sport routes. **Restrictions** - The Lulworth Estate have requested that no climbing take place on their land.
Stair Hole	10 min	Lots of sun	Restrictions	Tidal	Abseil in	Two magnificent caves presenting awesome steep faces. A deep water solo and hard sport paradise. **Restrictions** - The Lulworth Estate have requested that no climbing take place on their land.
Amphitheatre Roofs	15 min	Lots of sun	Restrictions			Hard sport routes featuring some major roof climbing. **Restrictions** - The Lulworth Estate have requested that no climbing take place on their land.

CONDITIONS

All the areas are south-facing, receiving plenty of sun. Stair Hole is a relatively sheltered sun-trap that is climbable in mid-winter. In summer the roofs at Stair Hole and Amphitheatre Roofs shelter the face, which means you can find shade here when you might not expect to. The cliffs are well-drained and there is little seepage although they can hold dampness on humid days. The rock is a bit rough in places and can be harsh on the skin, especially at the Amphitheatre Roofs.

HISTORY

The Lulworth history is included with the Swanage section of page 196.

GRADED LIST

Some of the routes are also included in the Swanage graded list on page 200.

Mike Weeks on the burly *Adrenochrome* (8a) on the East Cave at Stair Hole - *page 186*. Photo: Mike Robertson

TIDES

Low tide is needed at Durdle Door to access the ledge below the routes, and for the Amphitheatre Roofs, to enable an easier sea-level approach traverse. The other areas can be accessed during all states of tide but are best avoided in rough seas except Dungy Head which is well clear of the sea. Keep away from the Amphitheatre Roofs unless it is very calm since traversing in can be dangerous. The beach approach to Stair Hole can also be awash at very high tide but it is always possible to wade.

APPROACHES

Lulworth Cove is well sign-posted from the town of Wool on the A352 between Wareham and Dorchester. The main crags are approached from the big pay car park in West Lulworth. It is sometimes possible to park for free 500m back up the road into the village, by the church. The main car park is very expensive.

Dungy Head/Church Rock - Walk up the road, past the Cove Centre, and continue up the steep hill on the right. After 200m turn left up a hidden track, just past Stair House, and follow this steeply to gain a ridge. See page 182 for approaches from here.

Stair Hole - Walk up the road, past the Cove Centre, and continue over a ridge to descend into the Stair Hole basin. Do not bear left towards the telescope on the hill. See page 184 for approaches from here.

Amphitheatre Roofs - These are the cliffs situated on the far side of the main Lulworth Cove. See page 188 for approaches from here.

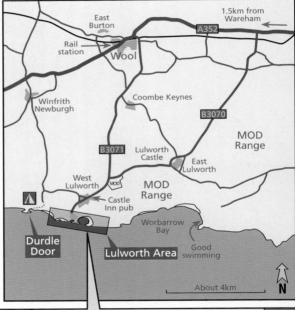

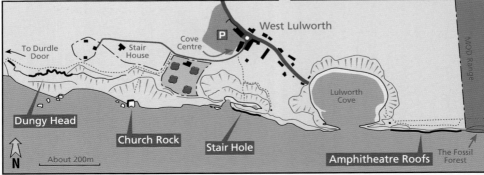

Abseil down the landward side of the arch from a block on the col with a thread

Easy escape on landward side of arch (VDiff)

Leave gear here on the seaward side of the ridge

From parking

Viewpoint

Small ledge at base of abseil

Hidden descent or escape (Diff)

DURDLE DOOR

The famous natural arch of Durdle Door has some fine well-bolted sport routes. They are situated on the seaward face of the arch and should be regarded as more serious undertakings than the average sport climb since they require a committing abseil approach in an intimidating position.

ACCESS - Durdle Door is on the same estate as Lulworth so climbing is not allowed here. It is only included in this guidebook for completeness. Additionally in the past there have been incidents where people on the beach have called out the coastguard to 'rescue' climbers.

APPROACH - Durdle Door can be easily reached by walking over the hill from Lulworth. Alternatively, park in the car park located at the far side of the Durdle Door campsite. There is a parking charge in the summer. A good path leads down to the arch. Once on the ridge, scramble rightwards to the col before the final summit. There is a hidden ledge for gearing up on the far side of the ridge. Abseil down the seaward face to reach the platform from blocks and threads.

TIDES - The platform from which the routes start is covered at high tide.

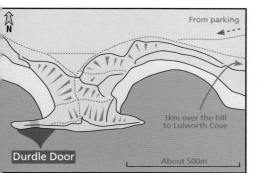

From parking

N

1km over the hill to Lulworth Cove

Durdle Door

About 500m

To get to the first route, abseil down the landward side of the arch to a bolt belay on a small ledge on the pillar.

❶ Arcwelder . . . . 🔆🧗‍♂️⬜ **7b**
25m. A hard start leads to a leaning wall above.
FA. Pete Oxley 25.4.93

The other three routes are reached by a direct abseil from the col. They all finish at double bolt belays. For those who don't like abseiling, or want to make a quick escape, there is a Diff descent scramble down the small chimney marked above.

❷ Riding to Babylon . . . . 🔆🧗‍♂️⬜ **7a+**
25m. A magnificent steep route with 10m of overhang in its 25m length. A bit of a stopper move to finish. It has been soloed but it is too long to be considered a DWS.
FA. Pete Oxley 22.12.92

❸ They Call Me Tall Man . . . 🧗‍♂️⬜ **6b**
10m. Short and steep, with the main difficulties at half-height.
FA. Joff Cook 13.12.92

❹ Unleash the Veins . 🔆🧗‍♂️🖐️⬜ **7b+**
12m. A gleaming white sheet of limestone. Follow good holds initially before more difficult moves lead eventually to jugs. Finish steeply on more good holds.
FA. Pete Oxley 16.10.92

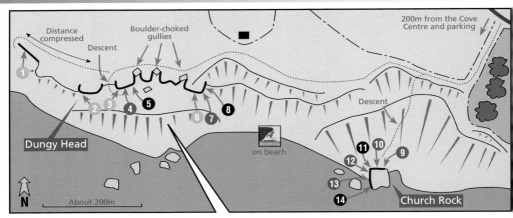

DUNGY HEAD

Dungy Head refers to the ridge of pinnacles situated high above the sea, just past Church Rock.

APPROACH - Walk along the main path above the pinnacles and drop down a gully, after walking past four pinnacles, and three boulder-choked gullies.

APPROACH (Route 1) - *The first route lies about 300m further along the path. Walk up the hillside towards Durdle Door. After the first stile, drop down the hill towards the sea, where the ridge hits the beach level. The route lies on the wall up and left.*

① Pickpocket . . . . 🔲🅱 [____] 5
20m. Old bolts up the central line.
FA. Tim Dunsby 5.4.87

On the far (west) side of the main descent gully is a lone route.

② Morris the Carnivore . . . . [____] 6a+
21m. Varied climbing starting from a bolt belay at the base. It is best approached by abseiling from a stake on the top of the crag. The stake is not easy to spot in the grass.
FA. Mike Robertson 24.4.94

The next routes are to the left (looking out) of the descent gully on a small buttress.

③ Beavis and Butthead . . . . . 📘 [____] 6a
13m. A poor route up the left-hand arete.
FA. Mike Robertson 19.2.94

④ Beers, Steers and Queers
. . . . 📙🕸🪓 [____] 6c
14m. The roof then a sustained wall above. The crux clip has seen some flyers. The lower-off is on a boulder.
FA. Steve Taylor 19.2.94

CHURCH ROCK
This is the isolated pinnacle down on the boulder beach west of Lulworth Cove. The rock has some very good short pitches and is well worth visiting. The rock may prove to be the venue of choice for those not interested in deep water soloing.

APPROACH - From the Cove Centre, follow the road up the hill towards Stair House. Turn left after the house and follow a steep path for around 100m to the cliff top where you can drop down a steep slope direct to the pinnacle at the water's edge.

⑤ Dungeons and Dragons. 🔲 7a+
14m. A roof leads to blind moves above and a shared lower-off.
FA. Pete Oxley 27.9.87

The next three routes are on the pinnacle nearest the parking.

⑥ Lost Souls . . . . 🔲 6a+
18m. The exposed face left of the arete.
FA. Mike Robertson 5.12.93

⑦ Looking Through the Infinity Window
. . . . 🔲 6c
17m. The arete is good value.
FA. Pete Oxley 23.12.88

⑧ Closing Time . . . . . 🔲 7a+
16m. A stamina test up the leaning white wall. Start from a belay in the base of a corner. Going left to the arete drops the grade to **7a**.
FA. Steve Taylor 27.3.94

CHURCH ROCK
The routes are described from left to right looking out to sea.

⑨ The Debt Collector . . . 🔲 6b
10m. The left-hand side of the inland face via a shallow depression goes on longer than might at first be imagined.
FA. Mike Robertson 10.7.93

⑩ Wall of Feedback . 🔲 6b+
12m. A vague crack just left of the right-hand arete is a good pitch with some pretty hard moves to get off the deck.
FA. Pete Oxley 13.12.88

⑪ Blow Daddy-O . 🔲 E4 5c
13m. A trad route up the spectacular arete, again with a stout start.
FA. Clarke Alston 20.11.88

⑫ House Nation . . . . 🔲 6c
11m. Excellent climbing up the steep pocketed wall, starting just right of the arete and moving rightwards.
FA. Pete Oxley 13.12.88

⑬ Jugmaster Funk Meets M.C Lane
. . . . 🔲 6b
10m. The juggy vein in the centre of the west face. A micro gem.
FA. Pete Oxley 13.12.88

⑭ Turn It On . . . . . . 🔲 7b
10m. A lovely little hard problem. taking on the leaning wall with fingery moves. Shared belay.
FA. Steve Taylor 3.7.93

BEACH BOULDER
There is a decent amount of bouldering to be found on the beach boulders between Chruch Rock and Dungy Head. There are around 20 problems at present up to V9 in difficulty.

STAIR HOLE APPROACHES

The main climbing area is on the seaward side of Stair Hole in and around the two caves which have various approaches.

APPROACH (Stair Hole West - Skeletor Approach) - From the beach make a VDiff traverse, around the end of the headland, just above sea level. There is a bolt belay on a pedestal in the cave entrance below *Never Kneel to Skeletor*.

APPROACH (Stair Hole West - Greyskull Approach) - Climb up onto the ridge and scramble along this to the central area just past an awkward slab. The gearing up spot is further on. Descend down a steep VDiff ridge on the far side between the two caves, past The Grotto on the right (looking in) to sea level. At sea level traverse back left (looking in) past various grooves to reach a bolt belay below the right-hand side of the West Cave.

APPROACH (Stair Hole East - Stage Divin' Approach) - Climb up onto the ridge and scramble along this to the central area just past an awkward slab. The gearing up spot is further on. Descend down a steep VDiff ridge on the far side to The Grotto. *Stagedivin'* starts here, the other routes are reached by VDiff scrambling down to sea level.

APPROACH (Stair Hole East - Mark of the Beast Approach) - Climb up onto the ridge and scramble along this to the central area just past an awkward slab and on to a gearing up spot. Continue scrambling along the ridge until you can drop down a short groove onto a slab below (VDiff). Scramble back left (looking in) along this below the big roof of the East Cave.

Gearing up ledge on other side of ridge

Tricky Step

The Laws Traverse

Approach

3

Finish of *The Maypole*

Start of *The Maypole* and the Skeletor Approach to the West Cave

Start of *Thieving Gypsy* in the East Cave

Tricky Step

Gearing up ledge

Laws Traverse

West Cave

Grotto

East Cave

Skeletor Approach

3

Greyskull Approach

Stagedivin' Approach

Mark of the Beast Approach

Once at the arete reverse the traverse back to the beach

LAWS TRAVERSE AREA

❶ The Laws Traverse   E1 6a
45m. An enjoyable low level traverse which is always soloed. Start by scrambling around to a ledge in the first cave. Make a wild swing onto the underside of the slab and then to a boulder in the back of the second cave. Continue to the arete. Now you have to go back since that is the only way out. Mid to high tide only to qualify as a DWS. **(S0)**
FSA. Pete Oxley and a team of locals 29.5.93

❷ The Walkin' Dude E4 5c
20m. A scary, 'pseudo' deep water solo up the rising break line to the arete. The hard bit is on *The Laws Traverse* but the rest is unnerving. Best treated as a conventional solo, even at high tide. **(S3)**
FSA. Mike Robertson 26.6.93

❸ The Maypole . . . .   HVS 5a
80m. A very good circular traverse and a fun introduction to the area. Start on the beach and head round the west tip of the Stair Hole Promentory. Continue into the West Cave at, or very near sea level, to emerge back on the beach. **(S0)**
FSA. Jon Williams 23.5.90

Bolt belays below ridge

Skull Cave

Descent from central section
of ridge between caves (VDiff)

Access from beach
(60m VDiff) along
first section of
The Maypole

Bolt belays

Portland West Portland East Lulworth Swanage Devon

STAIR HOLE - WEST CAVE
The west cave is somewhat overshadowed by its neighbour
but still offers some fine routes in a dramatic setting.
BELAYS - Bolt belays are situated over the lip for bringing up
the second, taking photos, or abseiling for gear.

APPROACH (Routes 1 to 6) - See the Skeletor Approach opposite.

❶ Truth, Justice and the Ragamuffin Way
. . . . **E2 5c**
15m. A deep water solo only which is a touch friable. **(S1)**
FSA. Jon Biddle 20.7.91

❷ Crazy Notion **E5 6b**
14m. Climb *Animal Magnetism* to its second bolt then move
straight up the overhanging wall. A committing pitch. **(S1)**
FSA. Mike Robertson 1990s

❸ Animal Magnetism. **7b**
14m. The ramp is short but intense. **(S1)** *Photo page 177.*
FA. Pete Oxley 4.6.92

❹ Journey to Eternia . . . . **7c+**
16m. A left-to-right diagonal link-up giving superb climbing.
Start up *Animal Magnetism*, reverse the crux of *Magnetic Gates*
and finish up *Gates of Greyskull*.
FA. Pete Oxley Summer 2002

❺ Never Kneel to Skeletor
. . . . **7c+**
14m. Start from a bolt belay in the cave entrance. Extremely
technical and powerful.
FA. Pete Oxley 5.9.92

❻ Hurbot the Turbot **E4 6b**
10m. A left-to-right solo across the hanging ramp above the
cave is often damp. **(S1)**
FSA. Jon Biddle 22.7.91

APPROACH (Routes 7 to 10) - See the Greyskull Approach opposite.

❼ Gates of Greyskull . . . **7b+**
14m. A superb route direct through the cave roof. **(S1)**
FA. Pete Oxley 4.6.92

❽ Magnetic Gates **7c**
16m. An exciting right-to-left link-up. Start up *Gates of
Greyskull* and break left, crossing *Never Kneel to Skeletor* via a
tricky sequence, to finish up *Animal Magnetism*. **(S1)**
FA. Damian Cook 7.2000

**❾ The Honorary Society of Self-Publicising
Water Rats** **E4 6a**
14m. The short overlapped roof into a groove right of *Gates of
Greyskull*. Not one to fall off! **(S2)**
FSA. Damian Cook 1990s

❿ Hairy Clamber **5**
17m. A solo. Follow the slabs diagonally rightwards under
the roofs before pulling over the narrowest section on jugs.
Scramble left to finish. The rock is friable in places. **(S2)**
FSA. Damian Cook 7.2000

*A number of deep water solos and boulder problems have also
been done inside the skull-shaped West Cave. These are very
esoteric and usually greasy and green; best reserved for summer when it is too hot outside.*

Portland West   Portland East   **Lulworth**   Swanage   Devon

STAIR HOLE - EAST CAVE

This is a major venue packed with some brilliant steep pitches on magnificent rock. Some of the routes are bolted but many have also been soloed at one stage although there are a few challenges still awaiting a solo ascent!
BELAYS - There are a number of bolt belays situated over the lip of the routes for bringing up the second, taking photos, or abseiling for gear.

APPROACH (Routes 1 to 5) - See the Stagedivin' Approach described on the previous page.

❶ Captain Bastard Got There First
. . . . **E2 5c**
10m. From sea level, move right and climb a blunt arete to finish back on the ledge. **(S0)**
FA. Joff Cook 21.7.91

❷ Anarchy Stampede . . . **E3 6a**
10m. The overhanging face is a good one for the timid-but-capable, with a steep blind crux not far above the sea. **(S0)**
FA. Jon Biddle 6.9.88

❸ Stagedivin' . . . . **7a+**
10m. Short and steep. Take care leaving the ledge if soloing; a spotter is advisable. **(S1)**
FA. Pete Oxley 5.92

❹ I Love Eszter **E3 5c**
15m. A solo only. Traverse in at a low level to the left corner of the arch, only at dead low tide. Graunch up the greasy chimney at the left-hand side of the arch to join *Horny Lil' Devil*. **(S0)**
FSA. Damian Cook, who else! 1990s

❺ Window of Opportunity . . . **E5 6b**
16m. Follow *I Love Eszter* until you can gain a line of good holds to join *Horny Lil' Devil* from below. **(S0)** *Photo page 174.*
FSA. Mike Robertson 1990s

APPROACH (Route 6) - Start from the beach side.

❻ Thieving Gypsy . . . **E5 6b**
15m. A very hard solo with some steep and blind moves. Starting on the beach, traverse to the boulder at the start of *Window of Opportunity*. **(S0)**
FSA. Gavin Symonds 13.8.03

APPROACH (Routes 7 to 16) - See the Mark of the Beast Approach described on the previous page.

❼ Hornier Than Thou . . **E6 6b**
15m. A solo just above the water taking the arch from right to left at a lower level than *Horny l'il Devil*. A hard dead-hanging start should see most in the drink. Reverse *Window of Opportunity* to finish. Very strenuous. **(S0)** *Photo page 176.*
FSA. Joff Cook 1990s

❽ Sliding Down the Banister . . **E4 6a**
10m. A wild and dark route, starting as for *Horny Lil' Devil*, and going through the arch to the beach in the cove. **(S0)**
FSA. Pete Oxley 23.5.92

❾ Horny Lil' Devil . . **7a**
14m. A brilliant bucket traverse across the bottom of the wall with an amazing hands-off rest. **(S0)**
FA. Pete Oxley 19.5.92

❿ Adrenochrome . . **8a**
15m. A brilliant, sustained test-piece which involves some highly dynamic climbing. May well be 8a+. **(S1)** *Photo page 179.*
FA. Pete Oxley 20.5.92. First repeat was soloed by Richard Bingham.

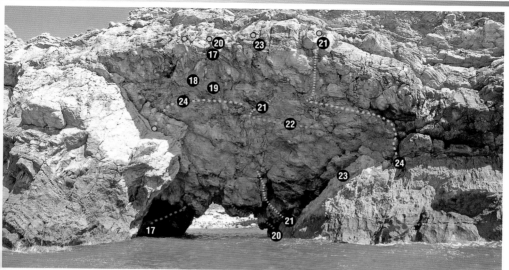

Portland East Portland West
Portland East
Lulworth
Swanage
Devon

11 Lord of Darkness `2` 7c
15m. A powerful traverse with some wild moves. Start up *Mark of the Beast* to the big flake by the 3rd bolt then traverse left across *Adrenochrome* at The Grotto ledge. **(S0)**
FA. Pete Oxley 1990s

12 Mark of the Beast `3` 7c
15m. One of the best 7c's around with good moves on large holds leading to a powerful crux at the lip. It is a popular route to attempt to solo. **(S1)**
FA. Pete Oxley 23.10.87

13 Burn Hollywood Burn
`3` 8a
15m. A desperate crux above the 3 pockets. After the crux it is just a matter of how long that you can hang on for. Possibly **8a+** for shorties.
FA. Pete Oxley 10.5.92

14 Lulworth Arms Treaty 7b
12m. Direct and powerful. It has been soloed but it is quite dangerous.
FA. Pete Oxley 23.10.87

15 Freed from Desire 7a+
11m. A smart addition with a low crux (left then right past the second bolt) to gain the big undercut on *Grimly Fiendish*. Then climb leftwards to finish on *Lulworth Arms Treaty*.
FA. Jim Kimber, Pete Oxley 1990s

16 Grimly Fiendish 7a
9m. A gentle warm-up? - Not!
FA. Pete Oxley 23.10.87

LINK UPS
The next routes link up sections of other routes already described and they require intimate knowledge of the crag.

17 Pump up the Beast. `3` E7 6b
22m. An awesome link-up of *Window of Oppprtunity*, *Horny Lil' Devil* and *Mark of the Beast*. A solo only. **(S1)**
FSA. Rob Sutton 16.8.03

18 Stage Fright 7b
15m. Reverse the last move of *Roof Predator* and finish up *Adrenochrome*.
FA. Pete Oxley 2000s

19 Centre Stage 7b+
15m. Extend *Stage Fright* into *Mark of the Beast*.
FA. Pete Oxley 2000s

20 Z-Cars E6 6b
14m. A fun solo. Follow *Hornier Than Thou* past its crux before making a testing move to gain the large 'Porthole' on *Horny Lil' Devil*. Finish across *Horny Lil' Devil*. Around 7b+! **(S0)**
FSA. Joff Cook Summer 2001

21 The Beast of Lulworth 7c
17m. A worthwhile link pitch. Start up *Mark of the Beast* to its high niche at 2/3 height. Swing right along a ramp to finish up *Lulworth Arms*. An easier finish goes past *Grimly Fiendish*.
FA. Pete Oxley 29.7.2000

22 Beast Club `2` 7c
17m. A diagonal line with some new climbing. Start up *Lulworth Arms Treaty* through its first crux then traversing left to reach jugs on *Burn Hollywood Burn*. Continue diagonally left to the high niche on *Mark of the Beast*. Finish up this.
FA. Pete Oxley 28.12.92

23 Burning Arms 7c
15m. A combination of two routes to give a fine 7c. Start up *Lulworth Arms Treaty*, clip the thread then move leftwards to join *Burn Hollywood Burn*.
FA. Pete Oxley 1990s

24 The Roof Predator. 7c+
18m. A big pump. Start up *Grimly Fiendish* and swing across to *Lulworth Arms Treaty*. A sloping ramp leads past *Burn Hollywood Burn* to a hard move into *Mark of the Beast*. Follow this left for 3m to a flake and then make a big move to a side hold on *Adrenochrome*. Go left again on pockets to a jug on *Stage Divin'*. Move down to The Grotto ledge to finish.
FA. Pete Oxley 28.12.92. Reverse Predator, 7c, is the pitch in reverse but traversing to easy ground once Grimly Fiendish is reached.

Portland West Portland East **Lulworth** Swanage Devon

Approach from Lulworth Cove

Coast path

Lower coast path

Amphitheatre

A

P 3

P

1 P

2

4 6 P

5

7

AMPHITHEATRE ROOFS

This roof playground gives similar routes to those at Stair Hole only steeper and shorter. The rock is good containing many pockets and flakes and the potential for new routes is huge, especially in the lower grades. The routes lie to the west of the MOD fence. The world famous Fossil Forest ledge is just beyond the fence.
ACCESS - No climbing is allowed on the Fossil Forest or any of the cliffs to the east of the MOD fence.
APPROACH - Walk around the shingle beach of the cove and follow a steep track on the far side. Take the lower coast path and after about 150m double back down the slope to a rock amphitheatre. From the far side of the amphitheatre, marked by a deep gully, scramble (Diff) or abseil down to just above the water-line. The starts are reached by scrambling along the base of the cliff which is easy at low tide but tricky at high tide (VDiff). It is also possible to abseil into the eastern end from a large stake 20m from the MOD fence. Leave gear well out of sight to avoid being 'rescued'!
TIDES - The starts can be reached at all tides although it is more awkward at high tide. **KEEP AWAY IN ROUGH SEAS.**

The first routes are 10m east of the descent gully.

❶ Bad to the Bone . . . 🔲🔲🔲 **7b+**
12m. Start at a bolt belay and make some reachy moves before powering up for some small holds at the lip.
FA. Pete Oxley 1990s

❷ Il Pirata . . . . 🔲🔲 **7a+**
12m. The central line. Cool moves and a definite crux. Tastier than anything served back at its namesake!
FA. Pete Oxley 1990s

There is a right-hand finish to Il Pirata which is still a project. The next routes are situated 20m to the right of Il Pirata.

❸ Dry Your Eyes Mate . . . 🔲🔲 **7c+**
12m. This is the right-hand line of the two. The left-hand line is still a project.
FA. Dan Knight 4.2005

The next routes are 40m further right.

❹ The Lemon Express . . . 🔲🔲 **7b**
15m. Powerful moves on big holds. Pre-clip the first bolt in the roof on the next route then step left 2m to start.
FA. Pete Oxley 1990s

❺ Breathe the Pressure 🔲🔲🔲 **7b+**
15m. Full of variety crossing the central weakness.
FA. Pete Oxley 1990s

❻ Granny Lifts Car. . . . . . 🔲🔲 **7b+**
12m. This is the right-hand finish.
FA. Pete Oxley, Andy Bell 23.01.2005

The next routes are in a bay of roofs which can be reached direct by abseil from a stake 20m before the MOD fence.

7 Let Ya Bones Hang 🏷️ 7a
15m. A good introduction to the steep roofs. Start at a bolt belay in the grooved rib. Climb the easy groove to the roof. Ape out across the roof on big pockets to jugs on the lip. Move slightly right on the rib to easier ground and the lower-off.
FA. Pete Oxley, Rob Godfray 18.2.01

8 Rigor Mortise 🏷️ 7a
15m. Great fun on (mostly) good holds. Start up the next route then move left at the break and out through the roof direct past a small niche.
FA. Pete Oxley, J.Biddle 1990s

9 A Storm in Heaven 🏷️ 7c
16m. A very hard route with an amazing inversion at the lip. Brilliant moves on a central line.
FA. Pete Oxley 1990s

10 Eye of the Storm 🏷️ 7b+
15m. A wild and acrobatic 10m roof. From the niche on *Storm in Heaven* break right to an intermittent finger rail. Reach a big jutting ledge and pull the lip to easier ground and a lower-off.
FA. Pete Oxley 25.2.01

11 Language of Nature 🏷️ 7b
16m. The obvious challenge of the diagonal crack in the right side of the roof to finishing up *Eye of the Storm*. The bolt on the lip needs a long sling.
FA. Pete Oxley 25.2.01

12 Weld's Mother 4+
16m. An escape pitch if your elbows blow out. It follows the left-slanting rib between two bays.
FA. Damian Cook 1990s

13 Monolith Monsters 🏷️ 7b+
14m. A blank-looking line through the widest part of the ceiling. Worth seeking out.
FA. Damian Cook 1990s

14 Mirrorball 🏷️ 7c
15m. Very powerful and graded for those with a big reach. Start up *Monolith Monsters*. Step right under the roof and make hard moves to cross the lip. Step right at the lip to finish on the difficult rock-over of *Shining Path*.
FA. Pete Oxley 4.2001

15 Shining Path 🏷️ 7a+
14m. Almost at the end of the cliff before the MOD fence. For guerrillas only!
FA. Dominic Cook 1990s. The first route here.

🔲 Beyond is the Fossil Forest which marks the start of the MOD land. Do not climb here, or even enter when the ranges are closed, or you are likely to be escorted off and ruin access to this area once and for all.

Swanage

Mike Robertson on the crux wall of the classic *Elysium* (E1 5b), Boulder Ruckle - *page 286*.
Good rock, solid gear and fine climbing make this a Swanage experience not to be missed. Photo: Mark Glaister

SWANAGE

Bottomless Buttress (HS 4b) at Boulder Ruckle - *page 280*. Photo: Chris Craggs

To the west of the bustling seaside town of Swanage (officially Britain's sunniest town!) lies the glorious Isle of Purbeck, an area of outstanding natural beauty famed for its varied scenery, geology and stunning coastal cliffs, interspersed with romantic little coves such as Lulworth and Durdle Door. The whole area is an excellent holiday venue with many good beaches offering swimming and scuba diving, plenty of campsites, country pubs and interesting places to visit. These factors, combined with the extensive sea cliffs and quarries, puts Swanage high on the list of major UK climbing venues.

For both traditional and sport climber, the limestone cliffs that run unbroken for 5km to the west of Swanage offer a unique climbing experience. Much of the rock is steep or overhanging, with many routes in the higher grades. For the accomplished climber, the style complements perfectly the more technical and fingery routes found on Portland. Some of the crags, such as The Promenade, Stair Hole and Blacker's Hole, offer incredible roofs of a scale not matched anywhere else in the country. However most of the climbs are not on such rugged terrain or of such an intimidating scale and the more popular destinations are the bolted quarries at Dancing Ledge, Hedbury and Winspit. Also popular are the gentler sectors such as Subluminal and the Cattle Troughs that offer novices the chance to take their first steps at Swanage. The other increasingly well-known draw of the area, and of great interest in the summer, are the superb deep water soloing venues such as Connor Cove and Stair Hole. The most recent high-grade developments have been in the more technical and serious 'head-points' - less steep routes but with minimal protection, in a 'gritstone style' - adding just one more dimension to the area's varied climbing.

Perfect evening conditions at The Promenade. Johnny 'Woody' Woods on *Crest of a Wave* (7b) - *page 262*. Photo: Mark Glaister

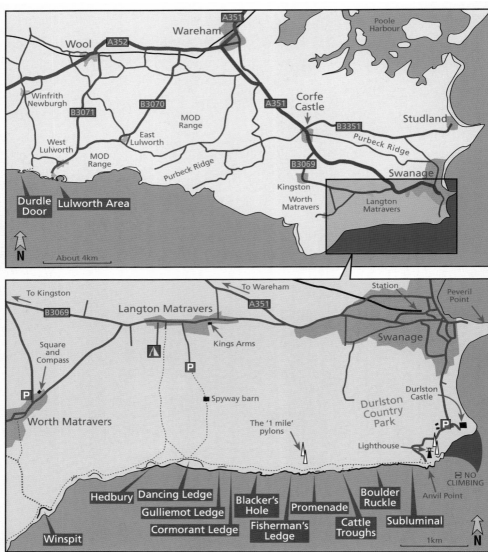

Swanage's climate is generally kind to the climber and more often than not is better than elsewhere in Britain. It is not unknown to be climbing in shorts mid-winter although the summertime heat can be unbearable. For the best conditions, cooler days in autumn and spring, and the crisp clear days of winter should be exploited and cherished. Nearly all of the Swanage cliffs face south and catch all the available sun. The following pages should tempt you to make a visit, it is surely insane not to leave the cold and dark north and the wet west behind for a while. Bring your shorts and some sunscreen, pack your quick-draws for the sport routes, a rack of gear for the trad, or at the very least a towel and a tankard of adrenaline for the odd solo or two.

The sheltered Quarryman's Wall at Winspit gives some of the best winter time climbing in the UK. Dave Pickford on *The Ancient Order of Free-Marblers* (7a) at Winspit - *page 206.*
Photo: Mark Glaister

1900 to 1950 - Unrecorded ascents by alpinists training for the War were undertaken in Boulder Ruckle.

1957 - The first recorded route *The Ramp* (Severe) at Boulder Ruckle by John Cleare.

Pre 1963 - Barrie Annette established the first classic in *Tatra* (VS). Subluminal and Cattle Troughs are quickly developed, with odd aid points used.

1963 - First Extreme is *Apex Corner* by John Mustoe - graded HVS, which set a trend for undergrading.

1965/66 - Tony Wilmott hits E2 and 5c with test-pieces such as *Philatus* (now E3) and *Stroof* (E1 5c). George Smith finds classics in the Ruckle such as *Lightning Wall* (HVS) and *Finale Groove* (HVS).

1967/1972 - Big Richard Crewe becomes a major driving force with many classic in the low Extremes such as *Squid* (some aid), *Conger* (E2) and *Buccaneer* (E2). However *Oceanid* (E2) by Pat Littlejohn becomes the big test-piece. Swanage Climbing Club spearheads the group of active locals.

1973/76 - Brian Snell blasts Guillemot ledge while Crewe finds the perfect route with his *Tudor Rose* (E2). *Squid* (E2) was freed to show that the big roofs predominant at Swanage, can be done. George Hounsome, a bold climber, entered the E3 zone with *The Last Hurrah*, using only three runners!

1978 - Young outsiders from Bristol and Portsmouth raise the level to E4. The brilliant Arnis Strapcans onsighted the awesome *Polaris* (now thought E5), Pat Littlejohn freed the pumpy *Melpomene* (E4) and other E4s were added by Nick Buckley and Kevin Turner, such as the future classic *Freeborn Man* (E4).

1982/84 - Martin Crocker enters the scene and creams through many modern classics, raising the game to hard E5 with *Fly Crazy but Free* and *Procrastinating Giant*. Pete Oxley also hits the scene.

1985 - Oxley equals the hardest routes yet done with his *Punks in Power* (E5). Crispin Waddy, a young Bristolian, joins in and explores some esoteric new stuff.

1986 - Oxley gives The Promenade some attention with many hard test-pieces including *Birth Pains* (E6) and the first sport route, *Tessalations* (7b). Waddy begins deep water soloing at Connor Cove with many fine routes.

1987/88 - Oxley adds numerous E6s, 7c and 7c+s plus the first E7 trad route with *Mark of the Beast* at Lulworth. Late in the year, Oxley completes the huge roof of Laughing Arthur, the first E8 in the South. The quarries are developed with *The Energy, The Faith, The Devotion* (7c+) setting new technical standards.

1989/90 - *Street Fighting Years (E7) is added to* Blacker's Hole. Dancing Ledge sees lots of new routes.

1991 - Oxley adds the first 8a with *Solid State Logic* at the Promenade then pushes the standard to 8a+ with *Palace of the Brine*. An excellent batch of four E6s go up at Smokey Hole and another fine E7 goes out over a big roof with *Godfodder* (E7) at the Promenade.

1992 - Lulworth is extensively developed including *Adrenochrome* (8a), one of the best around at the grade. One of the most overhanging pitches in Britain is climbed with *Infinite Gravity* (8a+).

1993 - A meeting decides which areas of Swanage are to be opened up for sport routes and which are to remain trad. Despite a few indescretions the agreement is probably more established now than ever.

1993/4 - Mike Robertson opens up many sport routes at Winspit and Dancing Ledge. Deep water soloing becomes more popular and the standard is pushed with Oxley's solo of *Mark of the Beast*. Crocker makes a return with the likes of *Deaf Mosaic* (E6) at Guillemot Ledge. The first Dorset ROCKFAX is published which covers the sport climbing areas at Swanage.

1995 - *Gates of Greyskull* (7b+) is soloed by John Cook. Hedbury Big Cove sees a revamp from Crocker eliminating old (indescretion) bolts and re-establishing it as a major trad adventure crag.

1996 - A significant 'last great traverse' around Hedbury Cove leaves Crocker and Robertson with *No Where to Run* (E6). Amphitheatre Roofs opened by Oxley and Dominic and Damian Cook with brilliant sport roofs to 7b+. Connor Cove sees attention from Robertson and Crocker with classics like *Privateer* (E6).

1997 - Robertson adds a batch of necky E6s at Black Zawn and Connor Cove such as *Talisman* and *Terminal One*. Oxley's *Storm in Heaven* (7c) pushes the standard on the Amphitheatre Roofs.

1998 - Oxley solos and straightens *Privateer* (E6) and adds *For Whom the Swell Tolls* (E6) on the same day. The first deep water solo festival is organised by Robertson and results in a 'ground up' of *Mark of the Beast* tick by Leo Houlding and others.

1999 - *Adrenochrome* (8a) is soloed by Sheffield raider Richard Bingham. Oxley adds three E6s to Connor Cove including *The Drowning Pool*. Oxley returns to hard trad routes with *Full Circle* (E7) at Blackers and later he adds *Mile High Club* (E6) to Conner Cove. 18 year old Dave Pickford has an awesome summer repeating scores of routes and sets the scene for the next millennium by onsighting the *Schwarzechild Radius* (7c+) and *The Roaring Boys* E6.

2000 - A busy year of consolidation and repeats after the second ROCKFAX. Dave Pickford continues his repeat rampage including *Infinite Gravity*, and achieves a bolt-free ascent of *A Dose of the Malhams* (E6). The Promenade sees more development from Oxley with classics like *Rise of the Robots* (7b+). Damian Cook achieved a high point with a deep water solo of his *Magnetic Gates* (7c) at Lulworth.

2001 - The new craze of deep water soloing reaches a climax with a regular yearly festival attended by 100s on the Swanage cliffs. Products of this are the classic *Vanishing* at E6 6a, and an astounding solo ascent of *Riding to Babylon* (E7 6a) at Durdle Door from Robertson. Oxley develops a multitude of hard sport classics at Lulworth East and The Promenade up to 7c+ including *Eye of the Storm* and *The Incredible Hulk*.

2002 - A quiet year except for The Promenade again where Oxley carries out lots of retro work and finds some quality hard sport climbs such as *Atonement* and *The Futurist 2002*, both 7c.

2003 - Highlight of the year is the superb *Event Horizon* (8a+) from Rob Kennard at The Promenade. Oxley adds the excellent *Journey to Eternia* (7c+) at Lulworth, while Matt King spearheads a resurgence of new sport climbs at Winspit.

2004 - A bad year for the local scene with the tragic loss in May of two of its greatest characters. Damian Cook drowns in Mallorca in a freak soloing accident while Brian Tilley dies in Baghdad during security work. Elsewhere, The Promenade receives one its best with *State of Play* (7c+) from Oxley, and at Winspit, Rob Kennard raises standards with the big roof challenge *Disbelief Suspended* (7c). Wrapping things up at Stair Hole, visitor Rob Sutton overcomes *Pump up the Beast* (E7).

2005 - A new local star emerges as Dan Knight starts to deliver after a hard winter spent training up to V12 in his bedroom. At The Promenade and Lulworth East, he sorts out two old projects, which both turn into powerful 7c+'s. As with the 2000 ROCKFAX, Pete Oxley manages once again to get the last new route in the book just in the nick of time with his major *Haka Pereperu* in the Palace of the Brine Cave. This is Pete's first 8a for 6 years and a fitting final addition prior to his departure to New Zealand.

The Future - The Promenade will see the completion of the retro-bolt plan and Lulworth East still holds large potential. For those prepared to look, substantial trad lines still await and maybe the largest roof in the UK, *Laughing Arthur* (E8), will get a repeat!

Portland West | Portland East | Lulworth | **Swanage** | Devon | Winspit | Hedbury | Dancing Ledge | Guillemot | Cormorant | Blacker's Hole | Fisherman's | Promenade | Cattle Troughs | Boulder Ruckle | Subluminal

ROCK ON

BULGING WITH CLIMBING GEAR

Many shops claim to be climbing specialists.
At Rock On we sell Climbing / Mountaineering
equipment and books and absolutely nothing else.

NOTHING ELSE
Now that's *specialist!*

FIND US AT
Mile End Climbing Wall
Haverfield Road
London E3 5BE
Tel: 0208 981 5066

ALSO AT
Craggy Island
9 Cobbett Park, Moorfield Road
Slyfield Est., Guildford, GU1 1RU
Tel: 01483 565635

www.rockonclimbing.co.uk

randma's Groove (E2 5c) at
ibluminal, Swanage - page 296.

Since 2000 the routes in Dorset have been open for voting on stars and grades on the ROCKFAX web site and this graded list has been based on the many votes we have received. Some additional routes have been added to the list if the online database concensus wasn't sufficient. If you disagree with the list then please let us know by visiting the web site and placing your votes - www.rockfax.com.

The routes are listed in descending grade order and with each route are three tick boxes. You can use these three tick boxes as you see fit but the intention is that box 1 is for clean ascents, box 2 for clean ascents but not first try, and box three is for all other styles!

Trad Routes

1 2 3 E8
♦♦♦ ☐☐☐ Laughing Arthur

1 2 3 E7
♦♦ ☐☐☐ Godfodder
♦♦♦ ☐☐☐ Naked and Savage
♦♦♦ ☐☐☐ Street Fighting Years
♦♦♦ ☐☐☐ Monsters of Rock
♦♦♦ ☐☐☐ Vapour Trail

1 2 3 E6
♦♦ ☐☐☐ Once in the Jungle
♦♦ ☐☐☐ The Jesus Lizard
♦♦♦ ☐☐☐ The Mind Cathedral
♦♦ ☐☐☐ For Whom the Swell Tolls
♦♦ ☐☐☐ Rocket USA
♦♦♦ ☐☐☐ Privateer
♦♦ ☐☐☐ The Drowning Pool
♦♦ ☐☐☐ Centrepiece
♦♦ ☐☐☐ Paparazzi News
♦♦ ☐☐☐ Herman Borg's .....
♦♦♦ ☐☐☐ Relax and Swing
♦♦ ☐☐☐ Hornier Than Thou

1 2 3 E5
♦♦ ☐☐☐ Punks in Power
♦♦ ☐☐☐ Fly Crazy but Free
♦♦ ☐☐☐ Zoolookologie
♦♦♦ ☐☐☐ Swordfish Trombones
♦♦♦ ☐☐☐ The Lean Machine
♦♦ ☐☐☐ World in Action
♦♦♦ ☐☐☐ Polaris
♦♦♦ ☐☐☐ Wall of the Worlds

1 2 3 E4
♦♦ ☐☐☐ Vikings
♦♦♦ ☐☐☐ Mother Africa
♦♦ ☐☐☐ Impending Gleam
♦♦♦ ☐☐☐ Warlord
♦♦ ☐☐☐ Singing Winds
♦♦♦ ☐☐☐ Freeborn Man
♦♦ ☐☐☐ Tensile Groove Test

1 2 3 E3
♦♦♦ ☐☐☐ Limited Edition
♦♦♦ ☐☐☐ Facedancin'
♦♦♦ ☐☐☐ Crystal Voayger
♦♦♦ ☐☐☐ The Ritz
♦♦♦ ☐☐☐ Mickey Mouse
♦♦♦ ☐☐☐ Fathoms
♦♦♦ ☐☐☐ Ocean Boulevard
♦ ☐☐☐ Poetry in Motion
♦♦♦ ☐☐☐ Soul Sacrifice
♦♦ ☐☐☐ Philatus

1 2 3 E2
♦♦♦ ☐☐☐ Ximenes
♦♦♦ ☐☐☐ Buccaneer
♦♦ ☐☐☐ Vortices
♦♦♦ ☐☐☐ Gypsy
♦♦ ☐☐☐ Grandma's Groove
♦♦ ☐☐☐ Oceanid
♦♦ ☐☐☐ Calcitron
♦♦♦ ☐☐☐ Tudor Rose
♦♦ ☐☐☐ The Conger
♦ ☐☐☐ The Tool
♦♦ ☐☐☐ The Peccary
♦♦♦ ☐☐☐ Mars

1 2 3 E1
♦♦ ☐☐☐ Sapphire
♦♦ ☐☐☐ The Laws Traverse
♦♦ ☐☐☐ Strongbow
♦♦ ☐☐☐ Yellow Wall
♦♦ ☐☐☐ Stroof
♦♦ ☐☐☐ Sinbad
♦♦♦ ☐☐☐ Elysium
♦♦ ☐☐☐ Billy Pigg
♦ ☐☐☐ Rattler
♦♦ ☐☐☐ Eskimo Nell
♦♦ ☐☐☐ The Spook

1 2 3 HVS
♦♦♦ ☐☐☐ Thunderball
♦♦ ☐☐☐ The Golden Fleece
♦ ☐☐☐ Peacemaker
♦ ☐☐☐ Director's Groove
♦ ☐☐☐ Thunder Groove
♦♦♦ ☐☐☐ Jo
♦♦♦ ☐☐☐ Lightning Wall
♦♦♦ ☐☐☐ Behemoth
♦♦♦ ☐☐☐ Finale Groove
♦ ☐☐☐ Astrid
♦♦ ☐☐☐ Aventura
♦ ☐☐☐ Troubled Waters
♦ ☐☐☐ Ledgend Direct

1 2 3 VS
♦♦ ☐☐☐ Revelation Chimney
♦ ☐☐☐ Baboon
♦♦ ☐☐☐ Tatra
♦♦ ☐☐☐ Isis
♦ ☐☐☐ Botany Bay
♦♦♦ ☐☐☐ Freda
♦♦ ☐☐☐ Tensor II
♦ ☐☐☐ The Heidelberg Creature
♦♦♦ ☐☐☐ Benny
♦ ☐☐☐ Black Sunshine
♦ ☐☐☐ Spreadeagle
♦ ☐☐☐ Silhouette Arete
♦♦ ☐☐☐ Old Faithful
♦♦ ☐☐☐ Batt Crack
♦ ☐☐☐ Bunney's Wall
♦ ☐☐☐ Slip Road
♦♦ ☐☐☐ Hangover

1 2 3 HS
♦♦ ☐☐☐ Balcony
♦ ☐☐☐ Bottomless Buttress
♦ ☐☐☐ Thompson's Chimney
♦♦ ☐☐☐ Zig-Zag

1 2 3 Sev
♦♦ ☑☐☐ First Corner
♦♦ ☑☐☐ Second Corner
♦♦♦ ☐☐☐ Avernus

1 2 3 VDiff
♦ ☐☐☐ Chockney

Sport Routes

1 2 3 8a+
♦♦♦ ☐☐☐ Infinite Gravity
♦♦ ☐☐☐ Event Horizon
♦♦♦ ☐☐☐ Palace of the Brine

1 2 3 8a
♦♦♦ ☐☐☐ Burn Hollywood, Burn
♦♦♦ ☐☐☐ Adrenochrome
♦♦♦ ☐☐☐ Hell's Darker Chambers
♦♦♦ ☐☐☐ Haka Pereperu
♦♦♦ ☐☐☐ Solid State Logic

1 2 3 7c+
♦♦♦ ☐☐☐ The Schwarzechild Radius
♦♦♦ ☐☐☐ Total Seizure
♦♦♦ ☐☐☐ Drunken Butterfly
♦♦♦ ☐☐☐ Temple Redneck

1 2 3 7c
♦♦ ☐☐☐ Legendary Shadows
♦♦♦ ☐☐☐ Mark of the Beest
♦♦ ☐☐☐ Atonement
♦♦ ☐☐☐ The Futurist 2002
♦♦ ☐☐☐ Liquid Steel
♦♦ ☐☐☐ Rise of the Robots

The strenuous and tricky Sureshot (6c) at Hedbury Quarry - *page 212. Photo: Mark Glaister*

1 2 3 **7b+**
- ◆◆◆ ☐☐☐ The Gates of Greyskull
- ◆◆ ☐☐☐ Lunacy Booth
- ◆◆◆ ☐☐☐ Waves Become Wings
- ◆◆ ☐☐☐ Bust ya' Boiler
- ◆◆ ☐☐☐ Fat Chance Hotel
- ◆◆ ☐☐☐ Violent Breed

1 2 3 **7b**
- ◆◆ ☐☐☐ Crest of a Wave
- ◆◆ ☐☐☐ Avenging the Halsewell
- ◆◆ ☐☐☐ Lulworth Arms Treaty
- ◆◆◆ ☐☐☐ Tessellations
- ◆◆◆ ☐☐☐ Spacewalk
- ◆ ☐☐☐ A Short Story About Power
- ◆◆ ☐☐☐ Down in the Sewer
- ◆◆◆ ☐☐☐ Birth Pains of New nations
- ◆◆◆ ☐☐☐ Slave to the Cave
- ◆◆ ☐☐☐ Animal Magnetism
- ◆◆ ☐☐☐ Prophets of Rage

1 2 3 **7a+**
- ◆◆◆ ☐☐☐ Riding to Babylon
- ◆◆ ☐☐☐ The Pump will Tear us Apart
- ◆ ☐☐☐ Double or Quits
- ◆◆◆ ☐☐☐ Mariner's Garveyard
- ◆ ☐☐☐ Mexican Wave

1 2 3 **7a**
- ◆◆ ☐☐☐ Sugar Ray
- ◆◆◆ ☐☐☐ Horny Lil' Devil
- ◆◆ ☐☐☐ The Wonders of Wallkraft
- ◆◆ ☐☐☐ Mr Choo Choo
- ◆◆ ☐☐☐ Peppercorn Rate

1 2 3 **6c+**
- ◆◆ ☐☐☐ Hieronymous GBH
- ◆ ☐☐☐ Pump Me Tenderly
- ◆◆ ☐☐☐ Haunted by a Million Screams
- ◆◆ ☐☐☐ Red Rain
- ◆ ☐☐☐ Idiot Joy Showland
- ◆ ☐☐☐ Disco's Out, Murder's In

1 2 3 **6c**
- ◆◆ ☐☐☐ Queen Anne's Men
- ◆ ☐☐☐ Bad Day
- ◆ ☐☐☐ Daylight Robbery
- ◆◆ ☐☐☐ Gangster Lean
- ◆◆ ☐☐☐ Lucretia, My Reflection
- ◆◆ ☐☐☐ Hangs Like a Dead Man
- ◆ ☐☐☐ House Nation
- ◆ ☐☐☐ Sureshot

1 2 3 **6b+**
- ◆ ☐☐☐ Peprpetual State of Confusion
- ◆◆ ☐☐☐ Titter ye Not Mrs!
- ◆ ☐☐☐ Wall of Feedback
- ◆ ☐☐☐ Skinhead Clash
- ◆◆ ☐☐☐ Born Again
- ◆◆ ☐☐☐ Rambling Moses ....
- ◆◆ ☐☐☐ Slopin' and Hopin'

1 2 3 **6b**
- ◆◆ ☐☐☐ Jumping the Gun
- ◆ ☐☐☐ Squalid Walid
- ◆ ☐☐☐ Of Mice and Men

1 2 3 **6a+**
- ◆ ☐☐☐ Think About It
- ◆ ☐☐☐ Ammonitemare
- ◆◆ ☐☐☐ Stone Mason
- ☐☐☐ Moves for the Masses
- ◆ ☐☐☐ Ideal World
- ◆ ☐☐☐ All Fall Down

1 2 3 **6a**
- ◆ ☐☐☐ Chicago Pipe Dreaming
- ◆ ☐☐☐ Date with a Frog
- ◆ ☐☐☐ The Flail Trail

1 2 3 **5+**
- ◆ ☐☐☐ Borra Ring
- ◆ ☐☐☐ John Craven's Willy Warmer
- ◆ ☐☐☐ New Age, New Style

1 2 3 **5**
- ◆ ☐☐☐ So Naughty

1 2 3 **4+**
- ◆ ☐☐☐ Tethered by Gravity

Portland West | Portland East | Lulworth | **Swanage** | Devon
Winspit | Hedbury | Dancing Ledge | Guillemot | Cormorant | Blacker's Hole | Fisherman's | Promenade | Cattle Troughs | Boulder Ruckle | Subluminal

SWANAGE

CRAG	Page	Sport Routes				Trad Routes				Boulder Problem			
		up to 4+	5 to 6a+	6b to 7a	7a+ up	up to S	HS to HVS	E1 to E3	E4 up	up to V0	V0+ to V2	V3 to V6	V7 u
Winspit Quarry	204	1	14	22	12								
Hedbury Quarry	210	4	5	12	6		1		9				
Dancing Ledge	218		11	39	27				1			1	1
Guillemot	228						7	11	13				
Cormorant Ledge	234					2	2						
Blacker's Hole	236			3	8		3	6	22				
Fisherman's Ledge	244			3		2	6	39	42				
The Promenade	258		5	20	47		5	5	3		5		2
Cattle Troughs	268					7	8	7	4				
Boulder Ruckle	274					1	20	42	37				
Subluminal	292					14	26	17	8				

Approach walk	Sunshine or shade	Access	Sheltered	Tidal	Other	Best routes	Summary
20 min	Mostly all day sun	Restrictions	Sheltered			Sport	A sport climbing quarry with many great technical wall climbs. More sheltered from the wind than other Swanage crags. Easy access and level base make Winspit one of the few family-friendly locations at Swanage. **ACCESS** - There is no established access and climbing is not officially allowed. You may be asked to leave.
30 min	Mostly all day sun	Birds	Sheltered			Sport	Hedbury consists of a sheltered sport quarry, which is quieter than the nearby Dancing Ledge, which contrasts dramatically with the two most adventurous cliffs at Swanage situated just around the corner - big hard routes which are mostly unrepeated. **RESTRICTIONS** - No climbing on Hedbury Big Cove and Smokey Hole from 1 March to 31 July.
25 min	Mostly all day sun		Sheltered			Sport	One of the most popular cliffs at Swanage. A sport climbing quarry and some steeper routes on the sea-level roofs. Easy access and non-tidal. Often busy and popular with beginners.
25 min	All day sun	Birds			Abseil in, Trad		A huge wall with several of the longest routes at Swanage. Abseil approaches required to a non-tidal boulder beach. More reasonable finishes than other Swanage cliffs and it is never busy although most people will head for the same few routes. **RESTRICTIONS** - No climbing from 1 March to 31 July.
25 min	All day sun	Birds	Tidal		Abseil in, Trad		A long and remote section of cliff that has a few classics in the relatively easy grades. Only four routes covered in this book. Abseil approaches necessary. **RESTRICTIONS** - No climbing from 1 March to 31 July.
45 min	Mostly all day sun	Birds			Abseil in, Trad		A varied area with a huge and spectacular cave home to the most impressive routes in Dorset. Also a sport quarry (in need of re-gearing) and trad wall with some good hard routes. A long walk in and exposed to rough seas. **RESTRICTIONS** - No climbing on the Polaris Area and in the Great Cave from 1 March to 31 July.
40 min	All day sun				Abseil in, DWS		A superb and varied area with the best deep water soloing spot in Dorset in Conner Cove. Also has one magnificent cave with several semi-sport roof climbs. Many more great trad routes all with easy access. A long walk in and exposed to rough seas.
30 min	All day sun					Sport	The best of the sport climbing crags at Swanage although it is mostly routes in the higher grades. Steep bulging walls with some short and intense climbs. Easy approach and access via non-tidal ledge.
25 min	All day sun				Abseil in, Trad		Two contrasting walls near a couple of rock amphitheatres. One is a great beginner's area the other has some steep hard routes. Escape is easy and routes mostly start from a non-tidal ledge. Abseil approach.
10 min to 25 min	All day sun	Birds	Tidal		Abseil in, Trad		The most extensive section of Swanage which has major classic routes across the grades. It is a big and commiting area with free-hanging abseil approaches and loose top-outs being the norm. Keep away in rough conditions. **RESTRICTIONS** - Several areas restricted because of nesting birds from 1 March to 31 July - check sector notes.
10 min	All day sun				Abseil in, Trad		A great area to sample Swanage. Short routes above a good ledge and mostly at very reasonable grades. Quick and easy access from the car park. Also includes the more atmospheric Black Zawn.

Summary

Subterminal | Boulder Ruckle | Cattle Troughs | Promenade | Fisherman's | Blacker's Hole | Cormorant | Guillemot | Dancing Ledge | Hedbury | Winspit | Devon | Swanage | Portland East | Portland West | Lulworth

WINSPIT QUARRY

The introduction of sport climbing in this area has transformed Winspit Quarry into a very pleasant and sheltered climber's playground. It has an excellent set of steep routes, across the grade range, mostly on positive square-cut holds and in-cuts. There is some friable rock but most of this is at the very top of the crags and is avoided by the placement of the lower-offs below this band. One of Winspit's greatest attractions is its micro-climate, this often means that climbing is possible here when conditions are poor elsewhere. Should the sea be rough and access dangerous to the main cliffs, Winspit is a good alternative, being set well back and sheltered from southerly gales. The style of the climbs ranges from some extremely steep roof routes to more intricate face climbing but metre for metre, the routes pack in the moves whatever their grade or style.

The quarry is divided into two halves enclosing a rocky cove, which is a popular picnic and sunbathing spot throughout the year, making this one of the better family-friendly cragging venues in the Swanage area.

ACCESS

Winspit Quarry is on private land and climbing is not allowed. If you go climbing here you may well be asked to leave. If this does occur, please leave without making any fuss so as not to jeopardise any future access negotiations. Winspit is only included in this book for completeness.

APPROACH

Winspit Quarry is situated 1.5km south of Worth Matravers and is reached by a pleasant stroll down a picturesque valley. Park in the main car park which is situated on the right as you enter the village. The approach path starts down a lane below the village pond.

CONDITIONS

The Quarryman's Wall/South Face have the best climbing with both faces receiving plenty of sun and the Quarryman's Wall in particular gets sun until late in the day. It is very sheltered and suffers hardly any seepage. The steep faces offer dry climbing in light rain especially if the wind is blowing from the east or north. The very back of the Quarryman's Wall is sheltered from southerly gales. In showery conditions there are plenty of caves that provide shelter in the event of sudden downpours.

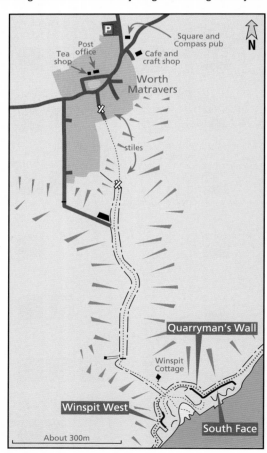

through arch on left

Portland West
Portland East
Lulworth
Swanage
Devon
Winspit
Hedbury
Dancing Ledge
Guillemot
Cormorant
Blacker's Hole
Fisherman's
Promenade
Cattle Troughs
Boulder Ruckle
Subliminal

WINSPIT WEST QUARRY

Winspit West is the least attractive of the quarries and is characterised by some impressive man-made caves and a good number of square-cut overhangs. Much of the rock should be treated with care.
APPROACH - On entering the quarry, head right towards some old buildings at the foot of the wall.

❶ The Skin Room . . . 🔲🔲🔲 **7a+**
12m. Steep and powerful climbing but dangerously loose.
FA. Jamie Hannant 10.5.2003

❷ Think About It. . . . 🔲🔲🔲 **6a+**
12m. The wall and groove just left of the through cave. The crux is at the top and is a bit on the reachy side. Some suspect holds by the third bolt.
FA. Kevin Turner 1977

❸ Things That Make You Go Hmmmm...
. . . . 🔲🔲🔲 **6c**
12m. A slightly friable route up the steep corner above the through cave. The start has lost a hold which has pushed the grade up a notch.
FA. Pete Oxley 22.9.91

❹ Restless Heart . . . . . . 🔲🔲 **6b+**
14m. The wall right of the corner is nicely sustained with good climbing and a no-hands rest in the niche.
FA. Mike Robertson 4.12.93

❺ Any Old Time . . . . . . 🔲🔲🔲 **6b**
14m. Aim for the upper arete which is followed on its right-hand side. Only short but featuring some exposed positions once on the arete.
FA. Mike Robertson 11.8.93

❻ Post-Coital Snooze 🔲🔲🔲 **6a**
14m. The cracks in the right wall of the corner. An honorary slate climb but without any positive footholds and it is very cruxy. This route has many varied opinions on its grade but the majority plumped for the upgrade from 5+.
FA. Mike Robertson 18.3.94

The next line of bolts out of the small quarried cave is a project.

❼ Book 3 . . . . 🔲🔲 **7a**
11m. The left side of the twin caves. Escapable climbing.
FA. Matt King 2003

❽ The Fantastic Mr Faz. . . . . 🔲 **6a+**
11m. Poor and loose climbing up the central pillar, moving right to a lower-off.
FA. Jamie Hannant 2003

❾ Idiot Village. . . . . 🔲🔲 **6a+**
11m. Climb the large blocky overhangs to the right of a deep cave. A little careful route-finding reduces the thuggery and once over the first roof the rest is straight forward - so long as you can jam.
FA. Mike Robertson 11.12.93

QUARRYMAN'S WALL

❶ The Genius of S.K. . . . . [＿＿＿＿] 6a
20m. The groove at the left-hand end of the wall has some poor rock and is high in the grade. A poor route.
FA. Mike Robertson 13.5.94

❷ Avenging the Halsewell 🔲🔳 [＿＿＿＿] 7b
20m. A strenuous outing up a series of roofs with three hard sections and a hard-to-spot no-hands rest. Now a popular test-piece. Excellent. A bit tougher (even 7b+) for the short.
FA. Pete Oxley 30.7.88

❸ Ancient Order of Freemarblers
. . . . 🔲🔳 [＿＿＿＿] 7a
20m. Steep stamina climbing following a finger-crack at half-height which is gained via a balancy yet powerful leftward pull low down. *Photo page 195.*
FA. Pete Oxley 13.11.87

❹ Billy Winspit . . . . . 🔲🔳🔳 [＿＿＿＿] 7a+
20m. A relatively easy lower wall and flake leads to a hands-off rest. The next move is hard and is very reach-dependent. The route has received various grades for those less than 6 feet tall ranging from 7c+ to a steady 7a+! Safe to say it won't be a route high on the list of those who are vertically challenged.
FA. Steve Taylor 28.11.93

❺ Peppercorn Rate . . . . . 🔲🔳 [＿＿＿＿] 7a
20m. A quality pitch, tough and unyielding, with a pumpy top wall and a blind crack.
FA. Pete Oxley 23.12.87

❻ Smiling Assassin . . . . [＿＿＿＿] 7a+
20m. The line just left of the arete is an eliminate in nature, it is easy to drift off the line.
FA. Matt King 2003

❼ So Naughty . . . . 🔳 [＿＿＿＿] 5
20m. A popular outing that has shed a hold on the crux but is still a grade 5 if a move right is made at the third bolt (**6a+** if taken direct). Start up the arete then make a tricky move into the corner which is followed to the top.
FA. Carol Robertson 5.12.93. The first new route from one of the local female climbers.

❽ Insanely Yours . . . . . . 🔲🔳 [＿＿＿＿] 7a
20m. A short route which is easier for the tall. The arete is off limits at this grade.
FA. Mike Robertson 20.3.94

❾ Jargon Eater . . . . 🔲🔳 [＿＿＿＿] 6b
20m. At the roof, move left and finish with difficulty.
FA. Nigel Coe, Tim Dunsby 20.12.87 retrobolted by Matt King 2003.

❿ Unseen Ripples of the Pebble 🔳 [＿＿＿＿] 6a+
20m. Nice climbing up the well-bolted crack-line.
FA. Nigel Coe, Pete Oxley 31.12.87 retrobolted by Matt King 2003.

⓫ Gallows' Gore . . . . . . 🔲🔳 [＿＿＿＿] 7a
20m. Good climbing on some fine rock, with a boulder problem crux, starting at the right edge of the cave.
FA. Pete Oxley 3.1.88

⓬ Red Rain . . . . 🔲🔳 [＿＿＿＿] 6c+
20m. A great route; nicely sustained and varied, featuring a tricky no-hands rest and, near the top, one of the best finger locks in the world.
FA. Pete Oxley 3.1.88

⓭ Queen Anne's Men . . . 🔲🔳 [＿＿＿＿] 6c
20m. Class climbing with a definite crux section. Although the wall beneath the crux has lost a side-pull there is no change in the overall grade. Reaching the lower-off is a touch bold.
FA. Pete Oxley 31.12.87

⓮ Exuberance . . . . . 🔲🔳🔳 [＿＿＿＿] 7a
20m. A good outing for the ambitious boulderer. Steady climbing to a cruxy move close to the top.
FA. Mike Robertson 5.8.93

⓯ Stone Mason . . . . 🔲🔳 [＿＿＿＿] 6a+
20m. A fun, well-travelled pitch up the disjointed crack-line with the hardest bit near to the top where a hand jam assists progress at a tricky crack. *Photo page 210.*
FA. Tim Dunsby 20.12.87

⓰ Resin Devotion . . . . 🔳 [＿＿＿＿] 6a
20m. Climb just right of a groove/corner.
FA. Mike Robertson 13.5.94

⓱ Insect Graveyard . . . . 🔲🔳 [＿＿＿＿] 6b
20m. The centre of the wall provides a nicely sustained pitch that has shed most of its loose holds.
FA. Mike Robertson 5.8.93

⓲ Know What I Mean Pal . . . 🔳 [＿＿＿＿] 6a
20m. An enjoyable exercise up the right-hand side of the wall.
FA. Mike Robertson 5.11.93

Cave gives useful shelter in rain

19 **Playtime with Playtex** . . . . 6c+
20m. The ubiquitous mid-height traverse from *Know What I Mean Pal* to *Gallows' Gore*.
FA. Pete Oxley 30.7.94

20 **Tom's Patience** 4
20m. The once dirty flowstone groove now gives a useful pitch at the grade.
FA. Matt King 2003

21 **Pump Me Tenderly** . . . 6c+
20m. There is only one hard move but it's at the top. A heel-hook helps, but the move can be done without.
FA. Mike Robertson 9.11.91

22 **Nine Years Absence** 6a
16m. Climb the wall to the right of the corner. Only short but worthwhile and enjoyable
FA. Mike Robertson 1.9.93

QUARRYMAN'S WALL

The Quarryman's Wall is the most popular section at Winspit and is a very reliable venue being set well back from the sea and extremely sheltered from the wind. The routes are on good rock and are very clean and well bolted. The climbs furthest inland are steep, whilst the rest are vertical. This is an excellent place for teams of mixed abilities and a good venue to head for if sea conditions prevent access elsewhere.

APPROACH - On entering the quarry bear left towards the wall which is ahead of you to the left of the track.

Vixen Bitch From Hell

SOUTH FACE

The South Face of Winspit Quarry has become more popular recently after the addition of a few new lines. Most of the better routes are steep and powerful, crossing the low level roof stacks before finishing up the vertical headwall. A few of the starts utilise cairns to reach the first holds and these often need rebuilding. Although there are no lower grade lines, the area has some excellent grade 7s.
The face is well-sheltered and gets lots of sun.
APPROACH - On entering the quarry bear left and continue around the corner from the Quarryman's Wall.

1 The Vixen Bitch from Hell
. . . . 🎯🏞️🎞️ B ☐ **7a+**
20m. A last move that will be dynamic for some. Old bolts.
FA. Mike Robertson 31.7.93

2 Agonies of a Dying Mind 🎯🏞️ ☐ **7a**
20m. A powerful start and a friable finish. The start gives a good **V5** problem.
FA. Mike Robertson 4.3.93

3 Dick Dastardly. . . . 🎯🏞️🎞️ ☐ **7a+**
20m. A tricky route that is difficult to on-sight. There are only two or three hard moves, but they are tough.
FA. Mike Robertson 5.12.93

4 Lips of a Stranger . 🎯🏞️🎞️ ☐ **6c+**
20m. Surprisingly good moves over the shattered roof and up the groove.
FA. Mike Robertson 4.12.93

5 Fragile Mind . . . . 🎯🏞️ ☐ **6c+**
20m. The steep left-hand line up the impressive crack. Take care with a couple of holds at the start.
FA. Rob Kennard 2003

6 Card of Hearts. . . . 🎯🏞️🏞️ ☐ **7a+**
20m. More strenuous stuff taking the right-hand bolt-line after starting up *Fragile Mind*, with a technical bridging finale.
FA. Rob Kennard 2004

7 Chrissy . . . . 🎯🎞️ ☐ **6c**
20m. A nice thuggy start off a wobbly jug leads to a testing mid section and some very fine bridging in the groove. Excellent and reasonably committing; the best on this wall.
FA. Mike Robertson 31.7.93

8 Revhead's Hi-roller 🎯🏞️🎞️ ☐ **7b**
20m. A steep start leads to the exposed finishing arete.
FA. Pete Oxley 5.6.94. Named after Mark Higgs' incredible car crash.

9 Mackerel . . . . 🎯 ☐ **5**
16m. The groove and flowstone to a chain.
FA. Matt King 2003

Portland West
Portland East
Lulworth
Swanage
Devon
Winspit
Hedbury
Dancing Ledge
Guillemot
Cormorant
Blacker's Hole
Fisherman's
Promenade
Cattle Troughs
Ruckle
Boulder
Subliminal

10 Knickerless Crutches . . . . . 🗗🗗 ⬜ 6b+
16m. The thin crack, with one tricky move that is very run out.
FA. Mike Robertson 4.12.93

11 Damnation Game . . . . . 🗗🗗🗗 ⬜ 7a+
20m. A classy and sustained pitch to the left of the big cave.
FA. Mike Robertson 28.11.93

12 Frightened by the Sun . 🗗🗗🗗 ⬜ 7b+
20m. Make a difficult start to gain wild moves around the lip of the large roof. Good wall climbing finishes this spectacular line.
FA. Rich White 2003

13 Disbelief Suspended 🗗🗗🗗🗗 ⬜ 7c
20m. The same difficult start as *Frightened by the Sun* to a very spectacular roof. Finish up the wall above, joining *Frightened by the Sun*. Also can be finished out right - better and harder.
FA. Rob Kennard 2003 Right-hand finish Pete Oxley 2004

The line of bolts above the first cairn is a project (8a).

14 Lunacy Booth . . . . 🗗🗗🗗🗗 ⬜ 7b+
20m. An entertaining, big and burly roof climb starting from a pile of boulders in the centre of the cave. A good knee-bar above the large roof gives a quick hands-off rest. The first bolt might need to be stick-clipped by the short.
FA. Pete Oxley 5.6.94

15 Nosey . . . . 🗗 ⬜ 6a+
14m. A short pitch with a bold finish.
FA. Mike Robertson 12.11.93

16 Rampant Love Jugs . . 🗗🗗🗗 ⬜ 6a+
20m. Starts in the dip 8m right of *Nosey*. Highly enjoyable. No piling rocks under the start - jumping is the whole point of the route name!!
FA. Mike Robertson 12.11.93

The last two routes are over in the far corner of the quarry, above a 'through cave'.

17 Gorilla Tactics . . . . . . 🗗🗗 ⬜ 6c
20m. Good climbing but on very unstable rock.
FA. Mike Robertson 5.11.93

18 Flashheart Direct . . . . Ⓑ ⬜ 6b
20m. The buttress right of the cave entrance. Finish above the cave in a good position. The bolts are said to be fine but they are old.
FA. Mike Robertson 7.8.93. Includes a section of 'Born to Be Free', G.Jeffries 1989.

The mid-grade sport climbing at Winspit Quarry and nearby Hedbury and Dancing Ledge Quarries is some of the most popular and best sheltered in the south of England. Rob Kennard on *Stone Mason* (6a+) at Winspit - *page 206*. Photo: Mark Glaister

HEDBURY and SMOKEY HOLE

The Hedbury and Smokey Hole area encompasses four very different crags to the west of Dancing Ledge. The main interest for most climbers will be Hedbury Quarry which is like a more compact version of the main quarry at Dancing Ledge with similar style routes but it is usually much quieter. The rock here is steep and solid and dotted with some strange flowstone holds. It is a good place for an afternoon's sport climbing in winter, getting lots of sun and located away from the sea. Just around the corner from Hedbury Quarry, and in complete contrast, is the immense Hedbury Big Cove. Huge leaning walls, massive overhangs, slightly unstable rock and big grade trad routes make this a place for maximum intimidation and atmosphere - and all this straight above the sea. Smokey Hole, on the other hand, is more solid and less steep than The Big Cove but has a similar set of high quality, high grade trad routes in a sensational setting. Most of the routes in the Big Cove and Smokey Hole have had few repeats but their position as some of the most demanding challenges at Swanage is assured and they certainly deserve more traffic. Topmast Quarry has three steep and sheltered sport routes.

ACCESS
All the routes on Hedbury Big Cove and Smokey Hole are restricted because of nesting birds. No climbing from 1st March to 31st July.

APPROACH
See the approach for Dancing Ledge on page 218.
For Hedbury Quarry and Big Cove (Left) - Once on the coast path, above Dancing Ledge, turn right (looking out) and follow it for 800m over a gentle hill. At a stile drop down a ridge path on the left into a huge open quarry with a

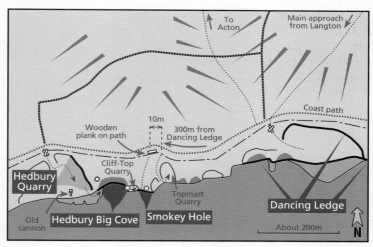

large cannon in its base. The quarry routes are on the wall on the left (looking out). To gain Hedbury Big Cove drop down some rock steps to a sea level ledge that leads left (looking out) into a cave.
For Big Cove (Right) and Smokey Hole - See page 216.

TIDES
All routes are non-tidal but keep away from The Big Cove or Smokey Hole in rough seas.

CONDITIONS
The central routes in the quarry have a waterfall running down them in winter but the rest are seepage-free and climbable all year round. It can get very hot in summer. The Big Cove and Smokey Hole both face south and hence receive lots of sun and are relatively unaffected by seepage, but keep away in wilder conditions.

THE QUARRY

Like many of the smaller sports crags in the area, Hedbury Quarry has now become a well-frequented venue and to be here on your own is a rare occurence. Most of the rock is good and the routes often pumpy. There is a very wide range of grades and The Quarry now has a degree of celebrity being home to the UK's first grade 1 sport route!
APPROACH - The climbable section of The Quarry is the first wall on the left as you enter it.

1 Tethered by Gravity . . . . . . 4+
12m. Great value for the grade. Climb just right of the blunt left-slanting arete, via a wide selection of large foot and hand-holds all the way up.
FA. Steve Taylor 12.3.94

2 Goddam Sexual Tyrannosaurus
. 5+
12m. A touch fluttery and getting polished which is good going for a route that gets no stars.
FA. Mark Williams 12.3.94

3 Ammonitemare. . . 6a+
10m. Sustained, technical, and hard for the grade.
FA. Steve Taylor 17.10.93

4 Of Mice and Men 6b
10m. The corner line has some thin moves high up. Don't get sand-bagged by the tempting ledge out right on the crux.
FA. Mike Robertson 18.3.94

5 Bad Day 6c
12m. Good technical climbing. A nice contrast to *Hangs Like a Dead Man*. The line is slightly left of the bolts.
FA. Steve Taylor 9.6.91

6 Moves for the Masses 6a+
12m. Weird and wonderful flowstone. A nice route with technical moves on small crimps. The direct start is called **One More Cheese Sarnie** and goes at **6c**.
FA. Pete Oxley 13.10.90. Direct start by James Mittens.

7 Hangs Like a Dead Man 6c
13m. A steep and popular route. Tricky moves to a hanging spike are the meat of the route.
FA. Pete Oxley 7.3.91

8 Under Starters Orders/
Realm of Radical Cool . . . 7a+
14m. The slight bulging groove left of *Jumping The Gun* to moves rightwards crossing *Jumping the Gun* to finish up rightwards.
FA. Pete Oxley 2004. FA. (RoRC) Mike Robertson 18.3.94

9 Jumping the Gun 6b
15m. The big diagonal flake is a delight in good conditions but unpleasantly slick if at all greasy. Not one for an unsure second as the start is tough and protection on the blunt end not good.
Photo page 217.
FA. Pete Oxley 7.3.91

10 Mouth Breather . . . 7c
15m. Hard and painful undercutting through the roof. A good hard testpiece for The Quarry.
FA. Pete Oxley 9.5.91

11 Sureshot 6c
15m. The big corner is often wet, but when dry is very good.
Photo page 201.
FA. Pete Oxley 8.10.90

12 Sexy Beast. 7a
15m. The striking leftward-slanting crack to the finish of *Sureshot* on good rock.
FA. Pete Oxley 2004

13 Alice In Pumpland . . . 7a
10m. A short lived teaser taking the appealing steep crack over the roof.
FA. Pete Oxley 2004

Portland West
Portland East
Lulworth
Swanage
Devon
Winspit
Hedbury
Dancing Ledge
Guillemot
Cormorant
Blacker's Hole
Fisherman's
Promenade
Cattle Troughs
Boulder Ruckle
Subluminal

⑭ Cinderella's Big Score

.... 🔲🔲🔲🔲 🔲 **7c**

16m. Since the loss of a big spike, the route is now an archetypal fitness test with a fierce crux entering the lower groove and a technical bulge to finish. One of the best hard quarry routes when dry.
FA. Pete Oxley 6.5.91

⑮ It Can't be Denied . 🔲🔲🔲 🔲 **7b**

16m. A really good short power endurance effort which joins *Cinderella....* near the top. A standing start off a boulder pile to reach the lip of the first roof makes it 7b, or climb from the back of the roof from the ground at 7b+.
FA. Mike Robertson 22.10.94. Direct by Pete Oxley 11.94

⑯ Glue Crux Clan ...... 🔲🔲 🔲 **6c**

16m. A fine direct pitch with interesting moves all the way to the last bolt, but especially in the first 5m.
FA. Pete Oxley 26.9.90

⑰ Produced by Fred Quimby

.... 🔲🔲 🔲 **6b**

16m. An easier diagonal start to *Glue Crux Clan* but still with a tough finish.
FA. Mike Robertson 29.6.91

⑱ Don's Long Gone .... 🔲🔲 🔲 **6b+**

12m. The roof crack. Good steep fun.
FA. Tim Dunsby 20.4.92

⑲ Mindless Optimism ...... 🔲 🔲 **6b+**

16m. The short upper arete. Good moves via a stuck-on finger flakes on the very lip of the arete.
FA. Mike Robertson 29.6.91

⑳ New Age, New Style .. 🔲🔲 🔲 **5+**

15m. Slabby and with a distinct crux.
FA. Jim Titt 2004

㉑ Very Ordinary Route ..... 🔲 🔲 **1**

14m. Yes a grade 1! The left-hand line in the blocky groove.
FA. Jim Titt 2004

㉒ Another Contribution ..... 🔲 🔲 **2**

15m. The righthand line in the blocky groove.
FA. Jim Titt 2004

㉓ Moral Flexibility .... 🔲 🔲 **5**

14m. The next line on the right, with a good finish.
FA. Jim Titt 2004

㉔ Sea View .... 🔲 🔲 **3**

14m. The far right line, closest to the cliff edge. A tough finish.
FA. Jim Titt 2004

Lots of sun / 30 min / Steep

Hedbury Quarry

Belay Stake

Pull out on pre-placed rope from fence post

Approach to ledge down ledges from quarry

Ledge

❶ Under the Sky, Above the Sea
. . . . **E5 6b**
An obvious challenge tackling the gymnastic roof crack above the centre of the platform. Start just right of a gap.
1) 6b, 18m. Follow a diagonal crack rightwards to a huge pedestal block. Power through the roof crack (small Friends) and belay on a slab above.
2) 5a, 12m. Climb the easy groove and step right to a finish as for *Sheffield Uber Alles* (thread).
FA. Martin Crocker 27.8.95

❷ Sheffield Uber Alles . . . **E6 6b**
25m. A top pump-out up a very overhanging wall giving sensational climbing. Start 8m right of the gap, at a short groove and (thread) at 5m. The first half is very steep (2 pegs) and leads to an open, left-hand groove. From halfway up this, a juggy line of left-trending flakes leads to the top. It has been done without clipping the single bolt.
FA. Pete Oxley 8.10.90. Without clipping the bolt - Martin Crocker 28.8.95

❸ The Jesus Lizard **E6 6b**
25m. Another awesome climb which crosses even steeper ground than *Sheffield Uber Alles*. A big rack is needed. Start 3m right of *Sheffield Uber Alles* and climb a slight prow (2 pegs) into another open groove. Continue up the right-hand wall of a corner (peg) to a steep set of left-trending flakes parallel to *Sheffield Uber Alles*. Follow these to finish. 2 bolts still in place.
FA. Pete Oxley 24.3.91. Without clipping the bolts - Martin Crocker 27.8.95

THE BIG COVE
This is a very impressive arena with some huge, overhanging routes on often suspect rock. The routes are significantly more adventurous than anything else in this guidebook and the lines which the climbs take are utterly gobsmacking. The big traverse of *Nowhere to Run* is the south coast's answer to *The Scoop* on Strone Ulladale.
For those who find the climbing too intimidating, this is a great place to hang out on a hot day and sunbathe with a private swimming spot in the cove to cool down in.
TIDES - All routes start above high tide but keep away in rough seas when the place could be a bit too exciting!
APPROACH - Routes 1 to 4 are easily accessible from Hedbury Quarry by dropping down some rock ledges to gain a rock platform that stretches across to the sea cave.
⊖ RESTRICTION - No climbing 1 March to 31 July because of nesting birds.

❹ Once in the Jungle **E6 6b**
Mercilessly steep climbing, up a huge arching line, on the left-hand side of the main cave. A heart-stopping line that is very committing. Start from the right-hand end of the access ledge.
1) 6b, 25m. Climb a short groove (thread) and from jugs swing right (thread) to a 'chert' nose. Thug through bulging rock above to reach a rising handrail. This leads to a niche then power out right to a rest on a white projection. Traverse leftwards (peg) and move up and left over a bulge to a foothold stance in an open groove.
2) 6a, 25m. Climb a slab diagonally right and continue to where it disappears between massive roofs (peg). Keep low until a bold swing right around a rib leads to a right-facing corner. Trend right up the corner to a broken finish. Belay and pull-out on a rope, pre-placed from the fence posts.
FA. Martin Crocker, Mike Robertson 31.8.96

Belay on fence post

Cliff-Top Quarry

Approach to Quarry

6

7

A

5

5

Smokey Hole →

APPROACH (Routes 5 to 7) - *The Cliff-Top Quarry is situated 50m further on from the open-cast Topmast Quarry, which in turn is 300m further on from Dancing Ledge. The abseil point is from the quarryman's thread in the right-hand (looking out) side of the cave. This leads to a ledge on the fault-line, just outside the cove and 15m above the sea.*

5 Nowhere to Run 　　　　　　　　**E6 6b**
One of the biggest adventure challenges in the area. A fantastic voyage crossing the entire cove from right to left at roughly half height. Massive commitment, huge exposure and some loose rock. Make sure you choose a long summer day since you will need plenty of time to complete the trip.
1) 6a, 27m. Traverse the break past a corner. Continue along a shelf in the fault until a drop down, and hand traverse, leads to a good stance on the lip of the cave. Peg and Friend belay.
2) 6a, 15m. Traverse easily left until squeezed by steep rock forcing a strenuous link (2 threads and a peg) to a superb stance on a perched slab in the centre of the cove. Peg, thread and nut belay.
3) 5c, 10m. Continue left with a tricky move to gain a slab. Follow this more easily to belay at its end. Nut and Friend belay.
4) 6b, 28m. Climb down left to a thread jug then finger traverse left to a short groove. Ascend the groove and pass two 'leg-over' breaks leftwards, before making breath-taking moves left (peg) and over a bulge to gain an open groove. (Possible stance as on *Once in the Jungle*). Climb diagonally down for 5m then horizontally to a belay on a spectacular hanging arete. Thread and nut belay.
5) 5c, 20m. Follow the break leftwards past *Jesus Lizard* and the other routes, to a corner. Continue using a thin break to the arete and make a final haul up (thread) to a projecting belay on the edge of the cove. Scramble left into the quarry.
FA. Martin Crocker, Mike Robertson 25.8.96

6 The Fabulous Professor Panic
. . . . 　　　　　　**E5 6a**
30m. A totally intimidating experience breaching the east side of the cove. Unbelievable exposure and good gear. Ascend a deep crack on the left but where that continues out right, pull left (thread) to a niche in a corner. Move up the corner then traverse left between roofs for 10m to a break in the roof (thread). Gain jugs above and a steep exit headwall. Belay to the fence.
FA. Martin Crocker, John Harwood 19.11.95 the second pleaded not to follow this one but to no avail, hence the name!

7 Figurehead . . . . 　　　　**E2 5b**
15m. Another exposed pitch but at a more friendly grade. Can be a bit dirty and dusty. Start as for *Professor Panic* by traversing left and up the deep crack. At its top, swing right to finish up the steep, hanging arete into the quarry.
FA. Crispin Waddy, Andy Ford 16.8.85

EXTRA NOTE - This is a bolt-free zone although 2 routes were done here before it was declared as such. The bolts on these routes are still in place, however both routes have been done without clipping them. They may be removed sometime.

Labels on image: Approach to abseil in Cliff-Top Quarry for Hedbury Big Cove routes 5 to 7 — Abseil point (stake not in place) — Topmast Quarry — Belay bolt above high water line — Lots of sun — 30 min — Vertical — Abseil in — ❶ ❷ ❸ ❹

SMOKEY HOLE

A huge leaning wall of good rock with routes to match those on the *Lean Machine* face. It is hidden from view except for a sideways glimpse from Cliff-Top Quarry. This little quarry is the gearing-up point.

APPROACH - The Cliff-Top Quarry is situated 50m further on from Topmast Quarry, which in turn is 300m further west from Dancing Ledge. The descent path is below some planks on the coast path that cross a dry stream bed. The four routes are gained by an abseil (no stake currently in place) from a point 10m left (looking out) of the descent to the Cliff-Top Quarry. The abseil leads down *Diving for Pearls* to a solid bolt just above high water (backed up by the abseil rope). You may need to swing the abseil or place nuts on the way down to stay in contact with the rock. All four climbs can be gained from this belay.

TIDES - The belay bolts are above the high tide mark but keep away from in rough seas.

EXTRA NOTE - This is a bolt-free zone but there is a useful bolt at the sea-level belay. Hopefully this won't be removed since it doesn't really alter the character of the routes.

RESTRICTION - No climbing 1st March to 31st July because of nesting birds.

❶ Slow Dive .... 🔩🎣🥾🧗 ☐ E6 6b
25m. A complicated and serious pitch on good rock. High in the grade. Trend left via a groove to a small ledge (runners on left). Boldly gain a layback edge above and step left (Rock 2). Make hard moves past a peg to a break then pull over a 2m roof (thread). Finish straight up the headwall (2 pegs) to a juggy break at the top (thread). Exit easily on right.
FA. Pete Oxley 31.7.91

❷ Diving for Pearls .. 🔩🎣🥾 ☐ E6 6b
25m. The central line is very sustained with a fairly bold start. From the bolt belay, climb direct up a slight groove (RPs and peg) to arrive shaken but not stirred at the fault (Friend 3.5). Cross a tough bulge (peg) to a hand-ledge. Move left and back right to a jug (peg on right). Reach some large flakes (peg) and finish up slabby rock on the right.
FA. Pete Oxley, M.Ford 1.12.90

❸ Vapour Trail .. 🔩🎣🥾🧗 ☐ E7 6b
25m. The best route here. A killer start leads to lactic-death higher up. Start from a hanging belay, 5m right of the bolt belay. Ascend the pillar (peg) past hard and serious moves to the fault (thread). Pass a peg to a spike then muscle left to a jug (peg). Move right to an alcove then climb through a series of bulges (peg and thread) to the headwall. More pumpy stuff leads to a solid top.
FA. Pete Oxley 13.12.90

❹ Rocket USA......... 🔩🥾 ☐ E7 6b
25m. Not as serious as *Vapour Trail* but steeper! It follows the groove system overlooking the zawn on the right. Start at a semi-hanging belay on the left arete of the zawn, 10m right of the bolt belay. A right-facing corner leads past an overhang to reach a fault. Swing up left (thread) to a handrail then power right to jugs and runners. Continue up the groove, past a hole, and over a wave to a jug (2 pegs). Finish up leftwards.
FA. Pete Oxley 31.7.91. Soloed by Mike Robertson (with fixed exit rope) 2001

TOPMAST QUARRY
This small cliff-top quarry has a set of short and powerful lines that are very well sheltered from the elements.
APPROACH - *Turn left before the planks and head down leftwards to the quarry - see map on page 211.*

❺ Bar Code ...... 🔩🥾🥾 ☐ 7b
12m. The line on the left-hand side of the deep cave.
FA. Pete Oxley 2004

❻ Bar King Mad .... 🔩🥾🥾 ☐ 7a+
12m. The central one links to the upper part of *Bar Code*.
FA. Pete Oxley 2004

❼ Isobar .... 🥾🥾 ☐ 7a
12m. The right-hand neighbour, but inishing by swinging left to the lower-off of *Bar Code/Bar King Mad*.
FA. Marty Hallett 2004.

Side margin (vertical): Portland West · Portland East · Lulworth · Swanage · Devon · Winspit · Hedbury · Dancing Ledge · Guillemot · Cormorant · Blacker's Hole · Fisherman's · Promenade · Cattle Troughs · Boulder Ruckle · Subliminal

Lee Proctor on the fine layback flake of *Jumping the Gun* (6b) at Hedbury Quarry - *page 212*. Photo: Mark Glaister

DANCING LEDGE

Dancing Ledge Quarry, and its lower tier of sea-level caves, form one of the most important areas at Swanage for sport climbers. The quality and variety of routes is good and virtually all are fully bolted with solid resin staples. The Quarry routes are mostly very solid and are, for the most part, friendly outings. The Lower Cave routes are intimidating, often committing and strenuous, though the rock, setting (and bolts) are mostly excellent. The beautiful scenery also makes this a great summer spot for picnicking and swimming and there is even a self-filling swimming pool in the ledge below the Mexican Wave Area.

At first sight the quarry may look a bit loose but in fact most of the routes are on solid rock and have lower-offs in place before the friable top section. Nearly all the climbs are strenuous and require a wide variety of techniques. The style of the climbing takes a bit of getting to grips with and the grades may feel a bit stiffer here than elsewhere. The accessibility and picturesque location make this a popular venue for non-climbing visitors which is not so good at weekends if you want peace and tranquillity.

ACCESS

There are no real problems here. The National Trust have requested that no top-roping or abseiling occurs over the cliff-top but all the routes have lower-offs so this isn't a problem.

APPROACH

Dancing Ledge, Guillemot Ledge and the Hedbury crags are approached from Langton Matravers. From just outside Swanage town, turn off the A351 towards Langton Matravers. Once in the village, go past the post office and turn left into Durnford Drove. The free car park is 300m down here (on a track for the last 150m) just beyond Langton House. From the parking, walk south on a good path past four fields and Spyway Barn. After the 4th field, head down a big hill towards Dancing Ledge which lies directly below the coast path. From here steps lead down into the quarry. For specific approaches from here see the notes with each area. Do not leave valuables in the car as break-ins are common in the summer.

CONDITIONS

This can be considered a year-round venue which offers some of the most sheltered climbing in Dorset. It is occasionally possible to climb here in shorts in January! The back wall of the quarry stays dry in light rain and only suffers from seepage in mid-winter. The lower walls suffer more from drainage and dampness if it is humid or if the sun is not out. It can be unbearably hot here. Bring the sunblock and water.

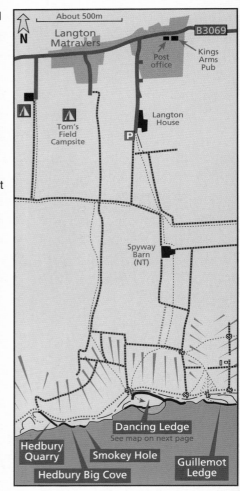

The atmospheric but easily accessed *Lover's Leap* (7a+) on the Hieronymous GBH Area at Dancing Ledge - *page 227.* Photo: Mark Glaister

DANCING LEDGE *Quarry - Left*

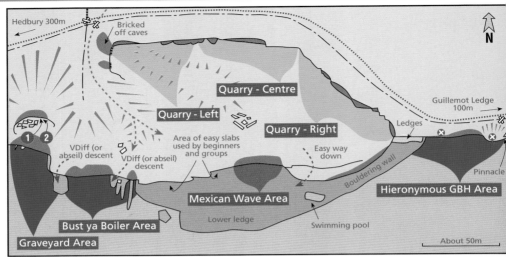

QUARRY - LEFT
The left side of the Main Quarry is a very popular place that has some great little pitches. The steep area around *Sugar Ray* is extremely sheltered, whilst to the right the less steep and easier lines dry very quickly.

APPROACH - On entering the quarry, double back left towards the wall.

Bricked off cave with window. No climbing on this wall.

Some good bouldering on the lower overhangs

There are two isolated routes in the small quarry to the right of the approach path (see map above).

❶ Birth, School, Work, Death . . . [ ] V4
An extended boulder problem up the left side of the overhangs.
FA. Pete Oxley 16.9.90

❷ This Should Move Ya! . [B][ ] 7a
The large rock stack just right of centre, with a jump for the lip.
FA. Pete Oxley 16.9.90

The main area of interest is the back wall of the quarry starting by the bricked-off cave. Two old routes, *For Your Arms Only* and *Volx with Friction* which were on the wall above the cave, have been de-bolted because the cave has been declared unsafe by the National Trust.

❸ Freedance . . . . [ ] V7
An extended boulder problem tackling the huge roof left of *Brutal Equation*. Finish up a small, hard corner and swing right to get back down.
FA. Pete Oxley 4.11.99

❹ A Brutal Equation . [ ] 7a
11m. Sometimes dusty. A boulder problem start from the back of the low roof is also possible - **V5**.
FA. Pete Oxley 6.6.91

Portland West
Portland East
Lulworth
Swanage
Devon
Winspit
Hedbury
Dancing Ledge
Guillemot
Cormorant
Blacker's Hole
Fisherman's
Promenade
Cattle Troughs
Buckle
Boulder Ruckle
Subluminal

5 Skinhead Clash . . . . . 🔲🔳 ⬜ **6b+**
10m. One of the steepest routes you'll find at this grade. Good thuggy fun. After the juggy roof at the start, climb rightwards to the belay of *Idiot Joy Showland*.
FA. Mike Robertson 19.6.91

6 Idiot Joy Showland . . . 🔲🔳 ⬜ **6c+**
10m. A hard rock-over to start, then climb direct on incuts. The start is a **V4** problem.
FA. Pete Oxley 19.5.91

7 Sugar Ray . . . . 🔲🔳 ⬜ **7a**
10m. A neat stamina pitch up a flowstone face. High in the grade. The start to a jug over the second roof is a **V3** problem.
FA. Pete Oxley 8.4.92. The first route in the U.K. to have staple bolts - how they have spread!

8 Names is for Tombstones, Baby
. . . . 🔲🔳 ⬜ **7a**
10m. Start at the end of the long strip roof. Two cruxes.
FA. Damian Cook 8.4.91

9 Transparent Birthday Suit . . . . ⬜ **5+**
10m. Start to the right of a grassy mound. A nice little route that requires a steady head at the top.
FA. Mike Robertson 20.1.91

10 Ideal World . . . . 🔲🔳🔳 ⬜ **6a+**
10m. A good climb with a couple of technical moves. Appears to need a steady head as a good number of people back off the route. Climb straight up past a flake to a tricky mantel finish.
FA. Brian Tilley 7.1.88. This line includes sections of Commander Cody and the Lost Planet Airmen.

11 Squalid Walid and the Druze Blues
. . . . 🔲🔳 ⬜ **6b**
10m. More sustained and slightly better than *Ideal World*, with a similar finish to the same lower-off.
FA. Gordon Jenkin 28.2.88

12 Ozark Mountain Daredevils . . B ⬜ **6a+**
12m. Not bolted.
FA. Tim Dunsby 28.2.88

13 Date with a Frog . . 🔲🔳🔳 ⬜ **6a**
12m. The interesting groove just left of the big, high roof is a good benchmark 6a.
FA. Mike Robertson 13.4.91

14 Fear of a Black Planet . 🔲🔳 ⬜ **7a**
12m. The bulges to a good finish on flowstone holds. It has lost a hold on the roof.
FA. Pete Oxley 26.9.90

15 Today Forever . . . . 🔲🔳🔳 ⬜ **7a+**
12m. A lovely balancy black wall and unobvious crux sequence. Climb the black streak to hard moves at the roof.
FA. Pete Oxley 23.3.91

Portland West | Portland East | Lulworth | **Swanage** | Devon | Winspit | Hedbury | **Dancing Ledge** | Guillemot | Cormorant | Blacker's Hole | Fisherman's | Promenade | Cattle Troughs | Boulder Ruckle | Subliminal

QUARRY - CENTRE

More good little pitches in the mid-grades, and once again on some good rock.
APPROACH - Turn left on entering the quarry and this is the centre of the back wall.

1 Chicago Pipe Dreaming . . . 6a
12m. A popular climb starting just left of a well hole. Although the runout between the 2nd and 3rd bolt appears to be significant there are jugs all around.
FA. Jane Wylie 5.9.93

2 Borra Ring . . . . 5+
12m. A neat route directly above the well hole. A good first lead at the grade.
FA. Jan Rostron 1.8.96

3 Perpetual State of Confusion 6b
12m. The wall to the ledge is the crux.
FA. Mike Robertson 26.8.93

4 Hiccup. 6c
13m. A poor route below the big loose roof.
FA. Mike Robertson 11.5.91

5 Empty Promises 6a
10m. An awkward wall climb.
FA. Steve Taylor 23.5.94

6 All Fall Down . . . . 6a+
11m. A fun route up the centre of the white wall via some tempting, but at times blind, breaks. Polished.
FA. Steve Taylor 23.5.90

7 Carol's Little Injection 6a
11m. A disjointed climb with a half-height rest.
FA. Mike Robertson 26.8.93

8 Slopin' and Hopin' . . . 6b+
12m. Nicely overhanging on sloping holds. Best done on a cold crisp winter's day; as the slopers feel like jugs then!
FA. Mike Robertson 26.8.93

9 Mr Choo Choo . . . 7a
12m. Stylish moves up a shallow, leaning groove at the left-hand end of a low roof. The route lost a hold a while back, this being the reason for the upgrade.
FA. Damian Cook 14.5.91

10 Seven Year's Solitary . . 7a+
12m. A very hard start over the big bulge.
FA. Pete Oxley 13.5.90

11 Disco's Out, Murder's In 6c+
12m. A hard start through the initial roof is not easy to read. Take care with the rock near the top of the pitch.
FA. Damian Cook 17.2.91

12 Daylight Robbery 6c
12m. A varied and interesting route up the leftward-leaning groove. Keep an eye on the footholds or things can quickly feel a lot harder.
FA. Steve Taylor 11.11.90

13 Double or Quits . . . 7a+
13m. The calcite wall just right of the bolt line. Further left is also an option at the same grade.
FA. Pete Oxley 7.91

14 Rambling Moses Weetabix and the Secona Park Seven 6b+
13m. The centre of the flat orange sheet is a fine route and one of the best of its grade in the quarry.
FA. Pete Oxley 27.6.87

15 The Honey Monster 6c
13m. Climb up leftwards from the bottom corner of the orange face. No grabbing the lower-off!
FA. Steve Taylor 21.8.93. An older route Hard Tackle took a similar line.

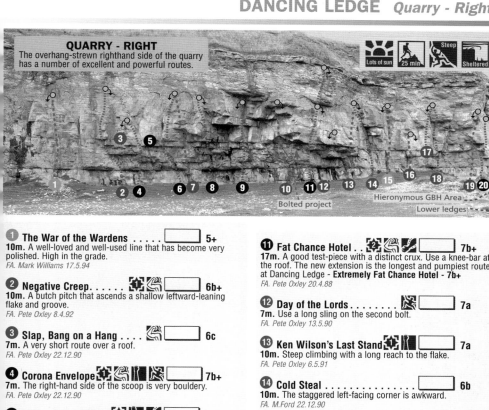

QUARRY - RIGHT
The overhang-strewn righthand side of the quarry has a number of excellent and powerful routes.

Lots of sun | *25 min* | *Steep* | *Sheltered*

Bolted project

Hieronymous GBH Area

Lower ledges

① The War of the Wardens . . . . . ☐ **5+**
10m. A well-loved and well-used line that has become very polished. High in the grade.
FA. Mark Williams 17.5.94

② Negative Creep . . . . . . ☐ **6b+**
10m. A butch pitch that ascends a shallow leftward-leaning flake and groove.
FA. Pete Oxley 8.4.92

③ Slap, Bang on a Hang . . . . ☐ **6c**
7m. A very short route over a roof.
FA. Pete Oxley 22.12.90

④ Corona Envelope ☐ **7b+**
7m. The right-hand side of the scoop is very bouldery.
FA. Pete Oxley 22.12.90

⑤ Corona Connection. ☐ **7b+**
13m. A pumpy link up from *Corona Envelope* into *Prophets of Rage*, via a short finger traverse and one new bolt.
FA. Pete Oxley 15.2.96

⑥ Prophets of Rage . . ☐ **7b**
11m. A tough but excellent route which has a right-hand variant on the mid-section also at **7b**. The direct start is **7b+** ish.
FA. Pete Oxley 7.5.90

⑦ Haunted by a Million Screams
. . . . ☐ **6c+**
11m. An excellent jug haul up some steep ground and a slight groove through the overhangs. A Dancing Ledge classic.
FA. Pete Oxley 17.3.88

⑧ The Ghost of Ian Curtis
. . . . ☐ **7c+**
11m. Steep knee-bars and a cornflake-sized crux hold.
FA. Pete Oxley 21.7.92

⑨ Atrocity Exhibition . ☐ **7a+**
12m. Some fierce moves up the blank groove.
FA. Pete Oxley 16.9.90

⑩ The Wonders of Wallkraft ☐ **7a**
12m. The steep crackline. Use long slings on some of the bolts to prevent krabs bending over the roof lips.
FA. Pete Oxley 2.12.90

The next line of bolts is a poor project which needs de-bolting.

⑪ Fat Chance Hotel . . ☐ **7b+**
17m. A good test-piece with a distinct crux. Use a knee-bar at the roof. The new extension is the longest and pumpiest route at Dancing Ledge - **Extremely Fat Chance Hotel - 7b+**
FA. Pete Oxley 20.4.88

⑫ Day of the Lords . . . . ☐ **7a**
7m. Use a long sling on the second bolt.
FA. Pete Oxley 13.5.90

⑬ Ken Wilson's Last Stand ☐ **7a**
10m. Steep climbing with a long reach to the flake.
FA. Pete Oxley 6.5.91

⑭ Cold Steal . . . . ☐ **6b**
10m. The staggered left-facing corner is awkward.
FA. M.Ford 22.12.90

⑮ John Craven's Willy Warmer ☐ **5+**
10m. Subtle bridging makes this well worth doing. Probably the easiest route in the quarry - if you can get off the ground!
FA. M.King 8.92

⑯ Taylor-made Tracking Damage . ☐ **6c+**
8m. Now harder due to hold loss and extreme polish.
FA. M.Ford 15.12.90

⑰ Alienation . . . . ☐ **7a**
12m. A technical eliminate. Start up *A Sea Without Water* then break left immediately to climb the difficult blank groove which becomes balancy, ending in a steep finish over a capping bulge.
FA. Chris Weedon 7.2002

⑱ A Sea Without Water ☐ **6c**
12m. A bouldery start gains some jugs from where increasingly technical and sustained moves lead with interest past a small roof to the belay shared with *Alienation*.
FA. R.Godfray, C.Parker 2000

A line here has had the bolt holes drilled (will be 5+).

⑲ Option B . . . . ☐ **6c+**
12m. The dusty shot-holed overhangs left of the arete.
FA. Damian Cook 6.9.93

⑳ Eye am the Sky . . . ☐ **7a+**
13m. Trend right around the arete. Crux reach for the belay.
FA. Pete Oxley 11.4.92

Abseil in from ledge or descend via VDiff down-climb

Lots of sun · 25 min · Steep · Abseil in

GRAVEYARD AREA

Hidden away under the west end of the quarry are two very eerie caves containing layers of tiered roofs. The rock is good with dramatic mega-steep pump-outs which are far more rewarding than the average clip-up in the quarry above, if you are up to them. This is also a great swimming and jumping spot for the hot summer days. Some of the routes here have been soloed, however most can not be considered as deep water solos.

APPROACH (Routes 1 to 5) - Abseil to the ledge on the right (looking in) of the cave. Once acquainted with the area it is possible to solo down the abseil line at about VDiff.

APPROACH (Route 6) -The last route requires a well-positioned abseil onto the start ledge, from bolts in blocks above. Alternatively it makes a great second pitch to *Mariner's Graveyard*, if you have enough strength left.

TIDES (All routes) - The cave is above high tide but keep away in rough seas.

The routes on this side are described as you would approach them, from right to left. All the routes finish at block belays in the main quarry.

❶ Here Comes the Hezbollah. 🏔 ⬜ **6b+**
10m. A direct line above the belay ledge, up a bulging wall. **(S2)**
FA. M.Ford 22.2.92

❷ F.Y.B. . . . . 🏔 🏔 ⬜ **6c**
10m. Start as for *Lucretia, My Reflection* then move out right and up to the top. **(S1)**
FA. Mark Higgs 7.10.95

❸ Lucretia, My Reflection
. . . . 🏔 🏔 🏔 ⬜ **6c**
140m. A cool route with great positions. Take a diagonal line through roofs onto a hanging slab. **(S1)**
FA. Pete Oxley 30.9.90

❹ The Pump Will Tear Us Apart
. . . . 🏔 🏔 🏔 ⬜ **7a+**
28m. Follow the monumental hand traverse to halfway then head upwards for the light. It has been soloed but is definitely not a deep water solo.
FA. Pete Oxley 7.10.90

❺ Mariner's Graveyard. . . 🏔 🏔 ⬜ **7a+**
A great traverse all the way across the narrow wall hanging above the zawn. Brilliant if you get good conditions.
1) 25m **7a+.** The long pumpy rail.
2) 10m **6b+.** Blast up the wall.
FA. Pete Oxley 19.10.90

❻ Corridors of Power. . . . 🏔 🏔 ⬜ **7a+**
14m. From the belay on the ledge, swing out left and tackle the bulging wall.
FA. Mike Robertson 27.11.93

Portland West · Portland East · Lulworth · Swanage · Devon · Winspit · Hedbury · Dancing Ledge · Guillemot · Cormorant · Blacker's Hole · Fisherman's · Promenade · Cattle Troughs · Boulder Ruckle · Subliminal

BUST YA' BOILER AREA

This steep section of roofs gives some great traverse pitches which can be climbed at any tide state.

APPROACH - Up to mid-tide you can walk across from the lower ledges, by the Mexican Wave Area, to scramble across the seaward floor of the small zawn. At higher tides abseil from blocks or down-climb (a Diff).

The first five routes share a starting point and initial section. Start around the corner in the huge cave by a one bolt belay in the side wall. There are also two sets of bolt belays on the top ledge for use with these routes.

❶ Slave to the Cave. 7b

This big right-to-left traverse line is poised above the lip of the cave and is similar to *Mariner's Graveyard*. It is possible at any tide and in rough seas for added adrenaline. Prussiks are advisable if you are uncertain.
1) 7b, 25m. The rail to a belay on small ledge.
2) 6c, 12m. Continue to a belay on the far side of the cave. Escape via an easy wall on the left or continue across *Mariner's Graveyard* if you aren't tired yet.
FA. Pete Oxley, Jon Biddle 3.2.98

❷ Hell's Darker Chambers

. . . . 8a

20m. Mindlessly strenuous roof climbing. Belay on the top ledge. Reverse to get the gear.
FA. Pete Oxley 3.5.92

❸ Legendary Shadows

. . . . 7c

15m. A sensational addition which forges a radical path through a very unlikely set of roofs left of *Bust ya' Boiler*. The bolts on this route have Petzl hangers. Belay on the top ledge. Reverse for your gear if you can't find a second.
FA. Pete Oxley 30.1.98

❹ Bust Ya' Boiler 7b+

12m. Superb power climbing. Pull over the roof and traverse along the hand rail for 3m, then climb direct through 3 roofs to a crux on the last lip. Large ring bolts. Belay on the top ledge.
FA. Pete Oxley 17.10.93

❺ Mucho Gusto! 7b

10m. A short, photogenic and very steep line across the roofs past a short crack. Belay on the top ledge (pre-place a sling over the edge to lower-off). If soloed, a spotter is needed for the first moves. **(S2)**
FA. Pete Oxley 23.1.98

The last three routes are in the small zawn crossed on the approach walk. They are the first routes you come to.

❻ Hard Act to Follow . . . 6c

10m. Short but very sweet and far steeper than you might imagine.
FA. Pete Oxley 23.1.98

❼ Dancing Fool 7a

10m. A tough roof problem on good rock.
FA. Pete Oxley 23.1.98

❽ Mariana's Trenchcoat . . . . 6b+

10m. Climb diagonally leftwards above the zawn.
FA. Pete Oxley 3.3.91

MEXICAN WAVE AREA

The next six climbs offer a fine venue for muscle junkies who like a bit of air beneath their feet. There is a full grade spread from 7a to 7c+. The area is popular with non-climbers so watch your swearing.

APPROACH - From the main quarry, follow the easy way down to the lower sea-level ledges. The Mexican Wave Area is at the back of the ledge in a small rectangular cave.

TIDES - The ledge is above high tide.

1 Whipping Boy 7a

10m. Short and strenuous with a tough last move. It has large ring bolts.

FA. Pete Oxley 8.2.97

2 Mexican Wave . . . . 1 7a+

10m. A fun jug haul with a novel leg-wrap near the lip.

FA. Pete Oxley 22.3.88

3 Armed and Dangerous . . . . 7b+

11m. Left out of the last guide since it had suffered a minor rockfall. It has now been cleaned up and bolted but there is still a large dodgy block on the final roof so take great care.

FA. Pete Oxley 24.7.87. Reclimbed - Mike Robertson 14.10.96

4 A Short Story About Power 1 7b

11m. Another route which has been cleaned up and now proves to be worthwhile. It offers plenty of shade.

FA. Pete Oxley 7.5.90

5 Circus Beach . . . . . 1 7b+

10m. Climb direct across the 3m roof to join *A Short Story About Power*. Superb acrobatic moves.

FA. Pete Oxley 1.2.98

6 The Ringmaster . . . 2 7c

10m. The longest and most involved arm-buster here, crossing a 7m roof stack. Top out or lower off the last bolt.

FA. Pete Oxley 26.1.98. The first roof was previously climbed as a direct start to A Short Story About Power which subsequently lost a crucial hold.

7 One Finger Trapeze . . . . 1 7c+

10m. Desperate stuff over the first roof including a one finger dyno. The second roof is also hard taken direct past the bolt to join *The Ringmaster* at the third roof. Top out or lower off the last bolt.

FA. Pete Oxley 28.2.98

Portland West Portland East Lulworth Swanage Devon Winspit Hedbury Dancing Ledge Guillemot Cormorant Blacker's Hole Fisherman's Promenade Cattle Troughs Boulder Ruckle Subliminal

Lots of sun | 25 min | Vertical | Abseil in | Windy

Fence post abseil points
Main Quarry
Winter waterfall
Eye am the Sky
Descent down big ledges

HIERONYMOUS GBH AREA

The next set of routes are on the face to the east of the quarry. The first few can be reached from the quarry , though those further right require committing approaches by abseil. They offer rewarding outings in superb situations.
TIDES (All routes) - None of the routes are tidal (including those reached by abseil) however keep away in rough seas.

APPROACH (Routes 1 to 5) - *Approach from the main quarry by a thin ledge traverse where there are belay bolts, or from the sea-level platform below, if the sea is calm.*

❶ Now and Always . . . . . 6c+
15m. An innocuous-looking route that is in reality steep, and has a tough crux. One of the better routes at Dancing Ledge.
FA. Pete Oxley 14.2.98

❷ Lover's Leap . . . . 7a+
16m. From the bolt belay 5m right of *Now and Always*, climb a series of bulges with a dynamic crux to a welded block.
Photo page 219.
FA. Pete Oxley 14.2.98. Valentine's Day!

The next 3 routes share a bolt belay on the lowest ledge.

❸ Born Again . . . . 6b+
18m. An elegant groove-line; groovy position, tasty grade. Worth seeking out - one of the best of the grade at Swanage.
FA. Pete Oxley 28.3.98

❹ Hieronymous GBH . . . . 6c+
18m. An atmospheric climb tackling the wall above and right of the cave.
FA. Pete Oxley 15.12.90

❺ Dante's Inferno . . . 7a
18m. A spaced-out hanging groove gained by a fierce pocketed crack and followed by a bulge and wall. Head left at the top.
FA. Pete Oxley 28.3.98

APPROACH (Routes 6 to 9) - *The next routes each require an abseil approach from above. The fence posts are located above and to the east (left - looking out) side of the quarry, just below the coast path. Take great care that you abseil in the correct place by using the detailed features on the photo above. It may even help to have a friend back in the quarry to shout instructions. Take some prussik loops in case things go wrong and avoid in rough seas.*

❻ Sea of Holes 6b
20m. The line of this atmospheric route is completely hidden, just left of a big sea-cave. Start from a hanging belay, before some low roofs, directly below the line. Follow the big line of pockets and pull out on the abseil rope.
FA. Mark Williams 25.8.94

❼ Song to the Siren . . . . . 7a+
26m. A great route which follows the huge pillar-face to some leaning tufas. Sadly, it is usually a drainage line in winter. To start, abseil to a hanging stance, with 2 bolts, just above the water line. Pull out on the abseil rope to finish.
FA. Pete Oxley 30.10.91

❽ White Rave . . . . 7a+
20m. A hidden route up the pocketed wall and slab to the right of the green drainage streak. Abseil to a hanging stance, with 2 bolts, 4m above the water line. There is a belay in an alcove below the top. Pull out on the abseil rope.
FA. Mike Robertson 25.8.93

❾ Ten-K-Rig E4 6a
20m. Start at the bolt belay of *White Rave*. Traverse right to the base of a crack then follow the crack through a bulge to a niche. Take a continuation crack in the wall above (to the left of a spike) and bear leftwards to the belay niche of *White Rave*.
FA. Martin Crocker, Pete Finklaire 21.1.96

Portland West | Portland East | Lulworth | Swanage | Devon | Winspit | Hedbury | Dancing Ledge | Guillemot | Cormorant | Blacker's Hole | Fisherman's | Promenade | Cattle Troughs | Ruckle | Boulder | Subluminal

Guillemot Ledge is a large and diverse area that is home to the highest section of cliff along the whole of the Swanage coastline. The big multi-pitch traditional routes on the West Face are amongst the most challenging in the south-west and almost all of them give tremendous climbing in wildly exposed situations. Across the two areas of the West and East faces, there is a reasonable grade spread from VS to E6 but Guillemot Ledge should be recognised and treated as a serious cliff where experience of committing and difficult climbing is essential. The rock is usually sound and the presence of a quarried top on the Tensor II Area will calm fears of possible loose finishes when topping-out on this section of the crag. The finishes of the routes on the West Face however are all loose and require much care when negotiating the last 5m of cliff top. A number of the climbs in this area rely on fixed protection from pegs all of which should be carefully inspected and backed-up where possible.

ACCESS

All the routes on the West Face are restricted because of nesting birds.
No climbing from 1 March to 31 July.

APPROACH

See main Dancing Ledge approach on page 218. Approach as for Dancing Ledge to the last stile before you drop down the huge slope to the quarry. Turn left (looking out) and follow the ridge track to cross the next stone wall. Drop diagonally right down a steep hillside to reach another stone wall. Follow the valley bottom to reach a rickety stile in the cliff-top fence. Cross here to find the lower cliff-top quarry on the left. The main abseil and gearing up ledge lies at the base of the deep gully on the right (looking out) of the stile. Steep rock steps lead down a gully to a small ledge. There is a stake cemented into the back of the ledge. An alternative abseil is from boulders in the quarry. Rucksacks can be safely left in the gully but be careful if approaching from the quarries.

TIDES

The boulder beach is well above high tide level and it even gives reasonable shelter in moderate seas. Access between the two faces can be cut off in moderate seas at a low section near the foot of the abseil.

CONDITIONS

This is yet another south-facing sun-trap with little significant seepage. It is possible to climb here all year round if the temperature is right. Avoid the place on the hottest days since it can become unbearable, especially if committed to some of the really long routes. If it is windy there will be little shelter on the big open faces.

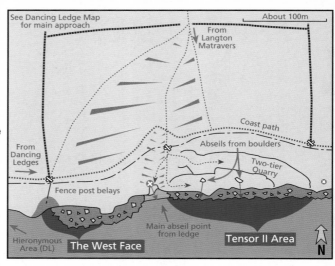

eraldine Taylor on the adventurous second
itch of *Oceanid* (E2 5b) at Guillemot Ledge
page 231. Photo: Mike Robertson

Fence post belays

White Rave
(Dancing Ledge)

Large
sea cave

Limit of boulder
ledge access

Boulder ledges well
above high tide level

THE WEST FACE

This is one of the best areas at Swanage with its famous high white face and its adjoining sea cave.

TIDES - The boulder beach below the face is non-tidal but calm seas are need to get to the face from below the abseil point.
APPROACH - From the abseil, boulder-hop right (looking out) around a large buttress for 100m to stand below the towering white face. Left of this is a brooding roof-packed sea-cave.

RESTRICTION - No climbing 1 March to 31 July because of nesting birds.

❶ Dougal the Great . . 🔳🔳🔳🔳 ⬜ **E6 6c**
A big route taking a huge diagonal line to finish at a high leaning chimney. Start near the right-hand side of the low cave roof.
1) 6c, 30m. Go direct over two roofs (peg and wedge) to join *Race for the Oasis*. Traverse 10m left under the roofs (thread and 3 old studs) to a peg. Power around the roof and continue up the steep wall (2 threads and a peg) to a small recessed ledge. Peg and nut belay. Watch out for rope drag.
2) 5c, 20m. Climb the bulging wall above from the left-hand side (thread) to a jutting ledge (thread). Finish diagonally leftwards, on shattered rock, to exit up the chimney.
FA. Pete Oxley, Jon Biddle 12.2.88. Formerly an A3 aid route.

❷ Race for the Oasis . . . . 🔳🔳🔳 ⬜ **E5 6a**
A wandering outing but with good pitches. Start at the very right-hand side of the low roof.
1) 6a, 25m. Gain a chimney then traverse left for 8m (peg under the strip-roof) then move up to a peg below another roof. Swing out to a bottomless small groove and climb its left-hand side via a fingery rib before trending right to join *Tudor Rose*. Hanging belay at the right-hand end of a narrow roof.
2) 5b, 10m. Move left for 3m and then climb a shallow groove. At the top of this traverse left again, and down, to the recessed belay on *Dougal the Great*.
3) 5c, 30m. Head diagonally rightwards to the fault and swing along to a good ledge (peg). From the left-hand side reach a peg, step left and move boldly up the wall to good finishing holds. Exit right then left up an easy groove.
FA. Martin Crocker, Jim Robertson 27.11.82

❸ Sons of Pioneers . . 🔳🔳🔳🔳 ⬜ **E6 6b**
Very intricate route finding and another set of bold and interesting linkups. Start as for *Race for the Oasis*.
1) 6a, 18m. A bold pitch. From the chimney move left for 3m then drop out and around the roof (crucial Friend 2) to follow a right-leading handrail for 3m. Cross the bulge above to the foot of a slight corner on *Tudor Rose*. Peg and nut belay.
2) 6b, 10m. From the top of the corner move up right to a horizontal break in a bulge (peg). Make wild moves over the bulge onto the lip. Multiple large to medium Friends belay.
3) 6a, 20m. Just right of an ammonite, climb the bold wall to wires. Trend right to a square-cut niche below the headwall. Climb direct (peg) to the top ledge. Move right to an exit corner.
FA. Martin Crocker, Nigel Coe 28.8.94

❹ Tudor Rose . . . . 🔳🔳🔳 ⬜ **E2 5b**
A brilliant and well-known classic with sustained and quality wall climbing. The first pitch is serious for the second. Start below a long crack right of the low cave roof.
1) 5b, 45m. Gain some cracks and climb the long left-hand one until it eases. Then traverse left to a good foot-ledge. Continue traversing past two slight corners (peg) and continue up past a jammed block to a small roof. Step left and climb up a groove, past the fault, to reach a stance in a corner. Large nut belay.
2) 5b, 20m. From the right-hand side of the ledge, a flake leads into a shallow groove on the left. Gain the horizontal crack then traverse right to finish up a short corner on *Oceanid*.
FA. Richard Crewe, P.Charman 5.5.74

❺ Facedancin' . . . . . 🔳🔳🔳🔳 ⬜ **E3 6a**
A fantastic direct line up the steep wall left of *Oceanid*. A tough route but well-protected where it matters. Both pitches are good. Can be climbed in a single pitch.
1) 5c, 25m. Start as for *Tudor Rose* to the good foot-ledge. Then ascend the wall and bulge via a groove to a belay at the fault.
2) 6a, 25m. Head diagonally right for 5m then back left to a ledge. Pass a bulge (peg) then step right and climb the thin cracks in the white headwall (peg) to the top ledge. Exit up the corner as for *Oceanid*.
FA. Martin Crocker, Jim Robertson 8.1.83

Portland West | Portland East | Lulworth | Swanage | Devon | Winspit | Hedbury | Dancing Ledge | Guillemot | Cormorant | Blacker's Hole | Fisherman's | Promenade | Cattle Troughs | Boulder Ruckle | Subliminal

❻ Oceanid . . . . 🔲🔲🔲 **E2 5b**
The dominating central line up the major crackline. Steep, strenuous and intimidating and with some loose rock on pitch two. Start 5m right of *Tudor Rose* on a boulder pile. *Photo 229.*
1) 5a, 20m. Traverse left for 3m and move up to a niche. Follow cracks above to a slab below the fault. Thread belay.
2) 5b, 30m. Climb up left to the fault and gain the wall passing a bulge on the left. Follow a steep groove direct, stepping left at its top. Avoid some big blocks above to reach the exit corner, (some of these blocks have now gone). A couple of large cams are useful on this pitch.
FA. Pat Littlejohn, K.Goodman 5.8.72

❼ Fly Crazy But Free . 🔲🔲🔲 **E5 6b**
Technical and pumpy climbing blasting up the white face just right of *Oceanid*. A fine position and high in the grade.
1) 5a, 20m. As for *Oceanid*.
2) 6b, 30m. Climb diagonally left then back right, above an overhang, to a small ledge (peg). Swing left and pass a niche to ascend twin cracks above. A hard move on the left gains a good horizontal break. Continue up the technical leaning headwall (2 pegs) to the top.
FA. Martin Crocker, D.Light 26.9.83

❽ Warlord . . . . 🔲🔲 **E4 6a**
A classic with strenuous and 'out there' climbing especially in the last few moves. Can be climbed in one long pitch.
1) 5a, 20m. As for *Oceanid*.
2) 6a, 25m. Climb diagonally left then back right, above an overhang, to a small ledge (peg) (as for *Fly Crazy*). Fire straight up the 'lightning crack' above, past a large wedged cornflake! to fingery wall moves at the top. Finish up some slightly unstable ground. Many pegs. Some of the pegs have small eyes so take a number of slim krabs.
FA. Brian Snell, Keith Knight 21.2.76 (aided).
FFA. Steve Monks, Steve Findlay 28.11.81.

❾ Vikings . . . . . . 🔲🔲🔲🔲 **E4 6a**
Three fine pitches right of *Warlord*. Technical and sustained with small wires essential. Start 20m right of *Oceanid* at two converging cracks. The finish to the top pitch needs care.
1) 5a, 20m. Climb halfway up the right-hand crack then step left into a scoop. Ascend a short corner to a slab then traverse along until is is possible to reach the higher slab (peg). Continue left to the belay on *Oceanid*. Friable rock.

Vikings continued...
2) 5c, 10m. Trend right to the roof (large Friend) then move over this. Undercut right along the lip then move up to belay (peg) below a short corner in the next roof.
3) 6a, 20m. Gain a corner and pull over the roof onto a narrow ledge (peg). Climb the wall just right (bold) to a rest in a flake-crack, then tackle the steep white wall on the left.
FA. Martin Crocker, Jim Robertson 21.8.83

❿ Caiaphas . . . . . . 🔲🔲🔲 **E3 5c**
A good bottom pitch, but a recent ascent has reported much loose rock. Start at a short corner on the right-hand side of the main wall, 3m right of a huge reclining pillar.
1) 5c, 25m. Climb the corner then trend right to reach a white sheet. Traverse 3m left and climb a thin crack to pass a strip-roof at the fault. Follow a long diagonal flake rightwards to a stance after 5m.
2) 5a, 15m. Continue along a flake to finish up a loose corner.
FA. George Hounsome, Scott Titt 22.9.79

⓫ Deaf Mosaic . . 🔲🔲🔲🔲 **E6 6c**
A desperately blank test-piece up the white face right of *Caiaphas*. Good gear.
1) 6c, 25m. Climb direct as for *Caiaphas* to a horizontal beneath the wall. Monodoigt holes lead up the centre (2 pegs) to the main break. A big undercut gains the shield above then proceed more easily to belay on *Caiaphas*.
2) 5a, 15m. As for *Caiaphas*.
FA. Martin Crocker, Nigel Coe 28.8.94

⓬ Zo Zo . . . . 🔲🔲🔲 **VS 4b**
An impressive climb for the grade that has an excellent first pitch, but a top out on some poor rock, requiring care.
1) 4b, 25m. The large corner needs some big gear. At the fault-line move left to a large ledge and belay.
2) 4a, 15m. The wall and groove above and to the right of the corner is steady but has some loose blocks.

⓭ Mistaken Identity . . . . 🔲🔲 **VS 4c**
A nice little route on good rock and with a relatively solid finish near to the approach abseil-pipe anchor.
1) 4c, 25m. Take on the left side of the black overhang and continue up the vertical wall with interest to finish on a good ledge on the right.
FA. Pete Finklaire, B.Etheridge 1976

TENSOR II AREA

This is a justifiably popular area of cliffs with easy access, good lower grade routes and clean-cut, quarried finishes. The routes are a bit shorter than on the West Face and many have a friendly feel to them although some of the high-grade lines are serious.

TIDES - All the climbs are possible at all tides and in moderately rough seas because of the boulder-field along the base.

APPROACH - The Tensor II Area is situated to the left (looking out) of the approach abseil and the routes are reached along the boulder-field below the wall.

BELAYS - The belays are on wires in the back wall of the quarry. There are also some blocks and a few stakes.

❶ Exit Chimney Two - The Sequel
. . . . **E4 6a**

30m. This once used to be the descent route before the chimney collapsed leaving a fierce and bold line. Start 10m right of the abseil. Climb past a roof crack then make bold moves up flakes to a mid-height roof (thread). Follow twin leaning cracks to the fault then climb direct on big holds to the top.
FA. Pete Oxley, J.Williams 5.12.87

❷ Sapphire **E1 5b**
A popular route with a solid and safe crux. Start 18m right of the abseil, beneath a sentry box near the fault.
1) 4b, 10m. Amble up the wall without much gear to the open sentry box (thread).
2) 5b, 20m. Gain the fault and swing left to an arete. Move over the roof (2 pegs) to reach the next roofs. Traverse right underneath these to finish up a crack, past a bulge to the top.
FA. G.Smith, K.Winkworth 3.4.72

❸ The Spook **E1 5b**
A well-travelled route which is thoroughly recommended. A great climb, one of Swanage's gems.
1) 5a, 18m. Climb the left-hand of two grooves and swing right beneath a roof. Layback a steep groove to the fault. Belay on right.
2) 5b, 15m. Step right onto the wall and climb up to the chert band, and an old hidden peg. There is an excellent half Friend around to the right and a bomber big nut up and left, these protect the pull through the overhang. Finish up the bold wall.
FA. Richard Crewe, P.Sharman 31.3.74

❹ Toiler on the Sea . . **E5 6b**
Good, clean climbing. Start at the arete right of *The Spook*.
1) 6b, 18m. Serious. Follow the arete to the roof (peg and threads) then pull around past a niche (peg) to safer ground. Pass another peg to finish up a shallow groove to the fault. Belay as for *August Angie*.
2) 5b, 15m. Ascend diagonally left (peg) to reach a protruding ledge. Gain a nose and continue to the top.
FA. Pete Oxley, G.Anstey 6.6.87

❺ August Angie **E1 5b**
Pleasantly sustained. Start at the groove right of the arete.
1) 5b, 25m. Take the groove (peg) to the roof (peg) then traverse right to clear it. Follow a corner to the fault and take a stance 3m to the left. Take care with rope drag.
2) 5a, 12m. Climb the wall on the right to a roof. Swing right around an arete then climb through the weakness in the overhangs, to the top.
FA. B.Snell, M.Colson. FFA. Richard Crewe 28.10.73

❻ Necromancy **E4 5c**
35m. Technical and bold wall climbing up the committing face 5m right of *August Angie*. Move up and pass a break in the roof. Trend right to a (peg) at a flake then run it out direct to a ledge (possible belay). Finish heading rightwards across a short blank wall to a clean-cut exit. Low in the grade.
FA. Pete Oxley 11.8.90

Belay point in Upper Quarry

Stake set back

⑦ The Heat . . . . 🔲🔲🔲 — E3 5c
A big pitch with quality moves but little gear. Start beneath a large roof at 15m.
1) 5c, 15m. A short wall leads to a ledge (peg). Move left (peg) then climb direct on blind edges to a ledge. Serious.
2) 5b, 20m. Follow a corner and trend right then left past a fault to a nose (peg). Traverse left to a V-shaped overhang.
FA. B.Snell, W.Lyons 7.4.74. FFA. George Hounsome, G.De Lacy

⑧ The Big Heat . . . . 🔲🔲🔲 — E4 6a
30m. A logical extension to *The Heat*. Climb the serious lower wall then press on (2 pegs) up the face left of the arete, in a good position. Finish up the final wall as for *Necromancy*.
FA. Pete Oxley, J.Williams 6.6.87

⑨ Funeral Pyre . . 🔲🔲🔲🔲 — E5 5c
Unprotected where it matters. The line follows the wall 8m right of *The Heat*, 5m left of a corner.
1) 5c, 15m. Ascend right then left to footledges. 'Go for it' up the blank scoop to a good stance as for *Tensor II*.
2) 5a, 15m. Finish as for *Tensor II*.
FA. Pete Oxley, Steve Williams 6.5.87

⑩ Tensor II . . . . 🔲🔲🔲 — VS 5a
The best route of its grade at Guillemot with two contrasting pitches. Start at a corner as for *Strapiombo*.
1) 4c, 20m. Climb the corner until undercuts lead out left. Pass a bulge and move up onto a good ledge and flake belay.
2) 5a, 15m. Technical slab moves (peg) gain the fault. Pass an overhang above to an exit groove.
FA. B.Snell, W.Lyons 8.12.73

⑪ Strapiombo . . . . 🔲🔲 — HVS 5a
30m. A direct corner and crack climb starting as for *Tensor II*. Follow a corner past a spike than a peg to pass a big roof on the right. A chimney allows access to the fault and a huge ledge (possible belay). Climb the continuation crack to the top. A helmet jam has been used to great effect by more than one team on this route!
FA. A.Webster, D.Hadlum 27.3.67

⑫ Ledgend . . . . 🔲🔲🔲 — HS 4b
The easiest way out if things go wrong. Start below a big flake crack, in a steep wall, 60m east (right - looking in) of the abseil, and 5m right of the corner of *Strapiombo*.
1) 4b, 25m. A crack leads rightwards to gain the flake. Follow this to its top. Climb a corner on the right to the fault then traverse right to belay on a ledge.
2) 4a, 15m. Step right off the ledge then move up for 5m. Traverse left to reach the quarry. Care required with loose flakes.
FA. D.Burgess, J.Allen, R.Colledge 11.4.66

⑬ Ledgend Direct. . . . . . 🔲🔲 — HVS 5a
A popular route up a gear-packed corner 9m right of *Ledgend* that gives exhausting climbing. It has taken a lot of scalps over the years and now fully merits its HVS grade.
1) 5a, 18m. Climb a wall to gain the corner which leads steeply to a ledge on the left, as for *Ledgend*.
2) 4a, 15m. As for *Ledgend* pitch two.
FA. P.Neame, A.Monnery 12.2.67

⑭ Batt Crack . . . . 🔲 — VS 4c
A popular route. Start as for *Ledgend Direct*.
1) 4c, 18m. Climb a short wall to a ledge then move right to enter and follow a corner to an overhang. Go right to belay.
2) 4a, 18m. Ascend a groove and flakes then move right and up to a ledge. Pass another ledge and a small roof on the left.
FA. D.Hadlum, G.Reynolds 25.3.67

⑮ Friends from the Deep. 🔲🔲 — E3 5c
An absorbing first pitch. Start just right of a chimney in an arete, 8m right of *Ledgend Direct*. An eliminate.
1) 5c, 25m. Gain a slot (thread) then pull out right to cross a bulge. Continue to a rest on *Yellow Wall*. Traverse left to a flake then follow the sustained crack (thread) to the fault. Belay on the left in the corner as for *Batt Crack*.
2) 4c, 15m. Move 2m right then finish rightwards through a V-shaped roof.
FA. Tim Dunsby, Nigel Coe 6.5.87

⑯ Yellow Belly Wall . 🔲🔲🔲 — E5 6b
40m. A fine hard eliminate on *Yellow Wall*. Follow a shallow groove, left of the normal start, past a bulge. Continue more easily to the down-pointing spike on *Yellow Wall*. Step right, boldly climb the wall to the fault, then pass the roof above (peg) to gain an undercut block on *Yellow Wall*. Finish direct, exiting up a white wall right of a broken groove.
FA. Martin Crocker, Nigel Coe 5.4.97

⑰ Yellow Wall . . . . 🔲🔲 — E1 5b
More fine wall climbing. Start just left of a big groove.
1) 5b, 20m. Climb the wall trending left to a down-pointing spike. Move left and past a bulge (peg) into a shallow groove. Continue to belay on a wedged boulder. Belay on left.
2) 5b, 20m. Trend steeply right under blocks then over to a small ledge. Move on and rightwards, around an arete, into a corner with a large flake. Finish up this, exiting left.
FA. Richard Crewe, A.Wilde, P.Crewe 3.4.72

⑱ Younger Days . . . . 🔲🔲 — E3 6a
35m. An unusual climb taking a prominent arete 8m right of *Yellow Wall* and with some orange streaks on its left-hand side. Start 3m right of the arete and climb easily until the arete steepens. Layback its right-hand side (thread) to the fault. Finish up the easy wall above direct.
FA. M.Saunders 6.6.87

233

CORMORANT LEDGE

Cormorant Ledge is a very long section of crag with a handfull of good low and mid-grade lines including a couple of classics. It is possible to gain access easily to either end of the area by abseil and a visit can be added on to a day at Gulliemot East without the need to move gear or abseil station. The tops of many of the routes in this area are very loose but on the routes described here they are either solid due to quarrying or regular traffic.

APPROACH

See main Dancing Ledge approach on page 218. Approach as for Dancing Ledge to the last stile before you drop down the huge slope to the quarry. Turn left (looking out) and follow the ridge track to cross the next stone wall. Drop diagonally right down a steep hillside to reach another stone wall. Follow the valley bottom to reach a rickety stile in the cliff-top fence. From this point, two approaches are possible:

a) Cross here to find the lower cliff-top quarry on the left. The main abseil and gearing up ledge lies at the base of the deep gully on the right (looking out) of the stile. Steep rock steps lead down a gully to a small ledge. There is a stake is cemented in at the back of the ledge. From the base of the abseil scramble right for 200m to access the Cormorant Area; low to mid-tide and calm seas only.

b) From the rickety stile follow the fence line left to a wall. Continue along the fence line and cross the fence at the 4th wooden stile (about 150m from wall). Drop down a steep path into a small quarry. An abseil stake is in the floor of the quarry 25m from where the path enters the quarry. Access at low to mid-tide and in calm seas.

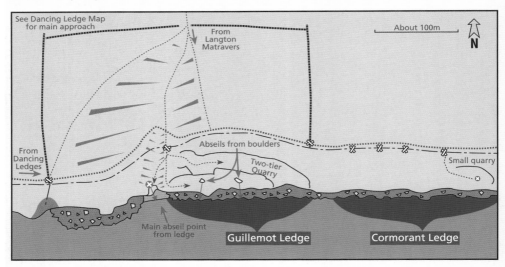

ACCESS

Cormorant Buttress West is restricted due to nesting birds.
No climbing from 1 March to 31 July.

CONDITIONS

Cormorant Ledge is a south-facing sun-trap with little significant seepage. It is possible to climb here all year round if the temperature is right. Avoid the place on the hottest days since it can become unbearable. If windy there will be little shelter on the big faces. There is little protection at the cliff base in moderate seas.

RESTRICTION (Route 1) - *No climbing 1 March to 31 July because of nesting birds.*

1 Cormorant Buttress West . . . VD 4a

The best route of its grade in the area. A remote setting and the need for the right combination of tide and calm seas make this a serious undertaking, and is not a good route for the inexperienced. Start from a large block below the large undercut buttress.

1) 16m, 4a. From the block make a tough step-up onto the wall - crux. Good holds lead up left into a shallow groove. The groove provides steeper climbing to gain the large ledge and good belays.

2) 15m. Climb up rightwards to the massive flake crack. Large nuts or cams protect the moves up the flake crack. From the top of the flake move right to an easy-angled but unstable ridge which with great care leads to the top.

FA. J.Yaldren, R.J.Crewe 11.10.1969

The next three routes are 100m to the right and best approached from the quarry abseil.

2 Quality Street . . . . HVS 4c

A superb pitch packed with excellent holds and climbing and with the added benefit of a very solid finish. One of Swanage's best HVS routes.

30m. Move up the wall on great holds to a flake at 10m, before climbing rightwards on steeper ground to gain the faultline (possible belay). Gain the steep wall on the left above the fault-line and take this to an overhang. Go left and up into a shallow corner with difficulty before easier bridging and crack climbing finishes this memorable pitch. Low in the grade.

FA. R.J.Crewe, P.Charman 10.2.1974

3 Wall Street . . . . HS 4b

A great little expedition at the grade, once again featuring good rock, holds and a solid top-out. Start just right of *Quality Street*.

1) 4b, 17m. Good holds lead up and right to an obvious crack. Keep on going on the same line past a ledge to the faultline. Traverse right to a stance on the arete just above the faultline.

2) 4b, 15m. The narrow groove above gains a solid top-out.

FA. R.J Crewe, K.Winkworth 29.3.1970

4 Oran . . . . Sev 4a

Smart climbing on good rock. Low tide and a calm sea is required to reach the start of the climb. Start 10m right of *Wall Street*.

1) 17m. Climb to and up a corner just right of the low roof. At the fault-line move right past an arete to a belay ledge.

2) 4a, 14m. Take the line above the stance bearing right towards the top.

FA. K.Winkworth, R.J.Crewe 27.3.1970

CORMORANT LEDGE

A limited number of worthwhile easier and mid grade routes in a remote area, that can be combined with the close by Guillemot Ledge Area.

TIDES - All the climbs are possible at low to mid tide and in calm seas.

APPROACH - The routes are reached by abseiling in at either end and then by scrambling along the boulder-field below the wall.

BLACKER'S HOLE

Blacker's Hole has the longest approach walk of any area in this guide but it also contains some of the greatest challenges to climbers along the whole coast. The amazing 25m wide roof of The Great Cave is a shock to the system when you first see it; this is the setting for *Laughing Arthur* and *Infinite Gravity* and these are amongst the hardest climbs of their type in the country. The undercut edge to the cave is tackled by Polaris which is another true sea cliff adventure. However, there is more on offer here in the shape of sport climbs in the quarry, quality (and accessible) trad climbs on the lower walls, and long serious trad adventures on the Polaris Area.

ACCESS
Access to all the routes in the Polaris and Great Cave area are restricted because of nesting birds.
No climbing from 1 March to 31 July.

APPROACH
The quickest approach is from the Durlston Country Park parking. Walk down past the lighthouse and turn right (looking out) along the coast path, past the Mile Pylons and around a wide bay, crossing over two stone walls. 200m past the second stone wall, locate a hidden descent ramp leading down to the left (looking out) side of the quarry. See the route pages for the specific approaches from here.

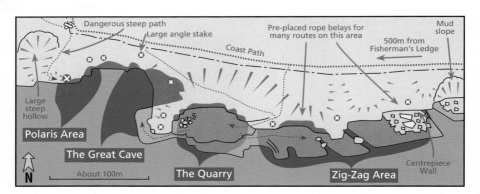

TIDES
The routes in The Great Cave and some routes on the Polaris and Centrepiece Areas are affected by the tides. More details are shown with the route descriptions. Keep well away in rough seas.

CONDITIONS
Most of the cliffs here get the sun all day except for The Great Cave which only receives some late evening light. The quarry is a useful winter suntrap but is best avoided when the weather is at its warmest. There is little seepage except in The Great Cave where dampness can linger on, and prove frustrating.

Very tricky descent down steep grass

Abseil stake. (difficult to locate)

The Great Cave →

Ledge covered at high tide

POLARIS AREA

100m or so left of the great cave are some very impressive routes centred on a huge bottomless groove (the main pitch of *Polaris*). All are very worthwhile expeditions in tremendously exposed positions. The rock quality is mostly good and the gear reasonable. Prussik loops are strongly advised on all routes here.

TIDES - Low tide is needed for the full versions of Routes 1 and 2. Routes 3 to 7 are possible at any tide although they could be a bit too exciting in rough seas.

BELAYS - Final belays for all routes are on the abseil rope. Pre-place a rope from the other stake for *Polaris*.

⊖ **RESTRICTION -** No climbing 1 March to 31 July because of nesting birds.

APPROACH (Routes 1 and 2) - *The abseil is from a single poor stake so bring another one to back it up. The stake is situated in a grassy hollow near the cliff edge, 150m west (right - looking out) of The Great Cave, and 20m left (looking out) of a deep gully with a mud slide at its top. Take great care descending the steep grass to the hollow. The abseil leads to a large ledge at sea level which is only exposed at low tide and in calm seas.*

①　Frank's Little Secret . . . . . 🔲 **HVS 4c**
A fine climb on good rock starting from the base of the abseil.
1) 4c, 25m. Climb the left-hand crack to an overhang. Traverse right and up to another then step left and ascend a crack until moves right gain a nut belay below a flake .
2) 4c, 10m. Follow a flake line above to the top.
FA. V.Dennis, N.Buckley 7.8.77

②　Polaris . . . . 🔲 **E5 6a**
Highly committing. A real south-west adventure with maximum exposure and reasonable gear. Start as for *Frank's Little Secret*.
1) 5b, 30m. Follow *Frank's* to below the second roof then traverse the fault right to the arete (or better, traverse at a lower level). Continue to belay below a large open groove.
2) 6a, 15m. Step down and onto the main arete. Tackle a steep thin crack then swing out right on a wild hand-traverse across a very steep wall. A graunchy move gains a ledge above the big roof. Nuts and peg belay. Very exposed!
3) 5c, 25m. The best pitch. Climb the side wall, 2m right of the corner, to a hidden peg. Move left and follow a slanting crack into the base of the large upper groove (good rest). Climb the pumpy groove past a bulge to an exit slab.
FA. Arni Strapcans, Gordon Jenkin, Frank Farrell 13.8.78

APPROACH (Route 3) - *Abseil down a groove just right (looking out) of the finishing corner on Polaris to a belay 10m above the sea on a scooped ledge just left of the lower arete. Nuts will need to be placed to keep in contact with the rock on the diagonal abseil.*

③　Exchange of Fire . . . . . 🔲 **E5 6a**
35m. A well-positioned route based on the left arete of the *Polaris* groove. Steep but with good rests. Dynamically climb the lower arete on its right-hand side to the fault. Follow *Polaris* up the steep thin crack then go over its capping bulge to a niche. Continue up the blunt arete to finish up the flake of *Nuke*.
FA. Martin Crocker, Mike Robertson 1.9.96

APPROACH (Routes 4 to 7) - *Abseil down the final groove of Polaris to its second stance on the lip of the roof. Nuts will be needed on the abseil to stay in contact with the rock.*

④　Nuke . . . . 🔲 **E4 6a**
25m. An exposed climb up the flake, trending left onto the arete, and finishing more easily on slightly suspect holds.
FA. Dave Ivory, Ed Hart 1.3.80 FFA. Crispin Waddy, Andy Ford 10.87

⑤　Bolt the Blue Sea . . . . 🔲 **E5 6b**
25m. A meaty number tackling a very steep crack in the left wall. Climb the back of the corner and pull over a bulge to join *Polaris*. Swing left (peg) and climb the thin crack steeply to good flake holds (peg). The flakes lead leftward onto the arete to easy ground beyond and on to the stake belay.
FA. Martin Crocker, John Harwood 15.10.94

⑥　Weapons of Sound . . . . . . 🔲 **E5 6a**
25m. Well protected. From the right-hand side of the stance, move rightwards to a pocket-line (thread). Gain a hand ledge and go up a short groove. Launch right across the steep wall, on a pocket line, to a break. Continue direct to easier ground.
FA. Martin Crocker, John Harwood 2.10.94

⑦　Enter the Void . . . . . . 🔲 **E6 6b**
25m. A superb climb in an awesome position, mainly on good pocket holds. Start out as for *Weapons of Sound* past the thread. From the hand ledge above, traverse right to another pocket line. This leads steeply (peg) to a good slot. Climb straight up the blunt white arete with hard moves to gain the ledge above. Step right to a broken but easy finish.
FA. Martin Crocker, John Harwood 2.10.94

Lots of sun | 45 min | Vertical | Abseil in | Multi-pitch

Portland West | Portland East | Lulworth | Swanage | Devon | Winspit | Hedbury | Dancing Ledge | Guillemot | Cormorant | Blacker's Hole | Fisherman's | Promenade | Cattle Troughs | Boulder Ruckle | Subluminal

Belay stakes set well back

Polaris Area

Blacker's Hole Quarry

Approach

Limit of easy access

Boulder beach above high tide

Routes hidden

Twin bolts for tyrolean into cave if needed

THE GREAT CAVE

The collection of mega routes in the cave are some of the most overhanging climbs in Britain and currently, even after fifteen years, they have seen hardly any repeats.

APPROACH - Descend from the quarry to a sea-level ledge below *Giantslayer*. The rest of the routes are reached by a serious solo traverse (about E1 5b) along the fault in the side wall. Alternatively abseil in direct over the lip of the cave to boulders, or, if one person gets into the cave a zip-line can be rigged from two bolts at the edge of the entry platform to a bolted boulder.

TIDES - You can reach the routes at high tide but it is better and easier at low tide. Keep away in rough seas.

AID CLIMBING - Please don't climb the routes in this cave as aid routes any more since vital nut/peg/thread placements may be damaged and crucial holds accidentally removed.

SPORT or TRAD? - This cave has been designated a sport climbing area but the *Giantslayer Wall* is not. However most of the routes still require a full rack of gear.

RESTRICTION - No climbing 1 March to 31 July because of nesting birds.

❶ The Schwarzechild Radius
. . . . 🔲🔲🔲🔲 ▭ **7c+/A1**

A vast arching line through the overhangs in the left side of the cave including an 8m roof crack. Pitch 2 has yet to be red-pointed but when it is done it will probably be linked with the first pitch to give a sustained 8a/8a+. To start, crawl leftwards from the pebble beach to a small ledge. This is non-tidal but requires calm seas.

1) 6b, 25m. The cave roof and leaning wall above provide a great pitch which is worth doing in its own right.
2) 6b/A1, 15m. The roof crack has yet to be redpointed.
3) 5b, 15m. Climb the 'easy' bulging pillar on the right.
FA. Pete Oxley 23.2.93

❷ Laughing Arthur 🔲🔲🔲🔲 ▭ **E8 6b**

Probably the biggest roof climb in Britain which still awaits a second ascent. It was originally a major aid climb but should no longer be climbed as such. Start at the back of the cave, left of the 'V' corner.

1) 6b, 25m. Climb the bulges (thread) to a large flake and rest (thread) above. Traverse right (peg) into the groove then surge out to good holds (thread and peg) and follow the main groove on more big holds (peg) until a short traverse left. Guano encrusted jugs above lead to ledges and a belay. This pitch will need cleaning before a successful ascent.
2) 6b, 15m. Climb the monumental roof crack, with occasional use of the side wall, to the lip. Pull around to an exposed hang-ing stance and bolt belay.
3) 6b, 8m. Follow the continuation crack, on blocky holds, to belay to the right of a slab (2 threads and a bolt).
4) 5b, 15m. Exit easily (as for *Schwarzechild..*).
FA. M.Boater, P.Deketelaere 6-8.8.70 FFA. Pete Oxley 3.12.88

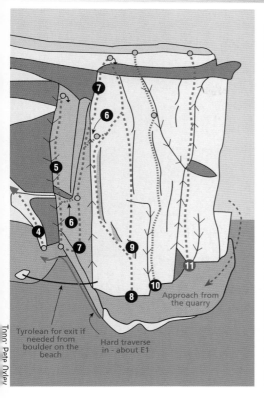

Tony Pete Oxley

Tyrolean for exit if
needed from
boulder on the
beach

Hard traverse
in - about E1

Approach from
the quarry

❸ Coma 2 . . . . 🖼️🖼️ [   ] E5 6b
18m. From the second belay on *Laughing Arthur*, climb direct past 3 bolts and 2 pegs to reach the belay on *Infinite Gravity*.
FA. Pete Oxley 25.11.89

❹ Infinite Gravity 🖼️🖼️🖼️🖼️ [   ] 8a+
45m. The outrageous 'ship's prow' arete overhangs at 45° for most of its length. This amazing route tackles it in one big pitch past 22 bolts and a peg. It has three hard sections with shakeouts in between. The first is a radical groove, then a crack bisecting a series of huge roofs and finally a less-steep arching crack and bands of horizontals with tough moves to reach the belay. The bolts are okay but a few nuts are needed in the first 8m.
Photo page 241.
FA. Pete Oxley 4.92

❺ Naked and Savage 🖼️🖼️🖼️🖼️ [   ] E7 6b
25m. A big steep pitch which is well protected by nuts and a few pegs. Start on the right-hand side of the boulder beach, below the overhanging groove line. Climb a thin crack (2 pegs) then up a corner (peg) to a niche (pegs). Gain the steep corner above and follow it to a crux undercling (peg and thread) which leads via a vertical exit crack to a bolt belay.
FA. Pete Oxley 23.8.90

❻ Procrastinating Giant 🖼️🖼️🖼️ [   ] E6 6a
A big challenge that is somewhat superseded by more recent direct routes. However, it is a great outing and gives the easiest of the cave routes. Accidentally missed out of the last guide.
1) 6a, 25m. Start up *Naked and Savage* to the niche then traverse out right via the overlap to a hanging stance at its end.
2) 5b, 10m. Climb a corner on *Monsters of Rock* past 2 pegs, and cross the right wall around the arete to a thread and peg belay.
3) 6a, 15m. Pull rightwards over bulges (thread) then climb up a left-trending crack (peg) to the fault. Surmount the capping bulge (peg) to reach a bolt belay. Climb out or abseil off.
FA. D.Fell 11.8.74. FFA. Martin Crocker, Jim Robertson 10.10.83

❼ Monsters of Rock . . 🖼️🖼️🖼️ [   ] E7 6b
A very impressive line taking the centre of the huge black wall and the groove above, bisecting *Procrastinating Giant*. Reasonable gear and low in its grade.
1) 6b, 20m. A very sustained pitch. Follow the exit traverse into the centre of the wall (old peg). Then climb straight up past 3 pegs moving right at the third to a flake (thread). Attain the overlap above and belay at its right-hand side as for *...Giant*.
2) 6a, 15m. Climb a steepening corner past old pegs. Near the top roof, swing out right in a dramatic position (peg) to pass the top bulge (peg and thread) to a bolt belay. Lower-off or top out.
FA. Pete Oxley, Jon Biddle 3.9.89

The routes *Marble Halls* and *Cold Empty Cross* have been de-bolted since they retro-bolted sections of the established trad route *Giantslayer*, and they were outside the agreed bolt zones.

The next route starts 4m right of the cave edge and is easily gained by ledges from Blacker's Hole Quarry.

❽ Giantslayer . . . . . . 🖼️🖼️🖼️ [   ] E5 6a
35m. Really good climbing in an exposed position. Quite well protected but very pumpy with a strenuous finish and the crux near the top. Gives a good introduction to the hard routes at Blacker's Hole. Watch out for rope drag. Climb a rib then head diagonally leftwards to the arete. Follow a flake crack just right of the arete to a thread and peg on *Procrastinating Giant*. Finish as for that route.
FA. Martin Crocker, D.Light 24.9.83

❾ Cold Empty Gun . . . 🖼️🖼️🖼️ [   ] E6 6a
30m. A direct line avoiding the loop on *Giantslayer*. It is bold and sustained up the blind crack - take plenty of small wires.
FFA. Dave Pickford, Richard White 2000. The route was originally a bolt line.

❿ Coercri . . . . 🖼️🖼️🖼️ [   ] E4 6a
A varied climb up the centre of the west-facing wall starting at a groove/ramp just right of *Giantslayer*. Well protected.
1) 6a, 20m. Ascend the ramp to its top (peg). Then make tricky moves to start the crack out right which leads strenuously to a ledge.
2) 5c, 10m. Climb another ramp up left (peg) then pull direct over an exposed bulge to easier ground. Stake belay.
FA. Kevin Turner, Nick Buckley 1980
FFA. Martin Crocker, Jim Robertson 28.8.83

⓫ Cosa Nostra . . . . 🖼️🖼️ [   ] E2 5c
30m. Good exposed climbing up the right-hand arete of the west face. Climb a bulging crack on the seaward side then move onto the arete. Step right, level with a ramp on the left, and follow the arete past a bulge and crack to easier ground. Stake belay well back.
FA. John Williams, Pete Oxley 21.4.88

Portland West | Portland East | Lutworth | **Swanage** | Devon | Winspit | Hedbury | Dancing Ledge | Guillemot | Cormorant | **Blacker's Hole** | Fisherman's | Promenade | Cattle Troughs | Ruckle | Boulder | Subliminal

THE QUARRY

A worthwhile spot for some sheltered fun on sport roofs. The bolts are rather old at the present time.

APPROACH - 200m past the second stone wall, locate a hidden descent ramp leading down to the left (looking out) side of the quarry. The quarry is where you descend to all the other sectors. It is non-tidal and well-sheltered.

NOTE - These routes still have old bolts but it is planned to rebolt them sometime in the near future. Until this is done, please treat all the bolts with extreme caution.

❶ Freedom Fighter 🔲 **B** ▭ **7a**
12m. Steep and entertaining.
FA. Pete Oxley 3.2.88

❷ Crack Gang Killing . 🔲 **B** ▭ **7b**
8m. There is also a desperate direct start (B9-ish, on which no boulders are allowed).
FA. Pete Oxley 18.11.88

❸ Roof Supreme . 🔲 **B** ▭ **7b+**
14m. A bicep-bulk-out.
FA. Pete Oxley 11.6.88

❹ Sunyata . . . . . 🔲 **B** ▭ **7b**
12m. A testing roof with a wild finish.
FA. Pete Oxley 6.2.88

❺ The Energy, the Faith, the Devotion
. . . . 🔲 **B** ▭ **7c+**
12m. A desperate, reachy roof and it is still hard higher up.
FA. Pete Oxley 12.3.88

❻ Plasma Stream 🔲 **B** ▭ **7c+**
12m. A hard roof to start, and nasty above as well.
FA. Pete Oxley 13.4.89

❼ The Nolans Meet Impulse Manslaughter
. . . . 🔲 **B** ▭ **7a+**
12m. A graunchy route which requires a huge reach..
FA. Pete Oxley 21.1.88

❽ Swimming in Jugs 🔲 **B** ▭ **6b+**
14m. As fun as the name suggests.
FA. Pete Oxley 6.2.88

❾ Les Hommes en Noir. . . . . **B** ▭ **6b+**
14m. The diagonal flakes on the far right are poor.
FA. Pete Oxley 3.2.88

Dave Pickford making the second ascent of *Infinite Gravity* (8a+) in he Great Cave at Blacker's Hole - *page 239*. Photo: Mike Robertson

Labels on photo: Belay stake · Preplaced rope top-out for routes 3 to 7 · Belay stake (set back) · Approach via quarry · The Quarry · Raised ledge at 2m · Ledge above high tide at this end

ZIG-ZAG AREA

The lower walls at Blacker's Hole give a good mixture of routes, some of these have been omitted due to their unstable finishes.

APPROACH - A short scramble down from the left (looking out) side of the quarry leads to a wave-cut platform. The first obvious features are a large slabby wall followed by a two-tiered cave.

TIDES - Most of the routes in both these areas start from the non-tidal ledge below the wall. The last 3 routes near *Centrepiece* need low-to-mid tide.

BELAYS - All routes finish at cliff-top stakes although some require pre-placed ropes on their upper sections.

❶ Zig-Zag . . . . 🔲🔲 VS 4c

As the name suggests, this weaves up the slab. Start at the foot of a diagonal crack.
1) 4a, 15m. Ascend the crack rightwards and over a bulge to come back left up another crack. Belay at an overhung ledge, next to the quarry.
2) 4c, 15m. Traverse a ledge on the right and climb a delicate slab rightwards to a finish that has suffered a lot of rockfalls in recent times hence the upgrade to VS.

❷ Credit in the Straight World
. . . . 🔲🔲🔲 E4 6a

25m. A good varied pitch taking the bold wall right of the slab. Starting 7m right of *Zig-Zag*, at an alcove. Climb the left-hand side of the alcove then go up a steep wall moving right to an undercut. Gain the slab and follow an easy flake before moving right and climbing another steep wall to a small groove. Move up and left to the top.
FA. Martin Crocker, Jim Robertson 20.8.83

❸ Absence Makes the Heart... 🔲🔲 E3 6a

30m. An enjoyable wall climb starting at a rib to the left of the roof stack. Climb the rib and a short groove to a ledge. Ascend rightwards passing a groove and follow the headwall (peg) trending rightwards to the top. Use a pre-placed rope to finish.
FA. Martin Crocker, Nigel Coe 23.2.86

❹ Street Fighting Years 🔲🔲🔲 E7 6c

A mighty challenge tackling the triple-roof-stack head on. Expect muscle damage! Fortunately it is well protected.
1) 6c, 12m. Climb to the roof and contort through the right-hand ceiling crack to belay around the lip on threads and wires.
2) 6b, 10m. Cross the next 3m ceiling, past a large jug, into a small corner. Swing up right to a semi-hanging belay at the break next to an old bolt stud (Friends).
3) 6a, 15m. Pull over the top roof and up an easy groove in the headwall before going leftwards to reach the belay of *Absence*.... Use a pre-placed rope to exit.
FA. Pete Oxley 22.8.89

❺ Full Circle. . . . . . . 🔲🔲🔲 E7 6c

Another sizeable roof test-piece through the right-hand side of the cave. Good gear on the crux but bold elsewhere, particularly at the start.
1) 6c, 18m. Move easily up then continue boldly over the first roof (peg on left is out of reach, unfortunately) to enter a slight groove. At the roof (thread), lean out then climb leftwards via a fading crack. Make hard moves past the lip to reach the next break. Semi-hanging belay as for *Street Fighting Years*.
2) 6a, 15m. As for *Street Fighting Years* or lower-off a pre-placed rope.
FA. Pete Oxley 14.6.99. Pete's comeback after leaving trad new routing for a long time .

❻ A Dose of the Malhams 🔲🔲 E6 6b

18m. Climb the dramatic steep prow then move over a 3m roof to the lip (currently 3 bolts but this is a bolt-free area so they may be removed). Swing left and pull up flakes to the break. Belay on the left as for *Street Fighting Years*. Finish up this or, better, lower-off pre-placed rope. Sport grade **7b+**.
FA. Pete Oxley 7.8.90 Without bolt by Dave Pickford 2000.

A traverse of the lower wall of the cave has been done. It is really only worth mentioning for its name - **It Sank the Ship, Now Eat the Lettuce, E1 5b.**

Belay stake (set back)

Pre-placed top-out or lower-off rope for routes 13 to 15 from stake here

Ledge tidal to the right of here

No access beyond this point

10   11   12   13   14   15

Portland West / Portland East / Lulworth / Swanage / Devon / Winspit / Hedbury / Dancing Ledge / Guillemot / Cormorant / Blacker's Hole / Fisherman's / Promenade / Cattle Troughs / Ruckle / Boulder / Subluminal

⑦ Sport Free World! . . . . 🔟 ☐ **E3 5c**
30m. A long line out of the right-hand side of the cave which can be split into two pitches. Take care to avoid rope drag. Start as for *A Dose of the Malhams*. Swing out up the leaning prow and traverse boldly right to a peg. Ascend direct up a shallow groove to a ledge then move leftwards via a short flake to a thin finger crack. This leads with increasing difficulty to jugs just below the top. Lower-off a pre-placed rope.
FA. Pete Oxley, Brian Tilley 10.6.99

⑧ Rufty's Roll Up . . . . 🔟 ☐ **E1 5b**
25m. A pleasant pitch away from the crowds. Start from the right-hand side of a raised ledge at 2m, situated 10m past the main cave. Climb the lower wall, past a prominent white jug, to finish up a vertical crack in the headwall.
FA. D.Simpson, A.Hedger 11.8.92

⑨ Tobacco Road . . . . 🔟 ☐ **VS 4c**
25m. Varied climbing on good rock. Start at the same point as the last route. Head rightwards and up two vertical cracks to a ledge below the headwall. Move left onto a ramp then out right to finish up cracks and a groove.

⑩ The Vapour Edge . . . . 🔟 ☐ **E1 5b**
25m. Nicely situated climbing on the edge of the wall. Start below the arete and climb it easily to a ledge at 15m. Trend right and ascend a thin crack, just left of the upper arete, finishing up the wall above.
FA. Martin Crocker, Jim Robertson 27.3.83

TIDES (Routes 11 to 15) - *At this point the wall turns a corner into another bay which is much more affected by the tide. The first two routes are just about clear but further right the ledge is only accessible from low to mid-tide.*

⑪ Snout . . . . 🔟 ☐ **E1 5b**
A strange first pitch requiring a whole variety of techniques. Start at a recess 8m right (looking in) of the left-hand corner.
1) 5b, 12m. From the recess gain the overhanging corner. Lean out to chimney up the hanging wall behind, trending rightwards into a groove. Climb the groove to a stance on the left.
2) 5b, 12m. Climb direct past a flake (thread) to a vague and serious finish - pre-placed belay rope advised.
FA. Richard Crewe, Des Marshall 11.10.75. Pitch 2 - George Hounsome, Scott Titt 1.6.80

⑫ Havana . . . . 🔟 🔟 🔟 ☐ **E4 6b**
25m. Quality climbing throughout including a technical crack up the flying headwall right of *Snout*. Well protected. Follow a direct line out of the right-hand side of the recess, passing a small roof crack to the undercut headwall. From good holds on the lip (thread) crank the thin crack to easier ground.
FA. Martin Crocker, John Harwood 15.10.94

⑬ The Equalizer . . . . 🔟 🔟 🔟 ☐ **E5 6b**
20m. Climb an easy flake (peg). Pull right over a roof (2 threads). Climb the desperate layback seam past a bolt and a peg to a ledge. Lower-off a pre-placed rope. The bolt runner may be eliminated and removed soon which will make it a bold E6.
FA. Pete Oxley 31.5.87

⑭ Centrepiece . . 🔟 🔟 🔟 🔟 ☐ **E5 6c**
20m. A great test-piece taking the dominating central line. Climb past a thread into a pod then make desperate moves up the calcite sheet. Pass a peg to a sloping ledge and belay on a pre-placed rope.
FA. Martin Crocker, Matt Ward 5.9.86

⑮ Not Forgotten, No Fade Away
. . . . 🔟 🔟 🔟 ☐ **E5 6b**
20m. Similar in quality to *Centrepiece* but more difficult to protect. Climb a direct line through the bulges and up the smooth face 3m right of *Centrepiece*. Belay as for *Centrepiece*.
FA. Martin Crocker, Matt Ward 5.9.86

FISHERMAN'S LEDGE

Fisherman's Ledge is one of the most popular and important areas at Swanage. There is a wide variety of climbing to be found including deep water solos, big trad routes, scary headpoints and bolted roof climbs. For the deep water soloist, Fisherman's Ledge (or Conner Cove as it is also known) is the place to be at the height of summer. Armed with only a beach towel and a supply of old boots and chalk bags, the climber can tackle some crazy solos or pull off an amazing 20m swallow dive. The main soloing areas are the Funky Wall and the Conger Cave.

The trad climbing of the Squid and Limited Edition Areas offers another attraction. Hereabouts are some classic routes that follow impressive lines above a solid and accessible platform. Further on is the awesome *Palace of the Brine*, home to some of the best and most spectacular roof climbing around. On the middle walls of Conner Cove are a series of high standard and often very bold trad routes - thin moves with minimal gear and without any deep water below. The rock is heavily weathered and yields some amazing pockets and gritstone-style slopers in places. On the whole, the finishes tend to be more solid than nearby cliffs which is very welcome if you are soloing or headpointing.

APPROACH

From the lighthouse, walk along the coast path to the stile before the mile marker pylon. Cross the fence and continue along its seaward side for 300m, to where a slight ridge descends to the cliff-top above *Helix* and *Freeborn Man*. The various areas require different approaches from here, these are described in detail with each section.

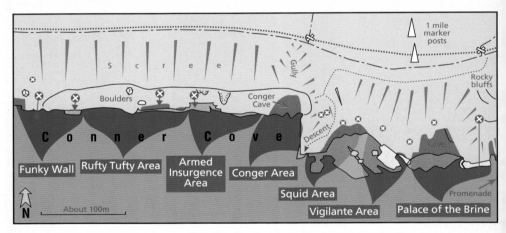

TIDES

Most of the areas are unaffected by high tide apart from the Palace of the Brine Cave which floods at mid-to-high tide, cutting off the walk-in approach. Many of the solos are safer at high tide although it isn't essential for the majority of the routes. The whole area is worth keeping away from in rough seas.

CONDITIONS

The cliffs get the sun for most of the day although Palace of the Brine is so steep that no sunlight actually touches the routes. It is usually considered as a summer venue because of the deep water soloing; however if you don't intend taking the plunge, then you can come here all year round and may benefit from fresh conditions in the cooler months. It can get very hot in mid-summer. There is some seepage in the Palace of the Brine, on the roofs of the Conger Cave and around *Captain Bloods..* but this is usually gone by early summer.

Abseil from two stakes (set back)

Main abseil to ledge from stake (set back)

Small foot ledge at high water mark

Ledge (Funky) at 5m above high water mark

Lots of sun | 40 min | Vertical | Abseil in

THE FUNKY WALL

The Funky Wall is a committing arena with routes which are mostly deepwater solos. The wall is completely hidden from view from above which adds to the air of commitment. Once you abseil in you will find superb weathered limestone, similar to the *Freeborn Man* wall, and almost gritstone-like in its appearance and feel. The best conditions are in summer and autumn but it can get very hot on this wall owing to the black rock. There is some seepage on Routes 1 to 4.

TIDES - All the routes are possible at any tide but keep away in rough seas.

APPROACH (Routes 1,2 and 5 to 15) - Abseil from a stake at the right-hand (looking out) end of the cliff-top ledge system to a sizeable ledge (The Funky Ledge) from where most of the routes start. If a 'splash down' has occurred, swim to the right-hand side (looking in) of this ledge to get out. Then either prussik up the ab rope, solo out via *The Rise and Dear Demise..* (HVS 5a), or swim a couple of hundred metres rightwards to *Helix* and solo out. Be careful, this is a serious spot. It is probably best to stay away from the routes in this area if you aren't confident of soloing up a HVS 5a which is **not** a deep water solo.

❶ ...And Captain Blood's Cavern

🔲🔲🔲🔲 E4 6a

40m. An atmospheric and beautifully structured classic poised over a hidden sea cavern. Seepage can affect this route. From the ledge, traverse the break a long way leftwards, until almost at the sea cavern. Launch up the leftward-arching corner for 10m and overcome the bulge on the left to gain an easier exit on the right. **(S1)** *Photo page 251.*
FSA. Joff Cook 8.8.90

❷ Davey Jones' Lock-off

🔲🔲🔲🔲 E5 6a

45m. At the end of the arch-traverse on *Captain Bloods*, step down and continue left to a jutting foot ledge. Climb the bulge above on undercuts and side-pulls to a rest. Finish up left. **(S2)**
FSA. Crispin Waddy 8.94

APPROACH (Routes 3 and 4) - *Abseil directly from two stakes above a large boulder, keeping a big swing going to reach a small footledge at the base of a corner at sea level (good large nut placement).*

❸ Privateer

🔲🔲🔲🔲 E6 6b

20m. *Captain Blood's* big brother which is dead scary with a high and exposed crux. Climb the corner above to join *Captain Bloods*' archway for 5m. Pull around a bulge to follow a tough right-facing groove which terminates in a committing finale to exit into a short crack. **(S2)** *Photo page 197.*
FA. Martin Crocker 12.10.96 - as an E5 6b trad route with a different start.
Line described above soloed by Pete Oxley 23.5.98

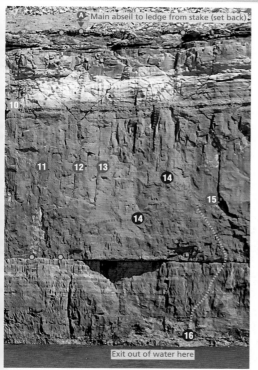

Main abseil to ledge from stake (set back)

Exit out of water here

8 Amazonia . . . . [symbols] **E3 5c**
20m. A great introduction to this sector for soloists. From the ledge gain a secondary small shelf then head leftwards to an arete and corner. Tricky low down. **(S1)**
FSA. Joff Cook 4.6.93

9 Amazon Emancipation
. . . . [symbols] **E5 6c**
16m. Hot and sticky and not a DWS. It follows the very narrow corner directly above the secondary ledge on *Amazonia*. Belay on this ledge then climb up to a desperate move over a bulge at 8m (should stop most attempts). Crucial Rock 2 at mid-height and hard-won gear in general.
FA. Martin Crocker 15.9.96

The next routes are not deep water solos. Presently they finish at stakes and drilled thread belays.

10 The Rise and Dear Demise
of the Funky Nomadic Tribes . . [symbols] **HVS 5a**
15m. Good incuts all the way up a slight groove starting from the left-hand side of the main ledge. Plenty of wires protect.
FA. Kevin Turner, Frank Farrell 27.8.79

11 Ten Thousand Spoons . [symbols] **E2 5c**
15m. A line up the wall above the middle of the ledge on seams and cracks. Hard for the grade.
FA. Mike Robertson, Barry Clarke, Mark Williams 3.8.96

12 The Friendly Ranger from Clontarf Castle
. . . . [symbols] **E2 5c**
15m. A tricky face climb on good rock, starting from the right-hand side of the ledge. Good gear and a slightly fluttery finish.
FA. Kevin Turner, Frank Farrell 27.8.79

13 Telomere . . . . [symbols] **E1 5b**
17m. A very pleasant pitch from the right-hand side of the ledge taking a rightward-trending line of holds into a small notch at the top. Good gear.
FA. Barry Clarke, Mike Robertson, D.Gilbert 3.8.96

14 The Talisman . . . . [symbols] **E6 6a**
22m. A serious eliminate. Start as for *Telomere* initially then head out right via a pocketed break (thread) to another thread and good wires. Step left and climb the blank unprotected scoop slightly left to good wires in a niche. Trend right easily to finish. Belay on drilled threads and a stake to the left or boulder to the right.
FA. Mike Robertson, James Dunlop 5.10.96

15 Gorillas in the Mist . . . . . . [symbols] **E3 5c**
22m. A quality line which starts as for *The Talisman*. At the thread at the end of the pocketed traverse, ascend a cracked layback rib to the top, exiting up a groove on the left. Belay as for *The Talisman*.
FA. Mike Robertson, Mark Williams 16.8.96

16 Charmed Life . . . . [symbols] **E6 6b**
20m. This route gives *The Talisman* a long direct start for a fine, balanced, hard route. Approach - abseil to the right-hand side of the very lowest ledge at sea level - **low tide and calm seas only.** Trend right to the low break (good wires) then make fingery pocket pulls (crux) above gear, to the thread on *Talisman*. Finish as for that route.
FA. Pete Oxley 3.8.99

4 For Whom the Swell Tolls
. . . . [symbols] **E6 6b**
22m. Three cruxes with some steep stuff near the top for maximum pump. Swing right at sea level for 2m and ascend a hard scoop to the big break. Continue up on good incuts then make extending moves leftwards to reach a giant undercut. Deep breath - 'go for it' with full power direct to a mantelshelf exit, passing a big jug mid way. May have lost a crucial hold. **(S2)**
FA. Pete Oxley 23.5.98. Includes part of a short-lived but nice route called In Too Deep, E3 6a in its mid section. This line started at the break and moved right into Fathoms to finish - still worth seeking out.

5 Fathoms . . . . . [symbols] **E3 5b**
26m. A 'rite-of-passage' route with a crux at the top. Approach as for *Captain Blood's*. Traverse the break left for 8m to a ledge then climb the first big groove diagonally leftwards to its finishing bulge. Leaving the big jug may take some will-power. **(S1)**
FSA. Crispin Waddy 8.9.86

6 Feeding Neptune [symbols] **E6 6b**
25m. A steep bouldery route with some 'big air potential'. Start up *Donald, Where's Your Trousers* then break left across difficult terrain to a thin finger flake. Excitement guaranteed! **(S1)**
FSA. Pete Oxley 24.7.99

7 Donald, Where's Your Trousers
. . . . [symbols] **E3 5c**
25m. Follow *Fathoms* to the small ledge below the big groove. Then break right up a lovely wall to finish up a short flake. **(S1)**
FSA. Crispin Waddy 8.9.86

A. Abseil from boulder (set back)

Gorillas in the Mist

Semi-hanging belay on abseil rope

Lots of sun | 40 min | Vertical | Abseil in

RUFTY TUFTY AREA

There are no deepwater solos on this section, it is back to trad lines on excellent quality rock. Once again, the routes are hard to spot from above so take care to plan your approach well.

TIDES - All the routes start from non-tidal ledges. Keep away in rough seas.

BELAYS - Belays are found on stakes, boulders and drilled threads on the cliff-top.

APPROACH (Routes 1 and 2) - *Abseil directly down a rib, from a big boulder, to a semi-hanging stance, 4m above sea level.*

❶ The Slant . . . . 🔲🔲🔲🔲 **E3 5c**
19m. Tackle a left-trending ramp starting up *The Friendly Landlord...* Good moves on mostly-perfect rock. Climb diagonally past two very thin threads (and not a whole lot of other gear) to exit at a boulder belay with drilled threads.
FA. Mike Robertson, Barry Clarke 17.8.96

❷ The Friendly Landlord of Durlston Castle
. . . . . 🔲 **E1 5b**
16m. Beautiful rock up the right-hand side of the rib, 5m left of the large rectangular recess. At two thirds height, move left 3m and finish past a thread.
FA. Crispin Waddy 6.9.86 (solo)

APPROACH (Routes 3 to 10) - *Abseil from a stake 10m west (right - looking out) of the finish of Aubergine. This leads down a brown scoop (Rufty Tufty Vivisects his Mummy) which drops over a large roof at the bottom to ledges.*

❸ Where the Land Meets the Sea 🔲🔲 **E2 5c**
20m. From the recess traverse left for 3m then follow a big diagonal flake to two sling placements. Finish direct via a run-out technical scoop.
FA. Pete Oxley 21.6.99 (solo)

❹ On the Third Day . . . . . . 🔲🔲 **E3 5c**
15m. Climb a groove from the left-hand side of the recess, finishing rightward past a roof via a flake line.
FA. Crispin Waddy, Toby Foord Kelsey 8.9.86

❺ Break Like a Wave . 🔲🔲🔲 **E4 6b**
15m. An unusual direct start to the next route, only the tall will reach the lip of the roof. From abseil, pre-place a sling over a jug on the lip of the recess, 3m right of the end of the overhang. Make wild moves (safe due to sling) straight past the roof then climb direct on thin flakes to the top past a mild runout.
FA. Pete Oxley, Dave Pickford 23.6.99

❻ Moving Away from Rufty Tufty 🔲🔲🔲 **E5 6b**
. . . .
16m. A serious route. Make a brutal pull up the roof-crack (as for *Rufty Tufty*) then move diagonally left up a 'grit-like' ramp to a vague crack. This leads to a hard finish shared with *Break Like a Wave*.
FA. Crispin Waddy 1988 (solo)

Abseil from stake
Abseil from stake (set back)
Armed Insurgence Area
Large recessed cave with ledge above high water level
Access possible via thin footledge
Ledge

Portland West
Portland East
Lulworth
Swanage
Devon
Winspit
Hedbury
Dancing Ledge
Guillemot
Cormorant
Blacker's Hole
Fisherman's
Promenade
Subliminal
Boulder Ruckle
Cattle Troughs

7 Rufty Tufty **E4 6b**
15m. Climb the roof-crack as for the last route but continue direct up the easier, pocketed crack above. Step right to finish.
FA. J.Preston, Jon Biddle 7.9.86. Once a gem of a route but now much harder than when it was first done after a rock fall removed the start.

8 Rufty Tufty Vivisects His Mummy
. . . . **E5 6b**
16m. Features French-style 'gouttes'. Start as for *Rufty Tufty* then make a hard traverse right to the base of a the brown-streaked scoop. Climb this to the top. Safe but very strenuous.
FA. Crispin Waddy 8.9.86 (solo).
Reclimbed by Pete Oxley, Dave Pickford 23.6.99

9 Hallucinating Freely
. . . . **E6 6b**
15m. High in the grade; it only has two runners. Start 15m left (looking in) of *Aubergine*. From the right-hand side of a recessed cave climb a series of layback fins (crucial Rock 6) then pull over a bulge to an incut (crucial Rock 2). Continue with difficulty up the headwall in an ethereal kind of way!
FA. Pete Oxley 29.8.89

10 End of the Innocence **E4 6b**
15m. A reasonably well-protected route with some great climbing. Start 3m right along the thin ledge and head out rightwards up a flake (a project heads left from this point) to follow the overhung corner diagonally right - hard!
FA. Pete Oxley 29.8.89

APPROACH (Routes 11 to 14) - *Abseil down Aubergine which follows a corner in the west (right - looking out) side of the central bay. All routes finish at stake belays.*

11 Tempting Truancy . . **E4 5c**
15m. Excellent fingery wall climbing taking the face 4m left of *Aubergine* but with negligible gear.
FA. Crispin Waddy, P.Windall, Toby Foord-Kelsey 9.9.86. The team beat Jon Biddle to this route as he had to go to school!

12 Terminal One **E6 6a**
15m. A very serious eliminate based on the 'grit-like' arete just left of *Aubergine*. A skyhook and poor thread protect the upper section. No side runners at this grade. Very photogenic.
FA. Mike Robertson 6.10.97

13 Aubergine . . . . **HVS 5a**
15m. Often used as an escape route but it is worthy in its own right. Climb the big flake crack in the corner past good gear and one stubborn section. *Photo page 245.*
FA. R.Kent, K.Winkworth, P.Charman, R.J.Crewe 1.3.70

14 Mile High Club **E6 6c**
15m. A cracking test-piece. From the bottom of the ramp on *Aubergine*, step right and climb up flutings to the break (gear). Undercut a flake and make a very hard move slightly rightwards. Finish direct with no more gear. Serious.
FA. Pete Oxley, Brian Tilley 16.12.99

ARMED INSURGENCE AREA

The final section before the Conger Area is another wall covered with some fairly hard trad routes. There is nothing of any great quality but all are worthwhile for those who have done a lot elsewhere.
TIDES - All the routes start from non-tidal ledges. Keep away in rough seas.

APPROACH (Routes 1 to 6) - *Abseil down Aubergine which follows a corner in the west (right - looking out) side of the central bay. The routes finish at various belays consisting of drilled threads, blocks and stakes.*

① Into You (Like a Train) ▮▮▮ **E5 6b**
15m. The steep, seamed bulge 3m right of *Aubergine* is very technical though with good wires when you really need them.
FA. Mike Robertson 3.9.96

② Armed Insurgence. ▮▮▮ **E3 5c**
15m. The centre of the black wall above a big ledge, trending right via the intermittent crack to a steep finish.
FA. G.Stace, S.Cook 15.4.84

③ Pariah .... ▮▮▮ **E6 6b**
15m. A good, bold line. From a small ramp 5m right of *Armed Insurgence* (wire), follow side-pulls direct until serious moves left gain a huge flake on *Armed Insurgence*. Finish up this.
FA. Pete Oxley, James Dunlop 3.5.99

The black wall right of Pariah is an excellent-looking project (Black Box Recorder) which will be one of the hardest and most serious routes in the south when it is climbed at E8 6c.

④ A Taste for Danger ▮▮▮ **E3 6a**
15m. The shallow black corner rising above a break in the ledge is harder than it looks. The gear is sparse but good. Exit rightwards via an easy slab.
FA. Pete Oxley, Brian Tilley 20.5.99

⑤ La Quebrada .... ▮▮ **E3 6a**
15m. Strenuous but reasonably safe. Start at a corner 3m right of *A Taste for Danger* above a small belay ledge. Climb into the corner then move out left to follow a central rib through steep black overlaps to an exit flake. Finish as for *A Taste for Danger*.
FA. Pete Oxley, James Dunlop 3.5.99. Named after the famous diving point in Acapulco.

⑥ Whack your Porcupine. **E1 5b**
15m. Climb the steep, tapering groove 3m right of the area of steep 'rooflets'. There is no real belay ledge at the bottom.
FA. Crispin Waddy (solo) 8.9.86

APPROACH (Routes 7,8 and 9) - *After a gap of 5m, past an easy corner marking the end of the shallow bay, are the next routes. Abseil directly into these from awkward nut and drilled thread belays.*

⑦ Barry's Route **E1 5c**
15m. Move left to the corner/groove.
FA. Barry Clarke 2002

⑧ The Caretaker .... ▮▮▮ **E6 6a**
15m. A serious headpoint taking a good line up the face left of *Ruurd Ruum* to arrive at an easy exit groove. Hard climbing above a nasty landing with no gear! A solo.
FA. Mike Robertson 6.98

⑨ Ruurd Ruum .... ▮▮ **E4 5c**
15m. Ropes needed. An under-rated pitch that starts as for *The Caretaker* then takes a fine series of rightward-slanting cracks to an exit groove. Difficult to protect, take RPs.
FA. Crispin Waddy, Toby Foord Kelsey 8.9.86

Mark Glaister DWS'ing a long way above the sea on the finish of
..And Captain Blood's Cavern (E4 6a) - *page 246*. Photo: Mike Robertson

Huge gearing up/diving ledge

Lots of sun | 40 min | Vertical | Steep | Abseil in

The John Williams Traverse, 6a

Routes 7, 8 and 9 reached from a boat or by swimming

THE CONGER AREA

This is the show-piece of all the deep water soloing venues described in this book. All the routes provide superb challenges with the additional benefit of some good viewing galleries and high diving areas adding to the interest.

TIDES - High tide is preferred for the solo routes though it is not a necessity.

APPROACH - (For the routes 1 to 3) - *Abseil in directly to the base of the corner of A Bridge Too Far from wires and blocks.*

❶ Leap of Faith **E3 5c**
16m. The arete left of the cave gives fine climbing, in a great position, on rock which is full of hidden pockets. Move left-wards around the bulge. Be aware of a submerged rock at the base, and be careful with the friable rock at the top. **(S2)**
FSA. Damian Cook 6.93

❷ Tsunami . .   **E4 6a**
16m. The direct finish to *A Bridge Too Far* with a tricky move around the bulge. An exposed and bouldery crux at the top focuses the mind! **(S1)**
FA. Damian Cook 6.93

❸ A Bridge Too Far . .   **E1 5b**
16m. A good line but with a friable finish. Start at the large corner left of the cave. Climb the corner to a roof then step down right to a foothold. Bridge (ouch) the chimney then continue rightwards to the exit of *The Conger*. **(S1)**
Yawn Yawn, VS 4c - The chimney direct is accessed via a traverse right from the belay.
FSA. Nick Buckley 9.79

SAFTEY - There have been nasty injuries here sustained after falling and jumping. Jon Cook ruptured his lung and Jon Biddle ripped his shorts off when he hit the slab on Freeborn Man whilst leaping off! Just because the route has been deep water soloed doesn't mean that you will be okay if you fall off. Always make your own decisions as to what you wish to attempt and make sure you keep your legs together when hitting the water.

APPROACH - (For the routes 4 to 6) - *Abseil to a hanging belay on an undercut pillar below and left (looking in) of The Conger exit. For those really into deep water soloing, the same point can be reached by traversing the fine technical wall between the base of A Bridge Too Far and the hanging stance. This link is* **The John Williams Traverse, 6a (S0)**

❹ Crime Wave **E2 5c**
16m. The face left of *Furious Pig* is a bit thin on gear. Makes a good descent solo when familiar with the area. **(S0)**
FSA. Damian Cook 6.93

❺ Furious Pig **E2 5c**
16m. Climb the left-hand pillar and flake to *The Conger* exit. **(S0)**
FSA. Crispin Waddy 3.89

❻ The Great Shark Hunt   **E4 6a**
17m. The right-hand groove from the hanging pillar start. One of the best deep water solos around. **(S0)**
FA. Crispin Waddy 3.89

Descent route
Helix (Diff)

A Twin abseil stakes

20

Squid
Area

19

16   17   18   21

Traverse ledge for start of routes

⑪ Snap, Crackle and Plop 　　　　　　　 **E3 5c**
20m. A direct finish above the chimney of *The Conger*. Friable holds make it even more exciting. **(S1)**
FSA. Damian Cook 11.9.90. Possiblby done before.

⑫ Jellied . . . . 　　　　　　　 **E3 5c**
22m. Another variation finish above the chimney of *The Conger*. Break rightwards above the big roof to a prow. **(S1)**
FSA. Jon Biddle 8.90

⑬ The Drowning Pool
　　　　　　　 E6 6c
20m. This follows an impossible-looking sister line to *Swordfish Trombones* through the left-hand side of the roof, finishing on the last holds of *Jellied*. **(S2)**
FSA. Pete Oxley 27.3.99

⑭ Swordfish Trombones 　　　 **E5 6b**
20m. A wild trip through the roofs above the hanging slabs of *The Conger*. The big roof provides most of the excitement with a hard pull over to finish. It does have good gear if you are thinking of leading it. **(S2)**
FSA. Crispin Waddy 27.9.87

⑮ The Musharagi Tree . . 　　　 **E2 5c**
18m. The diagonal hanging slab which can be started direct via the hanging arete (harder). Start at the niche of *Conger*. **(S1)**
FA. Jon Biddle, John Williams 1.8.88. Formerly known as 'The Great Durlston Prawn Robbery'.

⑯ Halcyon Days . . . . . . 　　　 **E2 5b**
17m. This tackles the fine overhanging corner above a good belay ledge to the finish of *Musharagi Tree*. Not a solo.
FA. Gordon Jenkin, Frank Farrell 9.79

⑰ Herman Borg's Basic Pulley Slippage
. . . . 　　　 **E6 6b**
17m. The left arete of the side wall is very technical. **(S2)**
FSA. Pete Oxley 1996. Originally climbed with a bolt by Pete Oxley in 1993.

⑱ Freeborn Man . 　　　 **E4 6a**
17m. A classic frightener with a soft landing which is traditionally attempted as an onsight solo. From halfway along the approach traverse, climb the slab and then the steep pocketed wall above to a big hole. Swing left and make some final tricky moves onto the top slab. **(S1)**
FA. Nick Buckley, Kevin Turner 8.79

⑲ Freeborn Borg . . . . . . 　　　 **E5 6b**
18m. Break left just below the crux of *Freeborn Man* to finish on *Herman Borg*. **(S2)**
FSA Pete Oxley (solo) 19.3.99

⑳ Freeborn Direct . . . . 　　　 **E4 6a**
17m. After the crux, exit direct onto the slab. **(S1)**
FSA. Mike Ford date unknown

㉑ Troubled Waters . . . . . 　　　 **HVS 5a**
17m. An line up the wall right of *Freeborn Man* is popular as a warm-up for the bigger challenges to the left. **(S0)**
FSA. Pete Oxley 15.7.85

⑦ The Appearing . . . . 　　　 **E5 6a**
25m. Approach by boat! Start in the back of *The Conger* cave at a bottomless chimney on the left. Climb to a good ledge where a winding series of cracks lead to the high point of *The Vanishing*. Follow *The Vanishing* to finish up *The Conger*. **(S2)**
FSA. Adam Wainwright 31.8.02

⑧ Red Bully . . . . 　　　 **E5 6a**
25m. Follow *The Appearing* to the good ledge. Move leftwards over a slab and bulge to join *The Vanishing* just before it reaches daylight. **(S2)**
FSA. Adam Wainwright 31.8.02

⑨ The Vanishing . . . . 　　　 **E5 6a**
28m. The first breach of the *The Conger* cave. Start on a ledge system on the right at the back of the cave gained by boat or swimming. Move up and left across a slab onto an arete (spotter needed). Climb the arete to the top of the cave and a good rest. Move down and out to *The Conger* chimney via some complicated moves. Finish as for *The Conger*. **(S1)**
FSA Mike Robertson 16.8.2001

APPROACH (For the routes 10 to 21) - *Solo or abseil down the route Helix to the sea-level ledge at its base.*

⑩ The Conger . . . . . 　　　 **E2 5c**
20m. A totally memorable solo in a very atmospheric position. It can be wet out of season. Start by traversing in along the break to a niche just before the cave. Continue past another corner and across slabs until stopped by a wall. Go round the rib and bridge out and up the chimney. Keep bridging then pull out left and up to finish. **(S0)**
FA. Richard Crewe 7.9.69. FFA. Frank Farrell 9.79. First soloed by Nick Buckley 26.6.83

Portland West
Portland East
Lulworth
Swanage
Devon
Winspit
Hedbury
Dancing Ledge
Guillemot
Cormorant
Blacker's Hole
Fisherman's
Promenade
Cattle Troughs
Boulder Buckle
Sublaminal

Approach from stile

Abseil stakes

Helix
(descent route)

Conger
Area

Ledge above high tide but awash in heavy seas

Limited Edition Area

SQUID AREA

This area is often ignored in favour of its more illustrious neighbours but it contains a good set of mainly harder routes that tackle the steep overlap-covered wall.
APPROACH - Reverse down *Helix* or abseil from stakes above the finish of *Quo Vadis*. The first route in this area is on the far left (looking in) of the sea-level ledges, just before the cliff turns a corner. All routes finish at cliff-top stakes.
TIDES - The ledges are above high tide but keep away in rough seas when the waves will reach the ledge.

❶ Helix . . . . **Diff**
15m. A superb climb for its grade - solid and varied. It spirals leftwards up a hidden slab above the Conger Cave. It is most often climbed as a descent to these areas.

❷ Felix . . . . **VDiff**
15m. Very pleasant climbing up the juggy black wall with a tricky high groove.

❸ Rough Boys . . . . **HVS 5b**
18m. Some good climbing but slightly escapable. Start 3m right of a wide crack. The hard bit is reserved for the upper crack. Hard for the grade.
FA. Nigel Coe, Frank Farrell 4.8.84

❹ Bon Firé **E1 5c**
18m. A great little expedition. Start as for *Rough Boys* then move right before traversing rightwards across the lip of the big upper roof before finishing straight up.
FA. Crispin Waddy, Dave Thomas 4.89

❺ The Wey of All Men **E3 6a**
Well-protected and varied. Start as for *Rough Boys.*
1) 4c, 10m. Climb up to clear the first overhang then traverse right above it to belay near the end of a slab.
2) 6a, 15m. Climb the roof crack on the left (crux) then continue direct via a thin crack.
FA. Dave Thomas, Crispin Waddy 25.3.89

❻ Quo Vadis Direct **E2 5c**
Despite the name, a wandering route up the buttress left of the impending roofs above the main ledge. The start is often wet.
1) 5c, 8m. Pull over the first roof then move out left and up a short groove. Continue through the next roof onto a slab and belay on *The Wey of All Men.*
2) 5b, 15m. Traverse right and break through the next overhang. Come back left to an arete then climb direct, via an open groove, past another overhang, to the top.
FA. Chris King, Pat Littlejohn 1.3.79

⑩ Squid . . . . 🔲🔲🔲 **E2 5c**
Similar to *The Ritz* but with a very definite crux roof. Be careful to avoid rope drag. Start beneath the right wall of the roofed central bay at a diagonal crack. A tough E2.
1) 4c, 10m. Follow the crack up left to a ledge and take a small chimney to the left of a roof. Belay on a good ledge on the right.
2) 5c, 15m. Assault the brutal roof to a breather in a chimney below the next roof. Traverse left into the light to join *The Ritz* at the arete and finish as for that route.
FA. R.J.Crewe, J.Yaldren 6.8.67. FFA. Falco Rech, Howard Lancashire 1975

⑪ Crackers . . . . 🔲🔲 **E3 5c**
A bold undertaking skirting the right-hand side of the roofs.
1) 5b, 10m. Climb direct above the start of *Squid* via a short groove. Trend left to the *Squid* belay.
2) 5c, 15m. Climb rightwards to make difficult and scary moves over the roof into a small groove. Finish straight up.
FA. Kevin Turner, Nick Buckley 9.79

⑫ Mental as Anything 🔲🔲🔲 **E4 6b**
30m. The very exposed stacked roof right of *Crackers* gives a safe and strenuous undertaking. Start above a diagonal crack. Climb past a ledge then up a groove to tackle the first overhang (2 threads). Pull straight over another roof to a scoop. Then undercut rightwards and cross a final overhang to reach an easier cracked corner. Climb this by its right-hand wall.
FA. Pete Oxley 22.12.87

⑬ Rock Around the Block Direct
. . . . 🔲🔲 **E3 6a**
30m. An enjoyable outing which is more sustained than cruxy. Start at the left-hand side of a rock pool. Trend right to gain a chimney then pull over the block roof directly on its left-hand side. Continue to the top via the big groove.
FA. Pete Oxley 15.2.88

⑭ Sting in the Tail . . . 🔲🔲🔲 **E4 5c**
30m. Highly underrated. Bold but with great rock on a good line up the left-hand side of the main face. High in the grade. Start on the right-hand side of a rock pool. Climb past a roof and up a flake on its left-hand side. Then move rightwards up a wall passing a shallow groove to gain the upper corner. Weave up this, first rightwards, then finish back left (poor peg). Save some 'umpf' for the final moves.
FA. Crispin Waddy, Pete Oxley 11.7.86

⑮ Limited Edition . . . . . . 🔲🔲 **E3 5c**
26m. Described here with a new start. One of the highlights of the sector which takes a big line up the centre of the wall. Start just right of an arete. Climb to a shallow right-facing corner. Climb this easily to a roof then move direct up the impending wall above (peg) to the top. The original start has suffered a rockfall and is now much bolder above the low hard section.
FA. Gordon Jenkin, Frank Farrell 17.5.80

⑦ Paternoster . . . . 🔲🔲 **E2 5b**
A typically awkward undertaking which was once given HVS. Start as for *Quo Vadis Direct*.
1) 5b, 20m. Climb into a niche and then up into a chimney/slot (2 threads). Break right to gain a blocky corner then traverse left, 4m along a break, beneath a strip roof. Climb into an open groove and belay on a perched ledge on the left.
2) 5b, 8m. Ascend the groove above to a snappy finish.
FA. Martin Barnicott, R.Henderson 30.5.76

⑧ Bad Young Brother . . . . 🔲🔲 **E4 6b**
30m. A wicked direct route but with reasonable gear. From the first niche on *The Ritz*, break left (crux) around a bulge (2 threads on the left) to gain the blocky corner on *Paternoster*. Go direct over the roof (peg) then climb straight up twin cracks, passing a large flake. Follow a crack above (thread) to the top.
FA. Pete Oxley 28.5.88

⑨ The Ritz . . . . 🔲🔲🔲 **E3 6a**
A brilliant outing for the grade, travelling through some awesome overhangs with good protection. Start below a niche.
1) 5b, 10m. Attain the small niche then move right into a chimney. Swing right along a roof and climb a groove to the next roof. Ape through this to an amazing hanging perch to belay.
2) 6a, 10m. Put on your cycle clips and power through the roof crack on the right to below another roof. Traverse left to an arete then climb the corner above to finish.
FA. Nick Buckley, Kevin Turner 11.78

Approach under Squid Area

Lots of sun | 40 min | Vertical | Steep | Abseil in

1
2
5
Limited Edition
3
4
6
Palace of the Brine Cave
Ledge above high tide
Approach
Approach via wave washed platform

VIGILANTE AREA

The right-hand end of the Squid area has a couple of huge boulders on the platform. The wall above this has a few routes which are of interest to the enthusiast.

APPROACH and TIDES - Scramble down *Helix* and walk right along the ledge. These routes all start from a raised ledge well clear of the sea. They can be done in moderately rough seas or at any tide by abseiling in direct.

❶ **Aquascrotum II** . . . . 🔲 **HVS 5a**
17m. Climb the corner, moving left around the bulge at the top.
FA. R.Snell, I. Howell 12.2.67

❷ **Slow Road to Ruin** . 🔲🔲🔲 **E5 6a**
17m. After an easy start, follow the bold, right-trending groove to finish on the last moves of *Vigilante* (shared peg).
FA. Mike Robertson 11.7.97

❸ **Vigilante** . . . . . 🔲🔲🔲🔲 **E6 6b**
18m. The central line direct up the wall gives intricate climbing that does not relent. It is bold low down then continues direct before trending left (peg) near the top. Small wires are needed. Two bits of fixed gear have disappeared hence the higher grade.
FA. Pete Oxley 3.4.88

❹ **Sue's Route** . . . . 🔲🔲 **E2 5b**
18m. Enjoyable. Climb the technical cracks and flakes on the right that form a long shallow groove.
FA. W.Church, R.Houston 1968

❺ **Girl from the Snow Country** 🔲🔲 **E1 5c**
15m. A hidden gem. From *Sue's Route* follow a diagonal flake onto a slab and the lovely calcite pocket vein above. This leads straight over the roof and direct to the top.
FA. Pete Oxley 3.4.88

❻ **All Quiet on the Southern Front**
. . . . 🔲🔲 **E3 5c**
20m. An absorbing climb with tricky gear but in a good position. From the right-hand end of the ledge, swing out right to a spike and then continue fairly directly up the vague rib on finger flakes.
FA. Pete Oxley 20.6.87

PALACE OF THE BRINE CAVE

APPROACH and TIDES (Routes 7 to 10) - *Scramble down Helix and walk below the Squid Area on the low ledges. Low to mid-tide only.*

❼ **Impending Gleam** . 🔲🔲🔲 **E4 5c**
25m. A tremendous climb up the huge towering groove.
FA. Nick Buckley 1993

❽ **Temple Redneck** . . 🔲🔲🔲 **7c+**
30m. A sensational and highly-rated route up the arete on the left-hand side of the cave. Climb the right-hand side of the arete and over a large roof. Continue up the steep wall to the break on *Mind Cathedral*. Swing out left to situ lower-off krabs, or belay and finish as for *Mind Cathedral*.
FA. Pete Oxley 22.2.93

❾ **Haka Pereperu** . . . 🔲🔲🔲 **8a**
35m. A major stamina pitch and a worthy companion for *Palace of the Brine*. Start up *Temple Redneck* to the break and shake out by the thread. Pull up right to a haven with a difficult kneebar shake out. Drop down and execute a complex series of swings right under the roof, passing a strange fang to join the last section of *Project Lifeforce*. From big flakes at the lip more tricky moves lead up a short groove to the top.
FA. Pete Oxley 12.6.2005. Another last minute addition, the day the book goes to the printers.

❿ **The Mind Cathedral** . 🔲🔲🔲 **E6 6b**
The big groove in the roof gives well protected outrageous climbing - a classic. Recent loss of holds hasn't affected the grade.
1) **6b, 30m.** Climb the groove (2 threads) to a belay on the lip.
2) **5b, 8m.** Finish straight up a short wall.
FA. Pete Oxley 21.5.88

The next line of bolts is an open project.

⓫ **Palace of the Brine** 🔲🔲🔲 **8a+**
30m. A huge climb taking an amazing line through the roof of the cave. Start from a non-tidal ledge and trend right up a blank wall. Then ape out left to tackle the horizontal groove in the 15m roof.
FA. Pete Oxley 21.9.91

Portland West | Portland East | Lulworth | **Swanage** | Devon | Winspit | Hedbury | Dancing Ledge | Guillemot | Cormorant | Blacker's Hole | **Fisherman's** | Promenade | Cattle Troughs | Boulder Ruckle | Subliminal

Lots of sun | 40 min | Steep | Abseil in | Tidal

Large pylon 50m uphill →

Abseil possible from stake at any tide state

Traverse line

Ledge above high water

Routes 11 to 18 can be accessed via traverse from abseil at all tide states

Portland West | Portland East | Lulworth | **Swanage** | Devon | Winspit | Hedbury | Dancing Ledge | Guillemot | Cormorant | Blacker's Hole | **Fisherman's** | Promenade | Cattle Troughs | Ruckle | Boulder | Subliminal

APPROACH and TIDES (Routes 11 to 18) - *At low tide you can walk to the following routes from the Squid Area. At high tide abseil directly to the ledge below Calcitron. The abseil is from 2 stakes about 20m below and east of the pylon. For Routes 10 to 13 traverse leftwards to two small stances 5m up the wall.*

⑫ Drunken Butterfly . . . . . 🔲🔲🔲 **7c+**
25m. The hanging V-groove gives another big roof climb, intimidating and in an outrageous position.
FA. Pete Oxley 25.3.93

⑬ Paparazzi News 🔲🔲🔲 **E6 6b**
30m. A sensational pitch. Climb a blank groove above the belay to undercuts, then blast out right and through the roofs into a shallow groove. Exit via a corner on the left, as for *Drunken Butterfly.*
FA. Pete Oxley 17.2.88

⑭ Cave Rave . . . . . . 🔲🔲🔲 **E5 6a**
25m. A wild pump-out, with good gear, up the steep groove 4m left of a deep chimney. Start from a ledge at 6m. Climb the groove and roofs (thread) before moving left to a corner (peg). Finish up this.
FA. Pete Oxley 14.11.87

⑮ The Beautiful and the Damned
. . . . 🔲🔲🔲🔲 **E5 6a**
25m. Start as for *Cave Rave* but ascend the serious slab on the right to a peg. Pull over the roof and up a short hard groove to a thread. Finish rightwards (thread) to a pre-placed rope.
FA. Pete Oxley 12.6.88. Reclimbed after a rockfall by Dave Pickford 7.7.99

PALACE OF THE BRINE AREA

Back at sea level, is a great cave which is home to some of the biggest overhangs around. This area has been designated as a sport climbing area and some of the routes are fully bolted. The ones needing gear have the nut symbol.

⑯ D Sharp . . . . 🔲🔲 **HVS 5a**
25m. A good line at a bargain grade for this area. Climb the groove right of the big chimney to a niche then move right to finish up some steep cracks.
FA. George Hounsome, T.Daniells 1980

⑰ Test Department . . 🔲🔲🔲 **E2 5b**
25m. Fine climbing up the left-hand side of the wall. Take a crucial 1/2 Friend. Many old threads are in place but are in poor condition. However this does not alter the grade.
FA. Pete Oxley 10.7.86

⑱ Damage Case . . . . . . 🔲🔲 **E3 5c**
25m. The straight crack. Many old threads are in place but are in poor condition, again this does not alter the grade.
FA. Pete Oxley 11.7.86

⑲ Calcitron . . . . . . 🔲🔲🔲 **E2 5b**
25m. The crack in the middle of the wall has 3 threads. A classy mid-grade route and much better that it looks.
FA. Pete Oxley 11.7.86

THE PROMENADE

In recent times The Promenade has been re-equipped and a significant number of new lines have been forced through some impressive ground. These two events have pushed the area to the forefront of development at Swanage and it is now the best place to go for those after mid to high-grade sport climbing. The Promenade is the first of the sport climbing areas at Swanage reached when approaching from Durlston Country Park. This is one of the best steep roof and wall areas at Swanage with many superb power-packed pitches. Nearly all the routes overhang and range from monstrous roof climbs to the more continuous stamina tests on the occasional leaning wall. There is also a number of good traditional routes that should not be ignored. Unfortunately there are only a few routes below E3/6b+ since the rock is so steep. Most of the climbs are strenuous with very few pockets but lots of edges and incuts. The Promenade is destined to become the most popular sport crag in the area for those with "the Guns" needed to tackle the obviously high quality challenges of the crag. There is also some good bouldering that includes some great traverses. Conditions are often favourable in this area as the severely overhanging nature of the rock keeps many of the routes dry, and numerous east and west facing buttresses mean that sun and shade can be found in about equal measure. The big flat belay ledges at the base of the crag are another of The Promenade's enticing features

TIDES

The sea-level platform is non-tidal except for the odd section which gets struck by high waves. Keep well away in rough seas or on windy days.

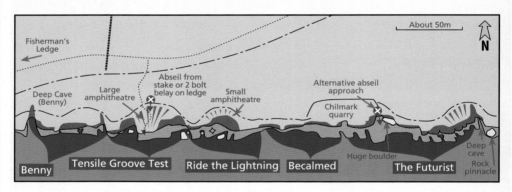

APPROACH

From Durlston Car Park, follow the road towards the lighthouse then turn west (right - looking out) along the coast path. Continue to a stile just before the two 'mile' pylons. From here, drop down a steep grass gully to a ledge above a large rock amphitheatre. Descend this (Diff) past a tricky step at the bottom to gain the platform. There are abseil bolts if required (the rope can be pulled down afterwards) and this is probably advisable on a first visit.

CONDITIONS

The Promenade receives all the sun that is going and is best visited on bright, fresh days to avoid the dampness that can linger on some of the holds. There is a little seepage on some of the steeper roof routes but most of the area is unaffected. The main roofs are always dry by mid-summer and are in the shade because of their steepness.

Just one of a host of easily accessible and superb steep sports pitches at the Promenade. Rob Kennard on *Tesselations* (7b). - *page 261*. Photo: Mark Glaister

BENNY AREA

The far western end of The Promenade is the location of this fine crag - high-quality, well-bolted, giving powerful routes above a non-tidal platform.

TIDES - It is non-tidal but keep away in rough seas.
APPROACH - The first routes start at the west end (left - looking in) of the ledge, where further progress is prevented by the big cave of *Benny*. Stake belays are in place for all the routes which top-out.

① Benny **A1/VS**

This serious but popular undertaking delves into the deep zawn at the western limits of the Promenade. Calm seas are essential for the first pitch, if it is remotely rough then keep away.
1) 15m, A1. Drop down and follow the side wall of the zawn just above the water pulling on fixed threads and nuts to gain a rock bridge at the back of the zawn.
2) 15m. Climb the dark chimney above on good holds until spat out of the blow hole, belay immediately. Lots of slings for threads needed.
3) 20m, 4b. Traverse awkwardly right to the arete, where a ledge leads right to easy ground.

FA. Scott Titt, D.Gumn, R.J.Crewe 24.4.76

② Clever Dick **E1 5c**

50m. A fine deep water solo gaining the rock bridge at the end of the first pitch of *Benny* from the other side of the zawn. Approach as for *Test Department* on Fisherman's Ledge (page 257). From the edge of the ledge, climb around, down and into the zawn. Finish up *Benny* or reverse to the ledge. **(S1)**

FA. Andy Donson 1989

③ Atonement **7c**

26m. A series of huge bulges above *Benny*. Start from the westerly edge of the platform. Lower off the single bolt belay once easy ground is reached. A future classic, in a great position.
FA. Pete Oxley 13.8.02

④ Crimes Against the Soul **7a**

26m. The steep rightward line leading into a deep groove.
FA. Pete Oxley 8.4.89

⑤ Hot Flush Down Under . . . **7b**

24m. A desperate chimney. Trend right to finish up the fine wall.
FA. Pete Oxley 24.9.93

⑥ Hot to Trot . . . . . . **7b+**

24m. A powerful roof to start, and the upper wall of *Hot Flush...*
FA. Pete Oxley 19.6.94

⑦ Gangster Lean . . . **6c**

26m. After a hard pull over a roof, the route follows a fantastic sustained leaning face, with no hard moves.
FA. Pete Oxley 22.7.86

⑧ Seppukku . . . . **6b+**

26m. Climb direct past two roofs to undercuts in a third roof. Move left to a vague rib which leads to the top.
FA. Pete Oxley 3.89

⑨ Chicago Peace **6c**

26m. Climb over bulges then trend right into a left-facing groove which leads to the top.
FA. Pete Oxley 31.1.87

Portland West
Portland East
Lulworth
Swanage
Devon
Winspit
Hedbury
Dancing Ledge
Guillemot
Cormorant
Blacker's Hole
Fisherman's Ledge
Promenade
Cattle Troughs
Boulder Ruckle
Subluminal

10 J.J.Burnell, King of the Bass
. . . . 6a
26m. Above a break in the ledge, move right up a slab then layback around the roof and climb the easier wall. Unlikely!
FA. Pete Oxley 7.4.89

11 Just Another Victim 7b+
18m. Super-steep climbing with wild moves. Initial bulges lead to a roof crack which requires good foot work.
FA. Pete Oxley 10.6.94

12 Godfodder. . . . E7 6c
26m. A good trad route through the mighty 4m roof crack in the central bay. Belay on a foot-ledge over the roof using a crack on the right. Climb out (4b) from here to escape.
FA. Pete Oxley 27.5.91

There is a desperate open project right of Godfodder.

13 A Bosch Boy, a Trad, and a Funky Dredd
. . . . 7a+
18m. A short roof problem. Swing left to a lower-off.
FA. Pete Oxley 14.4.91

14 Show of Hands 7a
15m. Some crazy roof moves that are easier for the short. Start up a shallow groove and gain the edge of the huge ceiling before making a hard rockover to finish. Lower-off on the right.
FA. Pete Oxley, Rich White 20.7.02

15 Empowerless 7a
15m. Short sharp roof climbing over the roof left of the zawn.
FA. Brian Tilley 29.8.94

16 Community Service . . . 7a
15m. A neat eliminate that ascends the steep prow right of *Empowerless*. Start up *Empowerless* before moving right onto the prow proper. Climb this without bridging across the chimney to a lower-off on the left.
FA. Pete Oxley, Rich White 20.7.02

17 Revelation Chimney VS 4c
25m. Great rock and a superb line. This trad classic tackles the huge chimney right above the zawn, via some sustained bridging and back and footing.
FA. George Hounsome, Scott Titt 28.3.76

18 Waves Become Wings 7b+
25m. A superb leaning wall. Best conditions are in the afternoon when the wall gets the sun.
FA. Pete Oxley 19.6.94

19 Birth Pains of New Nations
. . . . 7b
25m. The centre of the leaning face, joining *Waves Become Wings* at half-height, is also a high calibre line that again needs the sun on it for the best conditions. High in the grade.
FA. Pete Oxley 8.10.86

20 Tessellations 7b
25m. The overhanging arete right of *Revelation Chimney* gives this superb route that doesn't let up. Start direct up the lower arete. *Photo page 259.*
FA. Pete Oxley 10.7.86

TENSILE GROOVE TEST AREA

The Promenade has a relatively easy approach scramble down an open amphitheatre. To either side, the walls rear up steeply giving some powerful roof routes.
TIDES - It is non-tidal but keep away in rough seas.

❶ Carpe Diem . . . . . . 🔲🔲🔲🔲 **7b+**
25m. An excellent addition. Start up the easy groove (as for *Total Seizure*) then climb a roof to gain the groove before moving leftward on a steep and natural line to join *Tessellations*.
FA. Pete Oxley, Rich White 21.9.01

❷ Total Seizure . . . . . 🔲🔲🔲🔲 **7c+**
20m. A great route which tackles a huge set of bulges. Often in condition. Start as for *Carpe Diem* then weave through the bulges to a lower-off where the angle drops back.
FA. Pete Oxley 28.11.87

❸ State of Play . . . . . 🔲🔲🔲🔲 **7c+**
21m. Fine and super-steep moves that break rightwards over the wide roof right of *Total Seizure* to eventually finish up *Solid State Logic*. Start as for *Carpe Diem*.
FA. Pete Oxley 2004

❹ Solid State Logic . . 🔲🔲🔲🔲 **8a**
20m. A short and powerful climb over a 6m overlapping ceiling, and easier for the short. Reverse for the gear.
FA. Pete Oxley 12.5.91

The open project over the roof above the belay will be 7c+ (ish).

❺ Defining Moment 🔲🔲🔲🔲🔲 **7c+**
18m. Very powerful climbing up the right-hand side of the *Solid State Logic* cave. Needs good conditions. The nearby ledge is strictly off bounds if you had any ideas about sneaking a rest!
FA. Pete Oxley 21.9.01

A couple of poor and loose trad routes are just left of the descent scramble (Danglefoot - Diff). The next quality routes are in the caves to the right (looking in).

❻ The Flail Trail . . . . 🔲🔲 **6a**
11m. One of the few easier routes at The Promenade which gives some good climbing.
FA. Pete Oxley 29.5.85

❼ My New Top . . . . 🔲🔲 **6c**
10m. A short direct line below *Flail Trail* is not bolted. 'TR' it!
FA. Danny Woodward 12.7.96

❽ Violent Breed . . . . 🔲🔲🔲 **7b+**
12m. Reassessed as quite a hard power problem but at the bottom of the grade. Quite superb and photogenic, not to be missed and easier for the short! Start up the wall and then swing left and up the bulges.
FA. Pete Oxley 23.5.87

❾ Down in the Sewer. 🔲🔲🔲🔲 **7b**
18m. A striking and quality line up the leaning groove with sustained powerful climbing on great rock. Climb the hanging groove line, starting up the first few feet of *Violent Breed*.
FA. Pete Oxley 23.5.87

❿ Tensile Groove Test 🔲🔲🔲🔲 **E4 6a**
20m. A big overhanging line starting at the back of the cave. Good steep moves protected by decent trad gear. Can be damp and greasy.
FA. Pete Oxley 11.10.86

⓫ Crest of a Wave . . . 🔲🔲🔲🔲 **7b**
20m. An audacious line swaggering leftward through the roofs to finish next to *Tensile Groove Test*. The blank start is very technical. Lowering off the 3rd bolt gives a worthy **7a+**. The final bolt is hard to clip - pre-place a sling. *Photo page 193.*
FA. Pete Oxley 12.6.96

⑫ Crystal Voyager .. E3 5c
25m. A brilliant climb with a very exposed crux but with good gear. Follow an awkward crack to a niche, then swing right on the lip of a monster block. Before strength fades, ascend direct up a technical wall to finish via an easier groove system. A large cam is useful on this pitch.
FA. Gordon Jenkin, R.Dalgleish(aid) 14.11.76. FFA. Kevin Turner, P.Dawson 20.4.80

⑬ Star of Africa 7b
20m. The big 3m ceiling beneath *Crystal Voyager*. Start easily up the slab, cross the roof to a jug rail before heading diagonally rightwards up the blank headwall to lower-off the last bolt.
FA. Pete Oxley 29.8.01

⑭ Len's Rule of the Sea
.... E3 6a
25m. Another worthy line tackling the staggered flake-line in the bay 5m right. It can be wet low down and has a bold start.
FA. Dave Ivory, A.Ivory 2.8.83

⑮ Yorkshire Talk .... 7b+
15m. The photogenic arete right of *Len's Rule*. A quality route, with a campus style crux. Even better now than before it suffered a rockfall.
FA. Pete Oxley 12.6.96 (reclimbed post rockfall by Pete Oxley in 2001)

⑯ Shock to the System 7c+
15m. The heinous blank roof is very powerful.
FA. Pete Oxley 1999

⑰ The Resistor 7c
15m. Great moves over the big bulging overhang just left of *Electric Circus*. Start up *Electric Circus* and share its belay.
FA. Pete Oxley 20.8.02

⑱ Electric Circus . 7b+
15m. A fine route with an intense sequence on small holds. Pass a short, left-facing corner low down. Very technical.
FA. Pete Oxley 27.2.96

The second cave (right - looking in) from the descent scramble has a huge roof. The left-hand side has some short routes and the right-hand side has some powerful, all-weather bouldering.

⑲ Volts Discharge 7a
16m. Bulging rock and hidden pockets 2m right of *Electric Circus*. Easier when you know where the holds are.
FA. Pete Oxley 2.11.86

⑳ The Undertow Traverse . V6
18m. Start beneath *Volts Discharge* and traverse powerfully right around the roofed bay to a slab at the start of *Chasm Groove*. Can be linked to *Fat Lip*. Not marked on the topo.
FA. Pete Oxley 8.2001

㉑ Mr. Gymnasia 7a
16m. Fun moves following the slight crack.
FA. Pete Oxley 16.6.85

㉒ Gym'n'Tonic .... 7b+
16m. A bouldery link up from the first holds on *Load it for Me* leftward over the big roof to join *Mr. Gymnasia*. Good climbing but it is a bit of an eliminate.
FA. Pete Oxley 14.9.2001

㉓ Load it for Me 7b
16m. After a hard start, move rightwards into a shallow groove with a seepage streak. This has been known to form a free-standing icicle in winter. A direct start is also possible (**7b+**).
FA. Pete Oxley 4.10.86 Direct - Pete Oxley 27.2.93

㉔ Deep Puddle Dynamic . 7c+
16m. The tough roof and wall above.
FA. Dan Knight 2.2005

㉕ The Garage Mechanic 7c
16m. A powerful problem starting just left of a small pool.
FA. Pete Oxley 10.5.93

Portland West
Portland East
Lulworth
Swanage
Devon
Winspit
Hedbury
Dancing Ledge
Guillemot
Cormorant
Blacker's Hole
Fisherman's
Promenade
Cattle Troughs
Boulder Ruckle
Subliminal

RIDE THE LIGHTNING AREA

This short area has been developed mainly as a bouldering area. The problems here are short, powerful and mostly hard. They will stay dry in light rain but there can be some seepage and dampness from the sea.

TIDES - It is non-tidal but keep away in rough seas.
APPROACH - At the base of the approach scramble, turn left (looking out) and continue to the roofed recess.

❶ Coming In A Rush . 🗲🖐️B ⬜ **7b+**
21m. A hard roof to start before trending rightwards across *Chasm Groove* to climb the wall.
FA. Pete Oxley 21.2.87

2m to the right the roof can be crossed by **Jump Camp, V6** *though only the tall need apply.*

❷ Fat Lip . . . . 🗲🖤 ⬜ **V6**
12m. First recorded as a direct start to *Chasm Groove*, but now with a traverse in for added value. Squat start at a huge jug low on the left. Move up right along the lip of the roof before slapping up the hanging arete. Reverse back down *Chasm Groove*. Could be linked into *The Undertow Traverse* for a serious pumpout. It is bold, so come with a spotter.
FA. Pete Oxley 9.9.01

❸ Chasm Groove . . . 🖌️🖤🗲 ⬜ **E1 5b**
20m. The break in the crag angle above the pool on the ledge. Start to the right and traverse left above the overhang until the groove can be accessed and then climbed to a slabby exit out left. A peg for protection is not in place.
FA. M.Boater, D.Fell 19.4.69

❹ Ride the Lightning . 🗲🖐️🗲 ⬜ **V10**
25m. A long boulder traverse from left to right on the right-hand side of the cave. Often damp.
FA. Pete Oxley 3.93

❺ Drive By . . . . 🗲🖤 ⬜ **V6**
4m. An old project tackling the big bulge to a high pointed jug 3m left of *Juggernaut*. Powerful and bold.
FA. Pete Oxley 1.9.01

❻ Juggernaut . . . . 🖤 ⬜ **V7**
4m. A boulder problem to link two jugs, over the largest roof in the back centre of the cave. The right-hand start (*Jack Knife*) is the same grade.
FA. Pete Oxley 28.2.93. FA. (Jack Knife) Pete Oxley 3.93

❼ Techno Sketching . . . . 🖤 ⬜ **V6**
3m. Boulder up the blank groove 5m left of the seaward arete.
FA. Pete Oxley 3.93

❽ Puddle Jumper . . . . ⬜ **V5**
3m. Climb the right wall of the blank groove.
FA. Pete Oxley 3.93

The project through the roofs will be 8a.

❾ Baby-faced Assassin 🗲🎗️🗲 ⬜ **7a+**
17m. A well-positioned 'steepy' just inside the cave, starting via a short crack.
FA. Pete Oxley 25.6.96

❿ German New Order 🖐️🎗️B ⬜ **7b+**
15m. The wall 5m right of the cave.
FA. Pete Oxley 18.9.86

⓫ Blitzkrieg . . . . 🖐️🎗️B ⬜ **7b+**
15m. A hard fingery problem with a crux roof.
FA. Pete Oxley 14.12.86

⓬ Big Brother Is Watching . . B ⬜ **7a+**
16m. A mighty technical problem.
FA. Pete Oxley 14.3.87

Cliff-top quarry

Approach

1 2 3 4 5 6 7 8 9 10 11 12 13 P

Portland West
Portland East
Lulworth
Swanage
Devon
Winspit
Hedbury
Dancing Ledge
Guillemot
Cormorant
Blacker's Hole
Fisherman's
Promenade
Subliminal | Boulder Ruckle | Cattle Troughs

BECALMED AREA

The next section provides a welcome respite from the hard routes and boulder problems encountered so far on The Promenade. There is a good set of routes here although many of them are still in need of rebolting.

TIDES - It is non-tidal but keep away in rough seas.
APPROACH - At the base of the approach scramble, turn left (looking out) and continue past the recess to an area of staggered roofs directly below the cliff-top quarry.

① Distant Early Warning . 　6a
16m. A sharp, juggy roof is currently **E1 5c**, to a nut belay.
FA. Mick Ward 6.9.86

② Kool and the Gang . . . 　6a
16m. An easy corner *(Original Route - Severe)* leads to a 'kool' roof. Can be done at **E1 5b**, with decent gear, to a nut belay.
FA. Pete Oxley 26.4.86

③ Playing With Fire . . . . 　6c
12m. The slabby wall and roof right of *Kool and the Gang*. A weird crux where you swing leftwards over the roof. Enjoyable but don't wreck your rope lowering-off.
FA. Pete Oxley 13.6.96

④ Genetix . . . . 　6b
14m. A black groove leading through four roofs.
FA. Pete Oxley 12.4.87

⑤ Boiling Point . . . . 　7a
13m. The bouldery roof right of *Genetix*, starting at a hanging, left-facing corner.
FA. Pete Oxley 13.6.96

⑥ To Fever Pitch . . . . 　7a+
15m. A multiple roof stack with great moves.
FA. Martin Crocker 6.9.86

⑦ Becalmed . . . . 　7a+
13m. Good cranky stuff over a few bulges.
FA. Pete Oxley 27.2.96

⑧ Stakk Attakk . . . . 　6a
15m. A few tricky reaches past a small roof are gained by a short traverse from the left. Can be done at **E2 5c**, to a nut belay in the quarry.
FA. Pete Oxley 29.5.85

⑨ Geordie Pride . . . . . . 　7a
13m. A strenuous diagonal over the flying roof right of *Stakk Attakk*. Finish via a rockover onto the slab.
FA. Pete Oxley 27.2.96. Dedicated to Pete's dad, RIP.

⑩ Peggy's Cove . . . . 　6c
14m. A very hard move coupled with some rather poor bolting.
FA. Pete Oxley 27.2.96. Dedicated to Pete's mum, RIP.

⑪ Zeitgeist . . . . 　7a+
14m. Honest, there are no roofs on this one, just a sustained groove.
FA. Crispin Waddy, Pete Oxley 12.7.86

⑫ Spirits Rising . . . . 　7b
14m. The reachy roof and fingery wall just right of *Zeitgeist*.
FA. Pete Oxley 3.6.01

⑬ A Quantum Jump for Apekind 　7a
14m. Back to the roof stacks. Start just right of the arete.
FA. Pete Oxley 26.11.87

The open project to the right.

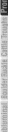

Lots of sun | 30 min | Steep

Possible abseil approach from block in quarry

Cliff-top quarry

Huge boulder

A Quantum Jump for Apekind

THE FUTURIST AREA

The final section of The Promenade contains more of the same - big steep roof routes with powerful lines. Just to add to the mix, there is a section with some good trad routes.
TIDES - It is non-tidal but keep away in rough seas.
APPROACH - Either walk left (looking out) from the usual approach, or abseil direct to this section from a belay in the quarry above.

❶ The Calling . . . . . . 7a+
14m. The central overlap with irresistible moves. Acrobatic.
FA. Pete Oxley 25.6.96

❷ Guided by Voices 7b+
14m. Sustained, gymnastic, and tough, especially on those without arms like a baboon.
FA. Pete Oxley 25.6.96

❸ Grossville 7a
15m. The huge ship's keel direct has some wild moves.
FA. Pete Oxley 18.10.86

❹ Spacewalk 7b
16m. A modern classic that makes the most of the *Grossville* prow. Very steep and pumpy. Start as for *Grossville* before trending right up the bulging wall to a roof crack. Cross the roof and swing out to the apex of the buttress. A good midway hands-off rest should not be missed.
FA. Pete Oxley 3.6.01

❺ Sea Ride . . . . HVS 5a
16m. A smart easier route with a safe crux. Start at the right-hand of two cracks in the back of the bay. Climb a slab and corner to a well-positioned roof crux. Block belay in the quarry above. This also acts as an abseil approach point if needed.
FA. M.Boater, R.Shergold 31.5.69

❻ Hackney's Hammer HVS 5a
17m. Varied climbing up the groove system parallel to *Sea Ride*, with a tough step left to attain the quarry. Block belay.

The next two routes start from the top of the huge block.

❼ Sexaphone . . . E6 6b
13m. A wild roof crack that requires specialist knowledge to overcome. Good gear but hard to place (1 thread and a peg in the upper groove). Stake belay.
FA. Pete Oxley 13.10.87

❽ Space Threshold. E2 5b
14m. A right-trending line through the roofs right of *Sexaphone*, finishing up a big flake. Stake belay.
FA. Pete Oxley 23.3.86

❾ Edward's Effort . . . VS 4c
23m. Start just right of the huge block and climb to a small sentry box. Trend right over three overhangs to the top. Stake belay.
FA. B.Heard 16.6.74

❿ All Apologies . . . . 7a+
20m. A long bulging arete with a low crux and a tenuous rounded rock-over to finish.
FA. Pete Oxley 29.6.94

⓫ Strangled in Black 7a
20m. A good line up bulges and a steep crack in the centre of the buttress. High in the grade.
FA. Pete Oxley 18.10.86

Portland West | Portland East | Lulworth | **Swanage** | Devon | Winspit | Hedbury | Dancing Ledge | Guillemot | Cormorant | Blacker's Hole | Fisherman's | Promenade | Castle Troughs | Boulder Ruckle | Subluminal

Ledge above high tide

---

⑫ Titter Ye Not Mrs! . 🖼️🖼️🖼️ ☐ **6b+**
20m. Climb direct up a slight groove after a steep start through the bulges.
FA. Pete Oxley 4.90

⑬ Fat Necrosis . . . . . 🖼️ Ⓑ 🖼️ ☐ **7a+**
18m. The first crack breaching the long, low-level roof.
FA. Martin Crocker 6.9.86

⑭ Rise of the Robots . 🖼️🖼️🖼️ ☐ **7c**
12m. A superb power endurance effort just left of *Liquid Steel*. Explosive moves cover unlikely ground to a jug rail. Overcome the last bulge to a shared belay with *Liquid Steel*.
FA. Pete Oxley 8.2000

⑮ Liquid Steel . . . . . 🖼️🖼️🖼️ ☐ **7c**
12m. A superb anaerobic challenge across the 6m roof.
FA. Pete Oxley 13.7.94

⑯ The Futurist 2002 . . 🖼️🖼️🖼️ ☐ **7c**
15m. This is an extended version of the original climb which is now harder and more sustained. Start just right of *Liquid Steel*. Spectacular moves rightwards gain the roof crack. Follow the crack with increasing difficulty (as for the original) to easy ground. Reverse for the gear.
FA. Pete Oxley 4.11.86. Extended in 2002

⑰ Event Horizon . 🖼️🖼️🖼️🖼️ ☐ **8a+**
15m. The awesome line out of the cave to the right of *The Futurist 2002* is The Promenade's hardest offering to date. Steep ground accesses the lip where thin cruxy moves may allow the belay to be gained.
FA. Rob Kennard 10.2003

⑱ Berserka . . . . 🖼️ Ⓑ ☐ **7a+**
22m. Climb rightwards to a gap in the ceiling then finish direct up the wall above.
FA. Pete Oxley 12.7.86

⑲ The Shape of Roofs to Come
. . . . 🖼️🖼️ ☐ **7b**
12m. A fun bicep-bulging test over the 4m roof right of *Berserka*. A long quick-draw is needed for the 4th bolt. No sneaking off rightwards at the top!
FA. Pete Oxley 24.6.01

⑳ War of Attrition 🖼️🖼️🖼️🖼️ ☐ **7c+**
12m. A desperate extended boulder problem over the double roof stack. Essentially a **V8** with bolts.
FA. Pete Oxley 17.9.00

㉑ The Incredible Hulk 🖼️🖼️🖼️ ☐ **7c**
12m. An excellent line up the 5m triple roof. Great climbing in a good situation despite moving into *Howling Stone* at half height.
FA. Pete Oxley 24.7.01

㉒ Howling Stone . . . 🖼️🖼️Ⓑ ☐ **7a**
20m. A strength-sapper up the final leaning pillar. Has a 2m roof and an exposed finish. Currently a bit muddy after a land slip so it is better to finish at the bolts of *The Incredible Hulk*.
FA. Pete Oxley 12.7.86

CATTLE TROUGHS

The Cattle Troughs Area is popular with novices and beginners although it is perhaps not quite as good a place to venture for your first taste of Swanage as Subluminal with its extensive flat and solid top and commodious belay ledges. The Cattle Troughs' routes are easy to reach and have generally sound rock; however gear can be a bit sparse on some climbs and it is a dangerous venue in rough or even moderate seas. Amphitheatre Ledge Area has some quality harder climbs on some good rock, whilst the slabs and short friendly walls of the Hangover and Isis Areas are favourites with novices and those looking for good easier and mid-grade routes.

APPROACH

From Durlston Car Park, follow the road towards the lighthouse then turn west (right - looking out) along the coast path. Continue to where, 150m beyond the 4th stone wall from the lighthouse (the western limit of Durlston Country park), the cliff-top path dips into a small valley above a slabby cove. Cross the fence here at a small stile. This is **Amphitheatre Ledge**. For the **Isis and Hangover Areas** follow an exposed narrow path along the cliff-top, contouring right (looking out). Pass several belay stakes until you come to a large gearing-up ledge after 200m (just beyond a large amphitheatre known as the Lecture Theatre). Alternatively continue along the main coast path, cross a stile and follow a steep path leading down through nettle beds (high summer only), and past a tall post, to the cliff-top gearing up ledge. See route pages for further approaches from here.

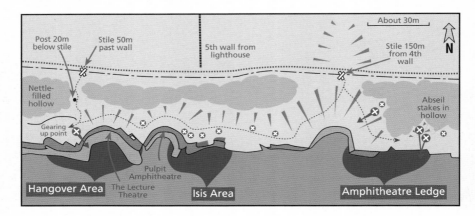

TIDES

All the climbs start from non-tidal ledges, however keep away in rough seas since freak waves can wash high up the walls. Always take a belay at the base of the routes.

CONDITIONS

The Cattle Troughs' cliffs are rapid-drying sun-traps and there is no seepage; this can be considered a year-round venue. Beware of the cliff-top path if it is at all muddy, as well as the descent into the Hangover Area which is a bit polished, fairly steep and at times can be covered in mud from other's boots. Keep away in high or moderate seas as the sloping ledges at the base of the crag offer little protection from waves. Cattle Troughs is a real sun trap with almost nowhere to get out of the sun on hot days. Bring plenty of water and sunscreen.

The ever-popular and friendly Cattle Troughs make a great place to begin an exploration of the Swanage sea cliffs. Johnny Woods on *Bunney's Wall* (VS 5a) at the Hangover Area of the Cattle Troughs - *page 270*. Photo: Mark Glaister

Way down from the coast path

Gearing-up spot

A

The Lecture Theatre

Pulpit Amphiheatre

Ledge at 4m above high water level

1 2 3 4 7 9 5 6 8

HANGOVER AREA

The cliff-line at Cattle Troughs comprises two semi-circular amphitheatres with a broken ledge-system running along their base, allowing easy access. The first few routes lie just west of the descent above a flat ledge system.

TIDES - The area is non-tidal but keep away in rough seas.

APPROACH - Descend down into the Lecture Theatre amphitheatre on its west side (right - looking out), below the clifftop gearing up ledges. There is a stake in place for abseil but most climbers will be able to scramble down. The first routes lie just to the right (looking out) of the descent.

1 Inspiration . . . . 🏷️ 6/05 **Sev 4a**
12m. A pleasant line up the centre of a flat face. Start just right of a large boulder. Easy but poorly protected climbing gains a ledge at half height. Climb the groove above and exit right.

2 Consolation . . . . 🏷️ 6/05 **Sev 4a**
12m. The right-hand side of the face via a short groove.

3 Chockney . . . . 🏷️ 🏷️ 6/05 **VDiff 4a**
12m. A 'classic' corner problem just left of the descent route makes a good first lead if you can get off the ground!

THE LECTURE THEATRE - *Right of the way down (looking in) and past the easy slabs, is the first route above the east side of the amphitheatre. The following four routes finish at a ledge above the wall or, futher back and safer, a stake belay by the cliff-top path.*

4 The Chimney . . . . 🏷️ 5/05 **VDiff**
15m. The unmistakable first feature reached along the access ledge. Exit on the right. Finishing straight up is a good and well-protected alternative finish at **Sev 4a**.

5 Hangover . . . . 🏷️ 🏷️ **VS 5a**
15m. A great little route up the steep wall 2m right to a large ledge. It has lost holds over the years hence the upgrade.

6 Resurrection . . . . 🏷️ **HS 4b**
15m. Right of *Hangover*, follow a lovely buttress-face to a recess. Exit rightwards to the good ledge.

7 Perfection . . . . 6/05 **Sev 4a**
15m. Follow the arete out right and finish up a groove.

8 Old Lag's Corner . . . . 🏷️ **VS 4c**
15m. The obvious corner above a large pedestal block. By-pass the top overhangs on the right to a good ledge. Direct is **5a**.
FA. Frank Farrell, Gordon Jenkin 13.8.84

Just before the end of the Lecture Theatre is a good bouldering wall.

9 Bunney's Wall . . . . . . 🏷️ 🏷️ **VS 5a**
15m. This climb takes the central line to the top with good moves, finishing up a slanting crack. The start is tricky. A good alternative is to swing right and climb the headwall. Nut and block belays. *Photo page 269.*

Approach from coast path

Pulpit Amphiheatre

Huge block

Ledge at 4m above high water level

ISIS AREA
Around the corner lies the second hollow known as The Pulpit Amphitheartre. All the routes finish at stake belays.
TIDES - It is non-tidal but keep away in rough seas.
APPROACH - Descend down into the Lecture Theatre on its west (right - looking out) side below the cliff-top gearing-up ledges. There is a stake in place for abseil but most climbers will be able to scramble down. The Isis Area lies to the left (looking out) of the descent.

1 Fallen Block Climb . . . . . . **VDiff**
18m. Take an easy line up the wall on the far side of the bay. The route is well-protected and has some fine positions.

2 Pulpit Route . . . . **Diff**
18m. A smart little route and a fine first climb. Follow the diagonal slab on the eastern (left - looking out) edge of The Pulpit. Move left near its top to finish on easy ground.

3 Pearly Gate . . . . **HVS 5a**
18m. Climb a crack on the right of the slab, then follow flakes leading to a roof. Move left to finish via a groove. Serious.

4 Eskimo Nell **E1 5b**
18m. An excellent pitch. Climb onto a huge block just right of *Pearly Gate* then head up to follow a groove just left of the half-height overhang.
FA. H.Evans, P.Deketeleare 16.2.69

5 Isis . . . . **VS 4c**
18m. A popular route with varied climbing in good situations. Start at the left-hand side of a high arched recess 5m right of a large block. Climb the groove on the left until moves left gain the lip of an overhang. Ascend a bulging groove on the left, trending right then back left and finish up two short walls.
FA. D.Rowlands 1963

6 Archangel . . . . **(E3 6a)**
18m. A scary route which has been affected by a recent rockfall and may not have been reclimbed. The line follows the centre of the arch wall and continues over the middle of the roof.
FA. S.Evans, R.Evans 5.5.74

7 Peacemaker . . . . **HVS 5a**
18m. The last good route on this area goes up the right-hand corner of the arch to a foot-ledge near the top. Step up right onto a slab for a tricky finish. Good gear for a route in this area.
FA. Pete Oxley 8.2.89

Portland West · Portland East · Lulworth · **Swanage** · Devon · Winspit · Hedbury · Dancing Ledge · Guillemot · Cormorant · Blacker's Hole · Fisherman's · Promenade · **Cattle Troughs** · Boulder Ruckle · Subluminal

AMPHITHEATRE LEDGE AREA

Amphitheatre Ledge is a quiet and secluded area that deserves more traffic. The climbing is invariably steep and on good rock but the finishes require caution. Some of the routes are awkward to approach.

TIDES - The area is generally non-tidal although some of the starts are much easier to reach at low tide. Keep away in rough conditions.

APPROACH (Routes 1 to 5, and 10) - *Abseil from two stakes above The Amphitheatre on its east side (left - looking out). This lands you on a ledge system which leads along the base of the cliff.*

① Varina . . . . HS 4a
25m. A pleasant, though serious, route up the arete of The Amphitheatre, finishing up a short groove. Sparse protection from small wires is your lot. Belay on the ab rope. Take care as the route has lost a large block high up and maybe harder now.
FA. R.Heigh, W.Church 1968

② Uncry These Tears . . . E2 5c
25m. A strong line up the face right of *Varina*. Climb to an overlap (small thread) then onwards to a larger overlap. Pass this on its left (thread) and continue past a peg to reach an exit ramp on the left.
FA. Mike Robertson, Barry Clarke 2.5.97

The next three routes are situated on the gloriously steep orange wall to the right. For those who have enjoyed Lean Machine, these give similar super-strenuous pump-outs. It is best to pre-place a belay rope from the abseil stakes.

③ Atomic Road Hero . E5 6b
25m. Climb straight up an easy lower wall and attack the technical and intricate face above (3 threads, 1 peg) to a large undercut. Move diagonally left (thread) to a slight corner and continue rightwards to the top.
FA. Pete Oxley 14.12.86

④ Theory of Everything E5 6b
25m. This is the central line and has the most sustained climbing. Start 3m right of the last route and ascend the easy lower wall to beneath some spidery cracks. Power up these past a peg and continue in a direct line to a good finish.
FA. Pete Oxley 23.3.90

⑤ Zoolookologie E5 6a
25m. A full-body work-out with reasonable gear. Start easily as for *Theory of Everything* then take the big cracks to the right up the steep wall (thread) pulling over a bulge to a ledge. An easy groove leads to the top.
FA. Pete Oxley 8.8.86

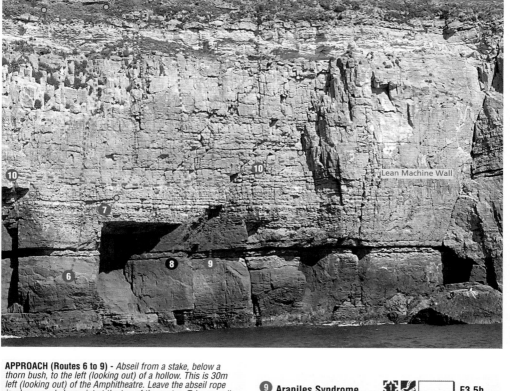

Within the photo:
- Belay on ab rope
- Pre-place belay rope for route 10 from twin belay stakes above Lean Machine Wall
- Lean Machine Wall

APPROACH (Routes 6 to 9) - *Abseil from a stake, below a thorn bush, to the left (looking out) of a hollow. This is 30m left (looking out) of the Amphitheatre. Leave the abseil rope in place as a belay point at the top of the routes. Take prussik loops down with you in case of problems. Routes 6 and 7 can be reached by a sea level traverse (Diff) at low tide.*

⑥ In a Big Sky E2 5c
30m. Start from a large sloping ledge, at a flake, 15m right of the big leaning wall. Move straight up to follow thin cracks past 5 threads. Near the top, move right with difficulty to an easier finish and a ledge. Belay on the ab rope.
FA. Pete Oxley, Gordon Jenkin 8.6.86

⑦ Land of the Leaning E2 5b
1) 8m. Start as for *In a Big Sky*. Climb the flake (thread) but then move right easily for 3m to a ledge above the zawn. Thread and nut belay.
2) 5b, 20m. Climb cracks rightwards then step left and back right at their end. Finish up easier rock to belay on the ab rope.
FA. Pete Oxley, Jon Biddle 7.6.86

⑧ World in Action . . . E5 6b
28m. A peach of a climb on lovely rock. It needs a direct abseil approach to gain an isolated small ledge at the fault 5m above the sea, 5m right (looking in) of the ledge of *In a Big Sky*. Climb the bulging arete above (peg and thread) to easier ground (thread), then move slightly left to beneath the orange headwall. Surge up a thin crack past lots of wires and 2 threads, to a jug. Before the pump wins, finish up the technical shallow groove to a cleaned exit. Belay on the ab rope.
FA. Pete Oxley, Steve Williams 11.4.87

⑨ Arapiles Syndrome . . . E3 5b
30m. Reminiscent of *Ocean Boulevard*. Abseil directly, from the stake, to a ledge beneath a diagonal crack, 5m right of *World in Action*. Start up a short groove then swing out left to reach the crack and follow it diagonally right to an overlap. Make two staggered short traverses rightwards again to gain an exit ledge. Belay on the ab rope.
FA. Pete Oxley, Nigel Coe 5.4.86

⑩ Mr Ruckle E1 5a
A fine, mid-height traverse of this exciting area all the way from *Varina* to finish right of *Arapiles Syndrome*. It can be done in rough seas. Before starting you need to pre-place a rope on the twin stakes above the *Lean Machine* area, for the last belay.
1) 5a, 18m. From 8m up *Varina*, traverse right (small thread) past a groove to belay on a cracked prow. This is reported to be a serious pitch with ground-fall potential and it can be avoided.
2) 5a, 30m. Drop down and rightwards across the *Zoolookologie* bay thread. Continue past a slight prow and vague scoop. Belay down and right of a cracked pillar.
3) 4c, 28m. Climb down and right to traverse a weakness past various old threads, in the centre of a bay, to a comfortable stance on the far side in a groove.
4) 4c, 15m. Follow the corner to the top and a terrace where you hope to find your pre-placed rope. Pull out on the rope to finish.
FA. Mike Robertson, Brian Tilley 28.8.97

Side tab (vertical):
Portland West | Portland East | Lulworth | Swanage | Devon | Winspit | Hedbury | Dancing Ledge | Guillemot | Cormorant | Blacker's Hole | Fisherman's | Promenade | Cattle Troughs | Boulder Ruckle | Subliminal

BOULDER RUCKLE

The white and yellow horizontally-banded vertical walls of the Boulder Ruckle make up the showpiece crag of Swanage. Boulder Ruckle runs westwards from Subluminal unbroken for over 1km and, at over 40m in height, it offers fear, exhilaration and many sensationally-positioned routes. The grade range of HS to E6 appeals to most at a first glance. However, when the seriousness of the free-hanging approach abseils, the awkward escape routes and the broken finishes are considered, it becomes a less attractive option for inexperienced teams. Nevertheless, for those in search of an adventurous mission, don a helmet, dust off the prussik loops and prepare to do battle on some fine atmospheric classics with little chance of having to queue. It is an especially good area in the HVS to E3 range. Fortunately gear is usually in good supply with the steepness of the rock accounting for the grade for most climbs, rather than any great technical difficulty.

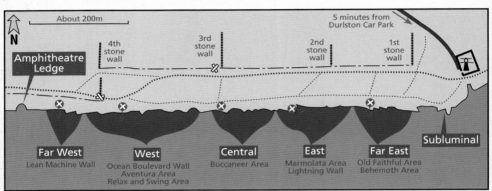

ACCESS

There are bird restrictions from 1 March to 31 July on Old Faithful, Behemoth, Too Precious, Aventura as well as Relax and Swing Areas. Check the text with the topos.

TIDES

Most of the areas are untroubled by the tides due to a large boulder-beach along the bottom but avoid the whole place if the seas are rough. There are a few isolated spots which require low tide; which are mentioned in the area notes.

CONDITIONS

The whole cliff faces due south and is a big sun-trap. This is good in winter but may be too hot in summer although it is shady after 6pm. It can be greasy in hot weather but the rock is rough and there is little polish. There is no seepage.

GENERAL APPROACH

Walk down the tarmac road from Durlston Car Park then head west (right - looking out) along the coast path. A cliff-top track runs below this and the abseil stakes are found near this lower path. The first area arrived at is a 10 minute walk and the furthest area takes 20 minutes. Precise details of the various approaches are listed with the Sector Notes.
Note - The boulder-beach is not continuous so you can not always move from area to area once committed to an abseil entry. Also, several of the abseils are free-hanging so avoid using thin ropes unless you want a rapid descent!

Chris Craggs on pitch one of *Jo* (HVS 5a) on the Relax and Swing Area of the Boulder Ruckle - *page 281*. Photo: Craggs Collection

LEAN MACHINE WALL

The most western area of the Ruckle is a very secluded section of the cliff-line. Either end is cut off by the sea and there is no easy escape. Most of the climbs are steep, pumpy, hardcore experiences, though with good gear.

APPROACH - 50m beyond the 4th wall (after 17 fence posts) climb over the fence and head down through a break in the bushes to the cliff edge. 5m to the right are 2 stakes directly above *Lean Machine*. This is a free-hanging abseil and you will only reach the boulder beach if the sea is calm.

TIDES - This sector is not advisable in rough seas although the approach described above will keep you above a calm high tide. It is also possible to reach it from the Ocean Boulevard Area at low tide.

NOTE - The easiest solid route out of this area is E3 and sea-level escapes are very awkward. Be sure you can climb this grade comfortably and take prussiks just in case. On most of the routes the abseil rope is essential to assist in finishing the top slab and/or for belaying on.

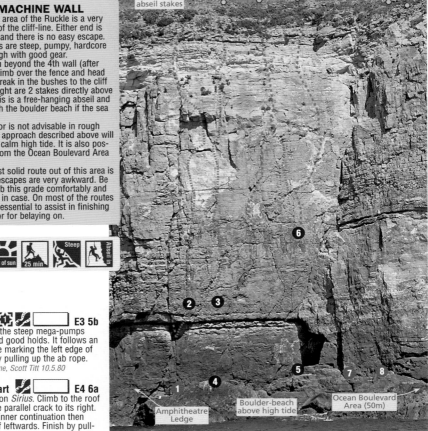

Pre-place a belay rope on twin abseil stakes

30m from coast path

Amphitheatre Ledge

Boulder-beach above high tide

Ocean Boulevard Area (50m)

❶ Sirius .. 🪨🥾 ⬜ **E3 5b**
35m. The first of the steep mega-pumps has good gear and good holds. It follows an obvious crack-line marking the left edge of the face. Finish by pulling up the ab rope.
FA. George Hounsome, Scott Titt 10.5.80

❷ Wild at Heart 🥾 ⬜ **E4 6a**
35m. A variation on *Sirius*. Climb to the roof but swing into the parallel crack to its right. Up this and its thinner continuation then cross the top roof leftwards. Finish by pulling up the ab rope.
FA. Tim Dunsby, Nigel Coe 19.9.92

❸ Punks in Power ... 🪨🥾🏃 ⬜ **E5 6b**
35m. A real arm destroyer. Start as for *Lean Machine* then weave up the cracked face to its left. The blank calcite sheet near the top provides a testing climax. Finish on the ab rope.
FA. Pete Oxley 15.9.85

❹ The Lean Machine .... 🪨🥾 ⬜ **E5 6a**
35m. The classic central line up the wall is perhaps only E4 if you have arms like a gorilla. The holds are mainly good and there are no gear worries, providing you can hang on long enough to put it in. Starting from a boulder leaning against the wall, climb a disjointed set of chunky cracks into a finishing groove. Finish by pulling up the ab rope.
FA. Martin Crocker 11.6.83

❺ Surge Control .... 🪨🥾 ⬜ **E5 6b**
35m. A superb stamina test up the cracked face right of *Lean Machine*. It shares the middle section of *Lean Machine* and has a tough start and finish. Finish by pulling up the ab rope.
FA. Pete Oxley 18.7.85

❻ The Roaring Boys . 🪨🥾🏃 ⬜ **E6 6b**
35m. The hardest route around - almost E7 for effort! Start as for *Surge Control* then swing right and up the right edge of the wall (crux at the top - thread). Finish by pulling up the ab rope.
FA. Pete Oxley 1.8.87

The big corner right of the main wall is E1 but is very poor and loose. The last two routes described are on a slab (!) just right of the corner. They have loose finishes.

❼ Charge of the Wild Horsemen 🧗 ⬜ **E1 5b**
35m. Climb the groove then the slab diagonally right, up a crack, to the fault. Take the groove above to the right of the prow to finish.
FA. Pete Oxley 29.8.88

❽ Charge of the Light Brigade 🧗 ⬜ **E1 5b**
35m. A counter-diagonal to *Charge..* starting at a small groove near the arete and pulling right onto the final prow from the groove to its left.
FA. Tim Dunsby, Nigel Coe, Scott Titt 19.5.91

Portland West · Portland East · Lulworth · Swanage · Devon · Winspit · Hedbury · Dancing Ledge · Guillemot · Cormorant · Blacker's Hole · Fisherman's · Promenade · Cattle Troughs · Boulder Ruckle · Subliminal

Lots of sun | 25 min | Steep | Abseil in

Geraldine Taylor working her way up the immaculate upper wall of *Soul Sacrifice* (E3 5b) on the Behemoth Area at Boulder Ruckle - *page 290.* Photo: Mike Robertson

PEGS and THREADS
Individual pegs and
threads are marked
on this topo as
they are useful in
identifying the actual
line on the otherwise
featureless wall.

Lots of sun / 20 min / Steep / Abseil in

Belay stakes

Line of abseil

Lean Machine (50m)

Aventura Area

Tidal ledge

Non-tidal boulder ledge

OCEAN BOULEVARD WALL
A fine wall with some great pumping classics.
TIDES - The boulder-beach is above high tide.
APPROACH - Follow the coast path to just before the 4th
stonewall as it drops down to the cliff-top. Continue over a
stile at the end of Durlston Country Park. The abseil stakes
are hidden above an earthy ramp 15m back towards the lighthouse from this stile. **NOTE -** The 2 stakes in a gully below
the wall are directly above the Ocean Boulevard Wall. The
usual abseil takes you down the upper part of *The Ramp*.

❶ Le Jaune Mechanique .   **E4 5c**
Good climbing taking the left edge of the huge *Ocean Boulevard*
wall. Start at a step in the rock platform. The pegs are rusty.
1) 5c, 22m. Climb onto the left wall of the arete (thread) and
continue (thread) to a shallow groove. Step right and up the left
side of the arete (thread) to a belay on the fault (peg and thread).
2) 5b, 22m. Pass the overhang above on the right (peg) to join
Barracuda to finish
FA. Pete Oxley, Crispin Waddy 21.6.86

❷ Barracuda **E4 5c**
45m. A 'mean fish' which is steeper than first appearances
might suggest. It tackles the first big crack-line on the wall and
never lets up. Safe, pumpy and excellent.
FA. Arni Strapcans, Gordon Jenkin 1.4.79. FFA. Dave Ivory, P.Preston 1.4.83

❸ Tuna Lick **E5 6a**
45m. An eliminate just right of *Barracuda*, joining this route
near the top. Very strenuous indeed.
FA. Pete Oxley 4.10.87

❹ Ocean Boulevard **E3 5b**
45m. An established pumpy classic which often gets the 'best
in Britain' tag. Lots of gear and plenty of holds. Start 5m right
of the edge of the wall. Climb the big flake line, veering left to
the fault. Then head steeply over via a crack and continue, easing all the time and moving left near the top.
FA. Kevin Turner, Nick Buckley, S.Bartlett 3.79
FFA. Steve Monks ,Gordon Jenkin 21.11.81

❺ Mother Africa **E4 6a**
45m. Very sustained - a mega pitch with no let up and high
in the grade. Start 4m right of *Ocean Boulevard*. Make good
holds to a small ledge then make some hard moves up a thin
crack to gain the fault (thread). Swing left (2 pegs) then follow
the continuous thin crack (pegs) to the top.
FA. Martin Crocker, Jim Robertson 5.6.83

❻ The Great Hunter House Milk Robbery
. . . .   **E4 6a**
45m. Start as for *Mother Africa* to the fault, then climb direct up
a blank wall (peg). Step left into the parent route near the top.
FA. Ben Moon 23.10.83. Ben uses a rest point on an E4!
FFA. Pete Oxley 16.10.85

❼ Wall of the Worlds **E5 6a**
45m. Arguably the best single pitch at Swanage. Hyper sustained climbing following a direct line up the cracked, central
line. Pegs and a thread near the top and lots of good wires
elsewhere. A mesmeric crux.
FA. Martin Crocker, Jim Robertson 12.6.83

Portland West | Portland East | Lulworth | Swanage | Devon | Winspit | Hedbury | Dancing Ledge | Guillemot | Cormorant | Blacker's Hole | Fisherman's | Promenade | Cattle Troughs | Boulder Ruckle | Subliminal

Lots of sun | 20 min | Vertical | Abseil in | Multi-pitch

Ocean Boulevard Area

Aventura Area - Right

Approach from Ramp abseil

14   15   16   17

AVENTURA AREA - LEFT
A section of roofs and corners which is home to the popular and excellent *Aventura*.
TIDES - The boulder beach is above high tide.
APPROACH - As for Ocean Boulevard Area, then walk left (looking out) along the boulder beach for 60m to the first quality route. This is just past a huge mid-height roof and just before a tall boulder. All routes finish at stake belays.

Portland West | Portland East | Lulworth | **Swanage** | Devon | Winspit | Hedbury | Dancing Ledge | Guillemot | Cormorant | Blacker's Hole | Fisherman's | Promenade | Cattle Troughs | **Boulder Ruckle** | Subliminal

8 The Last Hurrah of the Golden Horde
.... [symbol] **E3 5c**
45m. One of the worst single pitches at Swanage - loose and unpleasant. Start at the base of *The Ramp*. Climb to a large ledge then traverse left to ascend a crack to the fault. Follow the dodgy pillar and crack with care to the top.
FA. Jim Titt 19.2.72. An impressive route for its time.
FFA. George Hounsome 1976

9 The Ramp .... [symbol] **Sev 4a**
40m. A poor 'escape route' from the western section of the Ruckle. It follows the easy stepped ramp heading diagonally right underneath the right-hand side of the *Ocean Boulevard* wall. Pull out up your abseil rope - don't try and climb out!

10 Indian Pacific .... [symbols] **E5 6a**
40m. A tremendous girdle starting as for *Tartan Army*. Move out left to a peg, then follow a vague break (peg) to a niche on *Golden Horde*. Continue across (peg) to good holds on *Mother Africa* and then up left again to finish up *Ocean Boulevard*.
FA. Pete Oxley 15.3.86

11 The First Och Aye of the Tartan Army
.... [symbol] **E3 5b**
20m. Start from a stance two thirds of the way up *The Ramp*. (There is a poor lower pitch). Move up and traverse out left to a peg. Ascend the wall above, trending left to a shallow groove.
FA. Martin Crocker, Jim Robertson 23.7.83

12 Screaming Blue Messiah .. [symbol] **E3 6a**
18m. Start from the block belay on *The Ramp* (easiest reached by abseil). Climb steep thin cracks past a thread and peg.
FA. Pete Oxley 18.5.86

13 Queen of Carp .... [symbol] **E5 6b**
15m. An eliminate up the face just right of *Screaming Blue Messiah* past 2 pegs. Requires small wires.
FA. Mike Robertson, Mark Williams 28.7.97

AVENTURA AREA - LEFT

14 Black Sunshine .... [symbol] **VS 4c**
A solid and interesting route.
1) 4c, 20m. Climb a scoop, just left of the big boulder, then move leftwards around a roof. Traverse 8m back right to a corner and slab. The slab leads to a belay on the left at the fault.
2) 4b, 18m. Climb to an overhang, traverse 3m right and pull over. Continue to the top.
FA. Jim Titt, J.Thornby 24.10.71

15 Nassty Spider. ... [symbols] **E2 5c**
A typical Swanage roof test-piece. Start right of the large roof.
1) 5c/6a, 15m. Climb a wall and crack to the right-hand side of the roof. Swing out past a peg and surmount the roof leftwards into a crack leading to the fault. 6b for shorties!
2) 5a, 17m. Head diagonally right via two stepped roofs. Move right again and over a bulge to finish up a solid corner.
FA. Brian Snell, K.Knight 26.7.75. FFA. Gordon Jenkin, Tim Dunsby 10.6.84

16 Aventura .... [symbols] **HVS 4c**
Good, clean fun and very exposed. Start at a cave just west of a huge undercut buttress. Low in the grade.
1) 4c, 15m. Climb the corner above the cave, then at the fault, move right to belay on thread around an ammonite.
2) 4c, 15m. Ascend leftwards to a crack in the (detached?) roof and pull around in sensational position to continuation cracks. These lead to a ledge and the exit corner as for *Nassty Spider*.
FA. Pete Crew, P.A.Bell 29.8.64

17 Judgement Day ..... [symbols] **(E2 5c)**
An exciting harder version of *Aventura*, starting just to its right. A rockfall has affected this route and it may not have been re-climbed.
1) 4c, 15m. Climb steeply up a blunt arete which leads to the left-hand side of a triangular roof. Gain flakes on the right and continue to the fault and ammonite thread belay.
2) 5c, 15m. Step right and up to a niche below the roofs. Cross the 2m roof by a twisting crack, traverse left and exit up a wall.
FA. Tim Dunsby, Nigel Coe 10.4.92

AVENTURA AREA - RIGHT

The right-hand side of the Aventura wall has a few routes affected by bird restrictions.

TIDES - The boulder-beach is above high tide.

APPROACH - As for Ocean Boulevard Area (page 278), then walk right (looking in) along the boulder-beach for 60m to a tall boulder. Continue past the corner of *Aventura* to reach an undercut buttress. All routes finish at stake belays.

① Bottomless Buttress . . 🔳🔳   **HS 4b**

A worthwhile and enjoyable climb that is well-protected and on good holds. The big undercut buttress is started from its right. *Photo page 192.*

1) 4b, 15m. Climb the corner on the right and traverse left to gain the front of the buttress. Two cracks lead to the fault and a good ledge (large nut belay).

2) 4a, 15m. Climb up for 5m then move right to climb a corner to finish.

FA. I.Howell, A.Hartley, A.Rowe 16.6.64

⊖ **RESTRICTION (Routes 2 to 6) -** *No climbing 1 March to 31 July because of nesting birds.*

② Silhouette Arete . . . . 🔳🔳   **VS 4c**

The left arete of the huge roofs of *The Fin* is extremely exposed and gives extraordinary climbing for the grade. The second pitch is outstanding. One of the best VS routes in the Ruckle.

1) 4b, 15m. Climb a crack to a small ledge. Traverse right and up a short corner to a sentry box.

2) 4c, 15m. Traverse right along the fault for 5m then climb rightwards to gain the exposed arete, up this to an overhang. Pull over and climb past a large flake to an easy exit groove.

FA. Brian Snell, K.Knight 14.5.78

③ The Fin . . . . . 🔳🔳🔳🔳   **E5 6a**

Pump up your biceps; its a monster roof crack. Right of *Silhouette Arete* is a short corner, start at the groove right again.

1) 6a, 18m. Climb steeply up the groove and make serious moves leftwards over a bulge (poor peg) to a rest beneath the roof. Fight across the 3m jam crack, past a chockstone on the lip, and follow the easy crack above to the fault.

2) 4c, 15m. Traverse left onto the prow and continue as for *Silhouette Arete* to the top.

FA. Martin Crocker, Jim Robertson 24.7.83

④ Cima Petite . . . . . . 🔳🔳🔳   **E4 6a**

A similar experience to *The Fin* but a little safer to start. The first pitch is superb but the second is dirty.

1) 6a, 15m. Climb a crack right of *The Fin* and continue up a steep wall (poor peg) to the roof (poor peg). Head diagonally right across the wild roof crack to another easier crack above which leads to the fault. Belay on the left.

2) 5b, 18m. Climb a corner on the right then traverse right to the arete. Follow this over a roof then move left into a corner. Climb back right up the arete to the top.

FA. Brian Snell, N.Porter 6.11.77 FFA. Steve Monks,Steve Findlay 29.11.81

RELAX AND SWING AREA

The first climbs in this sector lie just before a bay and just after a large pointed block leaning against a yellow-stained wall.

⑤ Sun Streets . . . . 🔳🔳   **E2 5c**

A fine and exposed climb in a good position.

1) 5b, 15m. Ascend a short 3m groove to the right of the pointed block to its capping roof. Then move out left and up before coming back right to a hanging arete. Waltz up this to the fault.

2) 5c, 15m. Pull over a roof and climb a crack, just right of the arete, to a roof. Step left onto the arete and follow it and the short rib to the top.

FA. Pete Oxley, Crispin Waddy 31.8.86

⑥ Snowdrop . . . . 🔳🔳   **E1 5b**

An intimidating route. Start under the perfect groove on the edge of the bay.

1) 4c, 15m. Climb the groove to a hanging stance at the fault.

2) 5b, 18m. Move up to the roofs then make an airy traverse left to the arete which is then followed to the top. Intimidating.

FA. P.Holden, Howard Lancashire 31.3.75

Routes 7 to 10 have no restriction on them.

⑦ St Elmo's Fire . . . 🔳🔳🔳🔳   **E3 5c**

An exposed arete with quality climbing tempered by a necky start. Starts 3m right of *Snowdrop*.

1) 5c, 15m. Launch boldly over a low roof and up the left-hand side of the arete to the fault.

2) 5c, 15m. Climb the crack right of the arete, then the arete itself steeply all the way to the top.

FA. Crispin Waddy, Pete Oxley 13.7.86

⑧ Thunderball . . . . . 🔳🔳🔳🔳   **HVS 5a**

A typical Ruckle experience - steep, on good holds, weaving through overhangs. It begins from the edge of the bay, 5m right of the corner of *Snowdrop*. A tough proposition at the grade.

1) 5a, 15m. Cross low bulges to a rest, then climb diagonally right to an arete. Move into a corner right again and up to the fault to belay.

2) 5a, 20m. Climb the wall on the left, passing a mini-roof, then move back right below the big roof. Pull past a break in the roof strenuously to take a corner up to a final roof. Exit left to the top. Belay carefully to bushes if the stake is missing.

FA. P.Bell, T.Goodfellow 11.7.63

RELAX AND SWING AREA

The next set of routes lies deep in an atmospheric and intimidating shallow cove called Thunderball Bay.

TIDES - It is not tidal but rough seas can be a problem.
APPROACH - Follow the coast path to just before the 4th stone wall as it drops down to the cliff-top. Continue over a stile at the end of Durlston Country Park. The abseil stakes are hidden above an earthy ramp 15m back towards the lighthouse from this stile. The abseil takes you down *The Ramp*. Scramble left (looking out) along the boulder beach for about 200m. All routes finish at stake belays.

⑨ Jo . . . . **HVS 5a**
A brilliant route which is similar in style to *Thunderball*, with lots of variety. Start just inside the bay at a deep cavern. *Photo page 275.*
1) 4c, 15m. Climb the right wall of the cave to a ledge. Bridge past a roof into a corner, which is followed to the fault. Belay.
2) 5a, 15m. Climb the wall then move up right (thread) over a bulge to reach a smooth groove. Follow this, past good gear, to finish. Belay carefully to bushes if the stake missing.
FA. Richard Crewe and team 16.6.68

⑩ Relax and Swing . . **E5 6a**
A mind and body blowing experience. The highlight is a *Separate Reality*-style ceiling crack. Start 5m right of *Jo* at the large roof.
1) 6a, 10m. The big pitch! Gymnastically power out along the 7m horizontal jamming horror (great gear) to reach a hanging belay in a square-cut corner.
2) 5b, 12m. Traverse left to miss the next roof and follow an easy corner crack to the fault.
3) 5c, 20m. Climb a shallow groove then move rightwards beneath a blank headwall. Climb a thin technical crack, stepping left at the top to finish.
FA. Martin Crocker, Jim Robertson 23.7.83

⊖ RESTRICTION (Routes 11 to 13) - *No climbing 1 March to 31 July because of nesting birds.*

⑪ Sardine Special **E5 6b**
More roof work - not as wide as *Relax and Swing* but harder! Start beneath a short, hanging corner.
1) 6b, 12m. The original starting boulder has moved so combined human tactics are required to reach the first fingerlocks in the roof seam. Battle it out into the corner above then traverse right just below the next roof to a crack. Strenuously pass the roof to gain the left-hand groove. Belay.
2) 5a, 25m. Climb the groove, past the fault, to a roof. Move out right into a short exit groove.
FA. Brian Snell, K.Knight 19.9.76. FFA. Pete Oxley, Steve Williams 7.6.87

⑫ Jug Index **E4 6b**
Another fun roof problem.
1) 6b, 12m. From the raised ledge, cross the centre of the 2m ceiling (thread) past the jug, to a corner. Climb this in more normal fashion to the fault.
2) 5a, 15m. Move right along the fault to ascend a crack. This leads into a long groove that goes all the way to the top.
FA. Pete Oxley, John Williams 29.11.87

⑬ Future Primitive . . **E4 6b**
The final described route over the roofs here is a real beauty. However the serious start puts off many attempts.
1) 6b, 20m. Gain a groove and follow it to a small roof. Swing right to undercut around to a friable ledge. Swing left and attack the perfect 2m roof crack. An easy groove leads to the fault.
2) 5a, 12m. Take a groove on the right to a ledge then move back left to another groove system right of the arete.
FA. Martin Crocker, D.Light 5.11.83

BUCCANEER AREA

A fine sector which has some superb corner and roof climbs, pride of place being that taken the magnificent *Buccaneer*. The routes around *Grim Reaper* are less popular so take care with loose rock. All routes finish at stake belays.

TIDES - The boulder beach is above high tide.
APPROACH - 200m west from Marmolata Buttress, directly below the 3rd stone wall, a small path leads down from the coast path to twin yellow stakes. A free-hanging abseil takes you down *Prayers for Rain*. The main routes in the sector are to the left (looking out) of the long low roof of *The Grim Reaper*. *Larus* is the easiest escape route from this part of the Ruckle.

❶ Prayers for Rain . . . . 🔯☐ **E3 5c**
40m. This follows a line just right of the abseil, starting 10m left of the huge groove of *Scythe* (not described). Good holds lead to a thin crack in a smooth wall. From the fault, continue direct to cross a strip-roof. Use a good block to reach a short flake. Swing left then make a hard move through another overhang via a steep groove to an exit corner.
FA. Pete Oxley 29.10.89. Using a self belay system.

❷ The Grim Reaper . . . . 🔯☐ **E1 5a**
A fine sustained route that begins left of the huge groove.
1) 5a, 20m. Gain a small ledge (poor peg) then pass a bulge to follow a crack-line to a small, scary stance, 3m above the fault.
2) 5a, 20m. Traverse left under roofs and pull over, as for *Prayers for Rain*, at a good block. Skirt the roofs above and right, then move back left to a short corner. Swing right then pass some final roofs by another hand traverse rightwards to easier ground. Stake on the upper slope.
FA. Tim Dunsby, R.Lovett 6.6.84

❸ Alas, Poor Yorick . . 🔯☐☐☐ **E4 6a**
A great first pitch that tackles the bold arete. The second pitch is loose; *The Grim Reaper* provides an alternative escape.
1) 6a, 20m. Climb to a small roof then move right to a steep flake. Gain jugs above that lead to the arete. Technical and bold moves lead to the fault. Belay a little higher on *The Grim Reaper*.
2) 5c, 18m. Ascend rightwards to a roof on the arete. Pull over leftwards and finish past hollow rock up the exposed top wall.
FA. Crispin Waddy, John Alcock 5.6.87

The huge corner is taken by the route Scythe - E3 5b. This big Gogarth-style horror is best avoided owing to some loose rock in its upper section. Right of the corner is the sweep of Pillar Bay, characterised by the long low strip-roof.

❹ Razor Blade Smile . 🔯☐☐☐ **E5 6c**
15m. The only route to breach the strip-roof takes a line 5m left of the square-cut recess in the right-hand (looking in) side of the bay is a tough roof challenge. Pull onto the roof via juggy pockets and pass a blind crack by desperate moves to a thread belay in the break above. Continue up *Gold Fever* or lower-off.
FA. Pete Oxley 16.10.89

❺ Blow the House Down . 🔯☐☐ **E3 5c**
An intimidating route taking a traverse line above the roof.
1) 5c, 25m. Climb into and around the square-cut recess (tricky). Follow the horizontal break left into a groove. Ascend this to a small stance below the fault.
2) 5b, 25m. Climb the groove above the fault then move out left (thread) to gain an arete. Exposed moves up the long flake above lead to the top.
FA. Pete Oxley, Nigel Coe 10.11.85

❻ Gold Fever . . . . 🔯☐☐ **E4 5c**
Varied and sustained with a pumpy top pitch. A good route.
1) 5c, 10m. Start as for *Blow the House Down* by negotiating the square-cut recess. Then head diagonally left 5m to belay in the centre of the wall.
2) 5b, 30m. A big pitch. Pass a small ledge then climb the wall to the fault. Step right and then up, on small holds, to a metal spike. Step left and pull into a steep corner which leads strenuously to the top.
FA. Martin Crocker, Jim Robertson 23.10.83

❼ Larus . . . . 🔯☐ **HS 4b**
A worthwhile climb with good protection. A possible escape route.
1) 4b, 20m. Gain the groove from the right and follow it to the fault. Step left past a gap to a good belay ledge around the arete.
2) 4a, 18m. Climb past a flake and two roofs then come back left and up an exit corner.
FA. A.Hartley, R.Snell, I.Howell 8.5.64

❽ Joe 90 . . . . 🔯☐☐☐ **E5 6a**
35m. A fine sustained pitch, with some forceful moments, taking the wall right of *Larus*. Climb past a roof and trend left to the fault. Continue to another roof then climb over and right up a flake to a further roof. Finish up a long flake.
FA. Crispin Waddy, Dave Thomas 4.89

❾ Flying Finish . . . . . . 🔯☐☐ **E2 5b**
A varied route starting under the left end of a long roof at 10m.
1) 5b, 15m. Ascend to the roof then take a crack on the left to the fault. Hanging belay.
2) 5b, 20m. Follow a groove to a high roof. Swing right and over it leftwards finishing via a crack to the top.
FA. A.Strapcans, Gordon Jenkin 31.3.79.
FA. (P2) Crispin Waddy, J.Vlasto 28.3.85

Portland West | Portland East | Lulworth | Swanage | Devon | Winspit | Hedbury | Dancing Ledge | Guillemot | Cormorant | Blacker's Hole | Fisherman's | Promenade | Cattle Troughs | Boulder Ruckle | Subluminal

Approach
Boulder Beach above high tide level

Portland West
Portland East
Lulworth
Swanage
Devon
Winspit
Hedbury
Dancing Ledge
Guillemot
Cormorant
Blacker's Hole
Fisherman's
Promenade
Cattle Troughs
Boulder Ruckle
Subliminal

⑩ Billy Pigg **E1 5b**
A great introduction into the art of roof thuggery with good gear. Start beneath the break in the roof line, 8m right of *Larus*.
1) 5b, 15m. Climb to the roof and cruise over it!? Continue to the fault, stepping right to a belay ledge.
2) 4c, 18m. Follow a wall and groove to a roof. Go left then back right and follow a corner to the top.
FA. Richard Crewe, K.Winkworth 28.7.68. FFA. George Hounsome 11.3.78

⑪ Rattler **E1 5b**
A dominating groove line in a strenuous old style.
1) 5b, 18m. Climb the groove past a big flake. From a sloping ledge, climb a break in the bulge above to a good ledge at the fault.
2) 5a, 18m. Follow the groove past a huge dubious block and continue to the top. The block is the size of a mini car and has no visible means of support but seems sound - feeling lucky?
FA. Mick Nunn, Richard Crewe 17.7.68. FFA. Brian Snell, W.Lyons

⑫ Fish Supper **E3 5c**
An exposed second pitch. Start 5m right of *Rattler* below a left-facing corner crack.
1) 5a, 18m. Pass a roof and follow the crack until you can break right and climb a corner. Step left onto a hanging boulder then move up and right to follow a crack to the fault.
2) 5c, 20m. Move up left and take a corner to a roof. Go over on jugs and continue (peg) to another roof. Pass this then move right to finish up a groove. May be harder now.
FA. Nigel Coe, Tim Dunsby 8.12.84

⑬ Sinbad **E1 5b**
A very pleasant outing with lots of variety. Start at a V-groove in the buttress front. The start has the 5b move but the fantastic second pitch feels the harder of the two.
1) 5b, 18m. Thrutch up the groove to climb a crack (thread). Move left over a roof then right onto the face. Ascend a deep crack to the fault.
2) 5a, 20m. Gain the wall above and take a crack to a bulge. Pass this and climb slabs to a small exit-corner finishing rightwards.
FA. Richard Crewe, K.Winkworth 11.5.69

⑭ Mickey Mouse **E3 6a**
A wonderful and hugely impressive route with two completely differing pitches. If the second man falls off the top wall he will land in Brittany! Start beneath big leaning cracks in the side of the huge groove of *Buccaneer*.
1) 5b, 20m. Ascend the cracks in the left wall and thug up past a large poised block to the fault. Belay on a ledge to the left.
2) 6a, 25m. Climb a curving crack on the left to a niche. Gain the roof above then move out left with difficulty to reach the sensational wall above (peg). Move up and left to an exit corner as for *Sinbad*.
FA. Brian Snell, Richard Crewe, T.Tanswell 8.2.75.
FFA. Arni Strapcans, Gordon Jenkin 1.79

⑮ Buccaneer **E2 5b**
A truly magnificent climb which is one of the most travelled in the area, following the big narrowing groove to a wild finish. It gets an extra star for the line as the climbing is just a bit dirty, and a touch on the thuggy side.
1) 5a, 20m. Ascend the corner crack to a bulge. Shift right into a parallel crack then back left into the main corner to reach a small stance a short distance above the break.
2) 5b, 18m. Continue up the corner (peg) to the capping roof -superb large thread and resting place. Drop out and over to a strenuous exit crack.
FA. Richard Crewe, K.Winkworth 7.6.69.
FFA. Gordon Jenkin, Richard Harrison 2.78

⑯ Cutlass . . . **E5 6a**
40m. A good-looking direct line up the intimidating face 8m right of *Buccaneer*. Very bold. Ascend direct to a blind flake in a tiny groove. Push on with commitment to the fault and step left to a crack. Trend right above to reach the big roof, pulling over the central part and exiting right.
FA. Crispin Waddy, John Alcock 4.6.87

Buccaneer Area

Boulder-beach above high tide

MARMOLATA AREA

This is the most popular of all the traditional cliffs with the best lower grade routes in the Ruckle. There will often be people here at the weekends enjoying the high quality, solid and accessible climbs but it is still a potentially serious location should you get into difficulties. Keep this in mind before committing yourself to the abseil since the only escape route is up your ab rope. All routes finish at stake belays.

TIDES - All routes start from non-tidal boulders below the face but in rough seas the boulders beneath Marmolata Buttress may be impassable.

APPROACH - About 400m along from the lighthouse is the jutting bulk of Marmolata Buttress. Make a free-hanging abseil, from 2 stakes, down the face just to the east (left - looking out) of this. The path leading to it is 22 fence posts beyond the 2nd stone wall. The abseil leaves you at the base of *Marmolata Arete*. The first route is up a huge corner, capped by a mid-height roof, some 80m left (looking in).

❶ Koo-Koo . . . . 🔲🔲 **E2 5c**
A tough start leads to the big corner.
1) 5c, 20m. Surmount the roof then follow the corner. Traverse right to a pillar. Climb this to the fault and belay on the right.
2) 5a, 18m. Gain a ledge around a bulge. Traverse left around the exposed arete to a groove line which is followed to the top.
FA. Richard Crewe, P.Charman 2.9.73. FFA. Arni Strapcans, Gordon Jenkin 12.8.78

❷ Wide Awake in America
. . . . 🔲🔲🔲 **E6 6b**
Two contrasting pitches - a strenuous crack and a superb grey headwall. Start at a short, deep groove 15m right of *Koo-Koo*.
1) 6a, 18m. Ascend the groove to a rest on a slab (thread). Power through the impending bulge to a jammed flake and climb the hand crack to a belay at the fault.
2) 6b, 20m. Step left and 'go for it' straight up the wall (2 pegs but serious). At a small foot-ledge make hard moves up a grey headwall then leftwards to a jug. Easier ground leads to the top.
FA. Pete Oxley, A Blakely 11.12.84

❸ Boatpusher's Arete. 🔲🔲🔲 **E4 6a**
35m. The arete left of *Finale Groove*, has good climbing but with a serious start. Climb the steep arete direct (hard and bold) to easier ground which leads to the fault. Pull over, as for *Finale Groove*, for 3m, then move out left to ascend the seaward face of the upper arete.
FA. Pete Oxley, Tim Dunsby 4.11.84

❹ Finale Groove . . . . . . 🔲🔲 **HVS 4c**
35m. One of the classics of the area which follows an awesome line up a tapering groove that is packed with good gear and large holds. A great introduction to the big routes at Swanage. It lies 10m right of *Wide Awake...* and is 70m left (looking in) of the abseil point. Climb the right-facing corner past a bulge at 15m into a niche. Then climb leftwards past the bulge at the fault-line to ascend the narrowing continuation groove in a very spectacular position.
FA. G.Smith, D.Hadlum 12.4.66

❺ Sweet SA. . . . . 🔲🔲 **VS 5a**
The corner system 10m right of *Finale Groove*. The second pitch is very good.
1) 4c, 20m. Climb the corner past a bulge to a ledge. Continue to the fault and belay over to the left.
2) 5a, 15m. Ascend the grey wall (peg) to a shallow groove. Some bold moves up this lead to the top.
FA. F.Clarke, Al Alvarez 1963

❻ All Guns Blazing . . . . . 🔲🔲 **E3 6a**
The highlight is the lovely roof on the first pitch.
1) 6a, 20m. Start as for *Sweet SA* then, at 5m, traverse right out of the corner and cross the 2m ceiling to an easier crack (4 threads). Belay at the fault.
2) 5c, 15m. Overcome a bulge on the right and then bypass the upper overhang on its right (spike and thread) to a ledge. Finish more easily up the wall above.
FA. Pete Oxley, Crispin Waddy 29.8.86

7 The Heidelberg Creature . . VS 4c
A good testing first pitch, and an exposed second one. Start at a slightly overhanging corner 10m right of *Sweet SA*.
1) 4c, 20m. Climb the corner, passing a bulge, to a ledge on an arete. Follow the crack past another bulge and belay at the fault.
2) 4b, 20m. Pass an overhang then climb the wall and groove above to a ledge. Move right to exit.
FA. Tony Wilmott, A.Heppenstall 18.9.66

8 The Tool E2 5b
A fine sustained outing with good positions. Start 5m right of *Heidelberg Creature*. Worth considering doing in one pitch.
1) 5a, 23m. Climb steeply up parallel cracks to pass a blocky bulge on the left. Follow the deep hanging corner above past a large overhang at the fault line. Belay below a small roof above (nuts and a peg).
2) 5b, 15m. Step left around an arete and follow a thin crack and shallow groove to the top.
FA. Brain Snell, W.Lyons 6.7.74. FFA. George Hounsome 9.10.77

9 Tatra . . . . VS 5a
A wandering route up the huge abseil buttress. Very popular with some varied climbing and positions. Start below a huge sentry box 10m left of the abseil.
1) 5a, 18m. Enter the sentry box and cross it rightwards (awkward) to follow a steep crack more easily to the chimney. Large nut and thread belay. A tough pitch.
2) 4b, 10m. Traverse right then climb up a small corner. Hand traverse the big break rightwards to a good ledge on the prow of the buttress.
3) 4c, 18m. Climb the two corners above to the top.
FA. Barry Annette, P.Kemp pre 1963

10 Marmolata Arete . . E4 6a
Good climbing up the prow but with some serious moves.
1) 6a, 18m. Climb just right of the arete then step left and up a hanging groove to a short slab (optional stance as for *Marmolata Buttress*). Continue up the arete to belay on *Tatra*.
2) 6a, 18m. Ascend the arete on the right, past a peg, direct to the top in a superb position. Belay on the abseil point.
FA. George Hounsome, Pete Finklaire 31.3.79. Second ascent by Dave Cuthbertson in 1979 without any pegs because he didn't know any were needed! Direct by Pete Oxley 1986

11 Marmolata Buttress . . E3 5c
A gnarly first pitch leads to fine and varied climbing on the east face of the buttress.
1) 5c, 10m. Start as for the last route then climb a thin crack with difficulty to a large ledge on the seaward face.
2) 5b/c, 15m. Traverse around the corner (peg) to a groove leading to the fault. Traverse right again to a second groove which leads onto a ledge. Belay in the corner climbed by *Marmolata*.
3) 5b, 10m. Step left out onto the wall where a lovely flake system leads to the top. Belay on abseil point.
FA. G.Smith, Richard Crewe 2.6.73. FFA. George Hounsome, Scott Titt 20.11.77

12 Marmolata Combination E2 5b
The route *Marmolata* tackles the huge overhanging corner in two pitches, the second pitch being poorly protected and awkward. A popular combination is to climb *Marmolata* for one pitch then finish up *Marmolata Buttress*.
1) 5b, 18m. Climb the huge corner cracks to a big ledge belay.
2) 5b, 10m. As for pitch three of *Marmolata Buttress*.

Gearing up spot

Abseil down east face

Marmolata Arete

Boulder beach above high tide

LIGHTNING WALL AREA

This is one of the most popular sections of Swanage and not just because it is relatively close to the car park. The routes here are excellent with classics from HVS up to E2.

TIDES - The routes to the right (looking in) of Marmolata Buttress are very well shielded from the sea by a substantial boulder-beach which means access is possible in most seas.

APPROACH - About 400m along from the lighthouse is the jutting bulk of Marmolata Buttress. Make a free-hanging abseil, from 2 stakes, down the East Face (left - looking out) of this. The path leading to it is 22 fence posts beyond the 2nd stone wall.

① Director's Groove . . . . 🔲🔲🔲 HVS 5a
This rather worrying route starts up a wide groove just right (looking in) of the abseil arrival point, on the south facing wall.
1) 5a, 25m. Climb the groove, passing a roof on the right, then move left to gain an arete. Traverse diagonally right to belay below a wide crack. Scary stance with awkward belays.
2) 4c, 10m. Follow the wide crack to the top. Poor gear.
FA. D.Hadlum, P.Grainger 10.4.66

② Lightning Wall . . . . 🔲🔲🔲 HVS 4c
38m. A well-known classic with good holds and exciting situations. Start 25m right (looking in) of the abseil, at a groove left of a deep corner. Ascend the groove and at the fault pass the bulge on the right (old pegs) to gain a traverse. Follow this above the huge roof all the way to an arete which leads to a niche (peg). Head rightwards again and then exit via a corner.
FA. G.Smith, A.Webster 10.4.66

③ Elysium . . . . 🔲🔲🔲 E1 5b
38m. Interesting, sustained climbing with good gear. Start beneath the right-hand side of the big roof 5m right of a big corner. Climb a large crack to a ledge then a tricky thinner crack (peg) to reach the roof. Traverse right to an overhanging corner and jam up this (or easier, just right on the wall) to a second corner. Move left around the arete to join and finish up *Lightning Wall. Photo page 190.*
FA. Richard Crewe, K.Winkworth 7.1.68

④ Brisingamen . . 🔲🔲🔲🔲🔲 E5 6b
40m. A eliminate paralleling *Singing Winds*, starting as for *Elysium*. Climb a faint run-out groove (peg) and the short crack above. Then take the bold headwall, trending right up a thin crack, to finish more easily at an exit corner.
FA. Mike Robertson, Barry Clarke 27.8.96

⑤ Singing Winds . . 🔲🔲🔲🔲 E4 6a
40m. A big wall pitch just right of *Elysium* with some fine, bold face work. Start as for *Elysium*. Climb the initial crack then move right to a spike. Move up then launch up the blank, shallow groove to the fault (peg) - very bold! Climb direct to another peg, then move left to a thin crack and the finish of *Brisingamen*.
FA. Martin Crocker, Jim Robertson 24.7.83

⑥ Dune Dust . . . . 🔲🔲🔲 E3 6a
A good first pitch on fantastic rock. Combined with the top section of *Singing Winds* (above the fault line) this gives a 3 star E4 6a.
1) 6a, 25m. Climb *Thunder Groove* for 5m then go straight over a bulge to a horizontal. Follow the technical black streak above (2 pegs) to the fault. Go right over a bulge and up a corner to a ledge.
2) 4c, 10m. Ascend leftwards around an arete to an exit corner.
FA. Pete Oxley, J.Preston 5.9.86

Old Faithful Area

Very tidal from this point

7 Thunder Groove . . . . 🔧 [ ] **HVS 5b**
A quality route. Start at a small corner behind the highest boulder.
1) 5b, 20m. Head right for 5m then make a hard move upwards past a pinnacle block to a ledge. The groove above leads with difficulty to the fault. Place some good gear then tackle another groove to a large ledge on the left. Belay as for *Dune Dust*.
2) 4c, 12m. Step right and climb the groove past a ledge to reach an exit corner.
FA. Richard Crewe, K.Winkworth 16.9.67. FFA. Pat Littlejohn

8 Gypsy . . . . 🔧🔧 [ ] **E2 5b**
Pleasure guaranteed, pumpy and sustained. Start below a fissure in the wall below the fault.
1) 5b, 15m. Gain a ledge strenuously and ascend a corner to a roof. Continue past another roof to the fault.
2) 5b, 18m. Step right and gain an open groove. Follow this to below a small roof. Step right and head straight for the top.
FA. Richard Crewe, K.Winkworth 29.10.67. Pitch 2 used to be protected by two pegs which were removed by a falling leader (who survived).

9 Strongbow . . . . 🔧🔧 [ ] **E1 5b**
Similar quality to *Gypsy* with some nice steep climbing. Start at a right-facing corner. High in the grade. *Photo page 9.*
1) 5a, 15m. Climb the corner and move left around an arete to a ledge. Trend rightwards to another ledge and belay.
2) 5b, 30m. Climb cracks above, passing the fault with conviction and move up to a second roof. Traverse right to a shallow corner (peg) then continue to a bigger corner and an exit.
FA. Richard Crewe, P.Charman 19.5.74

10 Vortices . . . . 🔧🔧 [ ] **E2 5c**
More good climbing with reliable gear.
1) 5c, 20m. Climb the wall and overhang right of *Strongbow* to a hanging flake. Nip up a groove then swing right for 5m and take a thin crack to the fault to belay (nuts and peg).
2) 5b, 20m. Pull onto the wall above and finish up *Strongbow*.
FA. Pete Finklaire, D.Glover 21.4.85

11 The Mace . . . . 🔧🔧🔧 [ ] **E5 6b**
Bold and technical on both pitches. Recommended.
1) 6b, 18m. Ascend past a triangular niche (thread on right) and then move leftwards to beneath a shallow groove. Bravely work up this to the fault (a popular spot for flight time!) Belay on wires over the roof and a large Friend.
2) 5c, 20m. Step left and over to join *Strongbow* at its second roof. Swing left and climb a poky face prior to moving right into a hanging exit groove.
FA. Crispin Waddy, P.Windall 30.11.86

12 Acapulco . . . . 🔧🔧🔧 [ ] **E4 6a**
More strenuous than bold but with a committing start. Start 3m left of where the flat ledges drop away.
1) 6a, 18m. Climb the steep buttress just left of an arete to twin spikes. Cracks lead more easily to the fault.
2) 5c, 18m. Go rightwards into a curving groove and up to a roof. Cross this to easier ground and finish slightly left.
FA. Crispin Waddy, P.Windall 5.4.87

These next two routes start from a lower level and need low tide and calm seas to gain access.

13 The Planet . . . . 🔧🔧 [ ] **E3 5c**
A great trip - exposed and a bit run-out on the main pitch up the huge profiled prow. Start 5m right of a big corner.
1) 5b, 20m. Go over a roof and up an arete to spikes. Move left under the roof and up a crack to the fault. Belay on the right.
2) 5c, 25m. Follow flakes on the right then traverse out right over the roof to ledges on the arete. Hold your stomach and climb the wall just left of the arete past a spike to a break. Exit up a short groove.
FA. Crispin Waddy, Andy Ford 31.7.85

14 White Dwarf . . . . 🔧🔧 [ ] **E2 5c**
25m 5c. Variation to *The Planet* pitch 2. Climb the centre of the fine wall above the traverse.
FA. Barry Clarke 18.10.98. Cleaned by Brian Tilley

15 Ximenes . . . . 🔧🔧 [ ] **E2 5c**
A classic crack line which is sustained, athletic and protectable all the way. Start 10m right of the big corner below 'the line'!
Photo page 289.
1) 5c, 18m. Climb the crack and strenuously gain an overhanging corner which leads to the fault.
2) 5b, 18m. Pull through the roof above and move up to another one. Step right and over the roof then continue up the right-hand of two grooves. At the top step left to an exit scramble.
FA. G.Smith, Richard Crewe 4.9.71. FFA. Kevin Turner, Nick Buckley 1977

16 The Adventures of Portland Bill
. . . . 🔧🔧 [ ] **E2 5b**
A low-level high-quality traverse with lots of gear.
1) 5b, 25m. Climb the large crack on *Elysium* to a ledge then move right along a twin horizontal break until a step down gains a ledge on *Gypsy*.
2) 5b, 17m. Follow the breaks rightwards (peg) to a spike belay at the edge of the wall, on *Acapulco*.
3) 5b, 10m. Climb the flake crack on the right to the fault (strenuous) then belay on the right.
4) 4c, 20m. Ascend flakes on the right then move leftwards steeply to a roof. Cross this and continue up the exit corner.
FA. Pete Oxley, Jon Biddle 9.8.86

Abseil from the big
Old Faithful stake

A

Lightning Wall
Area (50m)

Behemoth Area

Non-tidal
boulder beach

1 **2** **3** **4** **5** **6** **7** **8**

Huge block

Large fin-backed boulder

Behemoth

Lots of sun | 10 min

Vertical | Abseil in | Multi-pitch

OLD FAITHFUL AREA

A great area with a famous abseil.
TIDES - The boulder-beach is non-tidal but keep away in rough seas when getting along the crag base is tricky.
APPROACH - 14 fence posts after the first stone wall passed on the Coast Path, a small path leads straight down to a large tubular 'Old Faithful' abseil stake (with back up). This is 200m from the lighthouse and leads to a large fin-backed boulder. All routes finish at stake belays.

RESTRICTION - No climbing 1 March to 31 July because of nesting birds.

❶ October Lady . . . . 🔲 **E1 5b**
Start at a small corner, 15m left of the huge block sat under the roof. Unusually thuggy climbing.
1) 4c, 15m. Climb the corner to the fault ledge.
2) 5b, 20m. Climb the crack above then undercut the long roof rightwards to an exposed exit groove (thread). Finish up this.
FA. Dave Gunn, George Hounsome 25.10.75

❷ Ice Queen . . . . 🔲 **E5 6a**
35m. An excellent direct start to *October Lady*, starting 8m further right. Climb the bottom bulging rib with difficulty (2 pegs) to the fault. Move slightly right then back left to the exit groove and thread on *October Lady*. Finish up this.
FA. Pete Oxley 29.12.85

❸ Sun King . . . . 🔲 **E4 6a**
35m. Start on the left of a massive block in an alcove. Climb direct to a crack (on *Jasper*) then swing left on the lip of the roof (hard) to a peg in a crack. Climb direct past the fault to eventually reach a large flake. Finish boldly up the white headwall via a horizontal crack finishing rightwards over a strip roof.
FA. Pete Oxley 29.11.90

❹ Jasper . . . . 🔲 **HVS 4c**
1) 4c, 15m. Climb the right-hand side of the massive block and then move left to ascend a crack to a belay at the fault.
2) 4c, 18m. Surmount a bulge and trend rightwards past a ledge and small corner to another smaller ledge. Exit to the left of a small roof at the top.
FA. Richard Crewe, K.Winkworth, R.Kent 4.5.69

❺ Old Faithful . . . . 🔲 **VS 4c**
The abseil line is the safest escape and also a worthy route.
1) 4b, 12m. Climb the crack above the fin-backed boulder, to a large fault ledge.
2) 4c, 18m. Climb the next crack boldly around a roof and continue to a ledge on the left. Move right into a corner to finish.
FA. R.Kent, Richard Crewe, K.Winkworth 4.5.69

❻ Argo . . . . 🔲 **HVS 5a**
A thin start but with good climbing above.
1) 5a, 16m. Climb over a bulge then move left to the main groove which leads to a belay in the fault.
2) 4c, 22m. Pull left onto the side wall and climb up to a niche. Follow the right-hand crack above to the top.
FA. Richard Crewe, D.Close 6.9.75

❼ The Golden Fleece . . . 🔲 **HVS 5a**
A superb outing which is steep and varied and has good gear when you need it. Start 15m right of *Old Faithful*, beyond a large corner, beneath an undercut buttress.
1) 5a, 18m. Climb a steep corner on the right to a ledge on the left. Continue up the wall (tricky) to belay on a prow at the fault.
2) 5a, 22m. Steep moves gain holds above and right. Pull into a groove and continue on jugs to a ledge. A corner leads to the top.
FA. Richard Crewe, Scott Titt 2.8.75

❽ Moose's Tooth . . . . . . 🔲 **E3 6a**
1) 5a, 18m. Start as for *Golden Fleece* but break right along a sloping ledge to the arete. Follow this to the belay in the fault.
2) 6a, 22m. Pull over a bulge on the left and pass an overhang above (hard) to finish up the left-hand side of the arete above.
FA. Crispin Waddy, C.Mullen 28.2.86. FFA. Crispin Waddy, Pete Oxley 29.9.86

Graham Parkes dispatching the first of two very steep pitches on *Ximenes* (E2 5c) in the Lightning Wall Area of the Boulder Ruckle - *page 287*. Photo: Chris Craggs

Abseil from the big Old Faithful stake

4

2

1 3 4

Old Faithful

Anger is an Energy

Large fin-shaped boulder

BEHEMOTH AREA

The closest section of the Ruckle to the parking is home to one of the best HVSs around - *Behemoth* - plus a few other gems worth seeking out.
APPROACH - 14 fence posts after the first stone wall passed on the Coast Path, a small path leads straight down to a large tubular 'Old Faithful' abseil stake (with back up). This is 200m from the lighthouse and leads to a large fin-shaped boulder. The routes start to the right (looking in) of this boulder. All routes finish at stake belays.

TIDES (Routes 1 to 4) - *The boulder-beach is non-tidal but access along the base is easier at low tide. Keep away in rough seas.*

❶ Behemoth . . . . 🔳🔳 ⬜️ **HVS 5b**
A well-protected mega-classic with a sensational top pitch.
It follows the steep corner 30m right (looking in) of *Old Faithful*.
1) 5b, 18m. Climb the crack and corner to a roof. A tricky move around an arete leads to a belay at the foot of the main corner.
2) 5a, 22m. Ascend the corner past a bulge then climb the arm-blowing cracks to a rightward exit via a cleaned ledge.
FA. Richard Crewe, G.Smith 14.11.71. FFA. Howard Lancashire, Falco Rech 1.75

❷ Soul Sacrifice . . . . . . 🔳🔳 ⬜️ **E3 5b**
35m. A brilliant pitch up the centre of the soaring face. It has good gear but is strenuous and sustained. Follow the starting crack on *Behemoth* then traverse right to take thin cracks to the fault. Fight through the short chimney and cruise up the rib (peg) and white headwall on pockets, to eventually exit onto a ledge. *Photo page 277.*
FA. Martin Crocker, Jim Robertson 2.2.83

❸ On Life's Edge . . . 🔳🔳🔳 ⬜️ **E4 6a**
Bold climbing up a rib above the zawn.
1) 6a, 18m. Hard moves lead over the bulge (peg). Continue up the front face of the arete (serious) passing a peg, to the fault.
2) 5b, 22m. Undercut right to the front of the buttress and ascend the easier wall direct past a thread on the last flake.
FA. Pete Oxley, Steve Williams 12.4.87

❹ White Horse . . . . 🔳🔳 ⬜️ **E1 5b**
Another big line following the right-bounding fissure.
The start is sometimes damp. In these conditions an alternative start can be made via *Soul Sacrifice*.
1) 5b, 20m. Move into the back of the zawn and climb out-wards to reach the corner which leads to the fault.
2) 5a, 22m. Ascend the crack steeply (peg) past a roof. Contin-ue in the same line (peg) to the top, finishing on a solid ledge.
FA. G.Smith, Richard Crewe 3.10.71. FFA. Howard Lancashire 1979

Fingery traverse
on approach

White Horse

5 6 7 8 9 10

Approach from abseil -
low tide and calm seas only

Subluminal Area (30m)
Escape/access possible
via HS traverse at sea
level (low tide and calm
seas only)

APPROACH (Routes 5 to 10) - *Cross the small zawn by the route White Horse. This is done via a fingery 5b traverse of the zawn wall. The first good routes lie 10m on from White Horse, past a buttress. All routes finish at stake belays.*
TIDES (Routes 5 to 10) - *Low tide is required to gain access to the starts although you can boulder hop in low tides and calm seas.*

❺ Anger is an Energy.   E5 6b
A bold face climb starting 10m right (looking in) of the fissure of *White Horse*.
1) 6b, 12m. Climb the centre of the smooth wall, past a poor peg, to the fault.
2) 6a, 18m. Layback around the overhang above then move strenuously leftwards up to a thin roof. Pull over this on good holds then follow the slab above to the top.
FA. Pete Oxley, G.Anstey 4.7.87

❻ Sparky   E5 6b
15m. Climb the centre of the broad pillar (left of *Let the Punka Burn*) past a thread on the right to a very committing last move for the fault. Finish up *Let the Punka Burn*.
FA. Martin Crocker, John Harwood 1.10.94

❼ Let the Punka Burn   E3 6a
A good technical first pitch.
1) 6a, 12m. Climb a thin crack, just right of a slight buttress, to the fault and a belay on the left.
2) 5b, 20m. Pull over a roof (tough) and move into a niche in the next roof. Continue direct up an easy crack to the top.
FA. Pete Oxley, Crispin Waddy 31.8.86

❽ Too Precious   E6 6b
30m. A superb but serious direct line up the blank face starting 5m right of *Let the Punka Burn* with a possible 'Desmond' from high up! Climb up easily and place runners on the left in a short crack then step right and take the centre of the face to the fault. Pull over on the right at a tiny corner then step back left to finish direct past an alcove to a finishing crack.
FA. Pete Oxley 14.8.87

The next routes are located in a smooth-walled bay 5m further on.

❾ Prudence   HVS 5b
The obvious line on the left-hand side of the bay features good rock and gear throughout.
1) 4c, 12m. Climb the right-hand crack out of a small cave to the fault. Belay on the left.
2) 5b, 20m. Pull over the overhang on the right and continue up the crack, past another bulge rightwards, to an easy finish.
FA. K.Cartwright 26.11.67

Two routes currently breach the face to the right but used some bolt protection. It is hoped these will be reclimbed without the bolts to give a pair of hard trad routes.

❿ Ganymede   E1 5b
Another good route taking the crack on the right of the bay.
1) 5a, 18m. Follow the crack to the fault. Move left then over a bulge to a belay (poor peg plus good nuts).
2) 5b, 18m. Traverse right for 5m and gain the right-hand side of the high roof line. Pass it leftwards (tricky) and take the groove above to the top.
FA. George Hounsome, T.Daniels 13.8.77

SUBLUMINAL

The low white line of sea cliff 'under the light' is the enchanting area of Subluminal. Subluminal is the place most folks head to for a first taste of Swanage steepness. The main reason for its popularity is the good selection of solid, short and amenably graded routes. Access is quick and there is a good ledge system running beneath the climbs that is well clear of the waves, giving the place a friendly atmosphere. Subluminal lies just west of the lighthouse and the Black Zawn, beneath open grass slopes. There is a clean-cut ledge above the climbs for gearing up and socialising, along with plentiful stakes for belays. Many of the climbs offer technical and fingery exercises as well as some bulging test-pieces in the Avernus Area. The Black Zawn is a place for the experienced only and has some of the best traditional pitches at Swanage in its confines. To its east are more routes worth searching out once the main classics have been ticked.

APPROACH

Walk down the tarmac road from Durlston Car Park. From the lighthouse, a track leads diagonally right (looking out) down the grass slope to cliff-top ledges situated 100m west of the Black Zawn. It is only a 10 minute walk from the car park and all the climbs are approached by a short abseil from stakes above. The best abseil line is down *High Street* which also doubles as a good escape route.

TIDES

The first three sectors start from the raised ledge so there are no tidal problems. Do not visit in rough seas as freak waves can drench the ledge and wash you out to sea. The Avernus Area running along to the Black Zawn needs calm seas and preferably lowish tides for some boulder-hopping.

CONDITIONS

There are no seepage problems at Subluminal and all the routes face south for maximum sunshine. The Avernus Area can be greasy (but then that route is virtually a caving expedition anyway!) Black Zawn can be damp and slow to dry due to its recessed and sheltered nature.

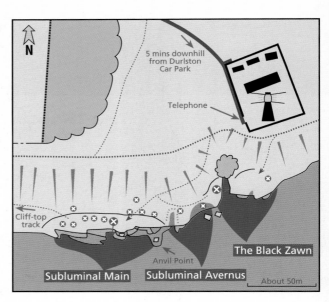

N

5 mins downhill from Durlston Car Park

Telephone

Cliff-top track

The Black Zawn

Anvil Point

Subluminal Main | Subluminal Avernus

About 50m

End of access ledge

11

Two lines
hidden in
the gully

Ledge 5m above high tide level

Boulder Ruckle

1 2 3 4 5 6 7 8 9 10 12 13 14 15

BABOON AREA

A fine and popular area with some good mid-grade routes.
TIDES - The routes start from a non-tidal ledge. Keep away in rough seas.
APPROACH - Walk left (looking in) from the High Street abseil to the end of the ledges. All routes finish at stake belays.

❶ Via Christina .... **HVS 5a**
8m. A wild route with great moves on big holds up the steep arete. Start just beyond the far end of the high ledges. Climb the final steep buttress starting from the left. Watch out for a loose but avoidable block at the top. Some people find it best to abseil (keep swinging in) directly to the belay of this line.
FA. K.Cartwright 1.4.66

❷ Dead Good **E5 6b**
10m. The left wall of the gully, starting from the gully as for *Greasy Chimney*. Move left and up the wall on small holds to a little corner. Reachy moves lead boldly to the top.
FA. Steve Taylor, Mike Robertson 19.4.92

❸ Greasy Chimney .... **VDiff**
10m. An atmospheric and slightly exposed start but easy climbing thereafter. Not always as unpleasant as the name implies.

❹ Suspension .... **Sev 4a**
10m. A great climb with lots of good protection and not too scary. Climb a short corner then move slightly left and ramble to the top. Can be a bit guano-covered at times.

❺ Dolphin .... **VS 4b**
10m. A nice pitch up the blank rib with no gear to speak of but with steady climbing.

❻ Curving Crack. ...... **Sev 4a**
10m. Safe bridging up the steep corner crack eases as height is gained. Take some large nuts.

❼ Face .... **Sev 4a**
10m. An unlikely-looking route at the grade which is well worth doing. Climb the left edge of the front wall which is well-protected once the first intimidating moves have been negotiated.

❽ Face Central ...... **VS 4c**
10m. Poorly protected but good climbing up the wall past a hole.

❾ Face Away .... **VS 4c**
10m. The groove and wall just right of *Face Central*. As with the previous line, the climbing is good but the gear is minimal.

❿ Baboon .... **VS 5a**
10m. A fun route which has seen some frustrated attempts over the last few years since the demise of THE hold on the crux. Pull over the roof to gain the corner above.
FA. Tony Wilmott 7.65

⓫ The Grobbler **E1 5b**
10m. A pumpy eliminate up the thin cracks and bulges just right of *Baboon*. Finish as for *Baboon*.
FA. Tony Wilmott 7.65

⓬ Transcript Direct. . **VS 5a**
10m. Good honest physical climbing up the steep corner right of the overhangs. A forceful approach pays dividends but don't forget to place the bomber gear.

⓭ Paralysis **E2 5c**
10m. A neat, committing test-piece up a blank wall.
FA. Tony Wilmott 7.65.

⓮ Balcony .... **HS 4b**
10m. An enjoyable, well-travelled line that features some difficult but well-protected climbing. Gain the jutting block by moving right beneath it and then its top (The Balcony). Finish up the small corner and the flake above.

Abseil from stake down *High Street*

Freda Area

Ledge at 5m above high tide level

14 · 15 · 16 · 17 · 18 · 19 · 20 · 21 · 22 · 23 · 24 · 25 · 26

Lots of sun · 10 min · Vertical · Abseil in

STROOF AREA

Another very popular spot with plenty of challenges including the short and sharp *Stroof*.
TIDES - The routes start from a non-tidal ledge. Keep away in rough seas.
APPROACH - Abseil direct down the route *High Street*.

⑮ Gangway . . . . **Sev**
10m. A decent warm up. Climb some rightward-trending flakes to a rest, then follow the ramp to its end and finish straight up. The start of the climb is the crux.

⑯ Juggler **E1 5b**
10m. A nice varied climb with adequate protection. Climb the roof, above a narrowing in the ledge, then direct up the smooth wall. Bold feeling to start and again to finish.
FA. S.Evans 1970

⑰ Stroof **E1 5c**
10m. A route for those who like them short, sharp and well protected. Amble up the lower section and assault the central crack in the white headwall.
FA. Tony Wilmott 12.65

⑱ Graunchy Grippers **E1 5b**
10m. Use side-runners in *Spreadeagle* to protect the slim upper groove. An eliminate with lots of graunch and not very much grip!
FA. Kevin Turner 1977. His first ever route on rock.

⑲ Spreadeagle . . . . **VS 5a**
10m. Great gear and superb moves on the upper section make this one a must do. Take a direct line to the roof then pull over into the interesting main groove. The finish is a touch polished.

⑳ Back Street . . . . **VS 4c**
10m. Contrasting features define this popular route. Easy climbing leads upwards to the delicate slab leading left to a fun roof. Unusual climbing for the area and a bit run-out.

㉑ High Street . . . . **Diff**
10m. A good route for a first trad lead, an excellent Diff on superb rock. Good jugs all the way - enjoyable, unserious and a 'must do' for any visitor. This is the easy way out (or in).

㉒ Bypass . . . . **Sev**
10m. Engaging, varied and well protected climbing direct up the rounded rib to an obvious left-facing layback flake.

㉓ Slip Road . . . . **VS 4c**
10m. An improbable-looking line for the grade, though very good fun, well protected and thoroughly enjoyable. Climb a short flake in the front of the buttress then pull over a bulge with some difficulty to gain the corner.

㉔ Thompson's Chimney . . . . **HS 4b**
10m. Awkward and exposed moves up the steep chimney above the break in the ledge.

㉕ Botany Bay . . . . **VS 4c**
10m. Quite a nice fun little route. The crux is low. Charge through the burly bulge before settling into the easier but poorly-protected higher section.

㉖ Battleship Bow . . . . **VS 4b**
10m. A serious lead up the rib above a gap in the ledge. Nice position but a bit bold.

Portland West
Portland East
Lulworth
Swanage
Devon
Wnspit
Hedbury
Dancing Ledge
Guillemot
Cormorant
Blacker's Hole
Fisherman's
Promenade
Cattle Troughs
Boulder Ruckle
Subluminal

Descent possible down
Pedestal Crack (Diff)

Lots of sun 10 min

Vertical Abseil in

The Pedestal

Avernus Area

Stoof Area

Ledge at 5m above high tide level

Bad step - TAKE CARE!

The Anvil

Descend rock steps to gain lower ledges
(can be covered in rough seas)

FREDA AREA

A popular and accessible sector with the classic *Freda* and plenty of other good pitches.

TIDES - The routes start from a non-tidal ledge. Keep away in rough seas.

APPROACH - Either abseil down *High Street* on the Stroof Area, or *Grandma's Groove*. An alternative approach is by scrambling down *Pedestal Crack* (Diff).

❶ Double Chockstone . . . 🔲🔲 ⬜️ **HVD**
10m. A route that leaves a lasting impression. Keep away in anything but clean and dry conditions.

❷ Skinhead . . . . 🔲🔲 ⬜️ **VS 5a**
10m. A worthwhile eliminate straight up steep ground, parallel to *Double Chockstone*.
FA. M.Hunt, A.Gilbert 28.8.77

❸ Bird's Nest . . . . 🔲 ⬜️ **Sev 4a**
10m. A good climb that is fairly high in the grade. Take a diagonal line rightwards from the start of *Skinhead*, passing a big ledge, to finish on the arete.

❹ Puffin . . . . 🔲🔲🔲 ⬜️ **VS 5a**
10m. An intense climb, direct to the ledge on *Bird's Nest*. Finish up the pleasant crack in the wall above.
FA. R.C.White 4.65

❺ The Indirect Route . . . . . . 🔲 ⬜️ **E1 5b**
10m. Good climbing but poor gear. Assault the lower roof and the more delicate arete above.
FA. Jim Titt, Scott Titt 14.11.76

❻ First Corner . . . . 🔲🔲 ⬜️ **Sev 4b**
10m. Excellent moves and good gear up the bottomless corner. Keep an eye out for a loose block near to the top of the pitch.

❼ Philatus . . . . 🔲🔲 ⬜️ **E3 5c**
10m. A real cracker of a face climb which is a must for aspiring hard men/women. Tiring to protect.
FA. Tony Wilmott 7.65

❽ Poetry in Motion . . 🔲🔲🔲 ⬜️ **E3 6a**
10m. A direct line parallel to *Philatus* but on smaller holds. Staying directly on line maintains the grade. Starting slightly left and moving right in the middle section makes things easier (**E2 5c**) but still worthwhile.
FA. Pete Oxley 19.2.84 Pete's first new route at Swanage.

❾ Second Corner . . . . . . 🔲🔲 ⬜️ **Sev 4a**
10m. A Subluminal classic with masses of atmosphere. Start by the break in the ledge. Classy, open climbing up the groove, finishing either left or right.

❿ Freda . . . . 🔲🔲🔲 ⬜️ **VS 5a**
10m. An all-time favourite of the area which pleases time after time. Start by the break in the ledge and follow the thin crack past a rusty peg to an easing. The appealing, smooth looking wall on the right is taken intricately to the top.
Photo on page 293.

⓫ Grandma's Groove 🔲🔲🔲🔲 ⬜️ **E2 5c**
10m. Boldly climb the fingery lower wall to safe, but still hard, moves up the narrow groove. *Photo on page 199.*
FA. Tony Wilmott 7.65

⓬ Grandpa's Grope . . . . 🔲 ⬜️ **VS 4c**
10m. Start up *Pedestal Crack* then step left to a tricky groove.
FA. Tim Dunsby 14.7.71

A Descent possible down *Pedestal Crack* (Diff)

Blow-hole exit

The Pedestal

Main ledge above high tide level

Lots of sun | 10 min | Vertical | Abseil in

18 19 20

16 17 21 22

15 23

Black Zawn

Access routes along cliff base boulders
Above high tide but only in calm seas

Portland West · Portland East · Lulworth · Swanage · Devon · Winspit · Hedbury · Dancing Ledge · Guillemot · Cormorant · Blacker's Hole · Fisherman's · Promenade · Cattle Troughs · Boulder Ruckle · Subluminal

AVERNUS AREA

The last routes at Subluminal are harder and more serious undertakings.
TIDES - Calm seas are required for access although you should be able to get to everything at all states of the tide.
APPROACH - Abseil down *Grandma's Groove*, or (if you are confident) reverse down Pedestal Crack. Then traverse left (looking out) at sea level, from the last routes on Freda Area, around to a cave inlet.

⑬ Pedestal Crack . . . . [ ] Diff
10m. This is the eastern descent or escape route taking the chimney corner at the right-hand end of the ledge to the top of The Pedestal, then easy ground. Polished at the base.

The next routes start from The Anvil, a block down at sea level.

⑭ Pedestal Face . . . . 🔲🏞 [ ] VS 4b
15m. Climb a crack, above The Anvil to the fault-line. Then move leftwards across the face of The Pedestal.

⑮ Pedestal Chimney . . . . [ ] VDiff
15m. Start as for *Pedestal Face* then climb the non-descript corner by the pedestal.

AVERNUS AREA

⑯ Graduation Day . . . . . 🔲🏞 [ ] E2 5c
20m. A good climb, requiring some bizarre contortions, up the left-hand wall of the zawn. Start at a corner and ascend flakes to the first roof. Traverse left, then over, to attain a full body-bridge. Climb direct up the chimney to a belay in the rock blow-hole. Takes a while to come into condition
FA. Scott Titt, Nigel Coe 24.6.89

⑰ Avernus . . . . 🔲 [ ] Sev 4a
20m. A hugely entertaining and fun outing exiting the same blowhole as *Graduation Day* but at a significantly easier grade. Start near the back of the cave and climb all the way through the chimney/roof to the rock blow-hole belay. Some find a head-torch a big help.
FA. M.Hurn, F.Higgins, D.Partridge 22.8.71

The following routes start from the higher ledge east of the zawn and offer steeper outings. They all finish at a stake belay.

⑱ Rainy Day, Dream Away . . 🔲 [ ] E2 5c
16m. A safe (hopefully) double-roof-stack above the first part of the ledge.
FA. Tim Dunsby, Scott Titt 7.7.91

⑲ All the Shakespearoes. 🔲🏞 [ ] E2 5c
20m. Start above the next rift in the ledge and follow the steep corner, finishing rightwards to skirt the roofs. Pumpy.
FA. Pete Oxley 11.12.88

⑳ The Great Rock 'n' Dole Swindle
. . . . 🔲🏞🏞 [ ] E3 6a
20m. The leaning buttress right of the last route has a hard pull over a roof in to a V-groove.
FA. Pete Oxley 27.11.88

The next set of routes are much more serious propositions. Drop down to sea-level boulders. **CALM SEAS ONLY.**

㉑ Tangerine Dream . . . . 🔲 [ ] HVS 5b
24m. In the left wall of the bay, climb a crack, overhang and steep groove to the top.
FA. George Hounsome, Kevin Turner 8.4.78

㉒ A Subtle Shade of Emptiness
. . . . 🔲🏞🏞 [ ] E5 6b
24m. The hardest route in this area traces a line through the overhung bay, with awkward gear and plenty of arm work. From the back climb an arete, traverse left then blast straight over a bulge. A shallow groove leads (thread) to the top.
FA. Pete Oxley 11.5.88

㉓ Close to the Sun . . . . . 🔲🏞 [ ] E4 6b
24m. More steep stuff through multiple roofs in the right-hand side of the bay. There are four threads on the route.

Beyond here the boulders disappear and the cliff turns a corner to form the impressive Black Zawn.

Twin stakes

Bushes 10m down
from the lighthouse

Approach

Abseil and gearing-up ledge

Avernus Area

Mellow Yellow

Abseil into the Astrid stance for routes 1 to 5

For route 6, abseil in from above the east wall
to a large boulder in the zawn bed that is only
exposed at low tide and in calm seas

Lots of sun   10 min   Vertical   Abseil in

SUBLUMINAL *Black Zawn - West*

Portland West · Portland East · Lulworth · **Swanage** · Devon · Winspit · Hedbury · Dancing Ledge · Guillemot · Cormorant · Blacker's Hole · Fisherman's Ledge · Promenade · Cattle Troughs · Boulder Ruckle · **Subluminal**

BLACK ZAWN

The Black Zawn consists of two contrasting walls. Black Zawn West is an enclosed atmospheric zawn with big, long routes requiring abseil approaches and a degree of commitment significantly higher than the nearby Subluminal Area. This is an awesome venue and the classic routes from the likes of Crewe and Littlejohn will leave lasting memories for all who venture in here. The Black Zawn East is much more open but the routes should still be regarded as major challenges. Both venues should be considered as places for more experienced parties only.

APPROACH - The Black Zawn is the section of cliff just to the east of the main Subluminal cliffs, below the lighthouse. To reach the abseil stakes follow a track to the right of the bushes then cut back left along a cliff-top track to reach a small ledge above the zawn. All the climbs are accessed by a 20m abseil. It is best to view the wall from the opposite side of the zawn so you know the score before committing. The abseil (place nuts to keep in contact with the wall) leads down the overhanging line of *Astrid* to its hanging stance . Keep the ropes out of the sea so the boulders don't snag them.

TIDES - *Achelous* and *Io* start from a low boulder in the zawn bed which is covered at mid to high tide. Otherwise all the routes are non-tidal but keep well away in rough seas when the whole face may be blasted by waves.
CONDITIONS - Although there is no seepage problem here, the West Face is prone to dampness owing to its enclosed nature. Most of the East Face actually faces south and gets sun all day. The West Face gives afternoon shade - handy for a hot summer's day. Do not enter in rough seas or on damp days when the zawn can become very greasy.

Routes 1 to 5 start from the same belay, from a spike and nuts, 4m above the sea at the base of Astrid. All routes finish at the abseil stake belays.

❶ Sweet Sixteen . . . . 🗿🏔️🧗 ▭ E5 6a
25m. Supersedes the climb *Just Seventeen* up the face left of *The Peccary*. It is bold low down with little protection. Traverse left past *The Peccary* from the *Astrid* stance and climb the bulging lower wall direct past a poor peg. Continue up the sustained face (thread) to finish up a thin crack.
FA. Mike Robertson, Barry Clarke 13.8.96

❷ The Peccary . . . . 🗿🧗 ▭ E2 5b
25m. A top little route although the best of it, the crack at the bottom, is over too quickly. Lovely holds, flowing moves, loads of gear and fair at the grade. Traverse left from the *Astrid* stance for 4m then follow the thin crack on fine holds to a niche and a finish up the wall above.
FA. George Hounsome, Martin Barnicott 31.5.76

❸ Astrid . . . . 🗿 ▭ HVS 5a
20m. Vast amounts of character, good climbing and an exciting abseil approach make this a memorable climb. The groove and crack-line in the centre of the wall gives steady climbing in impressive surroundings. Good gear. *Photo page 301.*
FA. Richard Crewe, S.Garner, Tim Dunsby 11.8.74

❹ Melpomene . . . . 🗿🧗 ▭ E4 5c
30m. Very fine climbing which is both steep and pumpy - the 'E' is for 'Effort' on this one. Good gear but beware of rope drag. Climb diagonally right into *Mars,* above the fault. Move up then swing right under a roof, to a arete. Sprint up the leftward-slanting cracks, saving some 'umph' for the top face, staying right of a square cut groove.
FA. Pat Littlejohn, Chris King 1978

❺ Mars . . . . 🗿🧗 ▭ E2
Stunning positions, excellent rock and sound protection. You can't go wrong - or can you? The grade has caused much debate over the years and is now up to E2 from HVS. For the best experience, wait until it is in good condition and has had a bit of sun on it. Whatever the grade, it is an awesome route.
1) 5m, 5b. Traverse right along the fault, or drop down to sea level and back up, to a sloping ledge beneath the roofs.
2) 20m, 5b. Climb the intimidating roofed corner and the stamina-draining groove above to the top.
FA. Richard Crewe, Tim Dunsby 11.8.74

APPROACH (Route 6) - *The next route starts from sea level and is approached by abseil from twin stakes, down the east wall of the zawn, to a rock platform in the zawn bed. Calm seas and low tide only.*

❻ Achelous . . . . . . 🗿🧗🏔️ ▭ E5 6a
35m. Even pumpier than *Melpomene!* It improves on the wandering line of another route, *Triton.* Protection is there when you need it. Climb a short arete to the fault, then a steep rib to a thin crack. Before an overhang is reached, swing left (hard) to a good knob, thread. Follow a thin crack leftwards to join and finish up *Melpomene.*
FA. Pete Oxley 11.12.88

Two traverses of the zawn have been done but these are very esoteric and not a patch on the quality of the vertical climbs.

BLACK ZAWN - EAST
The next two routes are on the east side of the zawn.
APPROACH and TIDES - Scramble down left of bushes to a twin abseil point which leads you down the line of the route to gain a platform in the zawn bed at low tide only.

❼ Io . . . . 🗿 ▭ VS 5a
40m. A pleasant outing up the crack in the East Face. Good gear. Low tide is required for the full route but you can start higher. Check the photo on the next page for another view of the line. Climb the crack past a rest out left to an overhang. Step right and up the groove to easy ground. Amble to the top.
FA. Gordon Jenkin, Frank Farrell 12.8.84

❽ Last Great Innocent 🗿🏔️🏔️ ▭ E5 6b
40m. Abseil to ledges on the side wall at 3m, or at low tide onto the boulder. Break out rightwards and boulder out the lower arete, at the edge of the zawn, on its left-hand side wall. Then continue more easily to the top. The first ascent was soloed above not-very-deep water at **E6 6b**, but there is gear.
FA. Mike Robertson 3.5.97

Twin stakes

Alternative abseil stakes for routes 5 to 8

Avernus Area

Io

Mars

Great Innocent

Ledge at 4m above high tide level

Boulders accessible only at low tide and calm seas

Lots of sun | 10 min | Vertical | Abseil in

BLACK ZAWN - EAST
The routes on this wall are more open than on the West Face and are generally in better condition. However they are still committing undertakings, for experienced teams only. All the routes finish at stake belays.
TIDES - The starting ledge is non-tidal.

APPROACH (Routes 1 to 4) - Abseil from the twin stakes down the seaward face, on the line of Ray of Sunshine, to reach the ledge 4m above high water. There is another abseil point further right (looking in).

❶ Mellow Yellow . . . . ▢ **VS 4c**
24m. A hidden gem. From the left-hand end of the ledge, climb a tough crack to the fault. Step right and follow a pleasing groove to an easy slab. Stake belay.
FA. Richard Crewe, Tim Dunsby 18.8.74

❷ Ray of Sunshine . . . . . ▢ **E2 5c**
24m. Highly recommended, on good rock but with sparse gear where it matters. From the ledge on *Mellow Yellow* head for the steep groove line and storm it up.
FA. Tim Dunsby, Ray Mardon 25.5.83

❸ Magic Mountain. . . ▢ **E4 6a**
24m. From the right-hand end of the abseil ledge, ascend cracks right of a pillar to the fault. Things begin to hot up now. Cruise steeply to an undercut block, then head left on to the upper face. Climb fairly direct to an excavated ledge to finish. Take plenty of wires.
FA. Martin Crocker, D.Light 6.11.83

❹ Fraggle Rock . . . . ▢ **HVS 5a**
24m. Quite varied. Start below and left of a jutting overhang at the fault. Climb past the corner of the overhang and swing right to its front face. Ascend the buttress to the top.
FA. Nigel Coe, Tim Dunsby 20.5.84

APPROACH (Routes 7 to 10) - The next four routes start from the ledge, just right of a jutting overhang. This can be reached by a scramble rightwards from the lower ledge or by direct abseil.

❺ Live at the Witch Trials . . . . . . ▢ **E1 5b**
24m. Climb diagonally left to finish up *Magic Mountain*.
FA. Crispin Waddy, G.Banks 7.84

❻ Hard Nose the Highway . . . ▢ **HVS 5a**
22m. Follow the last route for 5m to good runners. Then climb up and traverse right at a roof line to gain a groove that leads to the top.
FA. Tim Dunsby, Pete Oxley 7.4.84

❼ Harvest Gold . . . . ▢ **VS 4c**
20m. Climb the corner directly above, trending right to an overhang. Pass this on its right-hand side and continue to the top. Said to be a bit slick at the top
FA. A. Parker, S.Allen 17.5.75

❽ Yellow Brick Road . . . . . . ▢ **VS 5a**
20m. Climb diagonally right to a half-way ledge then direct up the tasty wall using a thin crack.
FA. Tim Dunsby, Pete Oxley 7.4.84

Some good routes lie further east but are difficult to reach without direct abseils which require some local knowledge.

Sue Hazel catching the morning sun and best conditions on *Astrid* (HVS 5a) in the Black Zawn at Subluminal - *page 299*. Photo: Mike Robertson

Devon

Devon's severely overhanging Ferocity Wall provides the south of Britain with its hardest sport lines. Ken Palmer crimping his way up *Postman Pat* (8a+) on The Ferocity Wall at Anstey's Cove - *page 311*. Photo: Mark Glaister

DEVON

The final attraction for travelling sport climbers in the South of England is found at Anstey's Cove in Torquay and the nearby Torbryan Quarry. These two locations will be of interest to those who have climbed on Portland and enjoyed what they found there even though they are not geographically very close being 85 miles apart.

The main area of Anstey's Cove is situated in the centre of "The English Riviera" and is about as close to its French counterpart as is likely to be found in the UK. This is a tourist town with all the trappings but the crag itself is in a fine and relatively secluded location overlooking the picturesque Redgate Beach. The routes are also very different to the mainly-vertical test-pieces found on Portland. Anstey's Cove is mostly about steep and powerful walls with some intense hard

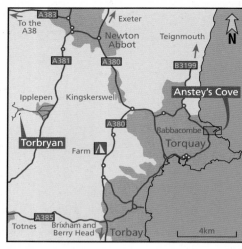

routes. The hardest sport route in this guidebook and the whole of the South of England is *Brian* at a whopping 8c, which tackles the centre of the awesome Ferocity Wall.

The less-imposing venue of Torbryan is well worth dropping into while you are in the area. It has a great set of well-bolted routes on a compact wall of tufa-laced limestone.

CRAG	Page	Best routes	Sport Routes				Trad Routes				Boulder Problems			
			up to 4+	5 to 6a+	6b to 7a	7a+ up	up to S	HS to HVS	E1 to E3	E4 up	up to V0	V0+ to V2	V3 to V6	V7 up
Anstey's Cove	306	Sport		1	6	32		2	5	8				
Torbryan Quarry	314	Sport			6	7			1	1				

	Approach walk	Sunshine or shade	Access	Sheltered	Other	Summary
Anstey's Cove	10 min	Lots of sun. One wall of morning shade		Sheltered	Dry in the rain	Very hard sport routes in a picturesque location above a beach. Conveniently located in Torquay. Very little in the easier grades.
Torbryan Quarry	5 min	Afternoon	Restrictions	Sheltered	Dry in the rain	A very well sheltered quarry with a single fine wall of perfect fused limestone. **Restrictions** - Access is sensitive since the area is an SSSI. Keep off the crag top and park carefully.

OTHER GUIDEBOOKS AND CLIMBING IN THE AREA

There is a lot more climbing in Devon ranging from the slabs, culm and granite of the North Coast on well known crags like Lundy and Baggy Point, to the high tors of Dartmoor and the wild lines at Berry Head. For a more complete picture of the traditional climbing in the area see *South Devon and Dartmoor* by Nick White (ISBN 1-871890-32-2 published by Cordee 1995). Dartmoor also has a vast amount of bouldering. Exellent online information on the bouldering can be found at **www.javu.co.uk**.

The fine west-facing wall of Torbryan Quarry serves up a high quality line up of gently overhanging routes in a quiet rural setting. The quarry classic is the flowstone face of *Thread Flintstone* (7a+) - *page 315*. Photo: GlaisterPhoto

ANSTEY'S COVE

Empire Wall and Mitre Buttress

Ferocity Wall

Cocytus Area

Sanctuary Wall (not described)

Long Quarry Point Cave

Anstey's Cove has some of the best and toughest sport climbing in Britain and its climbing style and rock is in good contrast to that found on Portland and at Swanage. During the late 1980s this small area around Torbay became a popular forcing-ground with many top climbers visiting to try and repeat the hard routes, more often than not with a frustrating lack of success. Since this time the desperate additions by Ken Palmer have kept on appearing at regular intervals and repeats of the hardest lines are rare. Those who are intimidated by the famous big grades of the gnarly routes of the Ferocity Wall should not be put off. The adjacent Empire Wall and Cocytus Area offer a good number of smart easier routes.

As on Portland, the climbs are staple bolted. Only 10 or 12 quickdraws and a 50m rope are needed although an abseil rope is required at Long Quarry Point. The few lines that are not fully-bolted are the quality traditional challenges like *Devonshire Cream* and *The Mitre* but these have some fixed gear so just a single rack of wires should suffice.

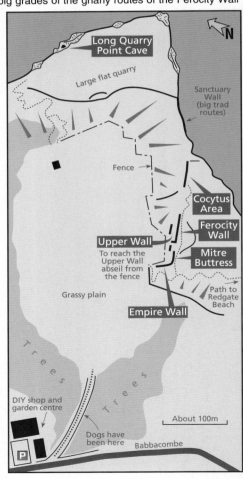

Long Quarry Point Cave

Large flat quarry

Sanctuary Wall (big trad routes)

Fence

Cocytus Area

Ferocity Wall

Upper Wall
To reach the Upper Wall abseil from the fence

Mitre Buttress

Grassy plain

Path to Redgate Beach

Empire Wall

Trees

Trees

DIY shop and garden centre

Dogs have been here   Babbacombe

About 100m

N

APPROACH and ACCESS

From Torquay seafront, follow signs towards Babbacombe, past three small roundabouts and up the long hill of Babbacombe Road. Eventually a DIY store and garden centre on the right are reached. Park at the DIY store and walk up a small path to its side. (You will notice that this lane is a popular place for people to walk their dogs - eyes to the ground). The main climbing areas are across the grassy plain above Redgate Beach. This beach has been closed after a rockfall and the path, which is used to access most of the routes, has been blocked off. However it is easy to get around this and climbing seems to be tolerated. Please keep a low profile to ensure that this continues.

BEST CONDITIONS

Anstey's Cove is a mega-suntrap which is great in cold weather but can foil red-point attempts in the summer. There can be seepage on the Empire Wall, and also on the *Cider Soak* area, which may give problems from about November to March. Many of the routes stay dry in light rain, however it shouldn't be relied on as a wet weather venue.

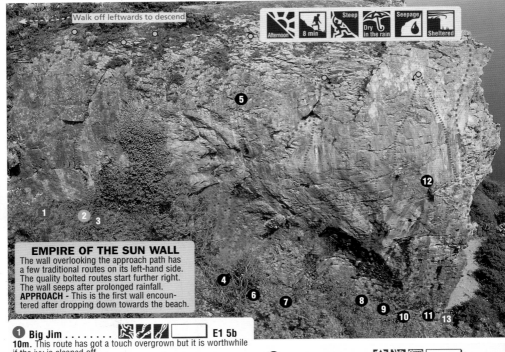

Walk off leftwards to descend

Afternoon | **8 min** | **Steep** | **Dry in the rain** | **Seepage** | **Sheltered**

EMPIRE OF THE SUN WALL

The wall overlooking the approach path has a few traditional routes on its left-hand side. The quality bolted routes start further right. The wall seeps after prolonged rainfall.
APPROACH - This is the first wall encountered after dropping down towards the beach.

---

① Big Jim E1 5b
10m. This route has got a touch overgrown but it is worthwhile if the ivy is cleaned off.
FA. Chris Nicholson, Ian Day 1.4.84

② Tiny Tim ....   HVS 5a
10m. A good little crack pitch which can be spoilt if ivy chokes the cracks.
FA. Pat Littlejohn, Ed Grindley, John Hammond 2.2.69

③ Timeless Skies ...   E2 5c
10m. Good pocketed wall climbing. Move up to a rounded pocket and then rightwards to a peg. Now climb the wall above passing a thread. Often needs cleaning.
FA. Paul Donnithorne, Tessa Meen 18.2.87

④ Crook Bruce ...   E4 6a
16m. Climb up left of the stuck on conglomerate pancake to a peg. Continue to a Z-shaped crack and then head right strenuously to a lower-off.
FA. Pat Littlejohn, Charles Wand-Tetley 14.4.77

⑤ Avant-garde ...   E5 6b
18m. Move directly up the wall above the Z-crack of *Crook Bruce* past a peg and thread.
FA. Nick White 4.91

⑥ Heathen Man 7b
16m. Very painful crimping in the first few metres but above things ease off.
FA. Martin Crocker 8.5.88

⑦ Sun of Righteousness .   7b+
17m. A tough beginning followed by some easier but still draining arm work.
FA. Dave Thomas 2.6.89

⑧ Uzi in My Pocket ..   7b+
17m. An impressive route with a short and intense crux. Finish on *Heathen Man*. The bolts are awkwardly placed on the crux.
FA. Mark Campbell 11.92

⑨ Empire of the Sun 7b
20m. A magnificent stamina test. After a slightly bold start, it becomes a race against time to the top. No hard moves.
FA. Nick White, Pete Bull, Andy Turner 3.88

⑩ Empire Direct ..   7b+
20m. The bold start can be avoided by a more technical right-hand variation.
FA. Pete Oxley 3.93

⑪ Just Revenge ..   7c+
20m. A superb, steep challenge which builds to a reachy climax.
FA. Martin Crocker, Jim Robertson 4.5.86

⑫ Avenged .....   7c+
20m. Move left after the 5th bolt on *Just Revenge* to join and finish up *Empire*. Pumpy.
FA. Nick White 4.6.89

⑬ Might and Main ..   6c
21m. The arete is taken mainly on its left-hand side. At the top, either swing left to the lower-off, or continue to the fence post. A crafty sling on a spike protects the first moves.
FA. Nick White, Bruce Woodley 1.6.89

⑭ Rise 'n' Shine ......   7b+
23m. A rising traverse line starting up *Son of Righteousness* and finishing as for *Might and Main*.
Variation - Rye 'n' Shy (7b+) finish up *Empire of the Sun*.

Empire Wall

| Lots of sun | 8 min | Steep | Dry in the rain | Sheltered |

22
21
Ferocity Wall
18
20
15
16
17
19

MITRE BUTTRESS
The weirdly-structured and well named Mitre Buttress provides a handful of absorbing and deceptively difficult pitches. Sloping holds, very steep ground and unrelenting climbing are the norm on this wall. The two routes on the wall to the right are useful for warm-ups.

MITRE BUTTRESS

⑮ Mitre Direct **E4 6a**
18m. Start up *Might and Main* then pull through the bulge to the right. Continue directly to some hard moves past a single bolt. Lower-off on the right or continue up the ramp to the final wall.
FA. Martin Crocker 5.5.86

⑯ The Mitre. **E3 6b**
18m. The original line of the buttress is a wild ride at the grade but has a very diifficult start. Follow the desperate slippery and slappy groove, past a bolt to the ledge. Now climb the wall right of the arete until it is possible to swing leftwards past a spike onto the Empire Wall. Move up and left to the lower-off on *Empire of the Sun*. **E3 6a** if started up the arete of *Mitre Direct.*
FA. (1pt aid) Frank Cannings, Peter Biven, Pat Littlejohn 1968
FFA. Steve Bell, Bruce Woodley 1979

⑰ How the Mighty Fall . . . **7a+**
17m. A very fine pitch on big slopy holds with three distinct hard sections separated by good rests.
FA. Nick White, Mike Barnes 6.6.88

⑱ The Waffle Supremacy . . . **7b+**
16m. A tough eliminate which is too close to other routes but it does have a few good moves.
FA. Dave Thomas 1990

⑲ The Mightier . . **7c+**
16m. Powerful. Steep climbing up the bulging right-hand side of the wall. No slinking off rightwards on the ledge by the crux.
FA. Martin Crocker 3.4.88

⑳ The Mightiest . . . . **7a+**
14m. Climb up to, and boulder past, the single bolt. Scramble off right or find another bolt to lower-off from. Poor.
FA. Jon Gandy 6.91

㉑ Time Bandits . . . . **6c+**
16m. The left-hand bolt line.
FA. Nick White, Dave Thomas 10.6.88

㉒ End of an Era **6a**
16m. The crack is bolted. At the top stretch left to lower-off.
FA. Nick White, Dave Thomas 10.6.88

Portland West | Portland East | Lulworth | Swanage | Devon

THE UPPER WALL
The Upper Wall is the short wall above the Ferocity Wall.
APPROACH - The best approach for the Upper Wall is from the grassy field above the wall. Abseil from the fence posts.

FEROCITY WALL
The continuously-leaning and colourfully-streaked Ferocity Wall is one of the UK's most difficult climbing venues with major pitches of extreme difficulty and quality side by side. The wall stays dry in light rain.
APPROACH - The wall is down the slope below Mitre Buttress.

THE UPPER WALL

1 The Creaming Dream . 🔲🔲 [____] **7a+**
9m. Climb around the left-hand side of the cave and cross the overhang via the crack. Move right up the wall above.
FA. Nick White 1.11.87

2 Peak 8b . . . . 🔲🔲 [____] **7a+**
9m. Climb direct to the same hard move as *Creaming Dream* through the crack. Move left to finish on the upper wall.
FA. Ken Palmer 10.89

3 Cry Creamdom . . . . 🔲 [____] **6c**
9m. The wall right of the cave.
FA. Nick White 1987

FEROCITY WALL

4 Devonshire Cream . . . 🔲🔲 [____] **E5 6a**
12m. The perfect trad wake-up call. You can leave your wires behind although a sky-hook might give some comfort on the crux which is carelessly situated before the first bolt.
FA. Chris Nicholson 4.84

5 Sole Fusion . . . . 🔲🔲 [____] **E5 6a**
13m. A variation to *Devonshire Cream*. Clip the first bolt on *Devonshire Cream* and then make a wild traverse rightwards to a hanging block on *La Creme*. Finish direct to the lower-off.
FA. Nick White 1987

Dalvinder Sodhi on *The Lynch* (7b+) at Anstey's Cove - *below*.
Photo: Mark Glaister

6 Cream Topping ...... 🎿🏞 E6 6a
13m. Another variation but this time move right from above the second bolt on *Devonshire Cream*.
FA. Nick White 22.7.87

7 La Creme .... 🎿🏞🪝 7c+
13m. A magnificent test-piece up the overlapping wall aiming for the hanging block. Cool conditions are essential.
FA. Nick White 7.12.88

The next two lines of bolts are outrageously hard projects, for which even Ken might need a finger transplant. The third line is the aid route Ferocity. The next route starts up this.

8 Postman Pat ..🎿🏞🪝 8a+
16m. A link-up route which enables the upper part of *Fisherman's Tale* to be sampled at a more amenable grade. *Photo page 302.*
FA. Ken Palmer 1996

9 Tuppence ..... 🎿🏞🪝 8a+
15m. The first of the original desperates is extremely technical, with three distinct hard sections.
FA. Ken Palmer 22.11.90

A link up with Postman Pat after the initial secton of Tuppence is **Cyberdog, 8a+** *(FA. Ken Palmer 8.2001)*

10 Tuppence Ha'penny ... 🎿🏞 8b
17m. A leftwards extension from above the hard climbing of *Tuppence* pushes the overall difficulty up.
FA. Ken Palmer 2002

11 A Fisherman's Tale
.............🎿🏞🪝 8b
16m. Another desperate where the clue is in the name.
FA. Ken Palmer 2.6.91

12 Poppy ......🎿🏞🪝 8b+
16m. Utterly desperate! Allow a slack rope when passing the third bolt since a tight rope reduces the grade dramatically.
FA. Ken Palmer 25.3.94

13 Brian .... 🎿🪝 8c
18m. An awesome link-up giving the hardest route south of the Peak District. Start up *Poppy* and where it joins *Fisherman's*, reverse *Postman Pat* into *Tuppence* then finish up *Tuppence Ha'penny*.
FA. Ken Palmer 2003

14 The Cider Soak ... 🎿🪝 8a
15m. Brilliant climbing up the faint left-facing groove. The third clip is tricky and the finish is airy. Unfortunately the midway pocket seeps after rain.
FA. Nick White 1988

15 The Lynch .... 🎿🪝 7b+
14m. The soaring crackline on the right-hand end of the wall gives a superb route featuring a bouldery start and a very strenuous upper two thirds. The direct above the start is another hard project. *Photo above.*
FA. Nick White 7.11.87

16 Pet Cemetery 🎿🏞🪝 8a+
15m. Although this link-up gives a miniscule amount of new climbing it is very worthwhile. From the 5th bolt on *The Lynch* make a very hard traverse left to join *The Cider Soak*.
FA. Mark Campbell 1996

17 Rawhide .... 🪝B 7a
12m. An uninspiring line and the bolts are old.
FA. Nick White 7.11.87

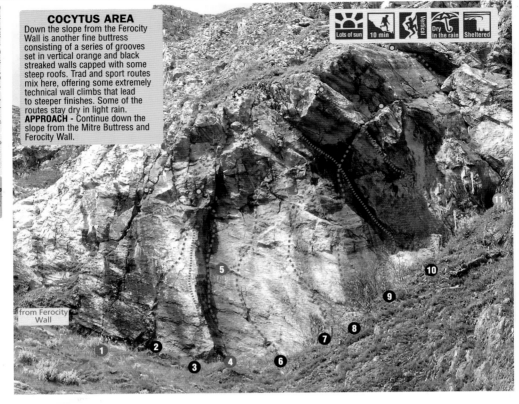

COCYTUS AREA

Down the slope from the Ferocity Wall is another fine buttress consisting of a series of grooves set in vertical orange and black streaked walls capped with some steep roofs. Trad and sport routes mix here, offering some extremely technical wall climbs that lead to steeper finishes. Some of the routes stay dry in light rain.

APPROACH - Continue down the slope from the Mitre Buttress and Ferocity Wall.

from Ferocity Wall

COCYTUS AREA

❶ Dumb Blonde **E3 6a**
10m. Hard and thin climbing gains a big block after which an easy traverse right gains a ledge and lower-off.
FA. Chris Nicholson, Nick White 4.3.84

❷ American Express . . . . **7a+**
10m. A little gem. The thin wall leads to a committing move towards a jug on the arete. The first bolt is quite high.
FA. Chris Nicholson, Nick White 5.84

❸ Torbay or Not Torbay . . **7b**
10m. An eliminate up the arete gives extremely sequency and insecure climbing.
FA. Chris Nicholson 9.85

❹ Cocytus **E2 6a**
A compelling line with immaculate moves on its first pitch.
Photo on page 307.
1) 6a, 10m. Climb the superbly technical groove to its top past two well-spaced bolts. Step left to belay.
2) 5b, 8m. Move up and across the wall rightwards behind the stance, finishing at a steep layback. Bolt belay on the right.
FFA. Pat Littlejohn, Dave Garner 31.5.76. Previously aided.

❺ Cocytus, More Steam Connection
. . . . **7a**
17m. A useful link up that gives one of the best pitches on the wall and at a reasonable grade. Climb to the second bolt on *Cocytus* and move delicately right to join the steep upper section of *More Steam, Bigger Women*.
FA. Mark Glaister 2003

❻ More Steam, Bigger Women
. . . . **7b**
17m. Great climbing up the thin, technical, orange-streaked wall. The first 8m is the crux, above the wall is steeper but with much better holds.
FA. Nick White 30.5.88

❼ Blonde Bombshell
. . . . **E5 6b**
17m. An adventurous number with a few bolts. Make technical moves up the wall to a steep finish.
FA. Pat Littlejohn, Tony Penning 29.5.83

❽ Blazing Apostles . . **7b+**
16m. The arete leads to hard moves up and right to gain the groove. Change angle and swing across the huge roof. Either belay around the corner or lower-off the last bolt in the roof.
FA. Nick White, Mark Campbell 4.91

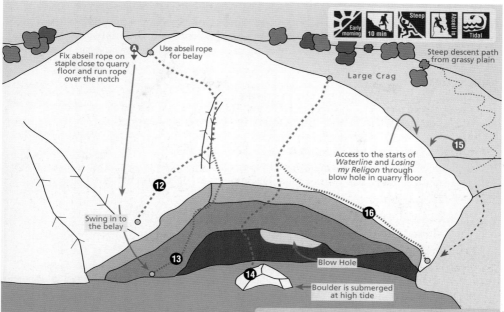

Early morning · 10 min · Steep · Abseil in · Tidal

Fix abseil rope on staple close to quarry floor and run rope over the notch

Use abseil rope for belay

Steep descent path from grassy plain

Large Crag

Access to the starts of *Waterline* and *Losing my Religion* through blow hole in quarry floor

Swing in to the belay

Blow Hole

Boulder is submerged at high tide

Portland West · Portland East · Lulworth · Swanage · **Devon**

⑨ The Shroud . . . . . 🔲🔲🔲 **E5 6b**
18m. The big, steep corner is disappointing.
FA. Dave Turnbull, Andy Grieve 18.7.88

⑩ Boy George . . . . . 🔲🔲🔲 **7c**
17m. A very steep arete with little respite. High in the grade.
FA. Ken Palmer 2002

⑪ Acheron . . . . 🔲 **HVS 5a**
20m. When clean this is a very good climb at the grade. Start a little way up the slope from the base of the huge overhanging corner of *The Shroud*. Climb the well-defined crack and continuation corner/groove on the right. Abseil off.
FA. Pat Littlejohn, Ed Grindley, John Taylor 3.1.68

LONG QUARRY POINT

⑫ Blue Planet . . . 🔲🔲🔲🔲 **7b+**
17m. A good route taking the large leaning wall left and above the blow-hole. The start is gained by a committing abseil from the top of the pinnacle; keep swinging in and right (looking in) to a white ledge with a staple belay. Move up the hanging rib and into the leaning crack/groove. Exit on pockets over the overhang. The hanging wall above is technical before easier moves left reach the notch on the pinnacle. Has been deep water soloed but needs a high tide. **(S2)** *Photo page 7.*
FA. Ken Palmer 8.2001

⑬ Christine . . . . 🔲🔲🔲🔲 **8a**
17m. An extremely steep line through the roofs right of *Blue Planet*. Use the same abseil as *Blue Planet* but continue to an old bolt belay and a large Friend in a crack at sea level. Move right to the line of bolts leading through the roof to join up with *Blue Planet* on its upper hanging wall. Has been deep water soloed but needs a high tide. **(S2)**
FA. Ken Palmer 2002

LONG QUARRY POINT CAVE

Long Quarry Point is the vast disused open quarry at the northern end of Anstey's Cove. There are a lot of trad routes in this quarry, and even a few semi-sport routes on the big dome of *Shadow Beast*. Included here are the only full sport routes in this area.
APPROACH (see map on page 306) - Walk across the grassy plain above Anstey's towards a white building. Pass this on the right and dive into the trees, descending rapidly towards the quarry floor. The routes are situated on the largest of the prominent pinnacles on the seaward-side of the quarry.

⑭ Losing My Religion 🔲🔲🔲 **(7b+)**
20m. A sensational pitch which has been deep-water soloed. Start on a small ledge in the cave (just above high tide). Climb out, out and out to daylight which involves more horizontal movement than upwards. Turn the lip with some wild bridging moves and a '360'. Finish easily above to a bolt belay on the ridge. Blocks have come away and the route has not been reclimbed. **(S3)**
FA. Nick White 17.8.91

⑮ Waterline . . . . 🔲 **6c+**
16m. A short route located inside the cave of the pinnacle, on the landward-facing wall, accessed by dropping into the blowhole. Climb outwards turning the lip on the landward side with difficulty.
FA. Mark Campbell 27.9.91

⑯ Waiting for Charlie
. . . . 🔲🔲🔲🔲 **7c**
17m. An artificial traverse but with good hard climbing. Scramble down to a small ledge on the seaward face, just by the outside cave entrance. Hand-traverse leftwards with your hands below the bolts and feet dangling uselessly below, to join and finish up *Losing My Religion*. Has been deep water soloed but needs a high tide. **(S2)**
FA. Mark Campbell 14.6.92

TORBRYAN QUARRY

Another attraction for sport climbers in Devon is Torbryan Quarry. Although only small, it has one of those faces that only quarrying can reveal. Along with the amazing organ-pipe rock and gently overhanging routes, Torbryan can be considered an excellent wet weather venue and a good training ground in winter. Most of the routes have solid resin staples.

CONDITIONS

The crag faces west and gets the sun in the afternoon. It is very sheltered and is also fairly rain proof. Some sections can seep a bit in the winter but this dries quickly and doesn't linger. The rock quality is superb, being totally fused and solid throughout.

ACCESS

Torbryan is an SSSI and discussions on whether to ban climbing have already taken place. The placement of lower-offs which prevent climbers from disturbing the rare cliff-top flora has eased this situation, however it is still a delicate issue.

Please **DO NOT WALK TO THE TOP TO PLACE TOP-ROPES.**

APPROACH

Torbryan is hidden away in the maze of small roads and villages to the west of Torquay. If approaching from Torquay, it is probably quicker to drive to Newton Abbot first. It is possible to take a more direct route but this not recommended. From Newton Abbot take the A381 towards Totnes. After 5km turn off to the right into the village of Ipplepen and follow signs for Torbryan. Around 200m beyond Ipplepen, a car park is located on the right, just as the road enters the woods. From the car park, walk down the road, keeping left for 200m, to a gated track on the left. The quarry is 50m up the track. Do not leave valuables in the car since there have been break-ins.

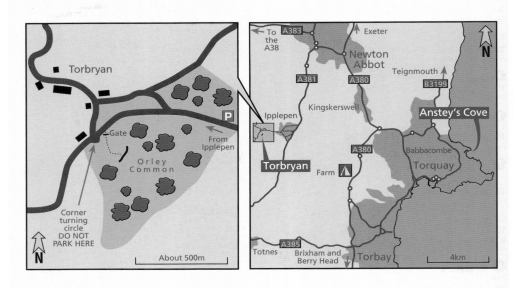

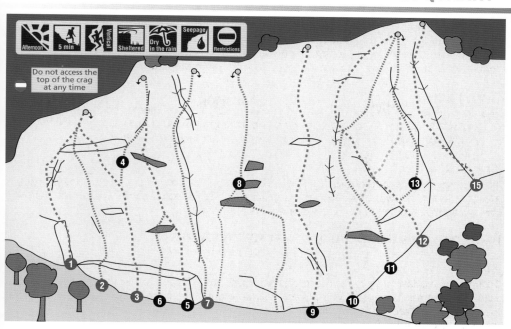

Do not access the top of the crag at any time

① Peggy Potato **6b**
12m. A short, technical route taking a small slanting corner on the far left of the crag. Start by a block/flake at ground level.
FA. Paul Donnithorne 10.11.87

② Pebbles **6c**
14m. Very technical climbing of the short and sharp variety.
FA. Nick White 4.12.89

③ The Wages of Fear . . . **6c**
15m. Gain a ledge from a slim left-leaning groove.
FA. Nick White 4.88

④ Viscious Delicious . . . **7b**
16m. A (slightly) harder right-hand finish to *Wages*.
FA. Nick White 15.9.93

⑤ Little White Lie . . **7b**
17m. A delightfully technical route with a tricky second clip. The red-point crux is the stretch for the ledge at the top.
FA. Ken Palmer 29.7.87

⑥ Little White Lie Direct
. . . . **7b**
16m. An slightly easier variation to its parent route.
FA. Pete Bull 1991

⑦ Mayday **6c**
18m. A superb route up the dramatic and sustained central groove. Well worth searching out.
FA. Andy Turner 1.5.86

⑧ Threadbare . . . **7c+**
21m. The long reach symbol is for your feet on the crux step but it is better to start up *Thread Flintstone*. A new start on the left makes the grade **7b+**.
FA. Nick White 18.8.91

⑨ Thread Flintstone . . . . **7a+**
22m. The best route here and one of the classic quarry routes of Britain. Superb rock, moves and flowstone pipes all topped off with a pumpy little finish. *Photo page 305.*
FA. Ken Palmer 19.6.87. With most gear from threads.

⑩ Bam Bam . . . . **7a+**
22m. A confusing eliminate. Take some wires. Cross *Boogie on Down* and then climb the wall to finish up the rib left of *Famine* past a bolt.
FA. Nick White 18.4.91

⑪ Barney Rubble . . . . **7a+**
22m. Smart and varied climbing with a pumpy finish.
Variation - Finish up *Boogie on Down* for another excellent **7a+**.
FA. Robbie Warke 18.4.89

⑫ Boogie on Down . . **6c+**
22m. The original line up this section is still very worthwhile. Take a few wires for the initial crack. Starting up *Bam Bam* gives a good variation - **7a+**.
FA. Andy Grieve 29.7.87

⑬ Look Back in Anger . . . **E4 6b**
22m. The crux traverse onto the ramp can be protected by clipping the bolt on the arete above. Check the peg is in place.
FA. Nick Hancock 25.6.87

⑭ Crosstown Traffic . **6c+**
34m. A right-to-left traverse. Start up *Boogie on Down* (wires). Follow a subtle diagonal line to finish at the ledge above *Little White Lie*, with plenty of bolts along the way. Tired yet?
FA. Nick White 24.4.88

⑮ Famine **E2 5c**
18m. The open groove is gained by a traverse from a tree on the right. The groove past a peg provides some tricky climbing to a bolt belay. Bold.
FA. Steve Bell 1980

ROUTE INDEX

GENERAL INDEX

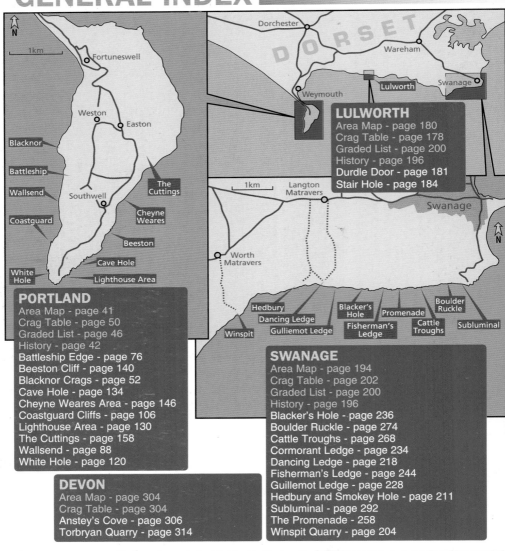